Chancellors, Commodores, and Coeds

CHANCELLORS, COMMODORES, AND COEDS

A HISTORY OF VANDERBILT UNIVERSITY

BILL CAREY

Clearbrook Press Publishing, LLC
Nashville, Tennessee 37205

 First Edition 2003

Printed in the United States of America
10 09 08 07 06 05 04 03 5 4 3 2 1

Library of Congress Control Number: 2002096716

ISBN: 0-9725680-0-X

Cover Design by: One Woman Show Design

Credits for cover and part lead photos
appear at image locations in the text.

Clearbrook Press

Nashville, Tennessee 37205
clearbrookpress@bellsouth.net

To my Family

TABLE OF CONTENTS

Part Four: Mr. Branscomb's School

Part Six: A new century

Preface

Like almost every other person who attended Vanderbilt in the latter half of the twentieth century, I have walked past Kirkland Hall, Cornelius Vanderbilt's statue, and Holland McTyeire's grave hundreds of times without giving any of those places a second thought. If prior to researching this book, someone had asked me about the school's history, I would have guessed that a very rich man named Vanderbilt had thought hard about the idea, then decided to give enough money for a great university in the South. Within a few years after that, I would have guessed, the school and its alumni became more or less self-supporting.

The fact that I graduated from the school with so little knowledge of its history is a shame.

In truth, the story of Vanderbilt University is fascinating. It's a story about how a man who never stepped foot in the South, didn't go to church regularly, and didn't attend school beyond the age of ten was talked into giving a million dollars for a startup college in the South by a young wife. It's a story about how a bishop in the Methodist church talked all the other bishops into a project that many of them wanted nothing to do with. It's a story about how a remarkable educator and administrator named James Kirkland turned a small school into one of America's great universities, taking on the nation's largest denomination and many of Nashville's power brokers in the process. It's a story about the struggle between academic excellence and academic mediocrity, between old and new, and between segregation and integration.

Along the way there are many subplots that are just as intriguing. America's most scandalous suffragette (Victoria Woodhull) develops a relationship with America's richest man (Cornelius Vanderbilt), causing Vanderbilt's children to scramble to find their old father a more respectable mate (Frank Crawford, the second Mrs. Cornelius Vanderbilt). A former governor of Mississippi (Henry Foote) flees his home state of to get away from his hated rival Jefferson Davis and marries a woman who owns a field near Nashville (that later becomes the Vanderbilt campus). An old woman (Mary Furman), terrorized by the death of her husband and oldest son, rewrites her will a week before her death so that the family will have a permanent monument (Furman Hall). A self-educated man (Edward Barnard) learns the basics of astronomy, stays up night after night, and discovers several comets while on the Vanderbilt campus. A university administrator (Kirkland) uses his friendship with America's most influential health care guru (Abraham Flexner) to turn Vanderbilt's medical school into one of the best in America. A group of young writers, ignoring the advice of the head of the English Department, forms a poetry club (the Fugitives) that evolves into one of the great literary movements in American history.

Then there are the more recent stories. Vanderbilt's controversial use of the federal government's urban renewal policy to effectively remove a neighborhood that formerly adjoined the southern part of campus. Chancellor Harvie Branscomb's successful battle to change Vanderbilt's Greek system, and his unsuccessful battle to reform intercollegiate sports. The divinity student (James Lawson) who was expelled for helping to train the participants in Nashville's successful sit-in movement. The political science professor (Denna Fleming) who helped develop the controversial theory that the Cold War was America's fault. The basketball player (Perry Wallace) who effectively integrated Southeastern Conference sports, to the dismay of many fans of his era.

There is much beyond the anecdotes that I wanted to capture in this book. Having been a Vanderbilt undergraduate in the 1980s, I I wanted to find out what it was like to be a student at other times in the school's history. I wanted to know what students studied, what rules they had to adhere to, and what rules they broke. I wanted to know why the school was built in Nashville and not in another city, and why it was built on West End Avenue and not in another part of town. I wanted to know why certain buildings were built when they were, where they were, and the way they were. I wanted to know why the Sarratt Student Center has such strange architecture and why Furman Hall looks so different from every other structure on campus. I wanted to know why there is a series of man-made tunnels underneath the campus. I wanted to know why the book *I'll Take My Stand* was such a big deal. I wanted to know how Vanderbilt was once a football powerhouse, and why it ceased to be one. Most importantly, I wanted to know something about the people whose names are enshrined on campus. I wanted to know what McTyeire and Kirkland and Barnard and Branscomb were like, to get these important men off their damned marble pedestals and make them walk around campus again.

I hope I've succeeded at this. As I have written this book, I've had many pleasant and amusing images. I could see Bishop McTyeire standing in a desolate place in the middle of one of America's worst economic depressions. His wife is standing beside him and asks the question, "Holland, are you going to put the university in a cornfield?" I could see Barnard proudly walking along a downtown Nashville sidewalk, carrying with him a check for $250 that he earned by discovering a comet. I could see James Kirkland in the year 1899 disembarking from a steamboat in an isolated corner of the rural south. He's dressed formally and he is carrying a briefcase; as his newly shined shoe sinks six inches into the mud, he tells himself that this arrangement with the Methodist church just isn't going to work. I could see a brilliant but unhappy student named Robert Penn Warren sitting in his small, cramped room in Wesley Hall working on his latest poem. I could see Branscomb and Harold Stirling Vanderbilt having a private discussion in Kirkland Hall about what to do about the school's race problem.

There are other, more amusing things that I could see as well. I could see a basset hound named George chasing the University of Tennessee's mascot out of Dudley Field. I could see students driving to the State Capitol to lobby against a bill that would have outlawed coed dormitories. I could see Vanderbilt medical students scurrying across their South Nashville campus in the 1880s, scared out of their wits because there had been so many reported sightings of a ghost of a cadaver in the area. I could see football coach Dan McGugin trying to organize a football team back when the sport really was just a sport; students marching against a fifteen dollar parking tax as if it was the most important thing on earth; even two male streakers running through Branscomb Quadrangle (something I didn't really want to see, but I saw it anyway).

In 2001 I began researching Vanderbilt history for a series of freelance articles for the *Vanderbilt Register* newspaper. (My first piece was about why Bishop McTyeire chose the West End Avenue site; my second was about Edward Barnard.) After I had written about a dozen articles, I became convinced that the subject was more interesting and rich than I had realized. I then decided to write an entire book on the subject, as sort of a successor to my 2000 book *Fortunes, Fiddles, and Fried Chicken: A Nashville Business History.*

In April 2002, thanks to a generous grant from the Ingram Charitable Fund and to administrative help from the Nashville Public Library Foundation, I left my job to work on the book full-time. I am happy to report that the book was written without any direct financial support from Vanderbilt, which means this book is entirely independent of the university's influence.

I hope you enjoy it.

Acknowledgments

I have many people to thank, but the most important by far is Martha Ingram. In March 2002 I told Mrs. Ingram that I wanted to get this book completed but had no idea how I could, given that it was a part-time project with a looming deadline.

After I explained the idea of the book to her, she got as excited about it as I was. She graciously agreed to support my research through the Ingram Charitable Fund and asked for nothing in return (she did not even request that I mention the family's generous donations to Vanderbilt; I wrote about that subject because any history of the school would be incomplete without it.) If it hadn't been for Mrs. Ingram, I don't know how I would have completed the book.

Here are some of the other people who have helped me along the way:

Skip Anderson, who as editor of the *Vanderbilt Register* started this whole thing with his agreement to publish a series of my history pieces.

The staff and directors of the Nashville Public Library Foundation, for offering administrative support in the execution of the Ingram Charitable Fund grant. Special thanks go to foundation director Susan Dyer, chairman Keith Simmons, and board member Margaret Ann Robinson.

The staff of the Downtown Public Library's Nashville Room: Sue Loper, Ronnie Pugh, Linda Barnickel, Kathy Bennett, Carol Kaplan, Louise Cox, and Deborah May. I would also like to recognize Beth Odle for the help she gave me in finding photographs in the *Nashville Banner* collection.

Thanks to Judy Orr of the Vanderbilt Creative Services Office for assistance in helping me to find recent photographs for the book and for her willingness to drop more urgent things to help me. And to Lynn Cradick, who was able to get the images we needed processed.

The staff of the Special Collections Office of the Jean and Alexander Heard Library at Vanderbilt: Juanita Murray, Kathy Smith, Molly Dohrmann, Teresa Gray, Hosanna Banks, and Strawberry Luck.

The investors who gave me the financial means to retain control over every aspect of the book's production: Alyne Massey, Ross Edwards, Edward G. Nelson, and Ridley Wills II. I would also like to acknowledge the late Herb Shayne, who had intended to be an investor but fell victim to cancer while the book was being edited.

Other people helped me along the way: Nicki Pendleton Wood, Tom Wood, Robert McGaw, John Beasley, Michael Schoenfeld, and Robin Patton.

I want to acknowledge another volume about Vanderbilt history: Paul Conkin's *Gone with the Ivy: A Biography of Vanderbilt University.* I have referred to Conkin and quoted from him numerous times in my text, and when it came to many subjects (such as the Lawson affair of 1960), I "piggy-backed" on the research done for that work. I don't believe my 2000 book *Fortunes, Fiddles, and Fried Chicken* would have been as successful without the two-volume Nashville history written by Vanderbilt history professor Don Doyle (*Nashville in the New South* and *Nashville since the 1920s.*) In the same regard, I hope this book can build on *Gone with the Ivy.*

Finally, I would like to thank my wife Andrea for tolerating me during the months in which we worked around the clock on this project, for encouraging me and giving me advice along the way, and for producing it as the art director of Clearbrook Press Publishing.

Bill Carey
March 2003

Part One

McTyeire's Mind to Methodist College

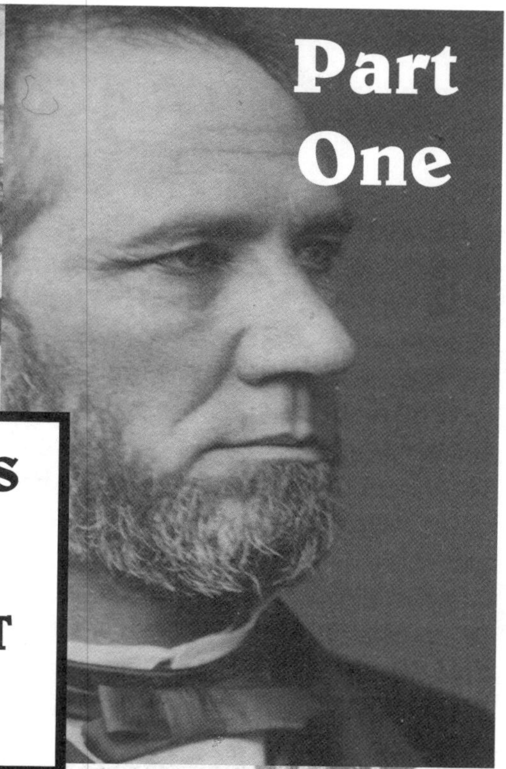

Mr. Aartson's ferry rides

First of all, the name wasn't "Vanderbilt," at least not in the beginning. The original surname of the family that gave money for a Methodist college in Nashville, Tennessee, was "Aartson."

Sometime around 1640 a man named Jan Aartson left the Dutch village of Bilt (now a suburb of the city of Utrecht) and came to the American colony of New Netherlands. Like thousands of other immigrants, Aartson was an indentured servant for three years, after which he set himself up as a farmer across the harbor from Manhattan. Jan Aartson had a son Aris, who became referred to by the name Aris van der Bilt, a description that indicated that he was from the Dutch town of Bilt.

Later the English took over the colony and changed its name to New York. People of Dutch descent were generally required to change their names to more English forms, and it was through this process that "van der Bilt" became "Vanderbilt."

Aris Vanderbilt's great-grandson Cornelius was born in 1794, the son of a farmer on rural Staten Island. Corneel, as he was known, hated going to school and hated farming but liked helping his father run the small ferry that the family operated as a side business. Corneel quit school at the age of ten to run the ferry full time. By the time he was a teenager he had a reputation as one of the most reliable ferry drivers in the area. He had also developed a sense of competitiveness that would remain with him through life; one of his favorite activities was racing other ferry drivers, to the delight of some passengers and the trepidation of others.

When Corneel was seventeen, his mother loaned him one hundred dollars to buy a small sailing vessel. Corneel worked even harder hauling passengers and freight on his own boat than he had for his father. Within months he had repaid his mother, married a woman named Sophia Johnson, and made enough money to move out on his own.

New York changed from a rural area to a large city during Cornelius Vanderbilt's lifetime, and his business grew with it. Rather than fight in the War of 1812, Vanderbilt used his boat to supply the six forts in the New York area. In the process he not only turned a good profit but also developed a reputation among business owners and military officers as a reliable boatman.

In 1817 Vanderbilt sold his sailing vessels and went into business with a man named Thomas Gibbons running a steamboat ferry from New York to New Jersey. In doing so, Gibbons and Vanderbilt competed with a ferry owned by a man named Aaron Ogden that possessed the only license from the New York legislature to operate that route. Eventually, Ogden sued Gibbons and Vanderbilt, accusing the partners of violating New York law. That case went to the U.S. Supreme Court. Led by Chief Justice John Marshall, the court ruled that no state could regulate the right of steamboats to travel from one state to another. The decision was one of the most important in the history of the high court, as it opened interstate trade and the expansion of the steamboat business into remote parts of the country (including Nashville).

With the opening of the Erie Canal in 1825, factories began appearing along the Hudson River, and Vanderbilt expanded his ferry business in that direction. By 1830 Vanderbilt had separated from his former business partner Gibbons and owned three steamboats of his own. During the next decade Vanderbilt made more money by running his business much the way children of later generations would play the game Monopoly. First he expanded his business by moving into new geographic areas. Then he would destroy the existing competition by reducing rates and improving service so that no one could afford to do business against him. As soon as his competitors would pull out, he would increase rates and make a killing. Vanderbilt repeated this pattern so many times that eventually he could make quite a profit just by threatening to expand his business. At one point a group of steamboat operators called the Hudson River Association paid Vanderbilt one hundred thousand dollars just to stay away from their part of the state.

As Vanderbilt built his wealth, his gruff personality and lack of social airs never changed. His afternoon refreshment consisted of a cigar and a glass of beer. And although he was an accessible man who agreed to see almost everyone who asked to see him, few people had the courage to do so. "State your business and be gone," or words to that affect, was how he usually greeted people who visited him in his office.

Like many powerful businessmen of his era, Vanderbilt was also far more concerned about winning than he was with safety. He instructed his captains to never stop for bad weather unless visibility was almost non-existent. Passengers were occasionally injured and even died during attempts by his employees to outrun other ferries or intimidate the competition by ramming other boats. In January 1840 one of Vanderbilt's ships, the *Lexington,* caught fire. Virtually all of the passengers on board died as they struggled for room on the *Lexington's* three small lifeboats.

By 1840 Vanderbilt controlled about one hundred steamboats and had been given the nickname "Commodore" by an article in the trade publication *Journal of Commerce.* The farmer's son was a millionaire, and his company had more employees than any other business in the United States. Vanderbilt, one biographer succinctly states, "was taking in money through every porthole." Within a few years, Vanderbilt moved into the railroad business.

CORNELIUS FIGHTS A WAR OVER NICARAGUA

Of all the episodes in the fascinating life of Cornelius Vanderbilt, none are as strange as his battle against the Central American adventurer William Walker over the fate of Nicaragua. Vanderbilt's fight with Walker was so bitter that it is ironic that the shipping and rail magnate eventually funded the development of a university in Walker's hometown.

One of the most important events in the history of the American West was the 1848 discovery of gold in California. Within a few months thousands of people migrated west, hoping to strike it rich. California was not yet linked with the rest of the country by rail, so early immigrants had a choice: take a stagecoach across the mainland (and run the risk of attack along the way by Native Americans), or board a ship that went all the way around South America.

Since people were desperate to get to California as quickly as possible, a few entrepreneurs came up with alternative routes. One was George Law, who founded a shipping company that ran passengers from New York to Panama before transferring them to stagecoaches for a trip across the peninsula to vessels waiting on the Pacific Ocean.

Cornelius Vanderbilt had no intention of being outdone by his business rival and decided to take passengers to California quicker by crossing Nicaragua instead of Panama. First, the Commodore tried to build a canal across Nicaragua. That effort was squashed by British banking interests, which had a major influence in Central America. Vanderbilt eventually settled on another plan that called for passengers to cross Nicaragua by riverboat and stagecoach.

Vanderbilt called his venture the Accessory Transit Co., and in 1851 the Nicaraguan government granted his business an exclusive charter to transport passengers across its territory. After Accessory Transit went into business, it cut two hundred dollars off the cost and two days off the time it took to get from New York to San Francisco. For about twenty-four months the business made money and carried about two thousand passengers a month, although it suffered a couple of shipwrecks in the process.

In 1853 Vanderbilt went on an extended vacation to Europe, leaving two men, Charles Morgan and Cornelius Garrison, in charge of Accessory Transit. Since intercontinental communication was difficult at that time, Vanderbilt had almost no means of keeping up with Accessory Transit's affairs while he was gone.

Meanwhile there was another prominent American venturing into Nicaragua. William Walker was a native of Tennessee; the site of his birthplace in downtown Nashville is marked with a plaque. After attending the University of Nashville, Walker worked as a doctor in Philadelphia and a lawyer and journalist in New Orleans. When gold was discovered in California, Walker took the overland route to California and became one of the editors of San Francisco's *Daily Herald* newspaper.

To understand how Walker got involved in Nicaragua, it helps to understand a little about how Americans viewed the world in the middle of the nineteenth century. At that time, the United States was a young nation that was growing fast because many of its citizens believed their country had a "manifest destiny" to grow west. Americans had no way of knowing that their nation would eventually settle on its twentieth-century boundaries with Canada and Mexico. Many Americans believed their nation might eventually include parts of Central America.

In this environment there arose a group of men in the 1840s and 1850s known as "filibusters" — people who would invade or aid in a revolution in another country to gain money and power. The American government did little to stop these people, partially because they were regarded as heroes by the general public and partially because the country was on the verge of Civil War and had enough problems at home.

"Commodore" Cornelius Vanderbilt
Detail of a print from The Carey Collection

Walker was not the first filibuster in American history, but he was the most famous. In 1854 he and a handful of followers invaded the Sonora area of northern Mexico, hoping to start a new colony that might eventually be admitted as a state. The Mexican army ran Walker's small army out of the country. But the small invasion helped lead to Mexico's sale of a part of Sonora to the United States, a transaction known as the Gadsden Purchase.

The next year Walker

conceived a plot to take over Nicaragua with the aid of Vanderbilt's trustees Morgan and Garrison. Walker promised the two men that if they gave him $20,000 and supported his overthrow of the Nicaraguan government of President Fruto Chamorro, he would revoke the Accessory Transit Co.'s charter and issue a new charter for a transit company that they — not Vanderbilt — owned.

Morgan and Garrison decided to betray Vanderbilt. In October 1855 fifty-eight Americans led by Walker invaded Nicaragua and, with the help of Morgan and Garrison, took over the government there. Once in power, Walker revoked the Accessory Transit Co.'s license and issued an exclusive license to operate to a new business owned by Morgan and Garrison.

Cornelius Vanderbilt was so angry when he learned he had been betrayed by Morgan and Garrison that he wrote them a short, ominous letter. "Gentlemen: You have undertaken to cheat me. I won't sue you, for the law is too slow. I'll ruin you. Yours truly, Cornelius Vanderbilt." During the next few months, Vanderbilt took several steps to regain control of the Nicaraguan steam route. He refused to allow his ships to take passengers to and from Nicaragua, effectively creating a blockade of that Central American country. He convinced Honduras, Guatemala, El Salvador, and Costa Rica to refuse to recognize Walker's government. He battled Morgan and Garrison in the courts and in the New York newspapers, a public relations contest called "The War of the Commodores" that delighted the editors of every publication there.

Finally Vanderbilt sent two soldiers of fortune to overthrow the new government of Nicaragua. With the help of about a hundred Costa Ricans, they did just that. In May 1857 Walker surrendered to the U.S. Navy.

To Vanderbilt's disgust, many Americans greeted Walker as a hero, and he was not prosecuted for his actions in Nicaragua. Having regained control of Accessory Transit, Vanderbilt shortly thereafter shut it down because the mad rush to California had slowed down. The Commodore then turned his attention to keeping his main business in operation during the American Civil War.

The Nicaraguan debacle didn't end Walker's career. In 1860 he led an invasion of the Bay Islands off the coast of Honduras. The

Honduran army attacked his army and captured its leader. On September 12, Walker was executed by firing squad. A few weeks later, a group of Nashville citizens asked Honduras to return the body to Tennessee, so that Walker could be given a hero's funeral. The Honduran government refused.

By the end of the twentieth century few Americans had heard of Walker. But in Central America virtually every child was told the story of how an American named William Walker invaded Nicaragua and was defeated.

NASHVILLE 60, LOUISVILLE 57

Vanderbilt University wouldn't be in Nashville if it weren't for the fact that the Southern Methodist Publishing House was already there. For that matter, the university wouldn't have existed if the Methodist church hadn't split in 1844. And as far as that story is concerned, it all started when a young woman died and left a female slave to the Rev. James Andrew of Oxford, Georgia.

Andrew wasn't just an ordinary country preacher. He was a bishop in the Methodist Episcopal Church. Andrew did not believe in slavery, but the laws of Georgia would not let him free the girl. He offered to send her to Liberia, but she did not want to go. He considered selling her to someone else, but was concerned she would end up with an inhumane owner. So he kept her and let her come and go as she pleased.

Because it had so many abolitionists in its flock, the 1840 General Conference of the Episcopal Church considered forcing Andrew to resign his position, but chose not to do so. By 1844 two things had changed. One was that Andrew had married a woman who had inherited a slave from her mother, making him the owner of two slaves. The other was that slavery had become a hot national issue because of the possibility of American expansion into Texas and the question of whether to allow slavery there.

On June 1, 1844, the General Conference of the Methodist Episcopal Church voted 110 to 70 to force Bishop Andrew to resign. Within days, Methodist leaders from the South decided that they

The Southern Methodist Publishing House's headquarters on Nashville's Public Square
The United Methodist Publishing House Collection

would form a separate denomination rather than allow an abolitionist church to minister to thousands of slaves.

It took years for the courts to decide how to divide up the money from the Methodist publishing concern, which had offices in New York and Cincinnati. In 1854 the settlement was finalized, and the Southern Methodists were given enough capital to start a new operation.

So why did the Southern Methodists pick Nashville as the home of their publishing house? Part of the reason was John McFerrin, a friend of President James K. Polk and the editor of a regional Methodist newspaper called the *Nashville Christian Advocate.* As the denomination considered where to put its publishing arm, McFerrin used his newspaper to argue in favor of Nashville. One story pointed out that New Orleans had "broken levees, deluged streets, deserted mansions, and epidemic diseases." Louisville, meanwhile, was a "border town," and "there is not a place in the South or West for which nature has done so much and man so little as the city of Louisville." But in Nashville, "Methodism is decidedly in the ascendant, and Tennessee is a commonwealth of primitive, real camp-meeting Methodists."

Nashville had other things going for it as well. In the three decades prior to 1854 the city had sent two presidents to Washington and was therefore considered the political center of the South. Civic spirit was high because a beautiful new state capitol designed by the renowned Philadelphia architect William Strickland was under construction. The city's economy had also received a boost from the new Louisville & Nashville Railroad, the first leg of which was under construction.

Nevertheless, when the General Conference of the New Methodist Episcopal Church, South, met in Columbus, Georgia, and considered the question of where to put its publishing house in May 1854, Nashville was hardly the unanimous choice. Eight cities petitioned the conference for consideration. On the first ballot, leading vote getters were Memphis, Louisville, and Prattville, Alabama (an industrial community near Montgomery). One by one, cities were eliminated from the list. On the sixth ballot, Nashville beat out Louisville 60 to 57.

McTyeire the Warmonger

If someone were asked to identify the person who deserves the title "Father of Vanderbilt University," they would probably point to one of three men. One is "Commodore" Cornelius Vanderbilt, whose money got the school started. Another is the first chancellor of the school, Landon Garland. A third is James Kirkland, who as second chancellor turned Vanderbilt from a small Methodist college into an independent university.

In fact, the person who deserves the most credit for the university existing was neither an academician nor wealthy. That person was Holland McTyeire, a bishop in the Methodist Episcopal Church, South, who convinced Cornelius Vanderbilt to contribute $1 million toward a university in the South. That being the case, it is surprising that there is a significant chapter of McTyeire's life that has remained buried since his death.

McTyeire, as editor of the weekly Methodist newspaper the *Nashville Christian Advocate* in the late 1850s and early 1860s, was a notorious and influential saber-rattler. Rather than use his paper to try to prevent the bloodiest war in American history, he used it to help whip thousands of southern Methodists into a frenzy. He told readers it was their duty to fight and send their children to fight. He told them God was on the side of the Confederacy. He was not above publishing misleading articles that led southerners to believe that if the Union Army conquered the South, thousands of innocent women and children would be exterminated.

McTyeire was chosen to replace John McFerrin when the latter retired as editor of the *Nashville Christian Advocate* in 1858. McTyeire had previously been the editor of the smaller and less influential *New Orleans Advocate.* At that time Methodist newspapers primarily reported on religious subjects. It was not unusual for the *New Orleans Advocate* and the *Nashville Christian Advocate* to contain front-page articles that sounded like sermons about the need to read the Bible, pray more, observe the Sabbath, and obey God's commandments. But as head of both publications, McTyeire found editorial

Bishop Holland McTyeire - circa 1880
Photographic Archives, Vanderbilt University

space to write about current events such as the Dred Scott decision and John Brown's raid on Harper's Ferry.

In the winter of 1860-61 McTyeire's *Nashville Christian Advocate* asserted in several editorials that preachers should avoid discussing secession from the pulpit. But when Ft. Sumter fell, the southern states formed a new government, and President Abraham Lincoln began increasing the size of the American army, McTyeire decided it was all right to use his newspaper for political purposes. In the April 25, 1861, issue he authored a long editorial headlined "Civil War – Our Duty." In the piece, which ran alongside an article asking congregations to improve their church music, McTyeire said there was no longer a way the country could avoid civil war. He said it had been the president's intention all along to wage war to "unite the North and consolidate his party." He described the Union troops as "trained bands and fanatic legions." McTyeire, who believed slavery was consistent with Biblical principals, also equated abolitionism with extremism.

Other excerpts from the editorial:

"We must meet the issue now and quit ourselves like men, or be slaves hereafter. We must fight for our altars and firesides – *fight*, that is the word . . . Witness the readiness with which Ohio and Pennsylvania and Indiana and Illinois, and the rest equip regiments and put them at the service of the Black Republican party, to overrun and subjugate the South. It is no time for half measures and dexterous trimming."

"Send your gun to the blacksmith and have it fixed. Pray God there may be no occasion to use it; but there may be occasion. Waste no more powder in idle salutes and at small game. Keep it dry. Hoard your ammunition; it may yet be scarce. He that hath no sword, let him sell his garment and buy one."

"The North has a large portion of worthless population to spare – food for powder. As a people they are by nature more cute than brave; and by profession more skilled in getting up wooden nutmegs than in handling arms. But we must not be deceived. The venom of abolitionism will make even a coward strike . . . Defending our own soil and institutions, one true Southern man can chase a dozen Yankees."

"Patriotism is a duty which the Christian religion enjoins and has illustrated by glorious examples. Let prayer be made at the head of regiments. And in the day of battle remember that 'He prayeth well fighteth well.' "

The next week McTyeire published an editorial in which he explained the reasons he felt the North intended to wage war on the South. One of these was the greed of northern capitalists. "They fight for their shops, we for our homes; they for their pockets, we for our independence," he wrote. "Every manufacturer, whether of locomotives or buttons, and every maker and every vendor of notions, and those dependent on them, realizes these facts . . . They would have no objection in the world to the flag being torn into shreds by hostile bullets, provided only they got the job of mending it. We must not underrate the number and spirit of this class. They are numerous. Their motive is low and mean, but strong . . . But under all their show of courage when confronting the weak or vacillating, there is a coward, dastard heart in them." At the time the wealthiest capitalist in the North was Cornelius Vanderbilt.

The *Nashville Christian Advocate* was also trying to sway public opinion in its news coverage. In April and May 1865 the paper published several articles from an unnamed correspondent in Cincinnati. The correspondent claimed that there were many influential people in the north who didn't just want southern slaves to be freed, but also wanted slave owners, their wives, and their children to be executed. "They don't care if the devil gets the slaves, so their masters and families are killed," the article said. The correspondent also said Southerners should be especially fearful, since the Union Army was being thrown together from the dregs of society. "A company in this city has been formed from the work-house, chain gang and prisons, or those recently released from confinement."

Letters reacting to McTyeire's two editorials came from all parts of the *Nashville Christian Advocate's* readership area, which at that time included Tennessee, Kentucky, and northern Alabama. To

McTyeire's credit, he published letters that supported his point of view and those that vociferously opposed it.

Among those opposed:

"I must request you discontinue my paper. With the first thought of treason I found breathed in the columns, I commenced praying for you; but either God does not hear my prayer, or you are past praying for, for that thought has grown into a monster of fanaticism and unrighteousness," wrote an unnamed lady from Middletown, Kentucky.

"Please discontinue our paper. . . . I do not wish my children to read the sheet that would not teach them to love their country, and be true and loyal citizens under a Government the most Christian-like on the face of the earth," scolded Sarah Prather of Newport, Kentucky.

"The minister of the gospel and editor of a religious paper should never do anything to stir up the waters of strife but endeavor to calm the warring elements, and proclaim peace on earth and goodwill to men. . . . Some of us have thought it would be as well to change the name of *your* paper, and print it *'Secession Advocate,'*" wrote N.C. Dewitt of Hart County, Kentucky.

"You have been hired to serve the devil. You have been hired to manufacture soul-damning lies, and publish them to the world under the garb of a religious newspaper. You old hypocrite. You are a goat in sheep's clothing. I tell you sir, there will be an awful and fearful reckoning before the throne of high heaven with you. Yes, you will hear the words 'depart from me you cursed' pronounced against you," predicted W.M. Boles of Cherry Grove, Tennessee.

The letters defending McTyeire's position were just as impassioned:

"I am proud to see my favorite paper enlisted in the Christian cause of the South. If the South is conquered, her States will be the Poland, Hungary and Ireland of a continent originally dedicated to freedom.

. . . Enclosed, I send you the names of twelve subscribers, with fifteen dollars," wrote an unnamed lady from Forest Hill, Kentucky.

"You will find the names of twenty-nine subscribers, and the money to pay the same. . . . I have looked upon you and admired your spirit, courage, prudence and patience in defending our rights in church and state, and pointing out the duty of the Christian in the patriot," said a letter from John Boring of Marion, Virginia.

"The *Advocate* is just the religious journal we need for the times . . . I am proud of its position and the boldness with which it maintains that position. . . . We have no fears of having the morals of our sons injured by the religious and patriotic tone of our beloved *Advocate*," wrote George Miles of Newbern, Virginia.

The *Nashville Christian Advocate* was also one of many publications that implied in its articles and editorials after the first Battle of Manassas (which the South won) that the war would be short one. "It may be that the end is not yet," a *Nashville Christian Advocate* editorial said on Aug. 1, 1861. "It may be that our best blood will continue, for a time. . . . But we have no doubt God is on our side, and will make us a great nation." But, of course, the war did not end, and in the end God did not give the Confederacy a victory. After Ft. Donelson fell to Ulysses Grant's army, McTyeire was one of thousands of Nashville residents who packed his possessions and prepared for the worst. "Silent as the grave was our publishing house," he wrote in his personal journal on February 19, 1862. "I spent an hour or two in *Advocate* office and burnt a bushel or more of papers and letters, putting things in order, if any of Lincoln's emissaries should come spying about. The best we can hope of the publishing house is that it will remain in status quo during the enemy's occupation. They can't stay there long. Nashville will likely be burnt, first or last."

A few days later McTyeire fled to Butler County, Alabama, where he spent the rest of the war. He continued to defend the institution of slavery and to claim that God was on the side of the Confederacy.

Immediately after the war the Methodist Episcopal Church,

South, held a conference in New Orleans. Since the war had decimated the economy and lines of communication of the South, the event was sparsely attended. At the conference, three new bishops were elected. It is impossible to know whether his status as the former editor of a defiantly secessionist newspaper contributed McTyeire edging out two others, including his predecessor at the *Nashville Christian Advocate,* John McFerrin, for the third bishop's spot.

McTyeire returned to Nashville in 1867 and turned his attention to helping rebuild the church. It was a couple of years later that his wife's thirty-year-old cousin married a much older and much richer man from New York named Cornelius Vanderbilt.

THE MAN WHO SLUGGED JEFFERSON DAVIS

"A bald and pugnacious little man," as he was once described, Henry Stuart Foote was kicked out of one southern state for dueling but managed to become governor of another. He was a man of many contradictions, the most notable being that he was a Unionist who served in the Confederate Congress. He was also a man of many enemies; he fought at least three duels in his life and once got into a fist fight with Jefferson Davis.

Among his other distinctions, Henry Foote has a place in Vanderbilt history, too. Parts of the campus were, for a brief time, his property.

Not that it was his only property. In an era in which people rarely moved, Foote was a nomad. He was born in Virginia and for much of the 1820s published a newspaper and practiced criminal law in Tuscumbia, Alabama. Foote was a good lawyer, but he had a hot temper. After he got into a duel with another lawyer, his legal license was suspended for three years and he moved to Vicksburg, Mississippi.

Foote loved living in Mississippi. By the middle of the 1830s he had restored his practice and become part owner of a Jackson newspaper. Then, in 1847, he was elected to the U.S. Senate. He immediately made a name for himself in Washington, becoming the chairman of the U.S. Senate Committee on Foreign Relations.

Vanderbilt campus in the late nineteenth century. Old Central (once owned by Henry Foote) and Old Science are in the foreground; the second Wesley Hall is in the background.
Photographic Archives, Vanderbilt University

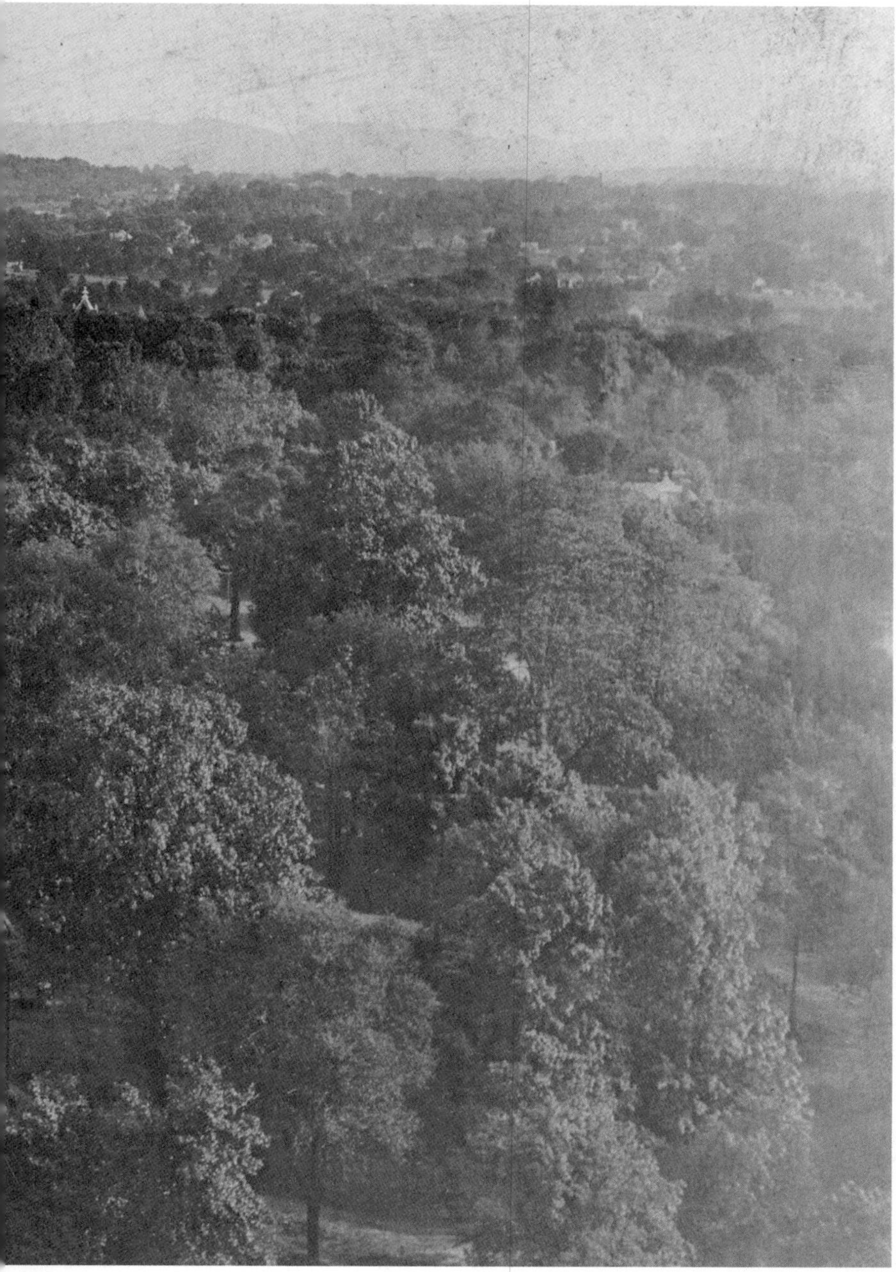

However, he did not get along with the other senator from Mississippi at that time, a man named Jefferson Davis. According to a story that was repeated in several biographies, Foote and Davis came to blows on Christmas Day 1847.

The animosity between Foote and Davis worsened as the years passed. In 1851 Foote defeated Davis in a bitter race for the Mississippi governorship. However, Foote lost his U.S. Senate re-election bid three years later. Disgusted by the spirit of secessionism taking over the South at that time, Foote moved to San Francisco, where he practiced law and was nearly elected to the U.S. Senate there.

In 1858 Foote moved to Tennessee and married a widow named Rachel Douglas Smiley, who had inherited land west of Nashville from her grandfather John Boyd. About the time of their wedding, Foote's new wife divided the land into different tracts and put it up for sale.

Civil War historians focus so much on battles that they rarely talk about how politically divided southern society really was. But Foote's actions and accomplishments as a Nashville citizen are ample proof that not everyone in Middle Tennessee was enthusiastic about the Confederacy. In July 1860 Foote officially nominated Illinois Democrat Stephen Douglas as president of the United States at a packed party meeting at the Nashville courthouse. In his long speech (which was reprinted in its entirety in Nashville newspapers the next day), Foote said he was opposed to both "Black Republicanism in the North and Secession in the South." He also had harsh words for political leaders on both sides. "Popular confidence in rulers is, for a time, at an end," he said. "Anarchy, licentiousness and lawless violence are everywhere displaying themselves. The Washingtons, the Jacksons, the Clays, the Websters, the Polks, have passed away. A generation of babbling factionists, noisy disclaimers, self-consequential, dreamy abstractionists, servile, sycophantic worshipers of ostentatious false greatness, has succeeded."

A few months after Abraham Lincoln was elected president, war broke out between the North and the South. In October 1861 the South prepared to elect its first Confederate Congress. Foote ran in the Tennessee's Fifth Congressional District, which encompassed Davidson, DeKalb, Smith, and Macon Counties. In his short campaign Foote claimed he was loyal to the Confederate cause but made few specific promises, pledging that he would "never be found wanting in industry, in watchfulness and in true devotion to your welfare." On November 6, 1861, the same day Jefferson Davis was elected president of the Confederacy, Foote won his Congressional race by an easy majority.

While in Richmond Foote became Jefferson Davis' bitterest enemy. During the war almost every time Davis proposed measures that would increase executive power, such as mandatory conscription or martial law, Foote stood up on the House floor and opposed him. Years later, in his memoirs, Foote accused the Confederate president of numerous improprieties, including making special arrangements to have his own crops spared from destruction during the war. "When Jefferson Davis ordered all cotton to be burned . . . and so many suffered so ruinously by the destruction of their cotton in this way, the crops of Mr. Jefferson Davis and his brother Joseph are understood, in some mysterious way, to have escaped the destructive flames," Foote said. Also after the fact, Foote defended the manner in which he conducted himself while a member of the Confederate Congress. "I did not intend to let Mr. Davis become an emperor if I could prevent it; nor allow his servitors in (the Confederate) Congress to organize a military despotism in Richmond upon the false pretext that they were extreme devotees of state's rights and Southern independence," he wrote.

Davis wasn't the only person annoyed by Foote's speeches, which were known to last as long as two hours. Years later one of Foote's colleagues in the Confederate House wrote that during legislative sessions, Foote "never spoke without indulging in denunciatory invective" against Davis and his cabinet. During one debate Foote called a colleague from Alabama named Edmund Dargan "a damned rascal," words that led Dargan to attack Foote with a bowie knife. On another occasion, outside of the chamber, a Tennessee Congressman named William Swan cut Foote's head with an umbrella.

The most notable thing that Foote did while a member of the Confederate Congress was try to bring about the end of the war. As early as September 1862 Foote proposed a resolution that the Confederacy send commissioners to Washington to negotiate a "just and honorable peace." That resolution was rejected, as was a similar proposal put forward after a series of Confederate military victories in June 1864.

Then, in March 1865, with Confederate forces soundly defeated on all fronts, Foote decided to go to Washington to meet President Lincoln and negotiate an end to the war. The first time Foote tried, he was arrested by Confederate forces and returned to Richmond, where he was censured by his peers but allowed to remain in office. On his second attempt, Foote made it to Washington, but Lincoln refused to see him.

Despite the fact that many Tennessee residents regarded Foote as a traitor, he made his way back to Nashville after the war and resumed his role as a leading Tennessee Democrat, albeit a pro-Union one. In March 1869 Foote was one of several political leaders who tried to push for the passage of the thirteenth, fourteenth, and fifteenth amendments to the U.S. Constitution (the amendments that abolished slavery and extended citizenship and the right to vote to former slaves). The next year, he actively supported his longtime friend A.S. Colyar in his unsuccessful campaign for governor. It does not appear as if Foote ever ran for public office again. But he remained a force in American politics; in 1878 the Grant administration named Foote the superintendent of the U.S. Mint in New Orleans.

By the time Bishop Holland McTyeire picked the West End site to be the future home of Vanderbilt University, Foote and his wife no longer owned it. By the late 1860s the land formerly owned by Mr. and Mrs. Henry Foote was owned by Daniel Dougheny (who bought the land where Twenty-first Avenue and West End met); C.A.R. Thompson (who bought the land where Kirkland Hall later sat); and A.B. Beech (who purchased the land where Old Science Hall later sat). When McTyeire bought the land, the only structure on the three parcels once owned by the Footes was the building later known as Old Central. Because building records were scant at that time, there is almost no way of knowing whether Old Central was built by the Footes or by Beech.

The Battle of the Bishops

Holland McTyeire was not only a marvelous preacher, but a great persuader, writer, and debater. He convinced his fellow Methodists to build a new university at a time when the church already had enough problems. He convinced Mr. Vanderbilt, who had never been to college, never been to the South, and was more superstitious than he was religious, to give $1 million for a Methodist university in the South.

The first of these two feats was probably the most difficult. Methodist Church leaders met (and continue to meet) at events called conferences. At conferences immediately preceding the Civil War, several bishops in the church promoted the idea of a new university that, unlike existing Methodist schools such as Wofford and Emory, would be sponsored by Methodists from all over the South instead of from just one state. McTyeire adopted the idea of a central university after he became a bishop in 1867. Then, at an 1872 conference in Memphis, the conference adopted a measure that called for the establishment of a college "of learning of the highest order" where "the youth of the Church and country may prosecute theological, literary, scientific, and professional studies."

However when the measure was adopted, the Methodist Episcopal Church, South, was in financial distress. Not only were many of its key clergymen and members still recovering from the tragedy and financial loss of the Civil War, the church's publishing house in Nashville had been plundered by the Union Army. Because of this, many Southern Methodists thought a new university was inconceivable.

The most fervent opponent of a central university was George Pierce, a bishop with a following at least as large as McTyeire's. Since radio didn't exist and travel was difficult at that time, the debate over the university took place in the *Nashville Christian Advocate.*

Between January and May 1872 Pierce and McTyeire each published three letters in the *Advocate* on the subject of the university. They were quite lengthy by today's standards; after all, it was an era when Americans could tolerate long sermons, lectures, and articles. Despite this, the letters make for wonderful reading.

In his three letters Pierce made it clear that he was opposed to the idea of a central university on several grounds. He argued that the church couldn't afford a new school and that the new university would drain resources from existing institutions such as Wofford and Emory. But the main reason had to do with the notion of the theological school. Pierce believed that the best preachers were the ones with no formal training, who learned by watching other preachers, reading the Bible, and praying. Because of this, the debate was about more than whether to build a college. It was about the future of the Methodist Church.

Here are some excerpts from Pierce's letters:

"Our people are afraid of it (the university) — do not wish it at all. The great body of the preachers are against it . . . All the Methodism in me (and there is a good deal of it) rises up in stern revolt."

"Give me the evangelist and the revival, rather than the erudite brother who goes into the pulpit to reconcile Moses with modern science . . . I do think breaking hearts with the hammer of the word is better employment than splitting hairs with metaphysical acumen. I do think evangelical sermons better than critical letters."

"Every dollar invested in a Theological School will be a damage to Methodism. Had I a million, I would not give a dime to such an object."

Here are excerpts from McTyeire's letters:

"The idea of a grand university . . . strikes the minds of the people in many places with an electrifying effect. They are delighted with the vision, and eager to see it realized . . . . On this subject, Bishop Pierce is a small minority, if any minority can be small that claims him."

"In the North, millions are annually bestowed in endowing literary, scientific and benevolent institutions; at the South, comparatively little has been done in this way . . . The establishment of such a university as that now in contemplation will greatly promote a general reinvigoration of the colleges in the South."

"What our enemies and patronizing friends have said of us is that Methodism will do very well for rude settlements and common people, but when they have become cultivated and refined, we are to turn them over to other churches prepared to take charge of them. I hope to be pardoned for declaring that I am not resigned to that condition."

Perhaps McTyeire's most persuasive argument had to do with the degree to which the American South and the Methodist church were changing. Prior to the Civil War, America was so rural that Methodist ministers were referred to as "circuit riders," who rode from small town to small town on horseback preaching at maybe half a dozen places as a part of their routine. Circuit riders usually gave the same sermon at every small church before they would write a new one and start the circuit all over again. They had few responsibilities other than preaching.

In his last letter McTyeire pointed out that the South was becoming increasingly urban, and that in the future, ministers would have to write a new sermon at least once a week (not to mention Sunday night services, funerals, and weddings). He cited the case of another preacher in the church who said he had once been opposed to theological seminaries but was now in favor of them. "The old plan of bringing in workers is gone," McTyeire wrote. "I saw it going out years ago & we must have something to take the place of the old plan, and a theological school, guarded and checked, and Methodized, is the best and the only substitute."

Pierce apparently never agreed with McTyeire on the idea of a central university. But on May 10, 1872, the two bishops met and put an end to their squabble, each signing a short letter that was published a week later in the *Advocate*. "The controversy between us, growing out of the proposed Central University, comes to an end," the letter said. By that time southern Methodist leaders had signed a document that took the university idea further. It requested that the institution be located "whenever the sum of $500,000 shall be pledged for the enterprise."

The problem was that no one had $500,000.

THE SCANDALOUS SISTERS AND THE BIG DONATION

The story of how Cornelius Vanderbilt gave $500,000 to start a Methodist university in Nashville has been repeated so often that the series of events that led to the donation are often overlooked. In fact, Vanderbilt University may owe its existence, in a way, to the odd and scandalous relationship between Mr. Vanderbilt and America's most radical feminist.

By the end of the Civil War Cornelius Vanderbilt had made the transition from steamboat operator to rail magnate and become one of the richest men in America. However, the man became lonely and eccentric. Vanderbilt had made so many enemies as he amassed his fortune that he had few friends he could trust. He had also never been especially close to his children.

Tennie Claflin (Tennie C.)
From the collection of CDR John W. Koster, USCG

After the death of his first wife Sophia in August 1868, Vanderbilt began to believe in ghosts and other types of supernatural phenomena. He instructed his barber to burn his cut hair because he believed that the person who possessed a lock of it would have power over him. He placed bowls of salt under his bed at night to ward off evil spirits. He believed it was possible to communicate with a deceased person as long as there was a photograph of them present.

Vanderbilt eventually began con-

Victoria Woodhull
From the collection of
CDR John W. Koster, USCG

sulting spiritualists in an effort to cure his physical ills and communicate with his late mother. Among those spiritualists were two sisters, Victoria Woodhull and Tennie Claflin. Whether it was because of their ability to get in touch with Vanderbilt's mother or other reasons, the Commodore became infatuated with the two women.

Woodhull and Claflin were the daughters of a destitute con man. Both were reputed to have scandalous personal lives; in fact, Woodhull was an outspoken advocate of free love who had left her husband and child for another man before she met Vanderbilt. Vanderbilt's children were horrified to learn that their seventy-three-year-old father was spending time with the two women and courting the twenty-two-year-old Claflin, who he affectionately referred to as "Tennessee." According to one of Victoria Woodhull's biographers, "Vanderbilt began spending more time with Tennessee, even bringing her to his office, where he would sit the 'little sparrow,' as he called her, on his knee and bounce her up and down as he talked railroad business. She told him jokes, read him the newspaper, and, pulling on his whiskers, called him 'old boy.' " Vanderbilt's children were so worried that they began to put other women in front of him to encourage him to take a liking to someone else.

About this time Vanderbilt received a visit from a respectable widow named Martha Crawford and her twenty-nine-year-old daughter, Miss Frank Crawford. Both were natives of Mobile, Alabama, and distant cousins of Vanderbilt's. Vanderbilt's children hoped their father would take a liking to Martha Crawford. Instead, he set his eyes on Frank. The next year he proposed to the young lady and she accepted.

Vanderbilt's sons and daughters probably had ambivalent feelings when they learned that their father was about to marry someone young enough to be his granddaughter. But they were probably relieved that this meant the likely end of their father's relationship with Woodhull and Claflin. They were probably even more satisfied when their father's fiancee signed a prenuptial agreement that gave her $500,000 as a result of the marriage — a tiny percentage of the old man's fortune.

Nevertheless, Victoria Woodhull and Tennie Claflin didn't fade into obscurity. About the time he married, Vanderbilt gave his old acquaintances enough money and stock tips to start a brokerage house called Woodhull, Claflin & Co. (Some biographies of Woodhull claim that Vanderbilt did so to pay Woodhull back for the many stock tips Woodhull picked up during seances.) The two women thus became the first female stockbrokers in America, and became known on Wall Street as the "bewitching brokers."

A few years later Woodhull and Claflin started a publication called *Woodhull and Claflin's Weekly*, becoming the first women in American history to own a newspaper. The publication combined business news, stories about spiritualism, and socialist political opinion, making it one of the most entertaining reads of its day. Among other things, *Woodhull and Claflin's Weekly* advocated free love, legalized prostitution, and birth control — extremely radical ideas at the time. The publication and its owners were so liberal regarding sexual opinion, in fact, that other women's rights advocates of that time, such as Susan B. Anthony and Lucy Stone, distanced themselves from Woodhull and Claflin.

In 1871 Victoria Woodhull ran for president of the United States, claiming that a fourth century senator named Demosthenes told her to do so during a seance. Despite the amount of criticism that she had received from other feminist leaders, Woodhull managed to secure the nomination of an organization called the Equal Rights Party. The Equal Rights Party nominated Frederick Douglass to be vice president.

Woodhull thus became the first woman to be nominated by a political party as president of the United States. But needless to say, the Woodhull/Douglass ticket didn't get many votes in the 1872 election (won by Ulysses S. Grant). For one thing, Douglass respectfully declined the offer by the Equal Rights Party to be the vice presidential nominee. For another, women weren't allowed to vote in 1872.

Appropriately, the relationship between the two sisters and Cornelius Vanderbilt ended with a bit of a scandal. During her failed presidential campaign Victoria Woodhull publicly criticized her mentor. "A Vanderbilt may sit in his office and manipulate stocks, or make dividends by which in a few years, he amasses $50 million from the industries of the country and he is one of the remarkable men of the age," she said in a speech. "But if a poor, half-starved child were to take a loaf of bread from his cupboard to prevent starvation, she would be sent first to the Tombs and then to Blackwell's Island." The speech was so radical for its time that most New York newspapers ignored it; but its contents apparently made their way back to Vanderbilt. From that point on, America's wealthiest man apparently stopped funneling money to its most radical feminist.

The Commodore died on January 4, 1877, leaving about 90 percent of his $105 million fortune to his oldest son William Henry. Three of Vanderbilt's other eleven children sued, claiming that their father had not been of a sound mind when he wrote his will. When he realized that it was his siblings' intention to produce the spiritualists Victoria Woodhull and Tennie Claflin as witnesses in the trial, William Vanderbilt reportedly paid the sisters more than $100,000 to leave the country (although Woodhull denied they were given that money). Woodhull and Claflin thus moved to England, where they both died in the 1920s.

THE BISHOP WITH THE BAD BACK

In March 1873 Cornelius and Frank Vanderbilt received a visit from Bishop Holland McTyeire, the husband of Frank Vanderbilt's cousin. McTyeire was visiting the Vanderbilts because he had a bad back and wanted to see a New York surgeon. While McTyeire was recovering, he asked Mr. Vanderbilt to give half a million dollars for the establishment of a Southern Methodist university. After a conversation that lasted several hours, the old tycoon agreed, putting only a few conditions to his gift. Among them were that McTyeire be named president of the school's board of trust for life, be given a salary of

$3,000 per year, and be allowed to live in a house on campus rent-free for the rest of his life. Also, the plans for campus construction had to be submitted to Vanderbilt for approval. Finally, Vanderbilt dictated that the school be located "in or near" Nashville.

Interestingly enough, Vanderbilt did not ask that the school be named for him. "He did not make this a condition, he did not request it, he did not hint it even remotely," McTyeire later said. But as a result of the Commodore's gift, McTyeire proposed to his fellow trustees that the name of the school be changed to Vanderbilt University. The trustees agreed, and the name "Central University" fell into oblivion.

So why on earth did Cornelius Vanderbilt – a man who was poorly educated, superstitious, not especially charitable, and who may have never stepped foot in the South in his life – give $500,000 for the establishment of a Methodist College in the South? The only three people who probably had anything to do with his decision were his second wife Frank, Bishop McTyeire, and Charles Deems. When Cornelius Vanderbilt married Frank Crawford in 1869, the railroad magnate was forty-three years older than his bride. By all accounts, Mr. Vanderbilt loved and doted on his second wife. According to John Tigert, who wrote a biography of Bishop Holland McTyeire, Frank Vanderbilt deserves

Woodcut of Bishop Holland McTyeire
The United Methodist Publishing House Collection

more credit than anyone else for swaying her husband. "Her love of Amelia [her cousin and McTyeire's wife], her confidence in the powers of the Bishop, and, above all, her deep devotion to the South and grief for its desperate plight, all prompted her hope of opening the Commodore's heart so that he would want to endow a university in the South," Tigert wrote. "She knew too that her husband was desirous of leaving some great memorial before his death."

Regarding his legacy, Cornelius Vanderbilt's original idea was to build a university on Staten Island to honor his mother. He had also considered the idea of building a massive monument to George Washington in Central Park. "Mrs. Vanderbilt did not attack this project, but she guided his thinking in another direction," Tigert said.

Since Cornelius Vanderbilt was not prone to give speeches, he never fully explained to anyone why he chose to give money to a Methodist college in the South. But he once gave a hint about what he was thinking in a letter he wrote to McTyeire, a letter the school submitted in an important lawsuit many years later. "I fitted out a vessel during the war to help suppress the rebellion and bring your people back into the Union, and I feel it is my duty now to do something for the South, especially as I have married one of Mobile's noblest daughters," Vanderbilt wrote.

In addition to McTyeire and Vanderbilt's wife, there is one other person who may have had something to do with the Commodore's decision to give money to a Methodist university in Nashville. Charles Deems was a native of North Carolina and the pastor of New York's Church of the Stranger, a congregation for transients and others without a church home. Shortly after they were married, Cornelius and Frank Vanderbilt attended the Church of the Stranger and heard a sermon by Deems that impressed Mr. Vanderbilt. Within a few months he had donated $50,000 to that church and become friends with Deems, a man whose son had fought and died for the Confederacy. Several accounts of Vanderbilt's gift that were published in New York gave Deems credit for swaying the Commodore.

In any case, no one will ever know who played the greatest role in influencing the Commodore, because no one apparently ever asked him. On October 4, 1875, the new Vanderbilt University was dedicated at a ceremony in the chapel of the school's Main Building. Vanderbilt did not attend the dedication (in fact, the man never stepped foot on the campus named for him). Attendees had to be content with a large portrait of the Commodore that was hanging on the wall.

A few months later a prominent Nashville citizen paid a call on Cornelius Vanderbilt to thank him for what he had done. "We found before us a man of somewhat more than medium stature – in his slippers and evening robe – with a frank, manly face, full of that force, energy and will, which impelled his remarkable career," the citizen later said. "You could see in it the determination which had led him from the humble position he held in his boyhood to the unsurpassed success of his extraordinary manhood." In June 1876 Vanderbilt increased his gift to the school, bringing the amount of his donation to a million dollars.

McTyeire ignores the local rags

Vanderbilt University has been linked with Nashville and West End Avenue for so long that it is hard to imagine it anywhere else. In fact, the school could have easily ended up in another city, or another part of town.

Nashville's citizens proposed many sites to Bishop Holland McTyeire, including a one hundred acre parcel offered free of charge by two property owners that is believed to have been located about where White Bridge Road was later placed. He also considered the idea of "sharing" a campus with the University of Nashville, an institution located south of downtown. Many Nashville residents wanted to see such a merger because their beloved University of Nashville was having trouble raising money — an ongoing problem that would doom it by the end of the century. However, McTyeire rejected the idea of a joint effort with the University of Nashville because, as he said in a letter to Mr. Vanderbilt, "we must control entirely or not at all."

Eventually McTyeire narrowed his choice to three locations. One was along the south side of West End Avenue, an area then several blocks from the edge of developed Nashville. The West End site totaled about seventy-five acres and was known in published accounts as "Litton Hill" or the "Taylor Property."

McTyeire's other two sites were in Edgefield, then a separate city east of Nashville and across the Cumberland River. One of those tracts was then known as "Confederate Hill," and is believed to be the eventual location of the Cayce Homes public housing project. The other was in the area of what eventually became Eastland Avenue.

Nashville's daily newspapers made no secret of which site they favored. The *Union and American* said Vanderbilt University should go in Edgefield because the local government there could better devote itself to the school's needs than the local government of Nashville. "No university has ever yet prospered in any city or town in the world in which its interests were not made the chief consideration in the local legislation of the place," the paper said. "The municipal legislation of Nashville will, of course, be directed mainly to the protection of her rapidly growing manufacturing and mercantile interests, while in Edgefield the proposed University would be the grand feature of the town and would be ever sure of receiving all the aid that local legislation could afford it."

The *Republican Banner* listed even more reasons Edgefield should get the campus. "It [Edgefield] has broader and more evenly graded and better shaded streets; it is quieter; it has more of a green sward and leafy wood and the scenic beauties of nature generally. . . . It combines the attractions of country with the conveniences of city."

The other reason Edgefield seemed to be the most likely site was money. Even though Cornelius Vanderbilt had pledged $500,000 for the university, McTyeire and his fellow trustees hoped to raise as much money as possible for land and initial construction through donations. To this end, the citizens of Edgefield pledged more than $49,000 if the campus were built there — more than twice as much money as the citizens of Nashville pledged in advance of the dec- ision. The *Republican Banner* criticized Nashville's residents for this lack of generosity. "It is with greater regret that we learn that some of those citizens who are most interested in the prosperity of the city and most able to help have refused to donate a dime," an editorial said.

On May 8, 1873, hundreds of Nashville citizens packed the sanctuary of McKendree Methodist Church to hear the final verdict. At that meeting, the University's board of supervisors announced it had decided to put the campus on the West End property as long as Nashville's citizens increased their pledge from $18,000 to about $48,000. (In the end, citizens donated $28,000 in cash and $15,250 in free land toward the campus.)

Since McTyeire had veto power over any decision the board of supervisors made, the board's decision was clearly his. To this day no one really knows why McTyeire (whose critics described him as secretive) chose West End over the other areas. But on May 21, 1873, he wrote this brief explanation of his choice to Cornelius Vanderbilt: "Of the many sites offered and which I examined, one was fixed upon as best. It is west of the city, beautiful for situation, easy of approach and of the same elevation as Capitol Hill, which is in full view."

Those Edgefield residents who pledged generous donations to Vanderbilt must have felt insulted when McTyeire chose West End. However, a *Banner* editorial written a few days after the 1873 decision pointed out that there were still reasons for Nashville residents to cross the Cumberland River into Edgefield. "If Edgefield has lost the location of the Vanderbilt University, there are some things that she cannot lose — her foliage, sweet-scented grasses, her beautiful homes . . . her genial men, her beautiful women, and last, though not least, her untaxed manufactories."

CORNFIELD TO COLLEGE

It's safe to say that in 1873 there was only one person in Nashville who could stand on rural West End Avenue, gaze at the cornfield in front of him, and see something great. That person was Bishop Holland McTyeire, who in less than two years turned an IOU from Cornelius Vanderbilt and a limited amount of authority from the Methodist Episcopal Church, South, into a university.

Not many records and stories survive about the original construction of the Vanderbilt campus. Still, enough material remains to offer glimpses of the early struggles, the determination of McTyeire, and the frustrations and pride with each new step.

When McTyeire first chose the site there were still remnants of a battle that had taken place less than a decade earlier. During the Civil War part of the Battle of Nashville occurred on the land that later became the Vanderbilt campus. The Union Army built trenches and rifle pits where the Vanderbilt Medical School was eventually built, although the Confederate forces never got close to them in their attempt to invade Nashville in December 1864. Some of these trenches were leveled and smoothed when the campus was laid out in 1874 and 1875. However, some of the Union Army fortifications remained in the 1880s as a part of Bishop Holland McTyeire's garden.

Very little is known about why campus planners built structures where they did, except one tidbit from a newspaper article. When McTyeire studied the land on which the campus was to be built, he had a hard time deciding whether to put the school's Main Building on a hill near West End Avenue or a hill to the south of it. "When I stand there, I think that is the better location; when I stand here, I think this is the better," he said in 1874. Since there was already a large house on the south hill, McTyeire put Main on the north hill. The building on the south hill served as the home of the Bible school for about five years and was referred to by students as Wesley Hall. In 1880 it was torn down and replaced with a much larger structure that was also called Wesley Hall.

McTyeire chose architect William Smith to design Vanderbilt's first buildings – the Main Building (which burned in 1905), the observatory (torn down in 1952), and eight residences. More than two decades after designing the buildings on the Vanderbilt campus, Smith was one of the chief architects for the Centennial Exposition of 1897 and designed the replica of the Parthenon.

For Vanderbilt, Smith designed an architectural wonder that contained two 150-foot-high towers. The Main Building contained just about everything a university needed at that time: one large and six small lecture halls, ten professors' offices, a library, a chapel, rooms for two literary societies, and a large chemical laboratory. Because of the laboratory, the interior of the building usually smelled of chemicals. Main also contained a public museum containing geological arti-

Vanderbilt's Main Building (later called College Hall)
The Banner Collection, Nashville Public Library, The Nashville Room

facts. The collection grew over the years and was so large by the 1920s that geology professor Willis Stovall made a public appeal for the school to build a separate museum for citizens of Nashville. That request was denied, and most of the artifacts were later sent to the Tennessee State Museum.

Main's general contractor was John Kilcoin of Nashville. In fact, McTyeire was proud of the fact that every contractor hired to build Main was a Nashville-based company except for one (which installed the steam heating system). "The reason why this contract was not let here was there were none among us who could do the work satisfactorily," the bishop later said.

The groundbreaking ceremony took place on Sept. 15, 1873, and was apparently only attended by one reporter, who later described the site as looking "bleak and desolate" at that time. McTyeire stuck the first shovel in the ground, saying the words "Except the Lord build the house, they labor in vain that build it" in Latin as he did so. During the subsequent six weeks about thirty-five workers removed four thousand yards of dirt by hand and mule from the Main Building site.

Seven months later, when the Main Building's cornerstone was laid, the Nashville Board of Trade took the unusual step of requesting that all local businesses be closed for three hours so that as many people as possible could attend the ceremony. Those who came did so despite rain and cold weather. That day a copper box was placed in the cornerstone of the Main Building. It contained over 60 separate items, including a picture of Cornelius Vanderbilt, a specimen of Tennessee coal, a current map of Nashville, and a copy of every single Southern Methodist newspaper published at that time (there were ten). Swan & Brown, the Nashville stone contractor that built the Main Building's foundation, even slipped a business card in the box. It is believed that the box was reopened when the Main Building was rebuilt in 1906.

Construction did not go smoothly. While Main was being built in the summer of 1874, Nashville suffered a terrible cholera epidemic. "Yesterday was the worst day we have had," McTyeire wrote in a letter to Chancellor Garland on June 21, 1873. "More deaths – 78 – in the city and suburbs. . . . Negroes get little attention – pressed are the doctors."

One thing that the original construction crew did not build was a dormitory. It was the strong opinion of McTyeire and Garland that it made more sense to let students board with Nashville families because dormitories promoted mischief and sin. (The fact that the school didn't have enough money to actually build dormitories may also have had something to do with this strategy.) The only problem with this idea was that there weren't many houses in the area of the campus. There were so few homes, in fact, that a Nashville newspaper asked residents to build houses in the campus area. "We set out to call attention to the fact that boarding houses will be needed," an article in a Nashville newspaper implored. "Now is the time for persons who have sons to educate, or who would make a pleasant living in a pleasant way to begin to get ready. Provide homes with room in each, or offices attached to each, for from four to a dozen young men as boarders. Land can be had now near the university for from $500 to $1,500 per acre, and the horse cars are running there."

At least one Nashville company did what McTyeire and Garland hoped and built a large boarding house near the campus. One month before classes started on campus, the *Nashville Daily American* contained an advertisement for a boarding house near the campus that had space for fifty men. "We shall endeavor to make our house rather more a home to students than a boarding house," the ad said.

For the first eight years of the school's existence, students frequently complained to McTyeire and Garland about the quality and cost of lodging near campus. In 1883 two graduate students organized a new boarding house and eating establishment. The two students leased a large house across West End Avenue, christened it Liberty Hall, and hired someone to cook meals and keep the place clean. For about five years, Liberty Hall was the closest thing Vanderbilt had to a dormitory. The students who lived there – up to sixty at a time — claimed it was safe and that the food was pretty good. But it became affectionately known as "The Stockyard" because the cook would keep live pigs and chickens in the backyard.

The success of Liberty Hall made McTyeire and Garland realize it was time to rethink the ban on campus housing, and in 1888 the school began building a row of two-story houses that eventually

A later view of Vanderbilt's Main Building
The Banner Collection, Nashville Public Library, The Nashville Room

became known as West Side Row. This plan was the first of many developments in the school's history that would cause consternation among Vanderbilt students. "A row of buildings which the authorities would likely put up would not add to the beauty of West End Avenue, and they would be a poor substitute for the beautiful grove which now stands there," stated an article in the November 1888 issue of the *The Observer* newspaper.

McTyeire ignored the student complaints; he had a tendency to do things his way and require that everyone else do them his way as well. For example, the bishop had a rule that no campus building could be built of wood. (The only thing that was built out of wood in the early days was the fence that surrounded the campus to keep cows and pigs from wandering onto it.) At one point in the late 1870s, McTyeire returned from an extended trip to find that Chancellor Garland and geology professor James Safford had violated the rule by building a wooden stable for their horses. Without saying anything to either man, McTyeire had the stables torn down.

One final observation on the original Vanderbilt campus was the size of the city's donation toward it. When McTyeire first chose the West End site for the university, Nashville's citizens pledged $43,250 toward its construction. (No one knows how much of that amount was actually collected.) Because the value of money changes so much over the years, it is difficult to generate a contemporary equivalent. But other cities were paying more for colleges at that time. The Memphis Chamber of Commerce made an offer of $200,000 for the school. And one year after McTyeire picked the West End Avenue site, the Tennessee Baptist Convention conducted a deliberate search for a place to build a college. Nashville was eliminated from the list because the Methodists had already chosen it for their college. But at least four cities petitioned for the Baptist school, and all four of them offered to give far more money than Nashville's citizens had offered to spend. Chattanooga offered $75,000; Murfreesboro pledged $74,000 plus the deed to a vacant college campus; Jackson offered $49,625 plus the deed to a vacant college campus; and McMinnville pledged $50,000 in real estate and $50,000 in subscriptions. The Baptists chose Jackson as the site for what became Southwestern Baptist University, and later Union University.

Part Two

The Bishop's School

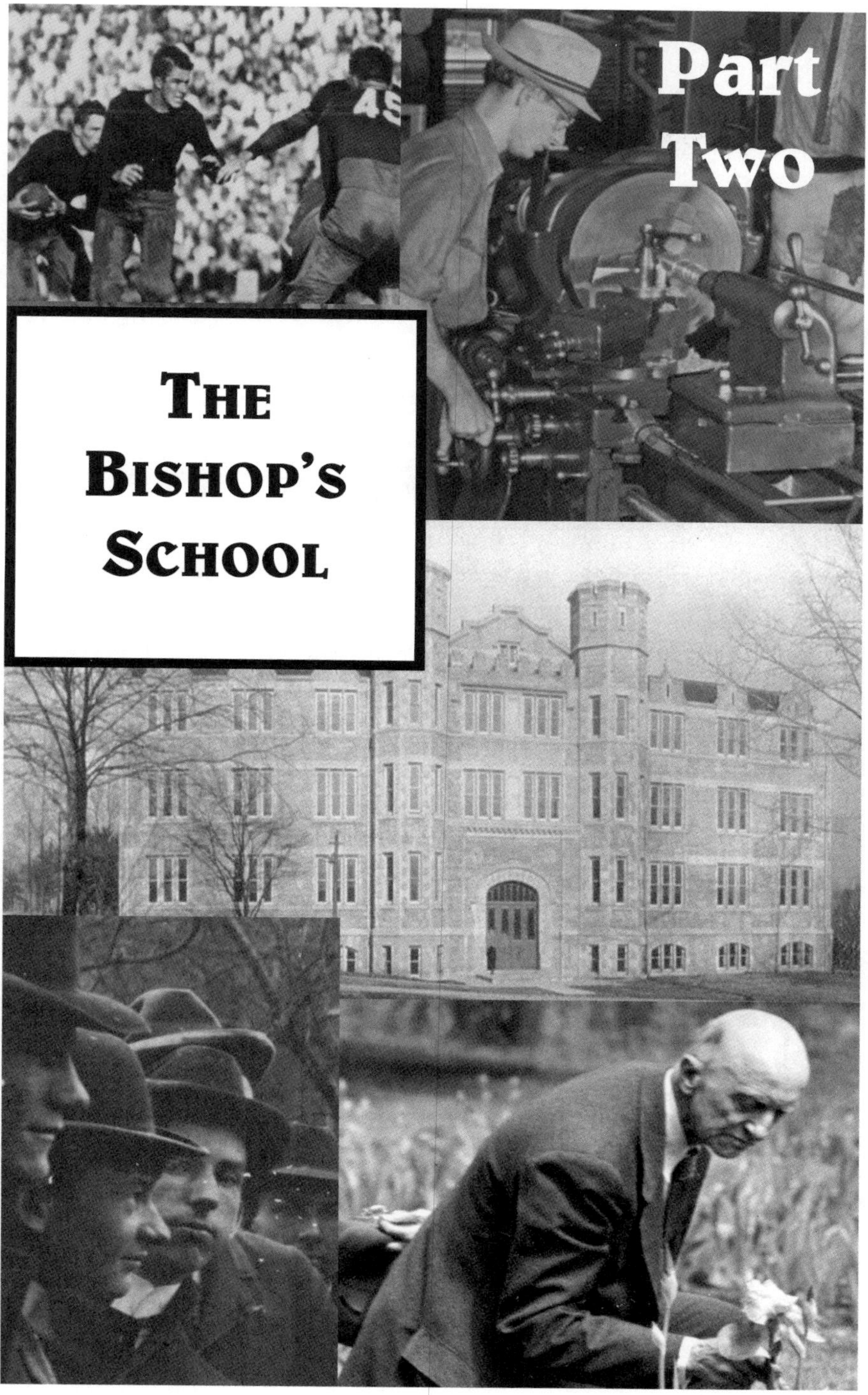

McTyeire hires and fires the Dream Team

"It is time for the Methodist Episcopal Church, South, to know that Vanderbilt University is conducted as an independent enterprise of Bishop McTyeire's, of which he is really president, chancellor, dean and spring-time lecturer, and that it is run very much in the interest of his own family."
– Alfred Shipp

In hindsight, it seems inevitable that there would have been problems. Holland McTyeire, whose background was in preaching and editing Methodist newspapers, was practically given dictatorial powers when Vanderbilt University was formed. When it came time for him to run the school, there were dissenters.

After the initial wave of excitement over Cornelius Vanderbilt's pledge and the selection of a site for a university, McTyeire began the arduous task of building an institution from scratch. One of the first things he did was offer Landon Garland the dual position of chancellor and professor of physics and astronomy. This selection surprised no one, since the relationship between McTyeire and Garland went back many years. Garland had been the president of Randoph-Macon College when McTyeire was a student there in the 1840s. By the end of the Civil War Garland was one of the most prominent Methodists in academia and an ally of McTyeire's in the struggle to get Vanderbilt University organized in the first place. Garland, who was in 1874 the president of the University of Mississippi, only reluctantly agreed to take the Vanderbilt job. He was sixty-five at the time and already suffering from fragile health.

McTyeire was a one-man committee (answerable to Cornelius Vanderbilt) when it came to decisions such as where the campus would be built and what the buildings would look like. He was also his own treasurer. During the 1870s most of the initial $500,000 donation went from Vanderbilt to McTyeire to vendor; the board of trust didn't begin acting more deliberately about university funds until the

1880s. But from all available evidence, Garland played a major role in the academic structuring of the school and the initial hiring of faculty. The chancellor thought big. As he explained to a colleague at the time, Garland's original intention was for Vanderbilt to be such a good school that "our sons need not go to England or Germany or

Chancellor Landon Garland
The United Methodist Publishing House Collection

France" to get an excellent education anymore. In other words, he envisioned a Harvard of the South.

In 1874 Garland proposed that Vanderbilt University have two departments in addition to medical and law schools that would be developed separately. Those departments were Biblical (with four professors) and Literature, Science and Philosophy (eleven professors). McTyeire and the board agreed to this structure, and during the next year McTyeire and Garland filled most of the positions, hiring some of the most highly regarded academicians in America.

Virtually every one of the new hires was in place by the time about two hundred students enrolled in the fall of 1875. But most of the professors wouldn't stay long. For various reasons, chairman McTyeire would effectively run off his first wave of faculty members by 1885. In one case, a faculty member was dismissed for allegedly being drunk. But in most other instances the reasons were more complex or political.

One of the most significant departures was Alexander Winchell. Winchell was a nationally renowned geologist who had been the chancellor of Syracuse University. When he was hired as a part-time lecturer in 1875, McTyeire knew that Winchell, as did most geologists, had a theory about the origin of man that was linked to Charles Darwin's theory of evolution. Apparently underestimating how controversial evolution was becoming in many circles, McTyeire offered Winchell the job anyway.

By 1878 evolution became a hot topic in many regional Methodist publications around the country, including the *Nashville Christian Advocate* and the *St. Louis Christian Advocate.* Although the editorial position of such publications varied, the idea that man evolved from a lower form of life was generally regarded as anathema by Methodist leaders. Winchell's evolutionary theories were also despised by Thomas Summers, a theology professor at Vanderbilt and an influential Methodist leader in his own right. Within three years of hiring Winchell, McTyeire realized his mistake.

In May 1878 McTyeire asked Winchell to give a lecture on his theory on the origins of man to the board of trust. (The only possible explanation for why McTyeire took this step is that he was setting up Winchell to be fired.) The next issue of the *Nashville Christian*

Advocate contained an editorial about the speech. "It was one of the most beautiful lectures we ever heard," the story said. "It made us almost sorry that we could not accept the nebular theory and evolution, its corollary," Shortly thereafter, Winchell was told that the board of trust had eliminated his position. His dismissal haunted the school for many years. Half a century later, in the midst of the national debate over the Scopes trial in Dayton, Tennessee, the school's handling of Winchell was cited in *Nation* magazine as an example of southern ignorance.

Another wave of faculty departures took place because of money. Every full professor hired at Vanderbilt in 1875 was offered $2,500 per year, plus free housing on campus. In 1879 the board of trust reduced all professor salaries to $2,213 per year, citing declining tuition income as the reason. A few months later, a group of seven faculty members, including Garland, wrote a stern letter to McTyeire asking that their full salaries be restored. The board did not do so – one of the reasons mathematician William Broun left the school in 1882, Greek professor Milton Humphreys departed in 1883, and chemistry professor Nathaniel Lupton left in 1885.

The most drawn-out dismissal was that of Alfred Shipp. In 1875 McTyeire offered Shipp, the president of Wofford College, a job as a theology professor. Shipp made it clear that he already had a notable disability – a throat condition that made it difficult for him to speak for long periods of time. McTyeire hired him anyway.

Within a couple of years, Shipp became very critical of the way the Biblical school was being run. The school had no academic standards; all a young man needed to be accepted was a letter of recommendation from a bishop or elder. The school also had no orderly curriculum. Beginner students were allowed to sign up for advanced courses in theology, often causing distress to students and faculty. Meanwhile, other Vanderbilt departments had entrance requirements and a more ordered series of courses, causing the rest of the faculty and students to look down on the Biblical school. "The impression prevailed that many of the 'theologues' were backward in their studies and took theology to conceal their lack of the elements of an English education and, in some cases, this was unfortunately the truth," an alumnus wrote around this time.

James Kirkland as a young Vanderbilt professor
The United Methodist Publishing House Collection

Shipp lobbied McTyeire hard to come up with entrance standards and a better curriculum structure. But the bishop was determined to run it his way and keep the Biblical school open to almost anyone who wanted to become a preacher. McTyeire was mindful of the fact that high academic standards might cause rank and file southern Methodists to resent his great university.

After Shipp and several of his colleagues sent McTyeire the 1879 letter complaining about salary reductions, Shipp said his boss started a systematic process of trying to get rid of him. McTyeire first tried to have Shipp appointed book editor of the Southern Methodist Publishing House, a plan that didn't work because Shipp made it clear to his fellow Methodists that he didn't want the job. Next, McTyeire increased Shipp's workload, promoting him to vice chancellor of the university and forcing him to teach separate classes on exegetical theology, systematic theology, and moral theology. Shipp was thus teaching twenty-three hours a week, while other faculty members (including McTyeire's recently hired sons-in-law William Baskervill and John Tigert) were each teaching less than ten hours a week.

After McTyeire and Shipp clashed on several other administrative incidents, the board fired the faculty member in December 1884. The official reason for the dismissal was Shipp's inability to speak at Methodist conferences. Shipp did not go down quietly, telling his side of the story in a long pamphlet that he distributed to Methodist church officials and published in a Nashville newspaper. Shipp accused McTyeire of nepotism, egotism, and covering up several of his own mistakes. One of those, Shipp said, was the time McTyeire ordered a disreputable young man to be admitted to the school who subsequently had to be hurried out of town "to escape the consequences of an offense that would have shut him up in the penitentiary."

Of course, it would be wrong to imply that life on campus during the first ten years of Vanderbilt's existence was dominated by faculty strife. True, many high-priced professors came and went. But in some cases, they were replaced by younger faculty members who fit in better and who became campus legends in the 1880s and 1890s. And one of the original faculty members who stayed for the rest of his career later said that he wouldn't have traded the experience of teaching during Vanderbilt's early years for anything. "A band of noble brothers was that (original) faculty," geology professor James Safford said. "I look back upon them with much affection."

By the late 1880s, McTyeire's "dream team" was gone. Vanderbilt had a new generation of faculty. Among them were a chemistry professor (with an interest in sports) named William

Dudley, another chemistry instructor named John McGill, theology dean Wilbur Tillett, and English professor William Baskervill. Less noticed at the time was a very young Latin scholar named James Kirkland and a theology professor named Elijah Hoss. Those two men, as chancellor and Methodist newspaper editor, would one day fight a huge legal battle over the school's future.

THE SEASON OF THE AUSTRAL

Vanderbilt University was a new place in 1879. It was located on a seventy-five-acre campus that didn't contain much more than two large buildings, eight houses, and hundreds of tiny trees. It had no traditions. It was completely dominated by the Methodist church and by the personalities of founder Holland McTyeire and Chancellor Landon Garland. But through the barren campus walked a new generation of students who felt a spirit of intellectual curiosity and quiet rebellion.

One of the most notable signs of this quiet rebellion was the debut of the school's first student newspaper. It was called the *Vanderbilt Austral* – austral meaning "coming from the south." Since the *Austral* didn't survive and was started anonymously, only a rough sketch can be given of how it came about and what became of it. Since they had no school funds with which to start their enterprise, founding students sold stock in the *Austral* for five dollars a share. Students did not distribute it on campus, but sold their publication at off-campus gathering spots for fifteen cents a copy.

The *Austral* was a twelve-page monthly publication that debuted in March of 1879. The front page was dominated by advertisers, such as J.L. Dismukes & Co. and Ordway & Co., almost all of which were clothing retailers located on Nashville's Public Square. The rest of the publication consisted of articles and editorials written anonymously.

Thanks to the *Austral* and to a few pieces that were written in the *Vanderbilt Alumnus* magazine during World War I, future generations can know bits and pieces about what life was life on campus in 1879. For example, all first-year students had to take courses in Greek,

Latin, and mathematics – the three subjects considered the foundation of a proper education in those days. Upon completion of those courses, students could move on to more advanced subjects such as physics and chemistry.

Another important aspect of student life in 1879 was the fact that Vanderbilt had no dormitories. Law, medical, and theology students could live anywhere in Nashville. But students of what would eventually become known as the Arts & Sciences division (who were then called literary students) were required to live in boarding houses west of the Union (train) Station. This rule was very unpopular, and the *Austral* editorialized against it because the cost of living was more expensive near the campus than in other parts of town. "Good accommodations cannot be obtained near the university for less than $20 a month, whilst in Edgefield and the city board equally as good can be obtained for prices varying from $12 to $16 a month," the *Austral* said. "Is not such a rule obviously unjust?"

Meanwhile, the school had no athletics of any kind, few student organizations, and no recognized fraternities. The largest sporting events on campus were croquet matches. The only social activities were ones put together by faculty members and the families who owned and ran boarding houses near the school. A group of young ladies who lived near the campus, for example, organized a "cooking club" that met every week or so at a different boarding house.

Because there was so little to do on campus, student life revolved around the classroom and activities with faculty members. One campus favorite was Greek professor Milton Humphreys. "He not only knew Greek, but he knew everything!" one alumnus recalled in an article written half a century later. "It was impossible to ask him anything that he didn't know." Another was mathematics professor William Broun. "Dr. Broun made all things simple," said an alumnus. "Dealing in the most abstract and to many the most difficult science, his clarity of vision was such that in terse, concise, almost snappy, but always kind words, he went straight to the point and made one feel almost ashamed that he even thought the problem difficult." However, students were completely intimidated by Chancellor Garland, a stern old man with a long beard whom respectful students called "Old Gray" and whom less respectful students referred to as

"Horsehead." The only way to break the ice with Garland was to ask him about his marvelous collection of physics and astronomy equipment.

Since most of the professors were young men who lived on campus, children were a big part of life at the school. These children were indulged by everyone, even stern Bishop McTyeire. Stella Vaughn, who grew up on the Vanderbilt grounds, said many years later that she had many fond memories of McTyeire. "The bishop was very fond of children," she wrote. "Whenever a snow fell, he would get out his one horse sleigh and drive from house to house picking up the little folks. All that couldn't get in the sleigh hung their sled on behind for his horse to pull. It was a funny sight."

The *Austral* bemoaned Vanderbilt's lack of activities. It suggested bringing outside lecturers to campus, saying that such speeches would make a good substitute for the weekly talks by Chancellor Garland "which are usually in the nature of reprimands." The paper also listed several reasons that Greek organizations would be good for Vanderbilt, saying that, "Cliques and factions are far more numerous and bitter in institutions where there are no fraternities than in institutions where they do exist . . . in a fraternity, the older members watch over the younger members with solicitous care, for the honor of one is the honor of all, and the disgrace of one is the common disgrace of all." Regarding the school's lack of athletic facilities, the *Austral* said it would make sense for Vanderbilt to build a gymnasium because "it is a well established fact that boys will not live without amusements of some kind, and if innocent ones are denied them, they seek the baser kinds."

What the students who wrote the *Austral* may not have known is that the school's lack of athletic facilities was only temporary. Later that year, Vanderbilt built a gymnasium – which had been planned all along — close to the West End Avenue side of campus. It was equipped with state of the art exercise equipment, such as parallel bars, climbing poles, a rowing machine, a vaulting horse, and a full set of dumb bells.

Without much to do on campus, one of the big events of 1879 took place after commencement, when Professor James Safford took a group of about fifteen students on a month-long geological expedition through southeast Tennessee. In the May 1879 issue of the *Austral*, students were advised to bring two flannel shirts, a pair of jeans, and a broad brimmed hat; but most importantly they were told to bring strong legs and a lot of energy. "There will be one or two wagons in which to carry provisions and other necessary articles and ride whenever necessary, but it must be borne in mind that the principal mode of travel will be on foot and that no unnecessary article should be taken," the story said. Students stopped on the way in Murfreesboro, McMinnville, Chattanooga, Cleveland, and Ducktown. The *Austral* came out a couple of nights after the group left on the excursion, and somehow kept up with their progress to McMinnville. "Where they are now, or what fate has befallen them, heaven only knows," a later story said.

Another interesting thing about 1879 is that two of the graduates that spring were a woman and an important abolitionist. The woman was Kate Lupton, whose father was a chemistry professor. Starting in 1875, Lupton began taking classes in various subjects on campus. Four years later, she had excelled at almost every subject, and in 1879 was given a Master of Arts degree for her effort. The abolitionist was George Hubbard. During the Civil War Hubbard was with the Union Army and got stuck in Nashville for a time because Confederate General Nathan Bedford Forrest had cut off the train line to Chattanooga. While stranded, Hubbard began teaching at a school for freed slaves. In 1879 Hubbard graduated from the Vanderbilt Medical School. He later helped start a Nashville hospital for black patrons that was named for him.

Besides the fact that it is one of the few glimpses into early campus life, the *Austral* is also priceless because it proves that as early as 1879, student journalists could be entertaining and offensive. At one point, officials at Ward's Seminary for Young Ladies invited Vanderbilt students to watch a calisthenics drill. A sarcastic reporter for the *Austral* said it was a fine event. "The way the girls did handle those wands, rings and dumb-bells!" he said. "Long may they wave with their little red bodies and dark colored skirts."

Another wonderful item by the *Austral* ridiculed medical students because, at that time, they had to resort to grave robbing to obtain cadavers. The March 1879 issue of the *Austral* reported that the medical school term was over, which meant that "the picking shop will be deserted, and the ghoulish ravages on the cemeteries will cease for a time." It went on to say that before they left for the year, the medical students had come on the main campus as a group to attend chapel. "The first place on the campus they visited, drawn by an irresistible attraction, was the two bishops' graves."

In its June 1879 issue, the editors of the *Austral* made it sound as if their publication would exist the next school year. But it didn't. According to a story repeated many years later in the *Vanderbilt Alumnus*, Chancellor Garland couldn't stand the *Austral*. "Young men, you should go to Jericho until your beards grow before you try to issue this publication," he reportedly told students at chapel. In the fall of 1879 Garland discovered the names of the students who had produced the *Austral*. According to a story that was handed down verbally, Garland told the students that they had to sign a pledge that they would abandon their publication if they wanted to graduate.

About two years later Vanderbilt students started a literary journal on campus called *The Observer*. But it would be nine more years before a new school paper, called *The Hustler*, made its debut.

BARNARD AND HIS $250 COMET

Edward Emerson Barnard was one of the first academic superstars at Vanderbilt and one of the few faculty members to have a building named for him. This in spite of the fact that he spent only four years at the university and had almost no formal education.

Barnard was born in 1857 and was a small child when the Union Army occupied Nashville during the Civil War. He grew up fatherless and in abject poverty. Fortunately for Barnard, there were no child labor laws at that time. At the age of nine Barnard took a job working in a photographic studio, doing a menial task no one else would do. In those days the process of enlarging a photograph was crude and required an intense source of light. At the van Stavoren studio at the corner of Fourth Avenue and Union Street, that source was sunlight, directed through the lens of a massive telescope on the roof. Barnard's job was keeping the telescope directed at the sun on long, sunny days. He did the job well enough to have it for six years.

Barnard worked with some intriguing people at the studio (which under later ownership became known as the Poole Gallery). Two were Ebenezer and Peter Calvert, who would go on to start a photography business called Calvert's Photographs that still existed at the end of the twentieth century. Another was James Braid, who started a company called Braid Electric that also still existed at the end of

Edward E. Barnard
The E.E. Barnard Manuscript Collection
Special Collections, Vanderbilt University

the twentieth century. A fourth was James Ross, an inventor who, along with Braid, conducted the first long distance phone conversation in Nashville by connecting a Western Union station in Nashville with one in Bowling Green, Kentucky, in 1877. Barnard witnessed that event. A few years later, Braid and Ross co-founded a business called Cumberland Telephone & Telegraph. CT&T remained Nashville's main phone company until 1911, when it was acquired by American Telephone & Telegraph.

There were so many fascinating people at the Poole Gallery that it is no wonder young Barnard developed interests in both photography and astronomy while working there. Braid gave Barnard his first homemade telescope and helped him build a second. By 1877 Barnard saved enough money to buy a $380 telescope that had multi-

The Barnard Observatory
The Banner Collection
Nashville Public Library, The Nashville Room

ple eyepieces. He spent entire nights looking through it, making observations about stars, planets, and other astronomical phenomena. At a time when there was high interest in things scientific, Barnard's interest in astronomy was contagious in Nashville. So many people would crowd on top of Poole's Gallery on some nights to look through Barnard's telescope that the rooftop evenings got a bit dangerous.

About the time he bought the telescope, Barnard had an experience that traumatized him. In 1877 the American Association for the Advancement of Science (AAAS) held its annual meeting in Nashville. The meeting was covered minutely by the daily newspapers. Sometime during the event, Barnard approached AAAS president Simon Newcomb, told him about his interest in astronomy but his lack of education, and asked his advice. Accounts of what Newcomb said to Barnard vary. However, years later, Barnard said that after meeting with Newcomb, he walked behind one of the columns of the State Capitol and wept.

Despite his experience with Newcomb, Barnard continued to look through his telescope and study the heavens night after night. He probably had encouragement and professional advice on how to record what he saw from Olin Landreth, an engineering professor at Vanderbilt who had experience working in observatories. In 1881 Barnard's long hours staring through his telescope paid off when he saw something no one else had: a comet that later became known as 1881 VI.

At the time a New York patent medicine manufacturer gave two hundred dollars for every unexpected comet discovered. The habitually broke Barnard used that money to help pay off the mortgage on his small home, which was located about where Music Row was later developed. "When the first note came due a faint comet was discovered wandering along the outskirts of creation, and the money went to meet the payments," he later wrote. A year later Barnard discovered another comet.

By this time young Barnard had become quite the local celebrity. And although his telescope was adequate to have helped him make two noteworthy discoveries, it was not the largest telescope in town. After all, Vanderbilt's first chancellor, Landon Garland, was a physics and astronomy professor. Years earlier he had supervised the construction of an observatory on the Vanderbilt campus.

In 1883 Barnard was invited to join the university. Since he had no formal education, his status was vague. He was required to attend class. But his main job was to stay up all night looking through the Vanderbilt telescope, and that is just what Barnard did. Among his discoveries at Vanderbilt: seven more comets, several new nebulae, and a small but discernible brightening of the sky called the gegenschein.

During his years at Vanderbilt Barnard frequently published articles about his work and was constantly being written about in scientific journals and daily newspapers across the country. Despite this fame and the unbelievable working hours he maintained, he got along fine with students and faculty. "Sleep he considered a sheer waste of time," Robert Richardson wrote in his book *The Star Lovers.* "You might suppose that a person who held himself to such a work-crammed schedule would be a neurotic who was continually at the breaking point. On the contrary, he was genial and even-tempered, always friendly with everybody around him." Barnard was happy to entertain amateur stargazers at the observatory, and on numerous occasions would enthusiastically give visitors a quick tour of celestial objects. The free publicity generated by these evenings was invaluable to Vanderbilt as the school grew in the 1880s.

In 1887 Barnard was offered a job at the Lick Observatory near San Jose, California, the site of what was then the largest telescope in the world. There Barnard discovered seven more comets and a fifth moon around Jupiter — the first new satellite of that planet discovered since the time of Galileo. Barnard later went to the Yerkes Observatory in Williams Bay, Wisconsin, where he remained until his death in 1923.

Considering the short period of time Barnard actually spent at Vanderbilt, the school went to considerable lengths to honor him after he left. Students liked Barnard so much that they named the yearbook *The Comet* in honor of his discoveries (it was renamed *The Commodore* in 1909.) A few years later the university named the observatory after him.

The Black School Across the Street

Events, homes, and institutions are sometimes erased so completely that they leave nothing behind. In Nashville there is no better example of this phenomenon that this: the land that eventually became Peabody College was once a black theological school called Roger Williams University.

During the Civil War a white abolitionist named Dan Phillips came to Nashville intending to start a school for African American preachers. By 1866, with the financial support of philanthropic northerners and the moral support of Nashville blacks, he started a school near Fisk University called the Nashville Normal and Theological Institute. The school moved several times and eventually fell under the sponsorship of the American Baptist Home Mission Society (a division of the northern Baptist denomination). In 1874, while Vanderbilt University was under construction, Phillips raised $30,000 from one of his former classmates at Brown University and bought a thirty-acre tract and three-story mansion on Hillsboro Road from Nashville resident William Gordon.

After the school moved to the site it added another floor and two wings to the mansion. A few years later the trustees renamed the organization after Rhode Island founder Roger Williams.

In the 1880s and 1890s Roger Williams University had about a dozen teachers and 250 students, most of whom were black and a third of whom were women. In an era when most blacks were former slaves and almost none had access to public schools, the institution didn't have the luxury of admission standards or specialized curricula. Roger Williams taught everything from reading to carpentry to algebra. But it still specialized in the training of black preachers, many of whom went all over Nashville every Sunday to preach at churches or the state penitentiary. Roger Williams University was so successful that, in the words of its founder, "I never in my life have witnessed more manifest and more cheering signs of the power of the Gospel," than through the work of the school.

Even though not everyone in the surrounding area was

thrilled about the presence of a predominantly African American college, the relationship with Vanderbilt was cordial in the recollection of one Roger Williams professor. "Relations between the two schools were entirely friendly," the faculty member recalled in the 1930s. "Vanderbilt students came over to join in religious meetings at the colored college. Roger Williams boys waited on tables at Vanderbilt. Vanderbilt football coaches coached the Negro team. Roger Williams students went to games at Vanderbilt and sat with the others on the bleachers – a practice which would not be allowed today. Individual students, white and black, formed friendships that outlasted school days."

Roger Williams also produced several people who would go on to be leaders in the African American community. Graduate Elias Morris became the first president of the National Baptist Convention. Graduate Charles Dinkins became the president of Selma University.

However, what may have been Nashville's only chance at an integrated part of town was doomed. The presence of an African American school in what was an increasingly affluent part of town became awkward with the emergence of Jim Crow laws and the development of residential areas near Vanderbilt. Starting in 1891, there were frequent offers from white developers to buy the campus. The Roger Williams trustees turned them down.

Eventually, acts of vandalism and terrorism began taking place on the campus. In 1903 a bullet flew through the chapel window during a music rehearsal. On Christmas Day 1904 someone fired into the home of school president Peter Guernsey, wounding Guernsey's wife.

At about seven in the evening on January 24, 1905, most of Roger Williams' students were attending a prayer meeting in the chapel of the school's main structure, known as Centennial Hall. A Roger Williams student was returning from his job as a waiter at Vanderbilt when he saw flames on the roof of the building. As the students rushed out of the structure, "the screams of the girls and the calls for help by the 140 boys were distinctly heard all over West End," the account of the fire in the *Nashville American* said.

Students from Roger Williams, with help from some

Vanderbilt students, spent the next few hours trying to save as much property as they could. There was little firefighters could do; at that time, the campus was outside the city limits and firemen could not get water to the site via hoses. Everyone present eventually formed a bucket brigade that kept the fire from spreading to the building's two wings. But by the next morning Centennial Hall was completely destroyed along with the entire science library and the personal possessions of 160 male students.

The next day, one of the coldest recorded in Nashville, it was hard for anyone to imagine the school continuing its operation. "The campus was covered with ashes and debris from the conflagration," the *American* reported. "Around the residences of Guernsey and (school) Treasurer Owen groups of students stood with quilts and blankets wrapped about them waiting for orders and money from the officers that they might return home or look for a permanent place to live." The students found shelter in nearby houses, and classes resumed within a week.

During the next few months there were conflicting reports as to whether the structure would be rebuilt or the school moved elsewhere. Neither Guernsey nor American Baptist Home Mission Society secretary H. L. Morehouse made any public indication that they wanted the school to leave. But on March 19, the *American* reported that a local real estate company was on the verge of buying the Roger Williams campus and subdividing it for residences – much like other areas, such as Belmont Heights and Murphy Place (later site of Baptist Hospital) were also being subdivided. Guernsey and Morehouse apparently turned down this offer also.

Then, on May 22, another part of Roger Williams' main building — the original Gordon mansion that had been converted into a female dormitory — burned down. Once again the fire brigade could do little to stop the fire because of a lack of running water outside of incorporated Nashville. But this time arson was publicly recognized as a possibility. According to a story in the *American* later that week, the only person sleeping in the building that night was a male student (other students had already gone home for the summer). After he went to bed "he heard a noise from the first floor, as of someone one falling over furniture. Hearing nothing further he went to sleep, to be awakened an hour later by cries of fire." Among the valuables that were lost in the second fire were six thousand books, two organs, and a piano.

No one ever proved that either fire was set by an arsonist. A few days after the second fire Guernsey said that despite the two fires and the acts of terror that most Nashville residents still treated the school well. "Prominent citizens, both ladies and gentlemen, have frequently gone out of their way to compliment me upon the good behavior of our students, and have called upon me at my home to express personal sympathy and regret," he said. "If it should develop that the fire of Monday night was incendiary, it would prove to be, I am sure, the work of some drunken tramp, or a dare-devil, or the work of some hare-brained miscreant with a mania for destroying school property in general."

However Guernsey and Morehouse decided it made no sense to rebuild the campus on that site. The school hired Nashville developer Adolphus Hill to subdivide the land and sell the lots. In 1905 Hill began developing a new residential subdivision in the area under the name University Place. But a couple of years after he started selling lots, he became aware of the possibility that he might sell the entire tract to Peabody Normal College, which was looking for a new campus to replace the one in south Nashville. Hill repurchased some of the parcels from their new owners to strike a deal with the Peabody trustees. In October 1910 he sold about twenty-five acres of the Roger Williams site to the Peabody trustees for $170,000.

Parts of the Roger Williams campus remained unsold for years. According to longtime Vanderbilt divinity professor and neighborhood activist Eugene TeSelle, who researched the history of Roger Williams extensively, the trustees sold the last parcels in 1925 to Nashville grocer H. G. Hill (no relation to Adolphus Hill). Three-quarters of a century later, those parcels constituted a large part of the area known as Hillsboro Village.

At first it appeared as if Roger Williams University would move to a thirty-acre tract somewhere east of the old campus. However those plans fizzled because of a deteriorating relationship between the American Baptist Home Mission Society and Roger Williams alumni and black trustees. When it became obvious that the northern Baptists were hesitant about rebuilding the college, some of Nashville's black leaders became embittered. "They built the old Roger Williams and turned it over to a society dominated by white men, and when the fire came and the winds blew, the Negroes woke up to realize that they had built on a sandy foundation," an article in the black-owned *Nashville Globe* opined. "An institution that belonged to them was swept away by the flames, the little sum of over $50,000 insurance was turned into the treasury of the society dominated by white men from the East, and the ground was cut up into building lots and is being sold so that the proceeds can go in the same direction. The university could not be rebuilt on the same ground because some white people objected."

In the fall of 1907 the American Baptist Home Mission Society agreed to contribute $20,000 toward the construction of a new campus. On January 1, 1908, a smaller and less-prestigious Roger Williams University opened on a twelve-acre site on White's Creek Pike. During the new campus' grand opening a representative of the mission society said the donation would end the financial relationship between the two organizations. In his words, "the time has come when Negroes in the South must work out their own problems and destinies." The school remained on White's Creek Pike for another two decades, when it moved to Memphis and merged with Howe Junior College.

THE GHOST OF BEN KING

There was a time when doctors and medical students weren't the most respected people in the world. In the late nineteenth century Americans so disdained medical training that there was almost no way for schools to legally acquire cadavers. Organizations like Vanderbilt had to find creative ways to acquire dead bodies. Often this meant that respectable institutions had to deal with not-so-respectable grave robbers.

For the most part Vanderbilt was able to keep its transactions with grave robbers out of the newspapers. But there was the time that the ghost of a cadaver was seen by several hundred witnesses strolling, crawling, and hanging from a tree near the medical school's campus, then located on a hill south of downtown that later became known as Rutledge Hill.

The trouble started in late summer 1885, when a few people noticed that almost every night around midnight, a curious-looking stranger would emerge from the medical school campus. The wandering spirit, dressed like a workman, would always head down Second Avenue toward downtown, carrying a bucket in his arm as if it had work to do.

After a few nights so many people said that they had seen the ghost that it became the talk of the town. Then on Saturday, September 12, several dozen men decided to establish watches in the area to get a good look at the person or thing that was causing the commotion. One group was stationed in the vicinity of a nearby drugstore when they looked up and saw a mysterious personage carrying a bucket and heading toward them. One of the men hailed the unknown thing, and to his utter surprise he "was greeted with a shriek that could be heard all over the neighborhood," a newspaper account of the event stated. "One swears positively nothing mortal could have produced that sound. Everyone asserts that not a vestige of flesh was seen on its face."

A few minutes later another group of people saw the ghost sitting on one of the medical college's gateposts and decided to charge it. It suddenly vanished into nothing before their eyes, then reappeared while suspended from the limb of a nearby tree, "as if struggling in all the contortions of one strangled." The crowd ran up to the ghost again. This time, wearing a white shroud, it took off running down the hill on all fours. One of the more eager mortals present, a young man named Dave Sweets, began throwing rocks at the spirit. The ghost turned around and came after Sweets. The young man panicked and ran, tripping over a rock and cutting his head in the process.

By this time there were about three hundred people present, yelling and running in every direction in a state of general panic. One of them, a black man who lived in the nearby slum area of Black Bottom, found a bucket on the rock wall near where the ghost had been sitting. The bucket contained a rabbit's foot, a horseshoe nail and a yellow piece of paper that contained the writing "1862, Nov. 19, Triune, Tenn. B.H.K," plus several smaller lines of writing that were harder to decipher.

According to an article a couple of days later in the *Nashville American*, a careful examination of the note (aided by a powerful microscope) indicated that the spirit was the ghost of a black slave named Ben Harrison King. King, the note stated, was hung for murder during the Civil War near Triune, Tennessee. The communication went on to say that King's body was taken from its grave, put into a sack, and taken to Nashville, "where it was sold as a stiff to the Medical College." The ghost of Ben King would never stop wandering until its bones were buried again, the note said.

The newspaper reporter who covered the story even tracked down someone named Jack Polk, who remembered the slave named Ben King. King, Polk said, was a strange person who many people believed was possessed. Polk went on to say that King had apparently made an appearance to his friends shortly after his death twenty-three years earlier.

As if this weren't enough to scare Vanderbilt medical students and residents of south Nashville, more creepy news came out a couple of days later. A group of workmen, digging a ditch for a new sewer line between Market and College Streets, unearthed a human skeleton buried in about three feet of dirt. From all appearances, the corpse had been buried for about ten to twelve years and would probably never be identified. "Who it was and why it was buried there will probably never be known," the paper said.

During the next few nights the people of south Nashville were a bit jittery. On one occasion a man who happened to be carrying a bucket in the area of the medical school was startled when a young girl named Sallie caught sight of him and started screaming so loud that it "lifted the hat off his head." Another time the apparition was seen sitting on the foundation of a building that had recently burned at the corner of Cherry and Demonbreun. When last seen, according to the *American*, the ghost "had begun his wandering in West Nashville."

KILL THE SPARROWS, SAVE THE STARLINGS

There is more to the Vanderbilt campus than buildings and sidewalks. From the time it was developed, the university and most of the people associated with it have understood the value of letting nature thrive, and because of that the campus has always had a park-like appearance.

For several decades after the founding of the school, the campus and the area around it were still rural and pristine. In the 1890s a man named John Hope was a professor at Roger Williams University, the predominantly African American institution located on what later became the Peabody campus. One of the things Hope liked about Roger Williams was that the campus was outside of the city. "Beyond the (Roger Williams) college farm not a house was to be seen for miles," Hope's biographer said. "Near the campus was a creek with a bridge across it. Persimmons grew along Hillsboro Road, which led out into the deeper country. On one side of this road lay Roger Williams University, on the other side Vanderbilt."

One reason that the campus had so much natural beauty is because it was designed as a tree-lovers paradise. Bishop Holland McTyeire loved trees and supervised the planting of many trees that were transplanted from the area that later became known as Green Hills to the campus in the 1870s. Once, when asked about what he did on those unfortunate occasions that trees had to be chopped down, McTyeire responded by saying, "I don't see it, sir. I can't stand it. I have to turn my back."

Several decades later Margaret Vaughan Branscomb, the wife of Chancellor Harvie Branscomb, came up with the idea of a row of magnolias around the campus. That wall of magnolias was planted in the 1950s and still lined the West End and Twenty-first Avenue edges of the campus at the end of the twentieth century.

Because of the efforts of McTyeire, Branscomb, and many other tree lovers, the Vanderbilt campus was granted membership in the American Association of Botanical Gardens and Arboreta in 1988. By that time seven trees on the Vanderbilt campus were recognized by the Tennessee state forester as the largest of their species in the state: a sweetbay magnolia, a southern hackberry, a Japanese zelkova, a swamp white oak, a Chinese scholar tree, an Ohio buckeye, and an English field maple.

Vanderbilt administrators and students have historically liked not only the trees, but the trees' inhabitants. In the 1880s Chancellor Garland would put out boxes of food for the squirrels to eat. Several decades later the school newspaper scolded students who were harassing squirrels. "Recently we have noticed that a number of freshmen are prone to chase the squirrels that make their habitat on the campus," the article said. "These uncivilized ruffians surely have not the love of nature and animals in their hearts when they do this."

In addition to trees, Bishop McTyeire loved birds, but killed English sparrows whenever he could because of their habit of destroying other birds' eggs. One day on one of his sparrow eradication expeditions, McTyeire fired at an animal that was perched on the roof of Wesley Hall and missed, sending small shot through the window of a young theological student's room. The student opened his window and began shouting invectives at McTyeire, not realizing who he was. "Well, my dear young brother, it seems to me that you have become rather easily perturbed," the bishop said.

McTyeire's hatred of sparrows caused great consternation to the engineering department, which in the 1880s was responsible for the maintenance of the school buildings. At one point engineering professor William Magruder sent Chancellor Garland a letter pointing out that the gutters and downspouts on campus were "full of small holes as if someone had tried to dislodge bird nests by shooting at them." Magruder's complaint fell on deaf ears. After McTyeire's death the tradition of sparrow hunting was passed on to campus policeman James "Cap" Alley. Before his passing in 1927 Alley claimed to have killed 14,765 sparrows.

McTyeire and Alley were certainly turning in their graves in February 1995, when the Vanderbilt campus was taken over by a huge flock of starlings, whose normal migratory patterns had apparently been thrown off by mild winters. "It's beginning to look like something out of Alfred Hitchcock's *The Birds,*" *The Hustler* said at the time. The starlings were in such great quantity that some students were

This photograph, taken from one of the Main Building's Towers toward Nashville in 1888, shows how rural the Vanderbilt area was at that time
Photographic Archives, Vanderbilt University

Chancellor James Kirkland enjoys a moment of peace with his irises.
The Banner Collection, Nashville Public Library, The Nashville Room

using umbrellas to protect themselves from bird droppings. Finally, the administration decided to do something about the problem. Rather than take care of the birds in the traditional method, the school spent weeks studying a sensitive way to solve the problem before using noise making devices, such as pre-recorded "starling distress calls," to run off the unwanted visitors.

Along with tree loving and squirrel loving developed a tradition of campus gardening. For many years, professors and administrators who lived on school grounds took great pride in their flower gardens. James Kirkland, who became chancellor in 1893, would spend about an hour a day tending his garden, in which he developed over 150 varieties of irises. Geology professor L. C. Glenn had a garden with about four hundred varieties of peonies.

One other part of Vanderbilt's natural terrain deserves mention: the campus cave. The underground chasm was located between and below the buildings later known as Benson and Kirkland Halls. In the 1870s and 1880s Vanderbilt used the cave as the campus sewage system. Built on top of the cave was a small, partially underground latrine commonly referred to by students as "Black Egypt." The city ordered Vanderbilt to stop using Black Egypt in 1891. But the school continued to dump its sewage into the ground until 1899, when Vanderbilt linked up with Nashville's sewage line on West End Avenue.

Nashville Gets a Teaching School

Nashville never would have gotten a school for teachers had it been up to the Tennessee legislature.

The George Peabody School for Teachers traces its origins to 1785. Back when Nashville was little more than a fort and its citizens still had frequent battles with Native Americans, the new residents of the area formed an institution called Davidson Academy. About two decades later Davidson Academy became Cumberland College. By the middle of the nineteenth century the institution had evolved into the University of Nashville, which for several generations served as Middle Tennessee's dominant college.

Like many other Southern educational institutions the University of Nashville was on shaky financial ground after the Civil War. The school's south Nashville campus was used as a hospital during the war and was in bad physical condition after the hostilities ended. Most of its alumni fought on the losing side in that war and were unable to support it financially afterward. When Vanderbilt University was formed most wealthy Nashville residents began sending their children to the new school on West End Avenue.

In this environment the University of Nashville's alumni and administrators had to get creative to survive. In the late 1860s a northern foundation called the Peabody Education Fund began looking for a place in the South to build a school for teachers (or a normal school, as they were then known). The foundation hired Barnas Sears as its agent. Under the influence of University of Nashville chancellor J. Berrien Lindsley, Sears homed in on Middle Tennessee, specifically the largely vacant University of Nashville campus.

However, Sears and Lindsley didn't have the final say in the matter. Since the University of Nashville was a public institution chartered by the state, only the legislature could authorize the transfer of the University of Nashville property to a new organization. Lawmakers, some of whom were bitter about the Civil War and distrustful of northern foundations in general, weren't in a hurry to do this. "Prejudice, suspicion, and distrust prevailed against any undertaking fostered by a man from north of Mason and Dixon's line," one of Peabody Normal College's first students recalled.

Despite the fact that almost all the money for the new institution was coming from the Peabody Education Fund, the legislature rejected proposals by Sears and the foundation to turn the University of Nashville into a normal school in 1871 and again in 1873. Finally the bill passed in March 1875.

Peabody Normal College, as it eventually became known, opened its doors in the fall of 1875 with about sixty students. However, the school still needed to raise about ten thousand dollars to build a new school building. In 1879 the Tennessee legislature rejected a request for that appropriation. At that point the government of Georgia offered two buildings, forty-seven acres, and an annual appropriation of six thousand dollars per year if the Peabody Normal College moved to Atlanta. Only then did Nashville residents and Tennessee legislators get concerned about losing the school.

On April 10, 1880, Nashville's citizens held a fundraising meeting for the Peabody College at the Maxwell House Hotel. Business leaders who attended that meeting raised four thousand dollars toward the immediate retention of the school and pledged to raise more. The next spring the Tennessee legislature finally agreed to spend six thousand dollars annually toward the school's operational expenses. That amount was raised to over twenty thousand a year by 1895.

It would be hard to overstate the importance of the Peabody Normal College to the South during the latter part of the nineteenth century. The school was set up as a professional school to train teachers from across the region. Although the school did not teach any subjects in great depth, it offered courses in Latin, English, literature, philosophy, art, mathematics, biology, chemistry, physics, geography, and history. With the support of the Peabody Education Fund thousands of people from all parts of the South were given two hundred dollar scholarships to go to the college. By 1911 the school had graduated 2,678 students from its three-year program, virtually all of whom became elementary or secondary teachers.

By the turn of the century, however, the future of Peabody Normal College was in doubt. Under the terms of the Peabody Education Fund's original grant the interest from the grant could be used to fund the college for thirty years, after which the trustees would reconsider the continuation of the school. By 1905 trustees were divided into two camps. One group wanted to liquidate the school and spend the money in a public relations effort to get local and state governments in the South to invest more in education. The other wanted to reorganize the school into a more prestigious degree-

The graduating class of Peabody Normal College in 1896, seated in front of the school's main building on the old University of Nashville campus in South Nashville.

Photographic Archives, Vanderbilt University

granting college, with the dual purpose of training teachers and educational leaders.

In 1903 the trustees of the Peabody Education Fund (which included President Theodore Roosevelt) decided to form a college. Then former Tennessee Governor James Porter began working on a financial package to build that institution on the old University of Nashville campus. Porter put together the largest incentive package the city of Nashville had ever seen: $250,000 from the transfer of old University of Nashville assets, $250,000 from the state, $200,000 from Nashville, and $100,000 from Davidson County.

Vanderbilt chancellor James Kirkland liked the idea of the Peabody College in Nashville, but he had another site for it. Around 1898 Kirkland began bringing up the idea of the teaching college building its campus on or near Vanderbilt. Using Columbia University as his model, Kirkland believed that Peabody and Vanderbilt would benefit from being co-located. (In fact, it was through this logic that he would eventually bring the Vanderbilt Medical School and the Vanderbilt Law School to the West End Avenue campus.) Kirkland knew that his plan wouldn't have many supporters in Nashville. So rather than go through local political channels, he tried to sell his idea directly to the Peabody Education Fund trustees. To this end Kirkland solicited the help of Wallace Buttrick, an old friend of his and the secretary of the Rockefeller-funded General Education Board.

Kirkland and Vanderbilt scored a huge victory in October 1906, when the Peabody trustees voted to appoint a committee to rethink the idea of putting Peabody College in south Nashville. A few months later, when that committee recommended that Peabody College be located near Vanderbilt, Porter was furious. The former Tennessee governor said that when he had put together the $800,000 Peabody incentive package that he had promised legislators and city councilmen that the new Peabody College would go on the old University of Nashville campus in south Nashville. "I have personally borne the heat and burden of getting the subscriptions required, and I assure you that the labor has not been light," Porter wrote. "I have stated on every occasion that the new college would be located on the grounds conveyed for the purpose by the University of Nashville. Had it been known by the subscribers at that or any other time that the action recently taken by the Board was ever contemplated, I never could have succeeded in getting a single one of the subscriptions, and I never would have attempted to do so because of the utter hopelessness of the task."

Opposition to the Peabody move also came from other camps. People who owned stores and boardinghouses in south Nashville were opposed for fear it would hurt their business. People loyal to the memory of the University of Nashville were opposed on sentimental grounds. "A great institution of learning transmitted to us from the Revolutionary period, numbering among its earliest trustees Gen. Andrew Jackson, Hon. Felix Grundy, Gov. William Carroll, Hon. John Bell, Gov. John Sevier . . . is to be cast aside like a worn-out garment," one citizen wrote at the time. "This school, venerable with age and traditions . . . is to be abandoned, and the buildings, no doubt, will be razed to the earth and the ground cut up and sold out in town lots, and the new institution moved near the Vanderbilt, so that its scholars may have the advantages and teaching at two colleges instead of one."

Another influential person opposed to putting the Peabody school near Vanderbilt was Elijah Hoss, a Methodist leader who was the biggest critic of James Kirkland in Nashville. Hoss said he didn't want to move Peabody for several reasons, one of which was the idea of mixing the two student bodies. "The majority of the students in the Teachers College will likely be young women," he pointed out in a pamphlet printed by the Southern Methodist Publishing House. "Personally, I do not think that it would be a wise thing to impart into the life of the university, either directly or indirectly, so large a number of women, especially if they are to be lodged in dormitories on the ground."

It may have been the most unpopular thing ever undertaken by a Vanderbilt chancellor. But Kirkland stuck by his plan, convinced that putting the teaching college next to Vanderbilt would be good for both institutions. And everything seemed to be going just the way Kirkland hoped it would in 1910, when the Peabody Education Fund began buying land near the Vanderbilt campus for use as a teaching college.

VANDERBILT IN 1901

In 1901, when many people still had memories of the Civil War, Vanderbilt was still searching for its role. The institution was beginning to struggle against the Methodist Episcopal Church, South, which had started it nearly three decades earlier. It was also becoming shaped by James Kirkland, the academician and administrator who became chancellor in 1893 and had visions of its future grandeur that almost no one other than him could see.

Of course, students had no way of knowing this at the time. The young men and women who then attended Vanderbilt lived, studied, and thought in ways that would be hard for people who lived a century later to imagine. A look through *The Hustler* and Nashville's daily newspapers from the 1901-02 school year gives an interesting snapshot of what life on campus was like at that time.

In the fall of 1901 Vanderbilt, along with the rest of the country, was recovering from the assassination of William McKinley, who was shot by an anarchist on September 6, 1901. During the first week of the school year the work of the school was suspended for a day in McKinley's honor. Students were required to attend a memorial service on campus and highly encouraged to attend another one in downtown Nashville, at the Union Tabernacle (later the Ryman Auditorium).

The Vanderbilt campus was still mostly empty, with structures such as Furman Hall, the Joint University Library, Garland Hall, Calhoun Hall, Alumni Hall, and the medical school not yet built. It was empty in other ways: many of the large trees that later made the campus beautiful were seedlings, or not yet planted. Vanderbilt was also located in a section of town that had only recently been developed. Virtually everyone reached the campus via the West End Avenue streetcar line, and the main Vanderbilt stop was located close to the Main Building (later Kirkland Hall).

Students spent most of their time in three places: the Main Building, where many classes met and where the university library was located; Kissam Hall, where most dormitory rooms were located and most student activities took place; and fraternity and sorority houses, which were located off campus. Students looking for something to do at night could still drop by the observatory in the middle of campus to look through the telescope at stars and planets.

The Vanderbilt football team enjoyed one of its most successful seasons ever, routing Georgia (47-0), Auburn (40-0), Kentucky (22-0), and Tennessee (22-0). The only loss was a 12 to 11 defeat at the hands of Washington University of St. Louis. The descriptions of these games by *Hustler* reporters make lively reading (Auburn's team played "the dirtiest game of football that ever has been"; Tennessee "resorted to dilatory tactics to kill time and keep the score down.") In those days the athletes were far less skilled and the game hardly organized by later standards. Vanderbilt head football coach W. H. Watkins also coached basketball and baseball. All the players were walk-ons, and some of the better ones were medical students. In fact, there was some concern at the beginning of the year that Vanderbilt wouldn't have enough players to field a team.

It wasn't inherently obvious what to do when watching sporting events; there was no band and few organized cheers. "Cheerleading was not an organization," Jim Robins, an 1892 graduate of Vanderbilt, said in the 1950s. "We yelled like old Confederate rebels. We just got up and made up yells. Our first yell was 'Ya Ya Yip Vanderbilt.' " Despite these limitations Vanderbilt students could get pretty excited after a big win. After defeating the University of Nashville 10-0, a near riot of several hundred Vanderbilt and University of Nashville students nearly broke out downtown. According to the account of the event in the *Nashville Banner* (which was repudiated in *The Hustler*), the trouble started when a number of Vanderbilt students "tried to paint the stone fence of the University of Nashville yellow and black."

Among the more popular organizations on campus were the Literary Society, the Dialectic Society, the Mandolin Club, the Young Men's Christian Association, and the Glee Club (a chorus of college men that performed to audiences all over the South). Campus debates, usually on national political issues, were frequent and often reported at some length in *The Hustler*. Meanwhile, the most frequent advertisers in *The Hustler* included clothing retailers, tailors, laundries,

Boscobel College, the future site of the Cayce Homes public housing project
The Carey Collection

banks, and public baths.

Vanderbilt students (and most other Americans) knew almost nothing about the part of the world later referred to as the Middle East. In October a Persian missionary named Koshaba Shimmon visited the campus and made a speech that did not paint Islam in a favorable light. "One can be a devoted follower of the faith, and at the same time be as great a thief and liar as anyone," *The Hustler* reported. "Their religion does not propose to regulate a man's conduct or change his life, but simply is a set of rules for ceremonies he must perform."

Since most students were men, meeting young women was quite a challenge. At one point a young alumnus named Arthur Dyer organized an outing to Mammoth Cave. (Tickets, which included round-trip train fare, cost $5.90.) In an article about the event in *The Hustler*, Dyer made it clear that he intended to recruit as many young ladies as he could from female schools such as Belmont and Boscobel College (an all-girls school located where Cayce Homes public housing project was later built).

Vanderbilt publications other than *The Hustler* included the *Comet* yearbook and *The Observer*, a monthly literary journal. In addition to fiction and poetry, *The Observer* contained articles about national and international politics, publishing articles in the 1901-02 school year about European politics, the idea of reforming municipal government, and the situation in China.

The prestigious Bachelor of Ugliness award was given to football star John Edgerton. Edgerton was so popular that advertisers in *The Hustler* used his name to sell their products. One such ad read: "John E. Edgerton will be glad to see his friends at Varley, Bauman & Bowers: One Price Clothiers, Hatters, Furnishers and Merchant Tailors."

The philosophy of the Vanderbilt Medical School was still affected by the university's affiliation with the Methodist Church. This was exemplified by comments made by Dr. G. A. Lofton, who spoke to medical students when the school year began. "There is a grand affinity between medicine and religion," Lofton told students. "The body, which is the temple of the soul, should only be looked into by those who possess religion, and I simply urge that you rise to the very highest point in your profession, for I believe that next to a preacher, a doctor is the noblest calling."

A DEPARTMENT OF TINKERS AND BUILDERS

Engineers are different from everyone else. Especially in the old days, it seems as if everyone who became an engineer did it because there was nothing else they wanted to do; they were tinkers and builders as children and wanted to be tinkers and builders as adults. So it stands to reason that the Vanderbilt School of Engineering has a history that is fundamentally different from that of the rest of campus. The school was at one time literally responsible for all the engineering functions on campus. So there are a lot of anecdotes within the engineering school about the campus' construction, power supply, and sewage system. Unlike the College of Arts and Sciences, which basically trains students to think, the engineering school has always trained students for a trade. Because of this, its curriculum has always been more linked to technology and market conditions than any other division of the school. Finally the Vanderbilt

School of Engineering has been more shaped by its alumni than other parts of the school, probably because both it and Nashville's engineering community have always been relatively small.

Under the basic structure of the school as first envisioned by Chancellor Landon Garland, Vanderbilt was supposed to have one engineering professor. It took a few years to fill that position, and in 1879 Vanderbilt awarded the post to a civil and mechanical engineer named Olin Landreth. For most of his tenure at Vanderbilt Landreth was almost a one-man department, teaching many of the classes and supervising those that were taught by a small number of assistants (most of whom he had taught in the first place). Landreth wore many hats. In a day in which engineering was a less-developed science than it later became, he worked with the physics, geology, and chemistry departments to develop a curriculum for students majoring in engineering. He helped students, including legendary scholar Edward

Vanderbilt students playing hooky sometime around 1900
Photographic Archives, Vanderbilt University

Barnard, learn to use the campus observatory. He was responsible for the maintenance of the school's buildings and the building of new ones. He was in charge of Vanderbilt's water, sewage, and steam power system in the 1880s. When Wesley Hall caught fire in January 1889, Landreth and assistant engineering professor William Macgruder were credited with extinguishing the blaze before it got out of control. As if this weren't enough, Landreth found time to help the city of Nashville build a new bridge across the Cumberland River at Hyde's Ferry.

The highlight of Landreth's tenure was the school's 1888 decision to build a separate home for the engineering department, a project made possible by a $30,000 donation by Cornelius Vanderbilt, the grandson of the school founder. The decision by the board of trust to construct a building for engineering must have caused consternation among other departments. It was also a sign that despite the heavy emphasis on the theological department that Vanderbilt intended to put a lot of emphasis on a type of practical education that could help the South rebuild itself. The Mechanical Engineering Building, as it was called, was designed by architect William Smith and had many unique architectural qualities, such as the handsome terra cotta and tile design surrounding its main entrance. After the completion of the engineering building, Vanderbilt hired two new professors and began offering separate majors in civil, mechanical, and mining engineering.

The early engineering department was housed for six decades in the ME Building, affectionately known as the Red Castle. It was a loud, busy place. Its basement contained the campus boiler and four steam engines used to pump water around the campus. Other floors contained foundries, machine shops, wood shops, and electrical labs. Regardless of what year you might drop by the ME Building, professors and students would be inventing or testing something. In 1892 an assistant engineering professor built a system of electric lights that was used in the chapel and observatory. At the turn of the century an instructor was hard at work designing a new automobile. Future generations would build airplanes and computers and operate a shortwave radio in the ME Building.

Landreth and his two main assistants left Vanderbilt in the mid-1890s. A man named William Schuerman was brought in to be the new dean of engineering; he would remain in that position until 1932. Shortly after his arrival the school brought in an instructor named C.S. "Shorty" Brown. The two men would effectively run the engineering school for the next two generations. But they did so with a limited budget. Vanderbilt's engineering department, a favorite of Chancellor Garland's, would remain noticeably small from the turn of the century until the end of World War II. The main reason for this was Chancellor Kirkland's decision to focus his efforts elsewhere, most notably the medical school and the sciences affiliated with medical training.

A laboratory session in the Mechanical Engineering lab - early 1940s
Photographic Archives, Vanderbilt University

As it had before, the engineering department made contributions to the school during the first part of the twentieth century above and beyond educating students. When Vanderbilt's Main Building burned down in 1905, Schuerman and Brown were two of the five people on the committee in charge of replacing it. "Schuerman's contribution to the reconstruction was to make it strong and durable," one alumnus from that time period later recalled. "Shorty Brown's was to make it cheap." A few years later Brown helped design an addition to the Old Gym that was meant to be temporary but in fact remained until 1963. And in 1914 Brown succeeded William Dudley as head of the Vanderbilt Athletic Association. In that role he worked on the development and construction of Dudley Field in 1922.

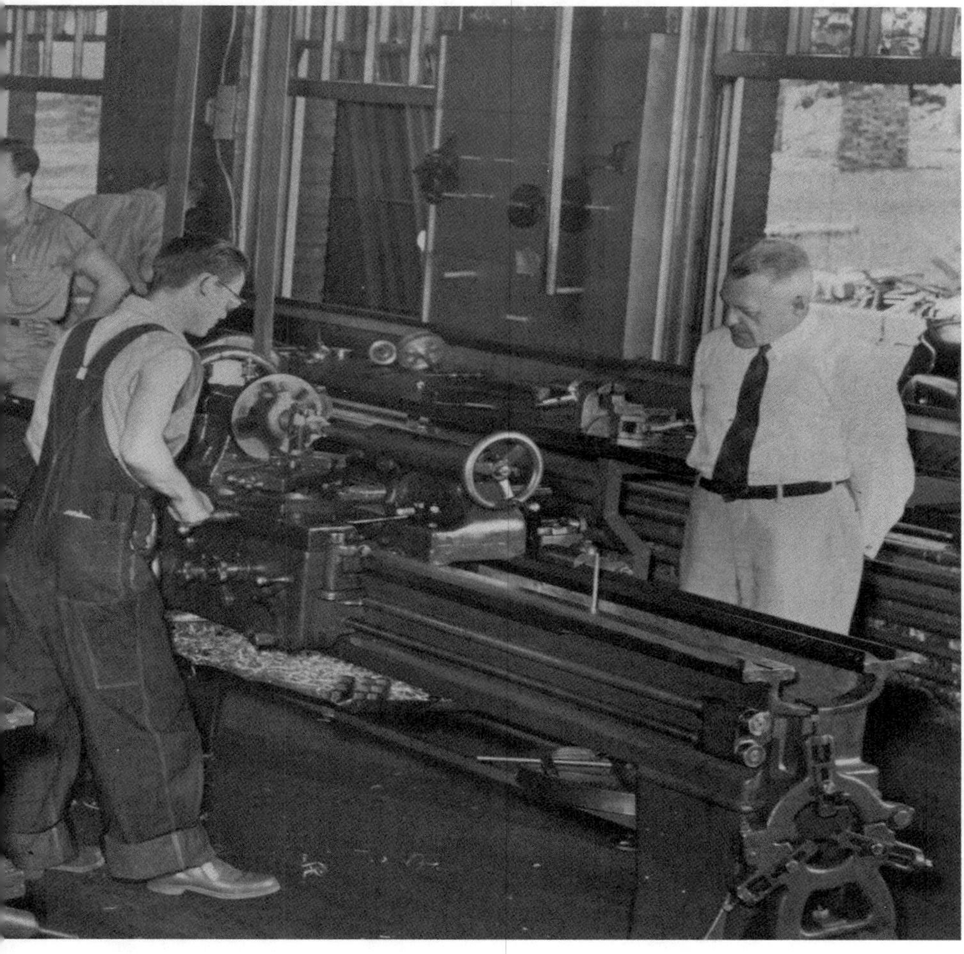

Meanwhile, engineering alumni played key roles in countless developments throughout Vanderbilt, Nashville, and the South. For many years the largest construction firm in Nashville, and one of the largest in the South, was Foster & Creighton Construction Co., co-founded by 1904 graduate Wilbur Creighton and later run by 1929 graduate Wilbur Creighton Jr. Among Foster & Creighton's many, many projects were Vanderbilt's Alumni Hall, the Joint University Library, and Memorial Gymnasium. H. Fort Flowers, a 1912 engineering graduate, invented the differential electric side-dumping car for use in mines, quarries, and mills. In the 1960s, he donated $250,000 to help Vanderbilt pay for an expansion of the Joint University Library.

The Schuerman era ended in 1932, when Fred Lewis became the new Dean of the engineering school. Lewis was bright and almost hyperactive. His nickname was "Fireball," and throughout his long career at Vanderbilt, he insisted on teaching a freshman class every year so he could make an impression on young students. During his first ten years Lewis tripled the engineering school's enrollment from about 150 to 450 while continuing to emphasize the civil and mechanical engineering undergraduate programs.

One of Lewis' ideas was a summer camp to train freshmen and sophomore engineering students to do surveying work. Just about every person who went to the month-long program at Camp Schuerman, as it was called, came back with stories about how much fun and how rustic it was. "All the buildings are within easy walking distance of each other, that is if you give yourself about an hour leeway and carry a big stick with you to beat away the snakes, horses, cows, and various other creatures that inhabit the place," read one story about Camp Schuerman. "At 6:30 in the morning there comes a gentle tapping on the door and everybody is awakened by the sweet strains of an atom bomb going off."

One of the many people who attended Camp Schuerman was a student from South Alabama named Dan Barge Jr. Barge came to Vanderbilt in 1939, intending to major in electrical engineering. "One of the first things they taught us to do was take an electrical motor apart and put it back together again," Barge said many years later. Barge had so much fun at surveying camp and at a summer job doing building work for the city of Nashville that he changed his major to civil engineering. In the 1950s Barge started an engineering and design firm that eventually became known as Barge Waggoner Sumner & Cannon.

By the end of World War II Vanderbilt had added a wing to the ME Building that was used primarily by the school's new chemical engineering program. A few years later the school got a new seventy-two thousand square-foot classroom, office and laboratory in the middle of campus (later known as Jacobs Hall). But as of the late 1950s the Vanderbilt School of Engineering still didn't have a graduate program to speak of. "Vanderbilt didn't give the department very much money under Lewis, and Lewis was not a big advocate of graduate work anyway," said Ed Thackson, a 1961 graduate who became a professor at the school four years later. "When I was a student, there were no graduate level courses in the School of Engineering, period."

The situation changed drastically under Robert Rowe, who came to Vanderbilt as Dean of the Engineering School in 1960 and may have been one of Branscomb's best hires. Rowe made many changes, the most tangible being in the number of Ph.D.s in the department. From only six in the late-1950s, the Vanderbilt School of Engineering grew to thirty-eight doctorates a decade later. Rowe's upgrades were a key factor in the 1969 decision by the Olin Foundation to make a major donation for a new chemical engineering building, aptly called Olin Hall. However, many alumni were sad to see one of the indirect results of Rowe's new emphasis on advanced research. In the mid-1960s Vanderbilt sold Camp Schuerman, and stopped requiring its undergraduate engineering students to spend an unforgettable month in rural Tennessee.

A SUICIDE AND A CASTLE

The story of how Furman Hall came to be is one of the lesser-known tales of Vanderbilt history, and many aspects of it are unique to the story of the school. During its early years Nashville residents made few large financial contributions to the university, except in the case of Mary Furman. Vanderbilt has historically remained clear of lawsuits that involved family squabbles, but found itself drawn into the one that involved the Furman family. And most buildings built on campus have been brick — except for Furman Hall, which is made of stone.

Furman Hall is named for Francis Furman, who emigrated from Ireland in the 1850s and made most of his money during the quarter-century following the Civil War. From about 1870 until his retirement around 1890, Furman & Co. Wholesale Dry Goods and Notions was located on Nashville's Public Square, the area surrounding what later became the Davidson County Courthouse. He and his wife Mary lived in a fashionable house on Spruce Street (later Eighth Avenue) and attended the McKendree Methodist Church. Naturally, Furman was familiar with Vanderbilt University. But neither he nor any of his family attended the school or apparently knew any professors there.

On Dec. 23, 1899, Francis Furman died of a stroke at the age of 81, something hardly noted in the newspapers at the time. About a week later the tragedy was compounded when his forty-three-year-old son Willie committed suicide by slitting his throat with a razor.

The death of her husband and her only son obviously devastated Francis Furman's widow Mary. About three months after her son's death Mary Furman died of Bright's disease. A few weeks later it was revealed that in her will, rewritten nine days before her death, she had left about $100,000 for Vanderbilt University to build a building named for her husband and $26,000 for the construction of a large monument to the family at Mt. Olivet Cemetery. In the will Mrs. Furman also wrote, "I am not unmindful of the fact that I have some distant relatives and I do not desire that any of the property herein disposed shall go to them."

Mrs. Furman's nieces and nephews were shocked by the will. They sued the executors and administrators of Mrs. Furman's estate, asking that the will be dismissed on the grounds that Mrs. Furman was insane when she rewrote it.

The case of the Furman will went to trial on November 4, 1901. Attorneys for the family members, led by a Vanderbilt Law School graduate named John Vertrees, presented several witnesses who claimed that after the deaths of her husband and son, Mrs. Furman grew depressed and absent minded. Several witnesses said that Mrs. Furman had never mentioned the remote possibility that she would give money to Vanderbilt. Attorneys for the family tried to prove that the exorbitant amount of money designated for the Mr. Olivet monument — more money than had ever been spent on a privately funded memorial in Tennessee — was in itself proof that Mr. Furman had lost touch with reality during the declining months of her life. They also produced a physician who knew Mrs. Furman and who said that during the last weeks of her life, she lost her short-term memory and was prone to sudden spells of weeping. "She was insane," the doctor concluded.

Lawyers defending the will included Walter Stokes and James C. Bradford, who had taught for a year at the Vanderbilt Law School. The two men produced several witnesses who said they had spoken to Mrs. Furman during the final weeks of her life and who described her as acting mentally sound at that time. Among them were two monument salesmen who had each met with her at some length, proof that her decision to build the large monument at Mt. Olivet was not made on impulse.

Bradford and Stokes's star witness was John Thomas, a friend

Furman Hall, shortly after construction
The Carey Collection

of the Furman family, an executive with the Nashville, Chattanooga and St. Louis Railway, and one of the chief organizers of Nashville's Centennial Exposition of 1897. Thomas said that a few months before her death, Mrs. Furman told him that in addition to the large graveyard monument, she wanted to erect a "living" memorial in honor of her husband. Thomas suggested she give money to Vanderbilt. Mrs. Furman asked Thomas to contact Chancellor James Kirkland and ask him about the needs of the university.

Thomas did so. And in a letter to Thomas dated March 5, 1900, Kirkland said that the university's most immediate need was $50,000 to establish an endowment for a new chemistry professorship. "This is a subject of so great importance that it will always remain one of the chief studies for every class of students at the university," Kirkland wrote. If he could secure funds beyond the $50,000, Kirkland said he would use it to build a structure that would house a chemical laboratory (thus replacing the one located in the school's Main Building).

Thomas' testimony helped convince the jury that Mrs. Furman knew exactly what she was doing when she rewrote her will. On December 2, 1901, the jury sustained the will of Mary Furman.

Legal appeals took time, as did settling the estate. So it was several years before Furman Hall became reality. Eventually, Vanderbilt negotiated an out-of-court settlement with the Furman heirs and received $80,000 in cash and $60,000 from the sale of real estate previously owned by the Furmans.

New York architect Garrett Snelling designed Furman Hall as an English Gothic structure made of stone. When it opened in 1907 it was regarded as the most modern chemistry and pharmacy building in the country, containing large offices, several chemistry labs, and a lecture hall. There was even a special system of fans through the building to eliminate odors emanating from the laboratory (unfortunately, it wasn't enough; the interior of Furman Hall smelled like rotten eggs throughout its life as a chemistry building). The university also placed a statue of Francis Furman in the structure named for him.

Furman Hall was a treasured landmark during its first few decades. Postcards of it became almost as common as postcards of

College Hall (which became known as Kirkland Hall in the 1930s), a sign that many people loved the castle-like appearance of the chemistry building. Still, there is no accounting for taste. Perhaps the most anti-Furman Hall piece ever was penned in 1944 by *Hustler* reporter Edyth Lasky. "About the only thing that can be said about Furman is that there couldn't be a drearier place on earth," the young lady wrote. "With those marble steps, vaulted ceilings, and coat of camouflage paint, the building has almost as much warmth and welcoming appeal as a very chilly ice cube." In 1967 Furman Hall was renovated and converted into a structure that housed the humanities departments.

As for Mrs. Furman's desire that a monument to her husband be built at Mt. Olivet Cemetery, it too became reality. At the end of the twentieth century, the largest monument at Mt. Olivet was the eighteen-foot-high memorial to the Furman family.

Dog breeders and X-ray experiments

Vanderbilt has had many great and memorable faculty members. Some of those professors' names were later enshrined in buildings on campus, while others left little behind except masterful reputations and thousands of student memories.

During the era in which Greek was a required subject, the greatest Greek professor at the school was Herbert Tolman. Tolman was a much-published international scholar on the Persian language and at one time was thought to be a candidate to be the American ambassador to Persia. From 1914 until 1923 he was also Vanderbilt's Dean of the College of Arts and Science, the second-highest ranking officer of the university at that time. When Tolman died after teaching a class in 1923, his students and colleagues were shocked. "When Dr. Tolman talked to you, he made you feel that, for the time being, you were the most interesting person in the world," one of his students said. Tolman also started Vanderbilt's Phi Beta Kappa chapter in 1901.

Another important faculty member was Wilbur Tillett. Were it not for Tillett, the Vanderbilt Divinity School would probably not have survived the Great Depression. Tillett became a professor at the

Biblical School in 1881. At that time there was enormous strife between the department and Bishop Holland McTyeire over the fact that the school had no admissions standards. Tillett became dean five years later and would remain in the department until the 1930s, presiding over it during the awkward time when the school went to court with the Methodist church over control of the university. Tillett seemed stern to his Biblical students; he forbade them from participating in school activities, such as sports and the Glee Club, that he considered sinful. But he was not above going to great lengths to save his department. According to Paul Conkin's Vanderbilt history *Gone with the Ivy*, Tillett repeatedly threatened to resign if his department didn't get more support from the board of trust. And in the 1930s, after Wesley Hall burned, Tillett disobeyed Kirkland's prohibition of professors soliciting members of the Vanderbilt family. This defiance resulted in a $150,000 donation by Frederick W. Vanderbilt to help give the Biblical school a new home.

Mathematician William J. Vaughn joined the Vanderbilt faculty in 1882, replacing one of the original faculty members who left in a pay dispute with Bishop McTyeire. Vaughn quickly became a fixture on the Vanderbilt campus and one of the few links between faculty members and Chancellor Garland, whom Vaughn had known many years earlier at the University of Alabama. Vaughn wore many hats during his thirty-year tenure at Vanderbilt. He taught math and astronomy and was the director of the Barnard Observatory. He was the closest thing the school had to a librarian for many years. Vaughn also founded one of Vanderbilt's most powerful family dynasties. His daughter Stella, who literally grew up on the Vanderbilt campus, was the unofficial school historian from the 1880s until the 1930s. His grandson William S. Vaughn was the chief executive officer of Eastman Kodak and the president of the board of trust from 1968 until 1975.

Edwin Mims was not only one of the most important Vanderbilt professors ever, but for the first half of the twentieth century he was considered one of the leading advocates of liberalism in the South. A Vanderbilt graduate hired by Kirkland in 1912, Mims was the unchallenged head of the Vanderbilt English department through World War II, turning it into the finest department of the undergraduate school and influencing two generations of students in the process. "I have no doubt that he is one of the great teachers of all time," a devoted student once wrote. "He is egotistical, but you cannot study with him without realizing how great is his love for literature and his reverence for the good of the past." Many remembered Mims for his requirement that every one of his students memorize a thousand lines of poetry.

Edwin Mims, who shaped the Vanderbilt English Department for two generations
The Banner Collection, Nashville Public Library, The Nashville Room

Outside the classroom Mims loyally supported Kirkland in episodes ranging from the the chancellor's battle with the Methodist church to Kirkland's decision to drop the Latin and Greek requirement. Mims was also one of the first Vanderbilt professors to regularly speak out on Nashville issues. In February 1918, in response to racial lynchings taking place throughout the South, he organized a group called the Law and Order League and wrote its charter. Ten years later Mims wrote a book called *The Advancing South* that he hoped would encourage the notion of progressive thought in the South. After Kirkland died in 1939, Mims wrote the late chancellor's biography, the first book ever published by the Vanderbilt University Press. With his white goatee and his cane, Mims was an ubiquitous presence on campus through the 1950s.

By the time he retired in the 1930s, physics professor John Daniel was criticized for his lack of energy and his boring lectures. But during the few years after his appointment as a faculty member in 1888, Daniel was considered brilliant and energetic. The best story about Daniel has to do with an experiment he conducted with a brand new invention called the x ray. In 1896 chemistry professor William Dudley asked Daniel whether an x ray of the head could reveal the location of a bullet that might be lodged there. Daniel said he did not know. The two men decided to conduct an experiment whereby Daniel would x ray Dudley's head while it lay on top of a coin to see whether the coin was revealed on the x-ray images. Daniel did so for an hour and found that he could not find any sign of the coin on the x rays. A few weeks later, Dudley's hair began to fall out, and the two men realized that it was happening because of the extensive x rays. Daniel immediately wrote an article about the episode to *Science* magazine. He was therefore credited with being the first person to discover the potential damage of extensive x rays to the skin.

A mainstay in the Vanderbilt philosophy department from 1908 until the 1950s, Herbert Sanborn was opinionated, eccentric, and influential. Unlike most of his colleagues, he was not afraid to speak out against Chancellor Kirkland regarding faculty issues such as tenure and pay. Sanborn was also quick to defend his native Germany, something he did right up to the beginning of both world wars. But Sanborn's main hobby wasn't politics; it was dogs. Between 1907 and

1930, Sanborn bred and raised about six hundred dachshunds, and spent countless hours conducting behavioral experiments on the hounds.

After he retired, Sanborn's name became a footnote in Tennessee political history. In 1954 a young man named Lyle Fulton died of cancer during his campaign for the state senate. At the last minute, the Democratic Party met and appointed Lyle's brother Richard to run for the office. Sanborn, an independent candidate who was by this time eighty-one years old, challenged the party's right to do this in court and said he would make a better state senator than Richard Fulton. "I am one of the very many who have lived far too long in the ivory tower, while rascals and traitors have betrayed our country," Sanborn told a reporter. Richard Fulton won the election and the case, launching a political career that would last for the rest of the century.

The School Without a Building

No school or department at Vanderbilt started as auspiciously as the law school. In September 1874 the newly organized university ran advertisements in newspapers across the state announcing the start of law school classes on the first Monday in October, to take place on the third floor of the Southern Methodist Publishing House building. The dozen or so students that showed up for the first day of class were greeted by the news that the rooms weren't ready yet. Most of the students left in disgust, but four remained. For the rest of the semester all law school classes were taught by one professor, a man named William Reece.

That first year must have been quite an experience for Reece and his students, but it set two precedents that would remain with the Vanderbilt Law School until the end of World War II. The first is that the Vanderbilt administration wanted to have a law school that was loosely affiliated with the university. The second is that the administration wasn't interested in spending a lot of time and money on it.

A year after its formation, Vanderbilt signed an agreement with Reece and two other prominent Nashville attorneys, Thomas

Malone and Edmund Baxter, to run the law school on Vanderbilt's behalf. For most of the remainder of the nineteenth century Malone, Baxter, and Reece served as the entire faculty of the law school, teaching everything from constitutional law to wills to contracts. From 1875 until 1889 law classes were taught on the second floor of the the Main Building. Then the law school moved to a building downtown shared by the Vanderbilt Dental School (an institution that ceased to exist in the 1920s).

Since the Vanderbilt Law School's history is poorly documented, not much is known about what it was like to attend the school in its early years. Faculty members were full-time attorneys first and teachers second, so classes were held in the afternoon. By reputation, law students were older than undergraduates and more serious than medical students. The highest honor for a law student was to be allowed to take part in the school's annual "Moot Court" proceeding, which took place graduation day. In the 1880s and 1890s Moot Court took place before a packed house and was usually covered in Nashville's newspapers.

With the retirement of its original faculty the law school changed quite a bit during the first few years of the twentieth century. After a couple of years of transition a man named Allen Hall became the first person to hold the position of full-time dean. During Dean Hall's tenure many part-time faculty members came and went. The most prominent was James McReynolds, who later became a member of the U.S. Supreme Court. Others included Jacob Dickinson, later Secretary of War in the Taft administration, and Claude Waller, a prominent Nashville attorney and the first of more than a dozen members of his family to attend Vanderbilt. Hall was also credited with lengthening the law course to three years and getting the Vanderbilt Law School recognized by the American Association of Law Schools.

One thing Hall was not able to do was toughen entrance requirements. For Vanderbilt's first five decades it was actually easier to gain admittance to the law school than it was the undergraduate division. The root of this problem was that the Tennessee Bar Association did not require an undergraduate education. Finally, under pressure from the American Association of Law Schools in the

1920s, the Vanderbilt Law School began requiring two years of college work for admission. But it was not easy; in fact, Vanderbilt's failure to fulfill the requirement led to the law school being temporarily dropped from the national association in 1927.

The Vanderbilt Law School was in financial trouble throughout the 1930s. Unlike other divisions of the university, it neither had a sizable endowment nor a home, which is why law school classes continued to meet in College Hall (the building renamed Kirkland Hall in 1937). In the Depression-era South, few people could afford law school, so enrollment slipped from more than two hundred in the 1920s to about sixty by 1935. By the late 1930s Vanderbilt was heavily subsidizing its law school and the board of trust was seriously considering discontinuing it. When World War II came, enrollment fell so low (twenty-two students) that the school decided to temporarily shut down the school.

By the time Harvie Branscomb became Vanderbilt's chancellor in 1946, the board of trust had decided to revive the law school. Although it is difficult to know which trustees took sides on this critical decision, it is safe to say that one of the key proponents of continuing the law school was Vanderbilt legal counsel Cecil Sims, one of the founders of the Nashville law firm Bass, Berry and Sims. As a part of restarting the law school, Vanderbilt University committed $500,000 from the Frederick Vanderbilt estate to law school endowment and began a fund drive to match that amount. The school hired a new dean, Dale Coffman, who assembled an entirely new faculty of nine professors. To Coffman's delight, more than 150 students — all of whom met the new requirement that students have a bachelor's degree — showed up for class in the fall of 1946. "Most of the students were just like me: poor before the war and fresh out of the military on the GI Bill," says Cecil Branstetter, a member of the Vanderbilt Law School class of 1949. "In those days, the school wasn't that hard to get into and it wasn't that expensive, nothing like it is today. Today it caters mostly to the rich in its attempt to be a national and international law school."

Within a year some of those students founded the *Vanderbilt Law Review*, a big step in the school's attempt to gain credibility. The fund drive only netted a disappointing $375,000 in addition to the

Frederick Vanderbilt money. But the momentum that the law school gained from its new faculty and enlarged student body was enough to get the organization into a new phase of growth. During Coffman's era the Vanderbilt Law School started a trend of hiring prominent law professors who had already retired from other institutions. In this way Vanderbilt hired three law professors who remained stalwarts through the 1950s and 1960s. The most eminent of them was Edmund Morgan, a professor of procedure and evidence who came to Vanderbilt from Harvard. "Morgan was a wonderful teacher," said 1957 Vanderbilt law school graduate George Barrett. "To this day, I remember the time that he called on me in class and asked me something about evidence that I got wrong. He acted like World War II had broken out all over again. It scared the hell out of me, but he reacted in a way that kept me from resenting it."

Coffman turned out to be the first of several deans who didn't stay long. In 1952 that streak was broken by John Wade, a tort law scholar who would remain for almost twenty years and is largely credited with building the law school into one of the nation's finest. By the time Wade became dean, the fact that the school was still meeting in the top two floors of Kirkland Hall had long since become an embarrassment. In 1950 the law school faculty specifically asked Branscomb not to install an elevator in Kirkland Hall to keep pressure on the board of trustees to fund a new law school building. That structure did not come until the early 1960s, when a new law school building and law library (named for trustee Alyne Queener Massey) were funded as a part of a $30 million university fund drive.

THE GAME THE WAY IT USED TO BE

A lot has changed since that late November afternoon in 1890, when a handful of Vanderbilt students met with a group from the University of Nashville and started playing a new game called football. "The game was interesting," read a brief account of the event in the *Nashville Banner*. "No one was hurt seriously, though some were more or less bruised." For the next few years coaches had to make do with the talent that showed up on campus every fall and players had to get by without much in the way of padding. It wasn't exactly the kind of sport people called football a century later. But it was fun nonetheless, as the following anecdotes show:

In the 1890s the forward pass was illegal, and most of the "plays" consisted of violent charges up the middle by the offense. Touchdowns were worth four points; field goals were worth five. There were hardly any penalties and only one referee to call them anyway. Substitutions were only allowed in case of a serious injury. "It was a story of a battle between giants, a titanic struggle in which strength and nerve played so important a part," enthused a *Banner* story about football at the turn of the century. "It was none of your pretty open play, your rapier slashes over tackle. It was a smashing, driving plunge into a line of men who met it with locked arms and legs and stout hearts." There was no room for young men with low thresholds of pain. One former Vanderbilt player bragged about how once "all the muscles in the side of his face were torn away. Yet he played all the game without a word of complaint or a time out."

Between 1890 and the Great Depression football players weren't nearly as large or as conditioned as they later became. A *Nashville American* article previewing the 1905 Vanderbilt football team noted that one of Vanderbilt's younger players "weighs about 200 pounds and is said to be very swift on his feet for a heavy weight." But so violent and injurious was the sport that many influential newspapers wanted it banned in the 1890s. In 1897 a reporter for the Methodist newspaper *Western Christian Advocate* attended a football game in Columbus, Ohio, and made the following comments: "I was perplexed out of measure at the exhibition of delight by Columbus mothers and daughters as they witnessed that dirtily-clad, bare and frowzy headed, rough and tumble, shoving, pushing, crushing, pounding, kicking, ground-wallowing, mixed-up mass of players, of whom any might come out with broken limbs, or be left on the ground writhing with ruptured vitals."

Between 1893 and 1922 Vanderbilt played its home games at a field at the corner of West End and Twenty-first Avenues, an area then known as Dudley Field and later renamed Curry Field. It was named in honor of William Dudley, a longtime Vanderbilt chemistry professor regarded as one of the founders of intercollegiate sports in the South. The north, east, and west sides of old Dudley Field each had about seven rows of seats. On the south side was a slope for standing-room only fans.

In 1903 a student named Wilbur Creighton was the manager of the Vanderbilt football team. Years later Creighton told his son that it was a part of his job to arrive in Knoxville the day before the game against the University of Tennessee. Since UT didn't have a regular place to play, Creighton and the UT manager had to scout around Knoxville for a good, flat field. They cut the grass, cleared the playing surface of rocks and debris, drew the lines on the field, and even built goalposts out of two-by-fours bought at a local hardware store.

Dan McGugin, Vanderbilt's most successful football coach ever, grew up in Iowa and played at Michigan. McGugin's father had been a part of General William T. Sherman's army during the Civil

War and had told his son how beautiful Tennessee was. Remembering this, McGugin wrote to Vanderbilt in 1904 and asked for the vacant job as head coach. Vanderbilt took him up on the offer, paying McGugin $850 a year plus board for his services.

That fall a *Hustler* reporter made note of the fact that new coach McGugin was so strict that he didn't let his players smoke cigarettes. "He believes in getting his men in the best possible physical condition, and to do this they must give up all kinds of intoxicants, cigarettes, etc. entirely. Not even on Saturday night or Sunday after a game must they smoke a cigarette." McGugin apparently knew what he was doing. During his first four years no southern team even scored against Vanderbilt, let alone win. Among the victories turned in by the Vanderbilt football team in 1905: a 97-0 win over Maryville; a 34-0 triumph over Alabama; and a 54-0 defeat of Auburn.

Vanderbilt vs. Alabama football game in 1926
Photographic Archives, Vanderbilt University

McGugin was actually a lawyer who coached football in his spare time. During working hours he could be found writing wills and performing other legal work at the law offices of Aust, McGugin and Spears. "He tended to his law practice during the day and in the evening he coached football," explained William "Dixie" Roberts, a star player under McGugin and 1932 Vanderbilt graduate. A man of many talents, McGugin served one term as a Tennessee state senator in the early 1920s. According to an article published during his term, McGugin didn't really want to get involved in politics, but he "was drafted into service by a citizens committee." McGugin's multiple careers led many people to speculate about just how good a coach he could have been if he had devoted all his time to football. "I believe Dan McGugin would have gone down in history as the greatest of all

The Vanderbilt football team in the 1920s. Head coach, lawyer, and state senator Dan McGugin is the man in the hat on the front row.
The Banner Collection, Nashville Public Library, The Nashville Room

coaches had he given all of his time to coaching," the sports editor of the *Birmingham News* wrote. "He was a great play-maker, but football was a sport for the beloved McGugin and law was his profession."

McGugin coached in a sport that was far more dangerous that fans of a later era would believe. In 1905 eighteen people died playing college football. At that point President Theodore Roosevelt invited officials from Yale, Harvard, and Princeton to the White House and told them he would ban the sport if it weren't made safer. A few months later a group of college officials developed new rules, most of which still existed a century later. The biggest change was the legalization of the forward pass, which was intended to open the game up and reduce its brutality. Other new rules defined and outlawed holding, clipping, personal fouls, and unsportsmanlike conduct.

The new rules eventually changed the game, but not at first. "Those who came out to see the much-talked-of new rules in force and expected to see some marvelously intricate new plays and formations probably went back disappointed," wrote a *Hustler* reporter of Vanderbilt's first game after the new rules were instituted. "It was good old straight football of the hammer and tongs variety." Injuries and the deaths continued for several more years. Sixteen people died playing football in 1915; eighteen in 1916; twelve in 1917; and eight in 1918. (One of the 1915 victims, a young man from the University of Tennessee named Bennett Jared, died from injuries he suffered in a game against Vanderbilt.) However, college football officials remained adamant about their intent to make football a safe sport. "The (death) figures will continue to decrease until fatalities in America's roughest outdoor game have been entirely eliminated," University of Chicago coach Amon Alonzo Stagg said in 1918.

Despite the fatalities the popularity of college football grew fast in Nashville during the McGugin era. When Vanderbilt played at Michigan on October 31, 1908, a ticker tape account of each play was wired to the Ryman Auditorium, and students and fans bought tickets to the Ryman that night so they could hear a report of each play as it came in. "While the telegraph keys were ticking, everyone had to be reasonably quiet," read an account of the event. "But the crowd gave the best exhibition of spirit seen for a long time at Vanderbilt." Michigan won 24-6.

Anecdotes from the McGugin era also indicate that there was a level of camaraderie between athletes that was unmatched in later years. In 1917 when the Vanderbilt football team traveled to the University of Chicago, McGugin and Chicago coach Alonzo Stagg arranged it so that the two teams could have dinner together the night before the game. After the meal the Chicago team sang some of their university songs to entertain the visiting Commodores.

The next year Vanderbilt defeated Tennessee 74 to 0. There are two footnotes about this game. One is that World War I decimated the ranks of most college football teams, Tennessee's included. As if that weren't enough, the season was nearly called off in October 1918 because of the influenza epidemic.

A few years later students and journalists began to criticize college football as too professional. McGugin and assistant football coach Wallace Wade responded with a letter to *The Hustler* explaining what was required of football players. The coaches said that practice started about two weeks after the school year began and that the season, from first workout until last game, lasted about ten weeks. Daily practices started at four p.m. and lasted until about 5:45, with the occasional after dinner meeting thrown in. "The total time in preparation and in the playing of the game will not exceed approximately 130 hours during the entire season," the letter said. "You are expected to put as much work on your studies during football time as at any other time during the year." The letter was written during a year in which Vanderbilt went undefeated.

Large taxpayer-funded schools like Tennessee and Alabama began putting more emphasis on football in the 1930s, making it tougher for small private colleges like Vanderbilt to remain dominant. In 1933 the Nashville media criticized McGugin for fielding a team with a 4-3-3 record. In a letter to *The Hustler*, McGugin defended himself. "I know our problems, our very limited number of freshmen, our expensive tuition, our scholastic standards for entrance and after entrance," he wrote. "Frequently upon teams which we play there are four or five splendid players who sought admission to Vanderbilt and could not enter for lack of credits or finances."

THE FUNDRAISING CAMPAIGN THAT FAILED

The legal split between Vanderbilt University and the Methodist Church took place in 1914. But when did it become obvious to Chancellor James Kirkland that the school and the church would have to go their separate ways? From available evidence, he made that decision around 1897, while climbing a muddy river embankment en route to another Southern city as a part of the most unsuccessful fundraising campaign in school history.

During Vanderbilt's early years the influence of the Methodist church on the school was evident in many ways: in the curriculum, in the mandatory chapel exercises, in the rules that forbade students from attending the theater, and in the hiring of professors (Methodists were given preferential treatment over non-Methodists). When Vanderbilt University was first organized, its relationship with the church appeared to be a permanent one. As one supporter of the University of Nashville wrote in 1873, "Vanderbilt University can never fill the place of the University of Nashville. It is intended to be a denominational institution. It is established for the benefit of the Methodist Church. It will be built up in the interest of the Methodist Church. And although . . . it will be conducted on the most general and liberal terms, still it will ever be, as it was intended, a Methodist University."

Nevertheless, the events that would eventually lead to Vanderbilt's split with the Methodist Church began a few years into the term of Kirkland, who became Vanderbilt's second chancellor in 1893.

When Kirkland took over, the school had terrible financial problems. After the financial panic of 1893 Kirkland became aware that returns were shrinking on the railroad bonds that had been left to the university by Cornelius Vanderbilt. Since these bonds constituted most of the endowment of the school at that time, this was a potential disaster. "The opinion prevails largely that Vanderbilt is rich and in need of nothing," Kirkland said in his 1893 inauguration speech. "I wish indeed this was so; but candor compels me to undeceive you. We are poor, and in need of many things. The income from our productive fund is, as I have stated, about $60,000 . . . It is absolutely impossible for a university to hold its position today without an income of several hundred thousand."

Kirkland also inherited a board whose trustees were appointed in a curious way. In 1893 the Vanderbilt board had twenty-four members. A third of them were Methodist bishops who automatically got a seat. The other sixteen seats were filled by eight separate conferences of the Methodist Episcopal Church, South (such as the North Alabama Conference, the Louisville Conference, and the Memphis Conference), which nominated two people each, one clergy and one lay person. The result was a board dominated by bishops, clergymen, and people unlikely to have much knowledge of higher education or business.

Kirkland thought about the school's financial problems on a whirlwind tour of Ivy League schools in February 1894. Upon his return Kirkland and the board made three important changes. The first was to sell the railroad bonds and invest the money in other ways. The second was to change the way that the sixteen non-bishop slots on the board were filled so that eight of the spots were filled by individual conferences, while the other eight would be filled by the quadrennial Methodist General Conference, without geographic consideration. (Kirkland reasoned that it would be easier to exert more power over a central organization such as the General Conference than it would to control the actions of eight separate conferences located in all corners of the South). The third step was when the board, at Kirkland's request, voted to admit three new members – Nathanial Baxter, S.J. Keith, and Samuel Cupples. The measure to accept these three men as trustees passed with little dissent, and there were few complaints about this step from within the Methodist church at that time.

About this time Kirkland began a fundraising campaign meant to appeal to Methodist church members. He approached the church and at one of its conventions got a motion passed declaring Vanderbilt University the denomination's "central institution" (a status above other existing Methodist institutions such as Emory College). Then the board of trust inaugurated what was known as the

"Twentieth Century Fund," a $300,000 fund-drive for Vanderbilt's theology department. For the next several months Kirkland traveled all over the South and asked Methodist congregations for money.

In an era before paved road, such travel was arduous. "I am tired of running around and stopping at these little fourth-class hotels without any of the comforts of life," Kirkland told his wife in one letter. "I believe I had rather camp out in the mountains than take much of this. Yesterday at Arkansas City (Arkansas), I had to climb down the banks of the river for several hundred yards in deep black mud, get on a little steamboat, pay fifty cents for passage across and climb up in the same way on the other side."

The Twentieth Century Fund was a bust. After three years Kirkland raised only $50,000, and most of that came from faculty, alumni, and citizens of Nashville. The experience convinced Kirkland that southern Methodists were not interested in giving money to a central university.

THE TRAMP OF THE UNBORN

Despite the failure of the Twentieth Century Fund there were those in the Methodist Church who believed that the church should exert more power over the school. The most important such person was Elijah Hoss, a former Vanderbilt theology professor who in 1895 became the editor of the *Nashville Christian Advocate*. While editor of the *Advocate*, Hoss became critical of Vanderbilt University and Chancellor Kirkland. Vanderbilt's athletic program, in Hoss' opinion, detracted from the purpose of the university. Dances that took place at the school promoted sin. Kirkland's willingness to hire non-Methodists for key faculty positions betrayed the church. "Denominational colleges are set up for the same reason as denominational newspapers – to advance the interest of denominations," Hoss said. Some people in the Methodist Church agreed with Hoss, including Bishop Warren Candler, the president of Emory College and a Vanderbilt trustee.

In 1904 Candler criticized Kirkland's hiring of non-Methodist faculty members at a board of trust meeting and proposed a measure to his fellow trustees that would have postponed the selection of non-Methodist Frederick Moore as Dean of the College. To Kirkland's mortification, the measure nearly passed. The vote was so close that Kirkland considered resigning. He probably would have had it not been for the support of board chairman Bishop Eugene Hendrix on the issue of non-Methodist faculty members. "I do not know of a great university in this country that limits membership in its faculties to any one denomination," Hendrix said.

The next year, with Hendrix's support, Kirkland proposed a measure regarding the number of bishops that could serve as trustees. Under Vanderbilt's original charter all bishops in the Methodist Episcopal Church, South – a group known collectively as the College of Bishops – were automatically given a seat on the school's board of trust. Since the number of bishops in the Methodist church increased over the years, this practice was impractical in the longterm. In 1905 the board passed a measure limiting the number of bishops that could serve on the board to five chosen by the church's education committee. This action brought the matter of Vanderbilt's relationship to the church to the forefront.

Hoss was in South America at the time of the 1905 board meeting. Upon his return to the states he began heavily criticizing the decision by Vanderbilt's board of trustees to limit the number of bishops to five. Under his influence the General Conference of the Methodist Episcopal Church, South, appointed five Methodist attorneys to "determine the relationship" between the school and the church. After months of research the commission decided that the church — not the board — had the authority to name board members and effectively run the school. However the next time the Vanderbilt Board of Trust met, it effectively discarded the conclusions of the commission and went on about its business.

For the next three years the issue of whether the denomination or the board ran the school simmered. It was foremost on the mind of Kirkand, who realized there was very little he could do to move Vanderbilt forward until it was resolved. The issue finally came to a head in 1910. That year, after a contentious debate, the Methodist conference passed a resolution naming three new bishops to Vanderbilt's board. A few weeks later Vanderbilt's board voted nineteen to eight not to accept them.

At that point the College of Bishops voted to remove Kirkland as chancellor and to remove the nineteen trustees who had voted against the three new members. The board of trust ignored those measures as well. The bishops then sued the board in Davidson County Chancery Court, claiming the board had violated the original charter of the university by declaring itself sovereign.

The matter went to trial in November 1912. Among the university's lawyers were James C. Bradford, Jordan Stokes, and John Ventrees (who only a few years earlier represented Furman family members in the case against Vanderbilt University). The church's lead counsel was Memphis attorney G.T. Fitzhugh.

The case was a long and complex one, and its filings totaled over ten thousand pages. In its filings the church claimed that Vanderbilt was started primarily as an institution for Methodist professors and Methodist students. Attorneys for the school, meanwhile, conceded that the Methodist Episcopal Church, South, had passed resolutions establishing the school, but claimed that the school was started for people of other denominations as well. During the trial the university produced evidence that showed that when the school was started, more than a third of the faculty were non-Methodists, a percentage that had remained about the same since that time.

Another important point was fundraising. The church claimed that its congregations had contributed a lot of money to the school over the years; it argued, for example, that most of the people who had donated money to rebuild the school's Main Building in 1905 were Methodists and did so because they were Methodists. In extensive testimony the university claimed otherwise, pointing out that the larger donations had come from members of the Vanderbilt family, from Vanderbilt faculty and students, and other individuals acting independently of their churches (such as Nashville resident Mary Furman). Kirkland testified about his failed attempt to generate funds from within the church through the Twentieth Century Fund. And as for the people who donated a total of thirty thousand dollars to help rebuild the school's Main Building, the school claimed that they had done so because they were Nashville citizens or Vanderbilt alumni, not because they were Methodists.

Another key point was Cornelius Vanderbilt's intention when he donated a million dollars to start the school. To this end the school produced a letter written by Mr. Vanderbilt in which he said that his main idea was to start a school to help the South. "I wish the university to be conducted with the best talent on non-denominational lines," Vanderbilt wrote. "I believe the education of the youth of the South on these lines will do much to harmonize the former strained relations. I put Bishop McTyeire at the head of Trust on a fixed salary for life not because he was a Methodist, but a man of talent and of fine executive ability, and because his wife and mine were cousins." Attorneys for the church countered with a key line from Bishop Holland McTyeire's will. In his last will and testament, McTyeire requested "that the religious character of the university be emphasized always. Insist on this. The institution is in care of the Methodist Episcopal Church, South."

At the heart of the matter was the question of who owned Vanderbilt University. That being the case, it is a certainty that Kirkland, as a witness, was asked who he thought owned the school. His answer was probably similar to one that he had given four years earlier to the Methodist attorneys who were conducting an inquiry into the matter. "I believe the owners of the institution are the generations for which they have to work, the public at large," he said at that time. "I hear the tramp of hundreds of thousands of feet of men and women who are to tread this campus and these halls in years to come, yet unborn; and if I read history aright, they are the true owners of this institution."

After the trial was heard but before a ruling had been sent down, two disputes between the church and the board took place. In 1910 the board of trust approved a land exchange that would enable the George Peabody School for Teachers to be built on a site adjacent to the Vanderbilt campus. The College of Bishops voted to reject this transaction.

Then northern industrialist Andrew Carnegie announced his intention to donate a million dollars to the Vanderbilt Medical School under the condition that the school be run by a non-denominational body. The Vanderbilt Board of Trust voted to accept the donation. Led by Bishop Candler, who called Carnegie's gift the "impudent proposal of an agnostic steelmonger," the College of Bishops voted to reject it.

In February 1913 Chancellor John Allison decided in favor of the church, ruling that the Methodist Episcopal Church, South, had the right to elect members to the Vanderbilt Board of Trust. The school appealed the ruling to the Tennessee Supreme Court. But for the time being it looked like a complete defeat for Kirkland. While awaiting the Supreme Court's decision, the chancellor began making plans to go elsewhere. One published account in April 1913 had Kirkland accepting the presidency of the University of Arkansas.

On March 21, 1914, the Tennessee Supreme Court handed down a historic ruling. The decision, written by Judge W.R. Turner of Knoxville, was a complex one that favored the university. Citing a comparable case related to Dartmouth College, Turner held that Cornelius Vanderbilt, not the Methodist Episcopal Church, South, was the founder of the university. The court ruled that the board of trust was a self-perpetuating body and that the bishops did not have power to veto its actions. However, it also held that the church's Board of Education had the power to confirm Vanderbilt's trustees. This was a bit of a hollow victory for the church, since the ruling went on to say that if the church should "contumaciously refuse to confirm members" that the board could act independently of it.

That night Vanderbilt students built a celebratory bonfire and paraded through Nashville's streets. From all accounts, the celebration got a bit out of hand, and managed to offend several local Methodists, among them Chancellor Allison. "What a spectacle in Nashville, 'the Athens of the South!' " Allison wrote in a letter of complaint to the *Banner*. *The Hustler* came out with a celebratory issue, which horrified Kirkland so much that he ordered every copy of it collected and destroyed. Meanwhile the national media weighed in with congratulations for the school. "For the same reason that we are glad to see the schools in France taken from under control of the Roman Catholic Church, for the same reason that we desire to see the schools in England taken from under the control of the Established Church, we are glad to see such an educational institution as Vanderbilt University taken from under the control of the Methodist Church," said the national opinion journal *The Outlook*.

Kirkland did not relax after the Supreme Court ruling, convinced that the church's power to deny trustees left the matter of control unsettled. However, as lawyers for the Methodist Church pored over the ruling, they realized that the idea of using confirmation power to control the board was a futile and destructive one. At the next Methodist conference, a resolution was passed severing all ties to the university.

At the time Vanderbilt University split from the church, many Southern Methodists viewed Kirkland as cold, arrogant, and somehow anti-church (others blamed Hoss for the divorce of the school and the church). But it should be pointed out that the controversy between the school and the church had far more to do with control of the university than whether the Methodist church would have an impact there. Even after the split between the church and the school, the theological department remained a part of Vanderbilt. The Methodist church remained the ubiquitous denomination on campus; a few years after the split, three Methodist bishops were the honored guests at the annual banquet of the Vanderbilt Alumni Association. Mandatory chapel remained a part of Vanderbilt life; whenever students complained about it in the 1920s and 1930s, Kirkland was the first to defend it. Finally, it should be pointed out that until his death, Kirkland, the son of a Methodist minister, remained a practicing Methodist.

The divorce between Vanderbilt and the Methodist church created two new universities. In 1915 Coca-Cola owner Asa Candler, the brother of Bishop Warren Candler, gave a million dollars to the Methodist Episcopal Church, South, to help start a Methodist university in the South to replace Vanderbilt. "What our country needs is not more secularized education, but more of the education that is fundamentally and intentionally religious," Asa Candler wrote in the letter in which he announced the gift. "I see no way by which such religious education can be supplied without institutions of learning owned and controlled by the churches." Asa Candler's gift was used to transform small Emory College into Emory University. At about the same time the Methodist Church started a school in Texas, giving it a name that would leave no doubt in anyone's mind about its origin. It was called Southern Methodist University.

Part Three

Mr. Kirkland's School

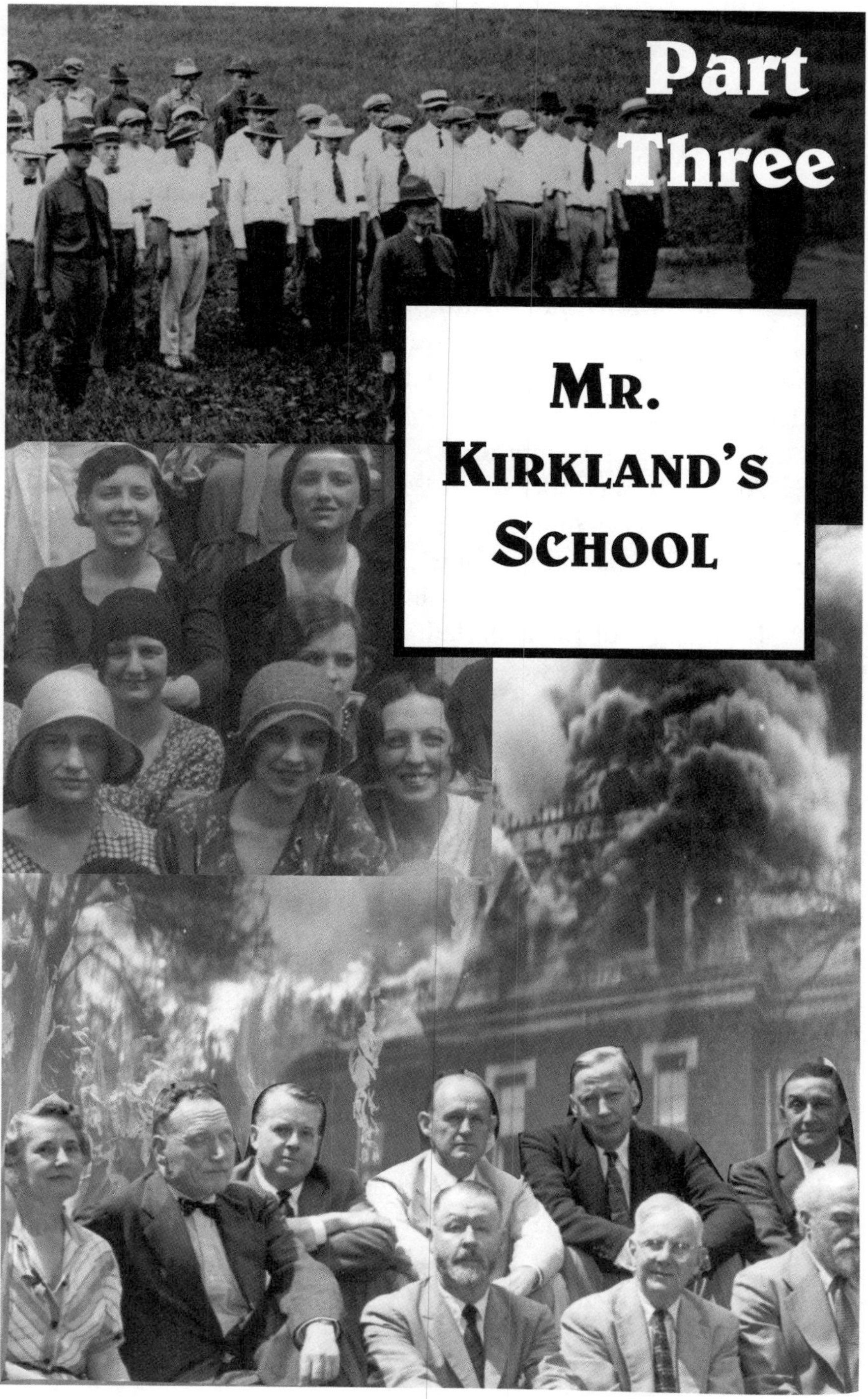

ONE CAMPUS, MANY PLANS

One of the things that makes the Vanderbilt campus so appealing is that its buildings represent so many architectural styles. But no one really planned it this way. There is a tale behind every part of the school grounds. More often than not it is a story about schemes that were half-executed, changed midstream, and merged with other plans. No one can be said to have molded the campus. But many people have left their marks on it.

For example: Vanderbilt's Main Building originally had two towers. After it burned in 1905 it was rebuilt with only one, mainly because of cost. New York architect J. E. R. Carpenter designed the Main Building's replacement (later called Kirkland Hall) and drew a lot of inspiration from the town hall of Siena, Italy.

By the end of the twentieth century the two open spaces on the main part of campus were Library Lawn and Alumni Lawn. They had both been there so long that they seemed permanent, even sacred. In fact, neither was planned. Library Lawn is the former site of Wesley Hall, the home of the Biblical College beginning in 1881. After it burned in 1932, Wesley Hall was not rebuilt because there was no money to do so. Alumni Lawn was the home of Kissam Hall, a huge dormitory where most male students resided from its construction in 1902 until the middle of the twentieth century. By the time it was torn down in 1958, it had fallen into such disrepair that almost no students or alumni expressed a concern for it. Some people have argued that it was the most beautiful building ever to be intentionally torn down on campus.

Kissam might have looked dignified from the outside, but many of the students who lived in it had a hard time appreciating its architecture. In fact, some of them later described the place a dump. "All the baths and toilet facilities were in one wing of the basement," Ralph McGill, a student at Vanderbilt between 1918 and 1920, wrote years later. "No student above the first floor entertained any save the most hostile feelings toward the memory of the playboy architect (Stanford White) . . . Indeed, I am sure Vanderbilt is the only university in America where toasts were drunk to Harry K. Thaw (who murdered White). Once in my time, during a particularly severe winter, a handsome, hand-painted poster was put up in the facilities quarter. It read: 'In grateful tribute to Harry K. Thaw, who rid the world of a damned bad architect.' "

When the fate of Kissam Hall was being discussed in 1954, Chancellor Harvie Branscomb said it was the school's intention to also tear down the Old Gym and build a new dormitory on that site, thus completing a quadrangle of dormitories around a new open lawn. No one apparently opposed those plans publicly, but by 1957 the administration had decided instead to renovate the Old Gym.

When Vanderbilt and Barnard Halls were completed and freshmen began using them as dormitories in 1952, upperclassmen complained that the newcomers were spoiled since they didn't have to live in the purgatory of Kissam Hall as they had. "They just can't get students quite as hardy as in the old days," an article in the *Vanderbilt Alumnus* said. "Then, it was different; it was Kissam, sink or swim.

Kissam Hall, which Vanderbilt built in 1902 and razed in 1958
Photographic Archives, Vanderbilt University

Some of the new freshmen would probably go through college and never see that cabinet plumbing of which all Kissam men are so justly proud."

To those familiar with the placement of the buildings on the Vanderbilt campus, Furman Hall seems a bit out of place. It doesn't face Kirkland; it doesn't face Twenty-first Avenue; it isn't even lined up with neighboring buildings such as Garland and Calhoun. Why? Because when Furman Hall was designed in 1907, Kansas City landscape architect George Kessler had just completed a campus plan that called for the main entrance to the university to be moved from West End Avenue to Twenty-first Avenue and for five stone buildings to built along that main drive, to be called the Court of Honor. Furman was supposed to be the first of those five buildings. But in the 1920s the administration changed its mind about the Kessler Plan, partly because a generous donor named Mrs. George Mitchell Neely didn't like it. The school hired another campus planner named Charles Klauder, who came up with the placement for structures such as Alumni Hall, Neely Auditorium, Garland Hall, and Calhoun Hall.

The adjacent structures known as Old Central and Old Science (later Benson Hall) have escaped demolition at least four times. The Klauder Plan would have torn down Old Science and Old Central, along with the Old Gym and West Side Hall. In the early 1950s another plan called for Old Science and Old Central to be torn down and replaced with a massive center for science, math, and engineering. However, when the university got around to executing that plan in the 1960s, students protested because the new center would get rid of much of the remaining open space in the middle of campus. About five years later the administration considered razing Old Central and Old Science and building a new student center there. Students didn't like that plan either, which is why the student center was eventually merged with existing Rand Hall. Old Science was about to be condemned in 1980. Then a member of the class of 1907 named Robert Benson donated a million dollars to restore Old Science and Old Central. Old Science was thus renamed Benson Hall, and the two structures became the home of the history department.

While Memorial Gym was being planned, it apparently did not occur to Vanderbilt administrators that it would cost money to operate the building. After the building opened in December 1952, each student was assessed a five dollar annual fee to help defray the cost of operating the facility, a move very unpopular with students.

During the debate about where to locate the Veterans Administration Hospital in the late 1950s, one faculty member at Vanderbilt who publicly criticized the idea of it being sited next to Vanderbilt was longtime English professor Donald Davidson. "It is hostile to genuine educational and intellectual interests to allow a university to become predominantly medical," Davidson said. "Why should there be a VA hospital at all? They're pork barrel projects."

When the university completed the functional but bland six-building Kissam Quadrangle in 1957, a few students opined that the project architecturally paled in comparison to everything that the university had built prior to that time. *Hustler* columnist Geoff Cooper wrote an article on what he perceived to be the Kissam Quadrangle's shortcomings. "It is hard to imagine how a man of (architect Edward Durrell) Stone's ability can make the same mistake six times," he opined.

Kissam Quadrangle received far less criticism architecturally than the 1969 addition to the Joint University Library. Typical of the complaints was a letter written by a student in 1968. "Who's in charge of general architecture at Vanderbilt?" the student asked. "If anyone occupies this position, let him come forth and explain what the hell that new library wing is doing on the old one. I don't mean functionally, I mean aesthetically. The combination of the designs of the buildings sets a new mark for total ugliness on campus, if not the city."

Prior to the 1960s no dorm rooms had telephones; students were required to share one phone with everyone else in the dorm. Finally, in the fall of 1967, housing dean K.C. Potter announced a policy whereby students in Barnard, McGill, and Carmichael Towers could get phones installed in their rooms for $6.90 a month. (Female students, who lived in Branscomb Quadrangle, were excluded from this early offer.) Within weeks 419 students had ordered phones, and Vanderbilt's seventeen full-time phone operators were deluged with more work than they could handle. By 1971 the school had installed phones in virtually every dorm room and replaced the operators with an automatic system.

Plant Operations originally produced steam by burning coal. Because of federal regulations, the facility switched to natural gas as fuel in December 1969.

By the 1950s and 1960s traffic on West End Avenue was much heavier than the road could bear. Many of the students who were attending Vanderbilt in 1970 remember the difference caused by the opening of Interstate 40 in Nashville. "All of a sudden one day we noticed that there weren't many loud trucks on West End Avenue any more," says 1972 graduate Steve Baker. "We knew then that the interstate had opened and that it had made that much difference."

In 1971 West Side Row changed from being a home for students and faculty to being office space. This administrative decision forced longtime Dean of Men Madison Sarratt to move. "I've lived there so long, I have no idea of living anywhere else," he said.

West Side Hall was originally built in 1887 as a dining and bathroom facility for the West Side Row dormitories. From the end of World War II until about 1990 it was the home of the Vanderbilt Navy ROTC unit. Navy ROTC kept quite a high profile on campus, and its midshipmen regularly marched on Alumni Lawn every Thursday afternoon. After McGill Hall (next door) became a "philosophy themed" dorm in the 1970s, the contrast between mostly left-wing "McGillites," as they were known, and mostly right-wing ROTC midshipmen created dozens of amusing incidents. (One year, McGill residents began playing Jimi Hendrix's version of the Star Spangled Banner during the formal ROTC parade.) In the 1990s West Side Hall was renovated and expanded and turned into the new Office of Admissions. Navy ROTC was moved from the heart of campus to the Baker Building, an office building across Twenty-first Avenue from the main campus.

The series of dorms near the south end of campus known as Mayfield is named for George Mayfield, a German and Latin professor who came to Vanderbilt as a graduate student in 1903 and remained on the faculty until 1947. Mayfield had a variety of interests and helped organize both the Tennessee Ornithological Society and the Nashville Children's Museum (later the Cumberland Science Museum). Mayfield was actually teaching a Latin class in Vanderbilt's

College Hall in 1905 when it caught fire. "A strange hissing and whistling noise was heard, as if air had been confined in a small space and was forcing its way out through a tiny opening," he said many years later. "Then suddenly there was an explosion above our heads, and a great pall of black smoke dropped over the windows like a dark curtain and the whole room became as dark as night. Then we all started toward the door. I don't know to this day who got downstairs first, but we all reached the front door quickly enough."

In 1985 the architectural firm Street and Street began working on plans to renovate Kirkland Hall. Architects decided that they wanted to lay new brick along the interior walls of the revered building. But to fit in, the bricks had to be old, and for several months it was

Firefighters try fruitlessly to save College Hall in 1905
The Stella Vaughn Family Collection, Photographic Archives, Vanderbilt University

The campus in the 1950s, showing Kissam Quadrangle under construction, while the old Kissam Hall remains
The Banner Collection, Nashville Public Library, The Nashville Room

unclear where they would obtain eighty thousand old bricks. As luck would have it, about that time a row of warehouses built around 1890 burned down on Nashville's Second Avenue. The firm made a deal with the wrecking company, took all the old bricks from the wreckage, and used them in Kirkland Hall.

By the end of the twentieth century Vanderbilt had put buildings on so many of the old open spaces on campus that it made alumni wonder if there would always be open space on campus. As it turns out, the school does have an obligation to keep a field or two. Under agreement with the U.S. Navy and Army, the school must provide a level, grass covered, unobscured, and readily accessible drill field for the Navy and Army ROTC units that measures at least sixty-four hundred square yards.

Finally, there is a little-noticed graveyard on the campus between the Vanderbilt Divinity School and Garland Hall. In 1876 Bishop McTyeire had the bodies of Methodist bishops William McKendree and Joshua Soule disinterred from neglected graveyards elsewhere in Middle Tennessee and reburied there. During his declining months Bishop McTyeire made it clear that he wanted to be buried alongside them, and asked that he "be buried in a suit that he had given a sermon in." Students filled the grave at McTyeire's funeral in February 1889. A few weeks later McTyeire's will was opened. There wasn't much to it, other than the introductory words "I die poor. I have laid up no treasure here."

PEABODY GOES ITS OWN WAY

In 1910 the Peabody situation seemed to be moving in just the way Vanderbilt Chancellor James Kirkland wanted. After four decades as a small teaching school on the old University of Nashville Campus, the Peabody Education Fund's trustees decided to form a more sophisticated teaching college. Many people, including former Peabody Normal College president James Porter and the residents and property owners of south Nashville, wanted the college to go on the former site of the normal school. But Kirkland wanted it next to Vanderbilt. He got his wish when the Peabody Education Fund decided to build the college on two large parcels: one, the former site of Roger Williams University (on the east side of Hillsboro Road); the other, on a part of the Vanderbilt campus (on the west side of Hillsboro Road).

At that point the Peabody-Vanderbilt arrangement took an unexpected turn. About the time of the land swap Peabody hired as its first president Bruce Payne, who had previously been a professor of education at the University of Virginia. As Payne traveled the country soliciting large donations for the new Peabody College, he became nervous about the school's evolving relationship with Vanderbilt. Without saying much to Kirkland, he decided to build the main part of the Peabody campus on the east side of Hillsboro, rather than the west side of Hillsboro as Kirkland had hoped.

Payne later claimed that architectural concerns were the reason for this decision. (He said that he wanted to build a quadrangle of pillared buildings dominated by a rotunda at the end of campus, just like at his beloved University of Virginia.) However, the real reason was that he didn't want his school to become a division of Vanderbilt. This change of heart infuriated Kirkland. By 1914 the chancellor was so upset with Payne that he demanded that the land on the west side of campus be returned. In the end Vanderbilt got the property back, and it later became the site of the new Vanderbilt Medical School.

George Peabody College for Teachers opened at its new site in the summer of 1914 with more than eleven hundred students and seventy-eight part or full-time instructors. At that time, the campus only had two buildings – the Industrial Arts Building and the Home Economics Building. Structures that followed included the Socio-Religious Building (1915), the Psychology Building (1915), the library (1918), West Hall dormitory (1923), East Hall dormitory (1924), Administration (1925), Fine Arts (1930), and Confederate Hall (1935).

It is impossible to give a complete history of Peabody College in this volume, but it would be irresponsible not to mention some characteristics of the school. First of all, George Peabody College for Teachers was a much different place than the Peabody Normal College. The normal college existed to train elementary and secondary teachers in a time when most southerners lived on farms. Peabody College also trained teachers, but its main functions were to shape

Peabody students studying home economics - circa 1920
The Peabody Collection, Photographic Archives, Vanderbilt University

educational thought, award graduate degrees, and train educational leaders.

Kirkland had hoped that Peabody would not develop its own liberal arts curricula in hopes that Peabody's students would cross-enroll at Vanderbilt. To Kirkland's dismay, Peabody did just that, offering college-level classes in biology, chemistry, history, and English. Peabody also had some very specialized programs. It had one of the nation's best training programs for librarians. It had a degree program for school administrators. It had a division that conducted surveys that was widely used by local and state governments as they tried to consolidate tiny school systems in the 1930s and 1940s.

Peabody also had one of the South's finest music schools (which eventually became the Blair School of Music). It had a demonstration school where students could learn how to teach and Nashville residents could send their children (which eventually became the University School of Nashville). Peabody even had a division called the Knapp School of Farm Life, located on a farm just southeast of downtown Nashville. Knapp demonstrated crop rotation methods, the benefits of scientific farming, and the value of farm machinery. Peabody operated the Knapp farm for several decades before selling the property in 1965 to Nashville general contractor Robert Mathews, who developed the Metro Industrial Park on the location.

Peabody developed a culture that differed from the Vanderbilt culture in two main ways. One was that the Peabody student body was primarily female; despite efforts by school administrators to recruit as many male students as possible, usually about three-fourths of the students were women. Peabody was also more regional than Vanderbilt. By 1917 more than half of the students in the teaching college were from outside Tennessee. As late as 1950 more than half of Vanderbilt's students came from Tennessee.

Many of Peabody's thousands of alumni developed close relationships with faculty members. One of the more legendary professors was Maycie Southall. Southall, like many women who attended Peabody in the first half of the twentieth century, taught for several years in a one-room schoolhouse before she came to Peabody as a student in 1918. Later, she was a high school principal and a rural county school supervisor — quite rare for a woman in the 1920s — before she came back to Peabody and earned her doctorate in 1929. At that point Southall became a professor of elementary education at Peabody. During the next thirty-five years Southall was a formidable figure in the world of elementary school teaching. "Elementary education was a sorry stepchild in educational circles until Dr. Southall . . . came on the scene," one of her former students said. "Her influence at national, regional, and local levels lifted the education of children from babysitting to profitable experiences for the child."

Another favorite faculty member was Alfred Leland Crabb, who taught education at Peabody from 1927 until 1949. For several years, Crabb conducted a weekly radio program on radio station WSM called "The Teachers College of the Air." But Nashville residents best remember Crabb as the author of several works of local historical fiction, such as *Journey to Nashville* and *Dinner at Belmont.*

MR. FLEXNER CHANGES EVERYTHING

The Vanderbilt Medical School is as much the creation of Abraham Flexner as it is of anyone. His effect on the institution is so dramatic that author Timothy Jacobson's 1987 history of the Vanderbilt Medical School is rightfully titled *Making Medical Doctors: Science and Medicine at Vanderbilt Since Flexner*.

Flexner was a native of Louisville, Kentucky, who attended Johns Hopkins University in Baltimore, Maryland. After graduation he moved back to Louisville and taught public school. For many years it appeared as if Flexner was destined to spend his life as an eccentric and demanding schoolteacher. But in 1905 he and his wife decided to leave Louisville to study at Harvard and then in Germany.

Along the way Flexner wrote a book called *The American College* that was highly critical of the college system employed in most parts of the United States and of what he saw as the American educational system's tolerance for mediocrity. "I had noticed all too frequently that the boys whom I had sent to Eastern colleges lost rather than gained enthusiasm for scholarship in the course of their college careers," Flexner later wrote in his 1940 autobiography *I Remember*.

The American College did not sell many copies. But it was read by a man named Henry Pritchett, the head of the Carnegie Foundation for the Advancement of Teaching. Pritchett was impressed by Flexner's outlook, and asked Flexner if he would make a detailed study of American medical schools. Flexner agreed, and in December 1908 he began his tour of 155 medical colleges.

Flexner's report was published in 1910 and is regarded as one of the most important documents in the history of medical training. Known as the Carnegie Foundation's "Bulletin Number Four," it was a complete indictment of the American system of producing physicians. Flexner argued that most medical schools weren't set up to train new doctors, but to give existing physicians a supplemental source of income. He pointed out that Germany, which had far better medical care than America, actually had fewer doctors per capita. There were far too many doctors in the United States and too many medical

The Vanderbilt Medical School Building, shortly after its construction in the 1920s
The Banner Collection, Nashville Public Library, The Nashville Room

schools. Most of the schools had loose admission standards and not enough equipment.

Flexner was not a man for subtlety, and his report was full of vivid and uncomplimentary details about individual institutions. He said that the California Medical College was a "disgrace to the state." The Baylor University College of Medicine had a "bare" laboratory. The Birmingham Medical College was "given over largely to surgical patients with gun-shot and other wounds." The Washington University Medical School in St. Louis "must be either abolished or reorganized." As for the state of Tennessee, it contained "more low-grade medical schools than any other southern state," including small medical schools in Knoxville and Chattanooga that Flexner described as "utterly wretched."

The Vanderbilt Medical School, then located in a group of buildings in south Nashville, didn't fare much better than most schools in Flexner's report. Flexner said that the Vanderbilt Medical School's entrance requirement was "less than high school graduation" and that the school had no full-time faculty. However, Flexner said that of Tennessee's nine medical schools, Vanderbilt's alone should be continued because it was "the only institution in position at this juncture to deal with the subject effectively."

It is impossible to know exactly why Flexner came to this extremely important conclusion. But it should be pointed out that Flexner had been a lifelong friend of Vanderbilt Chancellor James Kirkland; the two had neighboring summer homes in Canada. Flexner thought highly of the chancellor and described him as a "great man" in his autobiography. "I think the personal relationship between Kirkland and Flexner cannot be overemphasized," said Mary Teloh, a librarian at the Eskind Biomedical Library in 2002 who conducted considerable research into the medical center's history. Teloh also believed that Vanderbilt might have been more prepared for Flexner's inspection than other schools because of Kirkland's relationship with Flexner.

One person with first-hand knowledge of Flexner's relationship to Kirkland was Flexner's grandnephew John Flexner. "They (Kirkland and Abraham Flexner) were friends, neighbors, and fishing buddies," said John Flexner, a professor of medicine at the Vanderbilt Medical School Division of Hematology at the end of the twentieth century. John Flexner had many colorful anecdotes about his great-uncle Abraham. "He used to return all the letters that I would send him with all the grammatical mistakes corrected in the margin," he said.

Whatever the cause for Flexner's warm feelings toward Vanderbilt, the impact of his report on medical schools in Tennessee was far-reaching. Within years of the Flexner report most of the medical schools in Tennessee, including the University of Tennessee Medical School in Nashville, were shut down (the U.T. Medical School was later reopened in Memphis). In 1913, largely as a result of Flexner's conclusions about the future of medical education in Tennessee, the Carnegie Foundation gave a million dollars to the Vanderbilt Medical School to recruit full-time professors, equip laboratories, and raise standards. This took place at about the same time that Nashville's Methodist community was raising money for a new hospital building to be located on Vanderbilt's south campus.

Galloway Memorial Hospital, named for a Methodist bishop, broke ground in 1916.

On the eve of World War I the future of the Vanderbilt Medical School appeared to be good, and appeared to be permanently linked with several structures on the university's south campus.

THE ABANDONMENT OF GALLOWAY HOSPITAL

When Nashville Mayor Bill Purcell announced his capital budget for year 2000, one little-noticed item was the planned renovation of a long-neglected structure next to the Howard School office building. Few people knew that the building was once known as Galloway Hospital, and that it was originally supposed to be the medical facility affiliated with the Vanderbilt Medical School.

The Carnegie Foundation's million-dollar donation in 1913 to improve the Vanderbilt Medical School staff and laboratory was not enough to build a new hospital, something the medical school also needed. However, this shortage of money didn't appear to be an obstacle at the time because a new hospital called Galloway, funded by Nashville-area Methodist churches, began construction on Vanderbilt's south campus three years later. The proximity of the hospital to the Vanderbilt Medical School was not a coincidence; Vanderbilt Chancellor James Kirkland had urged the Methodists to build Galloway Hospital there so that the medical school could partner with it.

For a few years Vanderbilt's partnership with Galloway Hospital appeared solid. However, things changed by the time American troops came home from World War I. Nashville's Methodist community was unable to raise the funds to finish Galloway. Although it is difficult to say why this was the case, the fact that Americans were being asked to spend every penny to support the war effort in 1917 and 1918 may have affected it. In addition, Flexner left the Carnegie Foundation to work for the General Education Board, the foundation affiliated with philanthropist John Rockefeller. Finally, the catastrophic influenza epidemic of 1918, which killed twenty million people worldwide, reminded Americans just how much needed to be done in the area of health care.

Largely under Flexner's influence, the GEB in 1919 announced it would give another four million dollars to the Vanderbilt Medical School, the largest gift that had been made to the university to that time. With that amount pledged, Kirkland began to make plans for new medical school buildings on the south campus. He also hired a medical school dean named Canby Robinson.

Were it not for Robinson, the Vanderbilt Medical School probably would have spent the GEB's generous donation on the south campus. But from the moment he arrived in Nashville, Robinson was unhappy with the idea of the medical school separated from the rest of the university, since medical school students also needed training in undergraduate subjects such as chemistry and biology. Robinson lobbied heavily for a new combined medical school and hospital to be built adjacent to the main Vanderbilt campus. This stance aggravated Kirkland, who felt obligated to use Galloway Hospital and didn't think it would be appropriate to ask the Carnegie Foundation and GEB for more money.

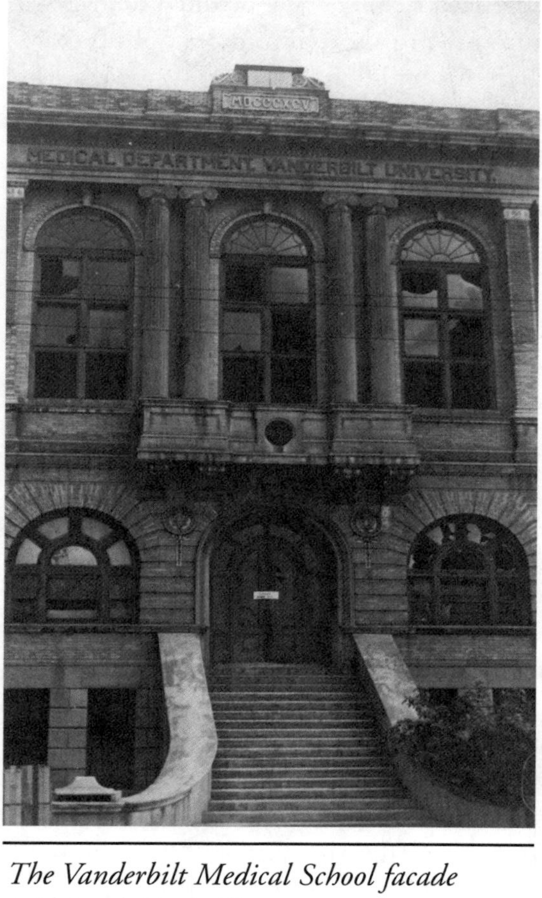

The Vanderbilt Medical School facade
Old South Nashville campus
The Banner Collection, Nashville Public Library, The Nashville Room

However, Robinson was persistent and even threatened to leave Vanderbilt if the campus weren't moved. "I am unwilling to assume the responsibility for the care of patients in a hospital in which thorough modern medical practices cannot be carried out and for the teaching of students in a school that is inadequate in facilities and staff," he wrote to Kirkland in February 1921.

Eventually Kirkland relented, and in the spring of 1921 the chancellor made a formal request to both the Carnegie Foundation and the GEB for more money. To Kirkland's surprise and delight, each promised an additional $1.5 million, bringing to a staggering $8 million the amount of money that the medical school had raised from the two foundations in just eight years.

Robinson and Boston architect Henry R. Shepley and Associates then began planning the new medical school, to be located along Twenty-first Avenue. They came up with a design for a massive six-story, Gothic-style building that, from the air, resembled a large tic-tac-toe board. Medical school departments such as anatomy, radiology, biochemistry, and physiology were given their own sections.

At the time it was the only combined medical school and hospital under one roof in the United States, something Robinson believed would make treatment better. "There would be no separate laboratory buildings at Vanderbilt standing in lonely grandeur aloof from the daily work of a teaching hospital," author Timothy Jacobson later wrote. "And there would be no ward or clinic not close enough to a laboratory so as to make the trek from bedside to bench easy and indeed obligatory." In keeping with the practice of the time, the new building had separate wards for white males (second floor), white females (third floor), and African Americans (fourth floor).

New York construction company Hegeman-Harris broke ground on the Vanderbilt Medical Center building in October 1923, and it opened with great acclaim two years later (even though many Nashville residents were still upset about the university's abandonment of the south campus). By that time Robinson had brought in about a dozen new full-time professors to replace the part-time faculty that had previously been affiliated with the medical school. Among the new faculty members was Ernest Goodpasture, a Clarksville native and Johns Hopkins graduate who was already making a name for himself as a brilliant pathologist. One of the few faculty members who survived the transition was Lucius Burch, dean of the school of medicine.

Nashville's Methodist community was generally upset with Vanderbilt's decision not to use the Galloway Hospital building, toward which many citizens had donated money. For a while it appeared as if Galloway Hospital would become the site of Nashville's first veterans hospital, but those plans also fizzled. Galloway remained unfinished for two decades. Then, in the late 1930s, the city of Nashville bought it, finished it, and turned it into a government office building.

Hazing and the Baldheaded Brotherhood

Like any institution, Vanderbilt has had its share of traditions; some still in place, but many long forgotten.

One of those was mandatory chapel, which began at the time of the university's founding and continued until the early part of Chancellor Branscomb's term. From available evidence, chapel was the most unpopular tradition on campus. Originally it was held at 8:45 a.m., but was moved to noon at about the turn of the century. Complaints about chapel made their way into *The Hustler* almost every year, but one of the more noteworthy exchanges took place in January 1917. "If it is true that brevity is the soul of wit . . . the chapel orators, who have the unhappy faculty of making moments seem eons of time, certainly have no claim to the distinction of humorists," the school newspaper said. A few days later German professor George Mayfield praised the editorial, saying he was willing to do what he could to make chapel more interesting. Chancellor Kirkland was not amused. "The days are passing when the college student will chew off a bit of truth, swallow, and digest it," Kirkland wrote in a letter to the school paper a few days later. "What delights college students most, I perceive, is some sort of mark and chess race on Dudley Field. Such things are enjoyable, it seems, but we would hardly say that they promote intellectual activity. When you come back to the final reason for conducting chapel, it is this: chapel is to bring one face to face with God." Nevertheless, *The Hustler's* editorial may have played a role in chapel being reduced from four times to twice weekly a few months later.

Another early tradition at Vanderbilt was the annual track meet at Sulphur Spring Park, an event that got everyone pretty excited since Vanderbilt didn't have many organized sports in the 1880s. Cumberland College and the University of Nashville would also participate in the event, which would feature events such as the shotput, tug of war, mile race, and bicycle race. When first organized in 1885, the meet was scheduled in the morning, to avoid conflicting with afternoon horse races that were held in Nashville at that time.

The 1890s was the golden era of clubs at Vanderbilt. Among the more creatively-named clubs on campus at that time were the Weinerwurst Eating Club, the Poker Club, the Baldheaded Brotherhood, and the Guitar and Banjo Club. The Glee Club, organized in February 1891, was one of the most active student organizations on campus for several decades. Like glee clubs at other college campuses, the Vanderbilt Glee Club was a chorus of college men that performed to audiences both on campus and far away. Only a year after it was organized the Vanderbilt Glee Club performed in Memphis, Little Rock, and Louisville. In 1907 a Glee Club member named R.F. Vaughan wrote new lyrics to the tune of a well-known song called "Acurci." It became the Vanderbilt alma mater.

For the school's first three decades the mass hazing of all freshmen by upperclassmen was a part of life at Vanderbilt. First-year students had to endure humiliating rituals such as having their heads forced under a fountain next to Kissam Hall, having their hair cut off, and having to wear green caps so that they could be recognized at all times. This tradition angered Chancellor Kirkland, who repeatedly spoke out against it. "The spirit of hazing is utterly contradictory to that highest aim of college life, character building," he said in September 1906. "The tendency of the development of character in Vanderbilt is directed away from mob law and toward personal liberty and individualism." Finally, in 1908, things got out of hand when the freshmen fought back. After a memorable night of pranks, vandalism, and violence parts of Kissam Hall were in ruins and several students were injured. The next day Kirkland made every student on campus sign a pledge that they would no longer haze. Violation of the pledge, the chancellor said, would result in immediate expulsion. After 1908 there were no more reports of mass hazing of freshmen.

The Vanderbilt band in the 1920s
The Banner Collection, Nashville Public Library, The Nashville Room

Of course, this is not to say that there was no hazing of any kind at Vanderbilt after 1908. Hazing went underground and became something organizations did to their members (which remained the case through the rest of the twentieth century). Usual victims of hazing included the pledging members of fraternities or honor societies, who were sometimes spanked, their heads shaved, and their bodies covered with itching powder and molasses during the Greek system's annual "Hell Week." But occasionally hazing affected Nashville's citizens, tarnishing the community's impression of Vanderbilt. "We injure people by running in mobs in the streets," read a 1933 *Hustler* article on hazing. "We jerk trolleys and stop already congested traffic."

By the latter part of the twentieth century campus polls showed that Vanderbilt students had Republican inclinations, a tendency undoubtedly linked to the fact that most of them came from affluent families. But there was a time when Vanderbilt students came from poor families and preferred Democrats. In 1908 more than ninety percent of students polled preferred Democrat William Jennings Bryan over Republican William Taft in the presidential election.

The first time Vanderbilt organized a marching band appears to have been the fall of 1909, when student B.E. Mitchell and faculty member Lee Ogle organized a band consisting of about eighteen students. From that point on the band had boom and bust periods, depending on student interest and faculty leadership. One example of a down time came in the 1950s, when the band had no director, no female members, lousy seats at football games, and no money for uniforms.

Starting in 1929 and continuing through World War II, an annual tradition on the Vanderbilt campus was a "Greased Pole Climb" during Homecoming Weekend, in which a team of freshmen and sophomores competed with each other in an attempt to capture a flag perched on top of a fifteen-foot pole. The event was quite violent and unpredictable. "Confidence is bubbling over in both rival camps, but past experience has proved that confidence is of little help in climbing a greased pole," *The Hustler* reported in 1939. "The outcome of this tussle depends on just one thing – namely, how greasy the pole is." Other Homecoming rituals of that era included a fraternity and sorority skit night, a bonfire, a fireworks display, a parade, and a dance.

Though it may seem offensive to the generations that came after the Civil Rights Movement, some of the most popular people on Vanderbilt's campus during its first seventy-five years were black men who occupied positions of servitude. One of the most respected was John Fulton, more commonly known as "Uncle Remus." Fulton came to Vanderbilt in 1887 to work as a butler of sorts for four faculty members (one of whom was James Kirkland). In his retirement Fulton lived in a tiny suite in the basement of Wesley Hall, where he frequently entertained students and alumni with teacakes and lemonade. His walls were literally covered with photographs of Vanderbilt graduates. Another campus favorite was Bowling Fitzgerald, who lived in Kissam Hall and informally played the role of football trainer through most of the McGugin era. According to one account in

1923, Fitzgerald "proceeds to be Daddy to each student, advises him, keeps his secrets, nurses him, encourages him when he is down and out, and also makes him behave, using force or strong speech when necessary. He has turned more than one star football player across his knee and supplied the place of mother."

In the 1920s and 1930s Vanderbilt students celebrated George Washington's birthday every year with a series of events culminating in the Washington Ball, at which girls would dress up in colonial costumes.

A routine that thrived in the 1930s was the annual "Turtle Trudge," where fraternities and sororities would race their pet turtles in front of Kirkland Hall. In the 1939 Turtle Trudge a reptile called Climax, sponsored by the Gamma Phi Beta sorority, edged out a contestant named Hold Tight, which led most of the way but then "proceeded to go around in circles instead of crossing the line."

Until the construction of Branscomb Quadrangle and Carmichael Towers, Vanderbilt did not have enough dorms for its students, which is why boarding house life was a Vanderbilt tradition for many years. A story typical of thousands is that of Dan Barge Jr. Barge came to Vanderbilt from southern Alabama in 1939 and did not know until he got to campus that he couldn't afford to live in Kissam Hall. "I had a scholarship that seemed to me as if it was enough, but when I got to school and told [engineering] Dean Lewis how much money I had, he told me that I would need to find a boarding house," Barge said many years later. Barge crossed Twenty-first Avenue and didn't stop walking until he had found a place to live for ten dollars a month, providing he help out and wash dishes every night. "At the time, ten dollars is what I would have been spending just to eat in Kissam Hall for a month."

Prior to World War II most students knew where professors lived and felt free to drop in on them unannounced. In the 1960s artist Puryear Mims recalled what it was like growing up as the son of Vanderbilt Professor Edwin Mims, who lived in a house in the middle of campus. "Students came into our house with out knocking, just like they were at home, which they were," he said. "They would come and wait to ask him (Edwin Mims) questions. There was a constant stream of students."

Members of the Vanderbilt senior class of 1904
The Elizabeth Vann Collection, Photographic Archives, Vanderbilt University

And, speaking of traditions, where did the Vanderbilt nickname come from? Although no one knows for sure, it is believed that the first appearance of the nickname "Commodores" for Vanderbilt students and athletes was in an article about a Vanderbilt-Sewanee football game in the Nov. 25, 1898, *Nashville American.* "In 1892 Sewanee scored a victory over Vanderbilt, but ever since that time until the present day the boys from the mountain have been struggling to overcome the Commodores," the article said.

According to an item in a 1906 *Hustler*, the use of the word "Vandy" to abbreviate Vanderbilt was started by students at the University of Virginia as a form of derision. "It sounds slangy, vulgar and cheap," the article said, pointing out that the word "Vandy" would not be used in the school newspaper that year. Two decades later an alumni publication would echo its distaste for the abbreviated version of the Commodore's name. "Its use does not tend to increase reverence for what is good and great at Vanderbilt," the article said. "It does not make for fine traditions; it does not thrill the teams to athletic conquest; as an inspiration its effect is nil. Do you get the soft, effeminate intonation of that word?"

In the 1950s *The Hustler*'s use of the abbreviation " 'Dores" rankled Leo Schwartz, a member of the class of 1926. "How sweet can you get?" Schwartz sarcastically wrote in a letter in the school newspaper. "Even typographical frugality does not excuse this. I think it would be better to limit this appellation to the distaff teams."

VANDERBILT'S WEIRD WAR EXPERIENCE

World War I brought profound changes to the Vanderbilt campus, and the changes peaked during the 1918-19 school year. It was the year the U.S. Army took over the campus, and the year women took over campus life. It was the year professors had to change the subjects they taught. It was the year of the influenza epidemic. It was the year a Vanderbilt professor secretly developed a horrible chemical weapon. And it was the year of Vanderbilt's first protest against the U.S. Army.

The first official presence of the military on the Vanderbilt campus came just before the end of World War I (although at the time no one knew that the end of the war was just around the corner). In the summer of 1918 the federal government organized the Student Army Training Corps to train and organize officer candidates as quickly as possible. Rather than run the SATC on military bases — of which there were few at that time — the government decided to operate it on college campuses.

Vanderbilt's SATC unit was inaugurated on October 1, 1918,

about the same time similar organizations were being formed on campuses all over the country. Almost immediately thereafter about three hundred young men from across the South descended on Vanderbilt's campus. Administrators such as Chancellor Kirkland became second fiddle to military officers, who ran the place as if it were a base. Wesley Hall, West Side Hall, and Kissam Hall became the homes of companies A, B, and C. SATC students were awakened at 5:45 a.m. and drilled for two hours before they marched, in formation, to class.

To train the SATC members, Vanderbilt's faculty had to alter its curriculum. A class in English composition became modified to teach SATC students how to write and read military messages. The chemistry department put together a lab class meant to train students to work at the massive gunpowder factory under construction in nearby Old Hickory, Tennessee. There were courses in sanitation, hygiene, surveying, map drawing, mathematics, and physics. Desperately in need of foreign language teachers, Vanderbilt brought in several part-time instructors to teach French and German.

All this was an inconvenience for Vanderbilt's faculty, staff, and regular students. But from available sources, it would appear as if everyone at the university was more than willing to do his part in the war effort. Patriotism ran high at Vanderbilt, and it ran higher every time there was news from Europe that an alumnus had given his life in the line of duty. One such death was Irby "Rabbit" Curry, a football star and the school's Bachelor of Ugliness in 1915. Curry was shot down over France in the fall of 1918. A few years after his death, the field on campus near the corner of West End and Twenty-first Avenues was renamed in his honor.

While SATC programs dominated the campus, Vanderbilt tried to maintain its usual curriculum for its 250 regular students. About half of them were young men who were either too young to serve in the military or had been rendered physically unqualified for military service. The other half were women, who, galvanized by their equal numbers, managed to take over what was left of campus social life. In the 1918-19 school year four of *The Hustler's* ten reporters were women. The leaders of the campus United War Charities fund drive were women. The editor of *The Commodore* was Dorothy Bethurum. The president of the senior class was Ednelia Wade, who tragically died in March of her senior year.

And if this all weren't strange enough, the worldwide influenza epidemic swept through Nashville in the fall of 1918. Between late September and early December of that year one in three Nashville residents contracted influenza, commonly known as the flu. One in 270 residents died from it—579 people out of a total population of about 155,000. For a couple of weeks virtually every aspect of life in Nashville came to a halt. Church was canceled for a month, and many sanctuaries were converted to wards for the dying. Schools, movies, and public meetings were called off for weeks. One of Vanderbilt's football games was canceled when the other team didn't show up for the game.

The Vanderbilt Hospital, then located in a building near the south campus, was overwhelmed by the influenza epidemic. Like every other hospital in the city it had to turn away patients at the peak of the panic. But courageous doctors and nurses treated as many people as they could. At least three Vanderbilt students on the main campus died of the flu that fall. Many more alumni perished; according to an item that appeared later in the *Vanderbilt Alumnus*, twenty graduates of the Biblical School alone died of influenza.

About this time one of the best-kept secrets in school history began to leak out. The Vanderbilt Medical School had a pathologist and bacteriologist named Dr. William Litterer. Several years earlier, while working on a formula for explosives, Litterer had inadvertently developed a gas that was so poisonous that he had to be taken out of the lab on a stretcher. When both armies began using chemical weapons during World War I, Litterer remembered his accidental discovery and found the formula for it in his notes. Before long Litterer was conducting experiments on Vanderbilt's south campus under the sponsorship of the U.S. Army Gas Commission, testing samples of his deadly gas with every known variety of German gas mask. At one point during the long and chaotic battle near Chateau-Thierry in June 1918, German troops were intentionally led to a series of trenches. What the Germans did not know was that the trenches had been filled with Litterer's formula – a gas that no mask could stop. All the Germans were killed instantly.

In November 1918 the influenza epidemic began to diminish

and the war ended. Within days the government shut down the SATC program. Hundreds of young men who had been sent to Vanderbilt by the military began to go home. After Christmas Vanderbilt students who had gone overseas for the war began to trickle back to campus. Young men began to elbow women out of positions of campus leadership. Fraternities began to resume meetings. Articles in *The Hustler* began to talk about the "good ole days" returning to the university.

No sooner did students begin to hope for a return to the careless days of going to class and hanging out at the fraternity house than a new type of militarism rose on the horizon. After the demise of the SATC Vanderbilt had agreed to form a Reserve Officers Training Corps program. Unlike the SATC, ROTC was a smaller, more professional organization that worked within a school's normal admission requirements. When it was first formed, the Vanderbilt faculty voted to make ROTC training mandatory for undergraduate men. Some students were furious, especially those returning from military duty in Europe. In January 1919 students called a meeting to discuss the matter. In one of the first acts of protest on the Vanderbilt campus, several students boycotted the mandatory drills.

A *Hustler* editorial by editor J. C. Higgins explained why some students were so opposed to ROTC. "An abhorrence of all things military still lingers from the SATC," Higgins wrote. "Even without the regulations and discipline of that defunct organization, the thought of mere drill is obnoxious. Were the war in progress, all would enthusiastically enter into it to get the best there is out of it. Now all are anxious to get back into the working harness and settle down to prewar work. Studies are heavy and time is precious."

It was the only time in his forty-four years as chancellor that Kirkland had to deal with a student protest. When a delegation of students came to him and expressed their displeasure with ROTC, he told them that he would not discuss the matter until the students stopped boycotting the drills. The students agreed to do so, and Kirkland formed a faculty committee to come up with a solution. In the end the committee recommended that starting in the school year 1919-20 that ROTC drill continue to be mandatory for freshmen and sophomore men.

Students drilled that year, although there is every indication that some did so grudgingly. *The Hustler* kept up its barrage of anti-ROTC editorials, publishing pieces that could have run in the school newspaper half a century later. ROTC "will impair the quality of students entering Vanderbilt," a *Hustler* editor named Joe Hatcher wrote. "Heretofore, Vanderbilt has catered to the cultured youth of the South, a class that does not believe in compulsory training to any

SATC students marching on Dudley Field during World War I
Photographic Archives, Vanderbilt University

extent. It certainly alienates the feeling of the students toward the officials of the University because of the fact that the students feel that the university is putting something over them." A few months later *The Hustler* called ROTC a "despicable organization."

Kirkland eventually changed his mind about the military's presence on campus. With little publicity the school canceled its ROTC program in the spring of 1920. Reasons for the decision are

unclear, but it is likely that Kirkland agreed with the general idea that a peacetime military presence on campus would interfere with his goal of building a great university. It should also be pointed out that, unlike the Army and Navy ROTC programs that Vanderbilt formed after World War II, the ROTC program the university canceled in 1920 did not bring with it a generous scholarship program.

By the fall of 1920 the chancellor was focusing his attention on other projects: a massive new medical center, a student center called Alumni Hall, a football stadium, and a new department of business administration. That spring, the departing leaders of the class of 1919 patted themselves on the back for keeping Vanderbilt's campus alive during the war. "We've run affairs at Vanderbilt for only four short years," a senior named Margaret White wrote. "But what she'll do without us is among our chiefest fears."

THE MAYOR AND CHAIRMAN DECLARE MARTIAL LAW

American patriotism and paranoia about communism were running high after World War I. Political tolerance was unfashionable; a Vanderbilt faculty member learned this the hard way.

Russell Scott was born in England, graduated from Oxford University, and traveled extensively in Europe before moving to the United States in 1912. Scott came to Nashville to work for the YMCA. After that post expired, he got a job teaching French to soldiers who were training at Vanderbilt under the short-lived SATC program.

Scott had become a member of the socialist party while in England. During his time in Nashville he made friends with Harry Goldfarb, a socialist who ran a shoe store at 1155 Broadway. Goldfarb introduced Scott to a group of leftists, union leaders, and intellectuals who met every Sunday afternoon at the office of the Nashville Trades and Labor Council at 411 Union Street.

A prominent issue of the day was the arrest of hundreds of political prisoners, including four-time Socialist presidential candidate

Eugene Debs, under the federal Espionage Act of 1918. Many Americans argued that the act and the arrests caused by it had more to do with stomping out political dissidence than catching spies.

Scott obviously felt this way, because he was scheduled to speak about the plight of American political prisoners at a labor rally to take place at the Ryman Auditorium on May 1, 1919. When Scott arrived at the meeting, there were between 25 and 500 and people in attendance (the *Nashville Banner* story claimed that the number of people was between 25 and 50; the *Nashville Tennessean* reported that it was between 250 and 500.) Among them were Nashville mayor William Gupton, district attorney Lee Douglas, a large group of police officers, and several federal agents. The officials ordered that the meeting be disbanded, impounding the following items from the meeting's organizers as evidence of sedition: a group of flyers that proclaimed that "Nashville Will Shake Tonight"; a copy of the Soviet constitution; the text of the speech for which Eugene Debs had been imprisoned; and a group of red carnations that the organizers intended to distribute to attendees.

The next day Douglas and Gupton called on Vanderbilt to dismiss Scott from the university. The student-run *Hustler* concurred in that opinion, as did Nashville's two daily newspapers. The *Tennessean* praised the mayor and district attorney as being "true to their oaths and to their duty as Americans" and said that the organizers were trying to "proselytize the gullible and distribute Russian propaganda – the Devil's own propaganda – conceived in the minds of imperial German junkers and the traitorous German agents, Trotsky and Lenin, who created chaos, rapine and slaughter in Russia."

The *Banner* said the organizers "have small right to plead any constitutional guarantee when their main purpose is to destroy constitutional government. Freedom of speech doesn't include the toleration of sedition . . . When the torch is at the temple door it is time for vigorous action and not to parley about claims of abstract rights presented through the sophistry of the nihilist."

Scott was bewildered, telling a student reporter that he had in the course of much travel only once seen a crackdown similar to the one at the Ryman Auditorium, that being twenty years earlier in

Germany. To a *Tennessean* reporter, Scott said that he was neither an anarchist nor a Bolshevik, but that he strongly advocated the immediate release of industrial, religious, and political prisoners. He also repeated a barb that was commonly repeated at the time by critics of the espionage act. "The people who oppose this [extending amnesty to all political prisoners] are trying to put truth into the jibe that Germany went to war for victory and America went to war for democracy, with the result that America got the victory and Germany the democracy," he said.

While all this was happening, Chancellor Kirkland was out of town. Dean Herbert Tolman, acting on his behalf, told the mayor and the district attorney that he didn't have the authority to dismiss Scott and that he would have to wait until Kirkland returned. Unhappy with that answer, Douglas and Gupton took the matter to a higher authority — board of trust president Whitefoord Cole. Though he didn't have the authority to do so, Cole immediately suspended Scott and scheduled a hearing in the matter.

Cole and other executive committee members held a hearing on the Scott case a couple of days later, after which Scott was formally suspended. A few days later Kirkland returned to campus. Noting that Scott had not violated any laws, Kirkland said he didn't want to fire him, and preferred to let the temporary suspension serve as the faculty member's punishment. Kirkland also appointed two members of the faculty to conduct an "inquiry" into the Scott case. Those faculty members concluded that Scott's behavior was "reprehensible," but concluded that Cole had no right to suspend Scott without a more in-depth hearing.

On May 9 District Attorney Douglas ordered Scott's home to be searched by three federal agents and the Nashville chief of police. "No 'red' literature was found," the *Banner* reported. "But quite a number of magazines and books on socialism were found. The authorities had been informed that Scott was to have received from Chicago a large quantity of Bolshevik literature to be distributed here, and it was for this literature the house was searched."

After the raid the Scott case faded from the news. Scott's contract to teach French was not renewed. Although details of his life are hard to come by after that, he probably left the country.

Philosophers and Poets

The most important literary movement connected to Vanderbilt University was started by a man with no affiliation with Vanderbilt University.

His name was Sidney Hirsch. Hirsch grew up in Nashville, attended public schools, and then went away to join the Navy. A few years later he worked his way back to town and by that time had a series of the most fascinating stories anyone in Nashville had ever heard. He had become the heavyweight boxing champion of the Pacific Fleet. He had traveled extensively through the Far East and experimented with mystic religions. He had spent considerable time in France, had modeled for Rodin, and had befriended Gertrude Stein.

Starting around 1914 a group of Vanderbilt students and professors began hanging out at the Hirsch's house near campus. The first to do so were English instructor Stanley Johnson and student Donald Davidson, who were first drawn to the Hirsch house because of a young lady named Goldie Hirsch. But it didn't take them long to become mesmerized by her brother Sidney. After all, here was a man who had (or at least claimed to have) been everywhere and done everything. Davidson and Johnson invited one of their English professors, a Vanderbilt alumnus, Rhodes scholar, and native of Pulaski, Tennessee, named John Crowe Ransom. He too became a part of the philosophy group.

World War I intervened, and several members of the group went off to join the military. After the war many of them filtered back into Nashville; Davidson, for instance, became an English professor at Vanderbilt. They resumed the visits to Sidney Hirsch, who by this time was living with his brother-in-law in a house at 3802 Whitland Avenue.

In the fall of 1920 the group began inviting several new students, such as a promising and opinionated young man from Winchester, Kentucky, named Allen Tate. By early 1921 the group shifted its focus from philosophy to poetic criticism. Along the way, they began calling themselves "Fugitives." The group chose this name, in part, because they were acting outside of the approval of Edwin Mims, the revered head of the Vanderbilt English department who did not care for Hirsch. Another reason was to acknowledge the fact that Hirsch, the group's spiritual leader of sorts, thought of himself as a wanderer and an outcast.

The practice of writing and studying poetry declined so much after the advent of radio and television that the Fugitive era needs a bit of explanation. By the end of the twentieth century a very small percentage of students actually studied poetry during their college years. But in the 1920s many students read and wrote poetry, not just in the classroom, but in their spare time. "There was just a tremendous interest in poetry among the students," one member of the Fugitives said in a 1977 interview. "There were two undergraduate writing clubs, junior and senior, where people would read poems and essays to each other. And there was the informal poet club which met about once a week. We'd read each other's poems and booze a little, crack corn [whiskey], and talk poetry. All kinds of people wrote poems then . . . it is hard to believe now." Ralph McGill, a Vanderbilt student in the 1920s who tried poetry but ended up a journalist, gave a similar account of life at that time. "The campus was in a ferment of talk and new ideas about books and poetry," he later wrote. "Some of us felt we were of the lost generation and if we could not be expatriates in Paris we would make do with what we had in Nashville."

By early 1922 more people joined the Fugitives, including students Merrill Moore, Jesse Wills, and an awkward-looking young man named Robert Penn Warren. The meetings became regularly scheduled and structured. A typical meeting would occur every other Saturday night, beginning at about eight and lasting until about eleven. Most of the attendees would bring with them several copies of a poem that they had recently written. They would hand them out to everyone and read them aloud, and then members of the group would comment on the verse's structure, meaning, and worth. "It was not enough for a poem to be impressive in a general way," Davidson said years later. "Poems that were merely pleasant, or conventional, or mediocre did not attract much comment."

Somewhere along the way one of the members suggested that the group publish a collection of its poems. Like many student groups that came before them and after them, the Fugitives couldn't think of a reason not to do so. The first issue of *The Fugitive* magazine came out on April 12, 1922. It contained more than twenty poems, written under pseudonyms such as Roger Prim and Robin Gallivant. Over the next three years eighteen more issues of the publication were released.

The Fugitive sold well in Nashville; five hundred copies of the first issue sold out almost immediately. The publication also garnered some favorable reviews from afar; *Baltimore Sun* writer H. L. Mencken said that it was "at the moment, the entire literature of Tennessee," a back-handed compliment that flattered the young poets but insulted everyone else in the Volunteer State. Nonetheless, *The Fugitive* didn't make much of an impact outside of Middle Tennessee and sold almost no copies outside of Nashville. In fact, it is safe to say that the only reason *The Fugitive* magazine became a collector's item was that many of its writers went on to prominence after the publication ceased publication.

The 1956 reunion of the Fugitive poets
The Banner Collection, Nashville Public Library, The Nashville Room

The first of these was John Crowe Ransom. Ransom came out with a book of poems about World War I in 1919, but two volumes that were published in the mid-1920s constituted most of the work for which he is best known. Ransom wrote short poems about sad, domestic, and routine tragedies. One of his best-known works was "Bells for John Whiteside's Daughter," concerning the death of a little girl; many Vanderbilt freshmen were required to memorize this poem in the 1930s and 1940s. In the late 1920s Ransom surprised many of his colleagues by announcing that he no longer intended to write poetry. He instead began to focus on writing essays related to the role of poetic criticism in academia.

Davidson's career took off in several different directions. In 1924 he had his first volume of poetry published under the title *An Outland Piper*. For the next few years, he remained a prolific poet, often choosing to write about historical themes such as the Civil War or the Southern frontier. In 1927 he published a collection of poetry entitled *The Tall Men* that largely idolized Tennessee's heritage. Meanwhile Davidson found time to edit the book review page of the *Tennessean* between 1924 and 1930.

Allen Tate moved to New York after he graduated and began pursuing a writing career on multiple fronts. By the late 1920s he had authored a volume of poetry which contained the well-known verse "Ode to the Confederate Dead," plus a biography of Stonewall Jackson. Tate then moved to Europe, where he met T.S. Eliot and Ernest Hemingway.

Like Allen Tate, Robert Penn Warren left the South after he left Vanderbilt – first for Berkeley and then to Yale. Throughout the 1920s Warren focused on his poetry. Then, in 1929, he hooked up with Tate in New York and, thanks to Tate's connections in the literary world, got a contract to write a book about America's most controversial abolitionist. *John Brown: The Making of a Martyr* was praised by critics when it came out in November 1929, but sold few copies because the Great Depression had just hit. At the beginning of the 1930s, Warren was living in Oxford, England, and homesick for his native Kentucky.

THE FIRST OF ITS KIND

Considering the fortunes of the Vanderbilt football program in the late twentieth century, it is extremely ironic. Dudley Field, the home of the Commodores, was the first football stadium built in the South.

Before the 1920s Vanderbilt usually played home games on the old Dudley Field, an open space near the corner of West End and Twenty-first Avenues. There were about forty-five hundred seats surrounding the field and no lights, no bathrooms, no concession stands, no dressing rooms, and, by the end of the season, not much grass on the field.

Since no college or university had anything better, the football field seemed good enough to just about everyone. But not William Dudley. Dudley, a longtime Vanderbilt chemistry professor regarded as one of the founders of intercollegiate sports in the South, dreamed about a real football stadium such as the ones in which Ivy League teams played. Under his leadership the Vanderbilt Athletic Association in 1908 began purchasing land about two blocks down West End Avenue from the main campus. When he died in 1914, Dudley left five thousand dollars toward the eventual construction of a stadium there.

Since Vanderbilt did not have an alumni organization, raising money for a football stadium was out of the question until the school began organizing one in 1915 (a year after the school officially split with the Methodist church). By the end of World War I Coach Dan McGugin and alumni leaders were pressing for Vanderbilt to build a stadium similar to the ones being built by other football powerhouses such as the University of Pennsylvania. Another person who encouraged Vanderbilt to build a stadium was McGugin's brother in law, Fielding Yost. Yost, who lived on Nashville's Craighead Avenue, spent several months a year in Ann Arbor, Michigan, where he coached the Michigan Wolverines. The pair were such good friends that Yost would often help McGugin coach, especially during McGugin's early years at Vanderbilt. Under Yost's leadership Michigan had become a gridiron great, with teams that scored so often that they became known as the "point a minute" teams. After Michigan built its stadium, Yost told friends and civic groups in Nashville that if Vanderbilt built a similar structure, crowds would fill it.

Finally, in 1921, football boosters asked the administration to loan the athletic department $75,000 in school funds for a new stadium (with the idea that another $75,000 would be obtained through a fundraising campaign). With the football team doing so well — Vanderbilt went undefeated that year — Kirkland reluctantly said yes.

The three people most involved in designing the new facility were McGugin, architect Russell Hart, and engineer Martin Roberts. Since they were building something that didn't exist in the South, the trio had to travel far to look at comparable facilities. In 1920 they visited stadiums at Princeton, Yale, Michigan, Wisconsin, and the University of Chicago. Eventually, they decided to build a horseshoe-shaped stadium similar to the one at Yale.

Meanwhile, the fund drive for Vanderbilt's new stadium succeeded in short order. Alumni Lee Loventhal and Frank Godchaux led a movement that raised most of the $75,000 in weeks. They were greatly aided by McGugin, a Rotarian, lawyer, and a Tennessee state senator. McGugin made several speeches for the fund drive; he frequently made the point that once built, the stadium could be used for other types of civic events and by Nashville's high schools. Supporters also raised money by selling reserved seats at the future stadium. A twenty-five dollar donation enabled the donor to have a "perpetual assignable privilege entitling the holder to purchase two season tickets" – a formal way of describing something that many years later would become known in professional football circles as a "personal seat license."

As plans for the new stadium came together, Nashville residents became enthusiastic about it. After all, the new facility was going to have about twenty-two thousand seats and could eventually be expanded to have fifty-five thousand seats – crowds larger than most people had ever seen. It would have restrooms and concession stands below its reinforced concrete frame. The field was even going to contain an underground tiling system to minimize mud. "This will remove the necessity of drowning again the Tigers in a sea of mud," a *Hustler* article quipped, referring to the final game of Vanderbilt's 1921 season against Sewanee.

Gould Construction Co. began working on the stadium on February 15, 1922. Rather than costing $150,000, the facility cost $232,000 (a difference that would eventually be made up by school funds). But as the new Dudley Stadium – as some called it — rose on West End Avenue, journalists from all over the South sang its praises. "That stadium is a stunning affair," an *Atlanta Constitution* reporter wrote. "Nothing like it in the South. Vanderbilt went about building a regular he-stadium and did not stop at one section." Many newspapers predicted that Vanderbilt's new stadium would cause colleges in other parts of the South to follow suit, a prognostication that turned out to be accurate.

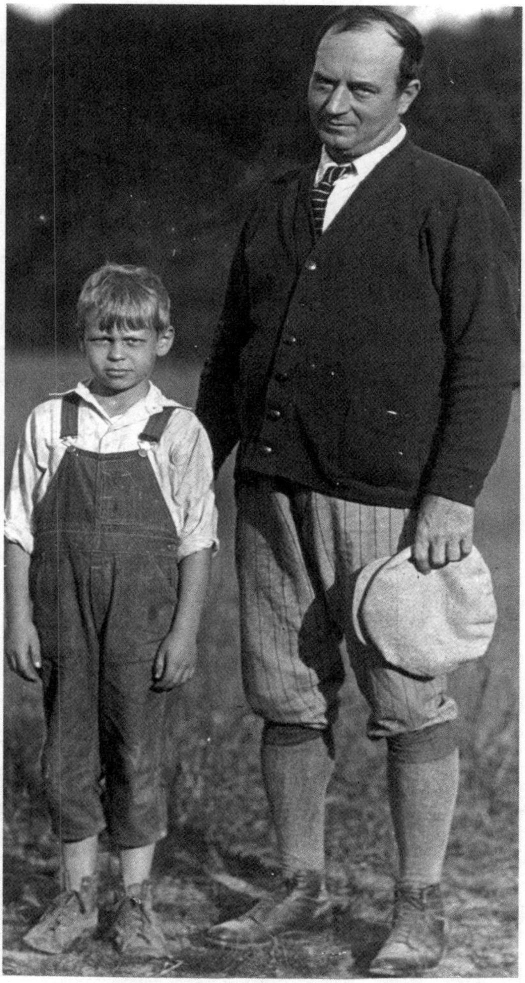

Coach Dan McGugin and his son Leonard
The Banner Collection, Nashville Public Library, The Nashville Room

The new facility was dedicated on October 14, 1922, in a contest between the Commodores and Yost's heavily favored Michigan team. It was a gala event, preceded by a dance, an alumni banquet, and a parade through downtown Nashville. "The city was ablaze with color – the gold and black mingled with a goodly display of maize and blue, while the stars and stripes waved over all," detailed one account of the proceedings. "The colorful gowns of beautiful women gave distinction to the scene, while the more sober dress of

Dudley Field during a game in the 1950s, when houses surrounded the stadium
The Banner Collection, Nashville Public Library, The Nashville Room

the men was touched up by arm bands of gold." In what must have been one of the first flight missions mixed with a football game in American history, a plane flew overhead the new stadium and dropped the game ball onto the field. McGugin caught it on first bounce, then ran across the field and handed it to his brother-in-law, the opposing coach. Among those in attendance that day were Cornelius Vanderbilt Jr., the great-great grandson of the man who had given a million dollars to start the university five decades earlier. But the game was not a sellout; there were about four thousand empty seats when the two teams came onto the field.

McGugin pulled out all the stops to fire up his team. "You are going against Yankees, some of whose grandfathers killed your grandfathers in the Civil War," he reportedly said to his team (failing to remind them that he was from Iowa and that his father had been an officer in the Union Army). Right off the bat, Michigan drove the ball to the Vanderbilt five-yard line. But they couldn't get a touchdown. "No more brilliant display of defensive play has ever been seen on a Vanderbilt gridiron," read an account of the game in the *Nashville Banner*. From that point neither team even threatened to score. The South's first football stadium was christened with a tie.

One reason that the Dudley Stadium fund drive was so noteworthy is that it succeeded while another failed. In 1915 Chancellor Kirkland began laying the groundwork for the construction of a student center, where students could meet, eat, have dances, play sports, and relax. After World War I a plan emerged to combine this project with a memorial to the forty-three Vanderbilt students and alumni who died during the war. Under its original plan, the building would contain meeting rooms, offices, a cafeteria, a bookstore, a post office, a barbershop, a swimming pool, a gymnasium, and a five-hundred-seat auditorium. No one was more excited about the project than Kirkland, who had plans to de-emphasize the Vanderbilt Greek system after the new student center was in place.

The fund drive for Alumni Memorial Hall, as it became known, began in March 1919. It got off to a good start, securing $165,000 in three-year pledges from alumni. But then the project – estimated to cost $400,000 — floundered. For the next several years school officials pleaded with alumni to give more money. "Here is a chance for a millionaire alumnus to make a name more enduring than marble," one of many letters to alumni said. But as word got out that the project was in trouble, some donors began to default on their commitments, making the project's future even shakier.

Without question, the 1921 fund drive for Dudley Field hurt the drive for the student center, which begs the question of why Kirkland moved ahead with a new football stadium before he took care of the needs of the other students. For a couple of years the Alumni Memorial Hall project was stagnated. Finally, Mrs. George Mitchell Neely, the widow of a Vanderbilt trustee, donated $100,000 toward the project in 1922. With that commitment in hand, the school scaled back Alumni Memorial Hall and turned it into two projects: a small, dignified student center with meeting rooms and offices called Alumni Hall, and an auditorium called Neely.

After Alumni Hall was completed, the school converted the chapel in College Hall into a new school library. Vanderbilt entered an agreement to allow students to use the swimming pool and gymnasium located in the new YMCA building on Twenty-first Avenue. It would be another five decades before Vanderbilt got a student center, and another seven decades before the school built a gymnasium for non-athletes.

The Name That Won't Die

When alumni returned to the Vanderbilt campus at the end of the twentieth century and saw the Wesley Place parking garage and apartment and retail building on Twenty-first Avenue, some said that they remembered the "old" Wesley building formerly on that site. In fact, the Wesley Hall they remembered was the third structure on the Vanderbilt campus to go by that name.

Little is known about the first. When the Methodist Episcopal Church, South, first organized Vanderbilt University in the 1870s, one of the buildings already on the land chosen for it was a house right in the middle of the future campus. In a speech given at the Main Building's cornerstone ceremony, Bishop Holland McTyeire referred to the house as a "commodious mansion," and said it would have to meet the needs of biblical students for the time being. The organizers of the university converted it into a dorm and classroom building. In deference to the founder of the Methodist Church, people called it Wesley Hall.

A much larger Wesley Hall building was built in 1880 and funded by a $150,000 gift from William Henry Vanderbilt, the son of founder Cornelius Vanderbilt. The building was located near the first Wesley Hall and housed the Biblical School and library, 160 dorm rooms for students and professors, lecture halls, and a cafeteria. Wesley Hall number two was a beautiful, five-story structure similar in architectural style to Old Science (later Benson Hall), which was built at about the same time.

For five decades Wesley Hall number two meant many things to many people. To the Vanderbilt administration it represented the Biblical School and the Methodist church that had organized the university but severed ties with it during the first two decades of the twentieth century. To Nashville residents Wesley Hall was one of the most beautiful buildings on campus, and its cafeteria was a favorite place to eat on Sunday afternoons. To students it was a major part of campus life. "No one is a true Vanderbilter who has not during his sojourn there spent a part of his life in Wesley Hall," a *Tennessean* article said. "Many have enjoyed the entertainment of sliding down the coal chute, pulling himself up in the elevator and jumping off before reaching the floor and keeping the banisters polished by sliding down them."

Some people even grew up in Wesley Hall. Allen McGill, whose father John McGill was a longtime chemistry professor, once described life as a boy in Wesley Hall. "As children of professors we were naturally interested in research, and we often dropped parachutes consisting of a small rock tied to four corners of a handkerchief, from the third floor," he said.

The most famous group of people to have roomed together in Wesley Hall were Robert Penn Warren, Allen Tate, and Ridley Wills, three members of the literary group the Fugitives who resided together in room 353 of Wesley Hall for a semester in the early 1920s. The trio did not keep a tidy room. "It was no place for the heathen," Tate wrote years later. "In order to get into bed at night we had to shovel

Wesley Hall on fire in 1932
The Banner Collection, Nashville Public Library, The Nashville Room

the books, trousers, shoes, hats, and fruit jars onto the floor, and in the morning, to make walking space, we heaped it all back upon the beds."

Wesley Hall number two burned down on February 19, 1932. No one was killed in the fire, but hundreds of rare books and students' possessions were destroyed. "Many of the students lost practically everything they possessed with the exception of the clothes they were wearing and the books they happened to have with them," read an account of the fire in the *Tennessean.* The university only had about $150,000 in insurance on the building, which had a replacement cost about three times that amount. Raising enough money to replace the second Wesley Hall was out of the question at the time, because the fire took place at the peak of the Great Depression.

For a few years it appeared as if the fire would doom the Vanderbilt School of Religion, which had been fighting for survival since the university's split with the Methodist Church two decades earlier. However, Fredrick W. Vanderbilt, whose father had funded the construction of Wesley Hall in 1880, gave $150,000 toward a new home for the religion department. (He did so in response to the personal plea of longtime School of Religion Dean Wilbur Tillett.) The university used that and other donations, plus the insurance settlement, to start an endowment for the School of Religion and find the school a new home in an existing structure that became the third Wesley Hall.

Wesley Hall number three was a large building with classrooms, a gymnasium, and a swimming pool situated across Twenty-first Avenue from the main Vanderbilt campus. The YMCA originally built it in 1927 as a training school for secretaries. For a few years, it was used jointly by the YMCA and Vanderbilt. However, the YMCA school went out of business during the Great Depression. Vanderbilt bought it in 1936, renamed it Wesley Hall and put its Department of Religion there. Meanwhile, the university, under a campus plan devised by New York architect Edward Stone, decided to leave the site of the second Wesley Hall undeveloped. The land on which it sat became an open space called Library Lawn.

The Vanderbilt Divinity School left Wesley Hall number three in 1960 for a new quadrangle next to the Joint University Library.

However, Vanderbilt continued to use the third Wesley Hall as home to its psychology department and a place for students to attend class, swim, and play basketball.

In the mid-1980s, after a study showed that the building would be too costly to rehabilitate, Vanderbilt tore down the third Wesley Hall. For a few years the university used the site as a parking lot. Then Vanderbilt came up with a plan to put a massive multi-use building on the site, with twenty-thousand square feet of retail space on the west side and an eight-hundred-unit parking garage on the east side. On the advice of trustee Nelson Andrews, the university also put forty-six townhouses on top of it. The new building's name: Wesley Place.

BUCK GREEN OF VANDERBILT

In the fall of 1925, a few weeks before a fiddle player named Jimmy Rogers went on WSM radio and spontaneously started a program that later became known as the Grand Ole Opry, Vanderbilt University did a very curious thing. The school made what was almost certainly the first motion picture produced in Nashville.

Chancellor James Kirkland went from one major project to another. First it was moving George Peabody College for Teachers across town. Then it was the legal break with the Methodist church. Next came the massive challenge of building a new medical school building. After the war ended, the school raised money for Alumni Hall, Neely Auditorium, and Dudley Field. Then came the school's semi-centennial celebration.

By 1925 Kirkland realized that Vanderbilt badly needed some new classroom buildings and new faculty positions. With a two million dollar matching commitment from the General Education Board in hand, Vanderbilt launched its first real alumni fund drive, hoping to raise two million dollars more.

Kirkland was determined to be organized and to get a clear message across to alumni as to why the money was needed. The chairman of the campaign was trustee Frank Rand, an executive with the International Shoe Co. of St. Louis. Through presentations to alumni groups and articles in alumni publications, Kirkland and Rand explained that the four million dollar campaign would provide money for three buildings (two for the physical sciences and one for the humanities); a $1.5 million endowment for graduate work; a $1 million endowment for the humanities; and a $700,000 endowment for the physical sciences.

Kirkland pointed out that in the past, most of the money that had supported Vanderbilt had come from big foundations and members of the Vanderbilt family. In fact, he claimed that every dollar donated by alumni had been matched twenty-five times over by money from people who didn't attend the school. Kirkland pointed out that it had been two decades since a classroom building (Furman Hall) had been constructed on the campus. Since that time enrollment had risen from three hundred to nine hundred. Kirkland also said that if Vanderbilt did not raise enough money to improve its undergradu-

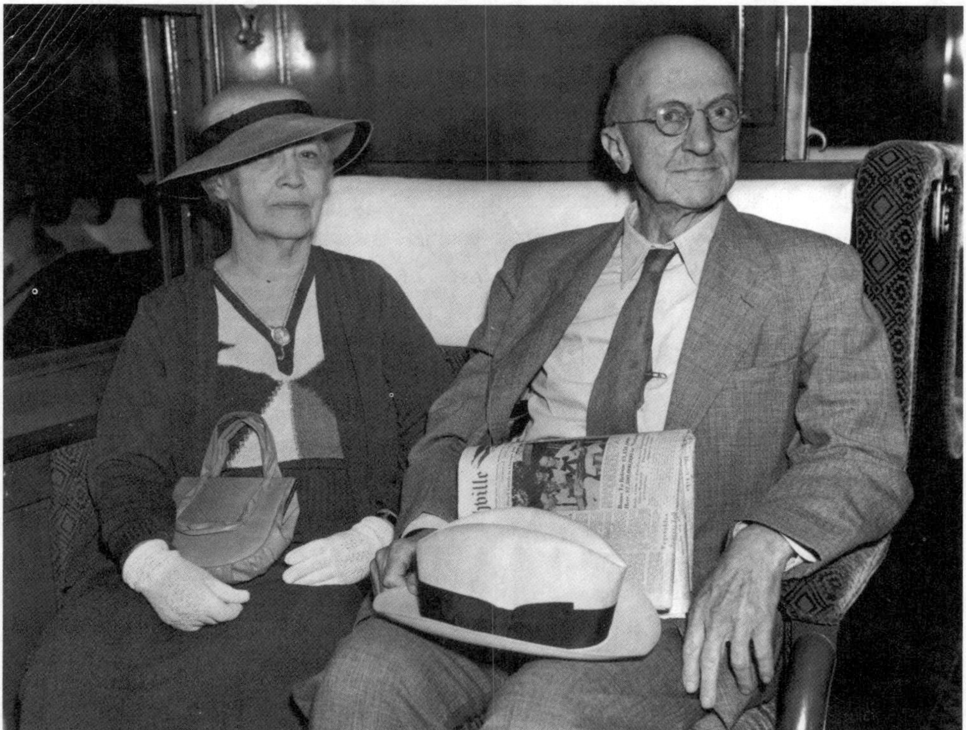

Chancellor James Kirkland and wife in 1936
The Banner Collection, Nashville Public Library, The Nashville Room

ate and non-medical graduate programs that the school was in danger of being overshadowed by its own medical school, a fear that was repeated frequently by faculty at that time. For example, English professor Edwin Mims nearly accepted an offer from Duke University in 1925 because he was concerned about Vanderbilt's increasing emphasis on the medical school.

Two million dollars was a lot of money in 1925, and it must have occurred to someone that the school needed to get creative to generate help from its alumni. The result was a motion picture filmed on the Vanderbilt campus in the fall of 1925 and shown to alumni groups around the south in 1926. The silent film was called *Buck Green of Vanderbilt.* Its purposes were to remind alumni what the campus looked like and to paint a picture of a university that was a force for good in the South.

In the film an actor portrays freshman Buck Green. When he first arrives on campus, Green goes straight to College Hall and, not knowing any better, says he would like to meet the chancellor. Kirkland (portraying himself) comes out of his office, shakes Green's hand, and takes him over to meet Dean Madison Sarratt (also playing himself). The film goes on to show Green greeting professors, attending class, leading a student meeting, courting a flirtatious young lady, and, with the aid of footage from a real football game, scoring the winning touchdown for the Commodores. The film also depicts eager students making their best of an inadequate physical plant. "The youthful spirit surmounts even the overcrowding of classrooms and halls," the picture says. In the end, graduate Buck Green is shown as a young businessman, supervising the construction of a new factory building. The film was eventually shown to more than twenty alumni clubs across the South.

About a fourth of alumni contributed to the fund drive of 1926. Several trustees came through with large amounts, such as Whitefoord Cole ($25,000) and Norman Davis ($10,000). The most generous donation came from medical school alumus Thomas Mitchell, who left $115,000 in his will for the creation of a scholarship program targeting students from Georgia. But most of the gifts were more along the lines of an alumna named Sarah Paris Prather. Prather said she would give the school all the money she earned from her cow Molly. She thus sent her alma mater ten dollars per year for the next three years.

In the end the 1926 fund drive succeeded not because of alumni involvement but because of members of the Vanderbilt family (who pitched in $650,000) and because of a lady named Mary Calhoun Foote. Foote, who spent most of her life in New York, died in the early 1920s and left $150,000 of her estate to Vanderbilt to honor her father William Calhoun. Like Francis Furman, William Calhoun never stepped foot on the Vanderbilt campus. He was a jeweler in Nashville who died shortly after the Civil War.

By the fall of 1927 the fund drive had raised enough money to allow Vanderbilt to break ground on three new buildings, later to be called Calhoun, Garland, and Buttrick Halls. At the time, the three structures were supposed to have been the first of several new buildings and dormitories to be built during the final years of Kirkland's tenure. But the Great Depression put a kink in Vanderbilt's plans. As it turned out, the campus construction in 1927 would be the last for Vanderbilt until the eve of World War II.

THEY TAKE THEIR STAND

The story of how a group of apolitical poets became defenders of the Old South begins, as many strange stories do, at the Tennessee legislature.

In the spring of 1925 a lawmaker and farmer from Lafayette, Tennessee named John Butler (who had reportedly never seen a railroad until he was twenty-one years old) proposed a measure that would make it illegal to deny "the story of the Divine Creation of man as taught in the Bible, and to teach instead that man has descended from a lower order of animals" in a publicly funded school. The bill passed easily.

A few weeks later a young teacher named John Scopes was arrested for expressing his intention to teach evolution at his public high school in Dayton, Tennessee. (Scopes was inspired to do so by the American Civil Liberties Union, which offered to defend anyone in Tennessee who challenged the law.) As the trial neared, it began to be followed closely by national newspapers, most of which interpreted it as a major test case of freedom of speech and of society's willingness to accept basic scientific thought. A fundamentalist group in Memphis recruited three-time presidential candidate William Jennings Bryan to help prosecute the case. The ACLU invited celebrated attorney Clarence Darrow to defend Scopes.

The trial took place in July 1925. Since there was little doubt about whether Scopes intended to violate the law, Scopes lost the case and was fined $100. Barrow appealed to the Tennessee Supreme Court, which eventually threw out Scopes's conviction on a technicality.

The so-called "Trial of the Century" didn't settle anything; the debate about evolution raged for the rest of the twentieth century. But it gave sarcastic members of the national media a chance to ridicule the South in general and Tennessee in particular. Story after story proclaimed residents of the Volunteer State to be old-fashioned, simple-minded, and just plain ignorant. In the middle of the trial a *New York Times* reporter described Dayton residents in some detail, saying bigotry was "bone of their bone and flesh of their flesh." He said women in Dayton were not interested in abstract subjects such as the evolution trial and that they "leave such affairs to the men folks." As for Dayton's chair of commissioners A.P. Haggard, he was delighted with all the attention that was being given his fair city and happy to report that Dayton was 99.5 percent fundamentalist, apologizing for the other half-percent.

Some articles spread blame beyond the confines of Dayton. One piece that was probably noticed by every educator in the state appeared in the opinion journal *The Nation* and was headlined "Tennessee: Where Cowards Rule." An excerpt: "If Tennessee has become the laughingstock of the world it is not because she has her villages which are intellectually a half century behind the centers of world thought but rather because among her sons who know better there is scarcely one who has the courage to stand up for what he thinks and knows."

While all this was happening there was the occasional dramatic reminder that many Tennessee residents were in complete agreement with fundamentalism. Within a few months of the Dayton trial, officials at a junior college in Ooltewah, Tennessee, raided their dormitories, seizing all novels, books on evolution, and items of women's makeup and tossing them in a big bonfire in the middle of campus. And only one month after the Scopes trial, thirty thousand members of the Ku Klux Klan (which started in Pulaski, Tennessee) marched on Washington.

Vanderbilt officials decided it wasn't a good time to remain quiet. In the fall of 1925 two of the most important people at the school answered the national media onslaught. The first response came in the form of a letter written to *The Nation* by Edwin Mims, the head of the Vanderbilt English department. Mims pointed out that among the evolutionists at Vanderbilt were Chancellor James Kirkland, geology professor L. C. Glenn, and biology professor E. E. Rienke. Mims also said that Dean of the Vanderbilt School of Religion O. E. Brown had written letters criticizing the state law. "Vanderbilt for a quarter of a century, and especially since its victorious struggle with the Methodist church over its control, has been generally regarded in the South as a citadel of modernism, higher criticism, evolution and other forms of heresy," Mims proudly stated. A few weeks later, in a speech given at the university's fiftieth anniversary celebration, Kirkland said that the best answer to the Dayton controversy and the narrow sectarianism demonstrated by it was do the two things Vanderbilt was doing: build new science laboratories and operate a school of religion. *The New York Times* was so impressed by Kirkland's speech that it held Vanderbilt up as an example of what all universities should try to attain.

Kirkland and Mims no doubt wished that every professor at the school agreed with them, but that was not the case. Within the faculty were dissenters, and chief among them was English professor Donald Davidson. In the mid-1920s, when the Fugitive literary movement was at its peak, Davidson was the most political of the group. Davidson's poems tended to concern historical subjects, and a reading of them reveals a lot of Old South romanticism. As Davidson read the accounts of the Scopes trial in northern publications, his blood boiled. Rather than get angry at the fundamentalists, Davidson became furious with the cynical and superior-minded news media and the way they described the people of Tennessee. The fact that Mims was in general agreement with the media's point of view of the Scopes trial made Davidson even angrier. Mims was generally disliked by younger faculty members; he ran his English department like an autocrat and a few years earlier had expressed no enthusiasm toward the Fugitives or their publication.

About this time Davidson, Allen Tate, and John Crowe Ransom conceived the idea of an entire book defending the Old South and attacking the conventional wisdom that industrialization was improving life. The three asked many of their friends and colleagues to help them by contributing essays to the project. Most declined. But among those who agreed to do so were Fugitive Robert Penn Warren (then studying in England) and Vanderbilt faculty members Lyle Lanier (psychology), John Wade (history), and Frank Owsley (history).

The result of the effort was a 1930 book titled *I'll Take My Stand*. The volume contained essays about economy, lifestyle, history, and race relations that some critics saw as visionary. "This symposium is the most audacious book ever written by Southerners," reviewer William Knickerbocker wrote. "Important as a vigorous declaration of social protest, it is even more important as a prescription for current economic evils." Prominent journalist H. L. Mencken was not so generous. "There is something dreadfully literary and pedagogical about their whole discussion," he wrote. "A thousand such books will never accomplish half so much for the suffering South as one concerted onslaught in plain English upon the nearest conspicuous fraud, whether political, industrial or theological, made by the same twelve men."

I'll Take My Stand was a commercial flop; its initial print run sold so slowly that the publisher didn't order a reprint. But the book created an intellectual stir in America, and has since become regarded as the best defense of the antebellum South ever put to paper. As the authors began to discuss the book's themes in public, they became known as Agrarians. And since so many of the Agrarians were Vanderbilt professors or alumni, the book turned Vanderbilt and its English department into a symbol of the Old South, to the mortification of "New South" disciples such as Kirkland and Mims.

Parts of *I'll Take My Stand* demonstrate a poor knowledge of economics and an overly sentimental view of the Old South's social hierarchy, not to mention a recurring theme of racism toward blacks. Nevertheless, it is an enduring document because its themes are more universal than its authors may have realized. The men who wrote the book talked about the decline of art, destructive business practices that rape the landscape, the numbing effect of mass production on the individual, and the absurdity of the idea that a fast-paced industrial lifestyle is more rewarding than a slow-paced agrarian one. Some of the points were as relevant in 1960 or 2000 as they were in 1930.

Consider, for example, what Davidson said in "A Mirror for Artists," a piece about the impact of the industrial lifestyle on art and leisure. "The furious pace of our working hours is carried over into our leisure hours, which are feverish and energetic," he wrote. "We live by the clock. Our days are a muddle of 'activities,' strenuously pursued. We do not have the free mind and easy temper that should characterize true leisure. Nor does the separation of our lives into two distinct parts, one of which is all labor – too often mechanical and deadening – and the other all play, undertaken as nervous relief, seem to be conducive to harmonious life . . . The leisure thus offered is really no leisure at all; either it is pure sloth; under which the arts take on the character of mere entertainment, purchased in boredom and enjoyed in utter passivity, or it is another kind of labor, taken up out of a sense of duty, pursued as a kind of fashionable enterprise for which one's courage must be continually whipped up by reminders of one's obligation to culture."

Many of the authors of *I'll Take My Stand* eventually developed ambivalent attitudes toward it. John Crowe Ransom repudiated Agrarianism in 1945, saying it was based more on sentimentality rather than reality. After he became nationally known, Robert Penn Warren wrote a small book called *Segregation* that contradicted the major points he had made in "The Briar Patch," an *I'll Take My Stand* essay defending racial segregation.

Of the Agrarians, Davidson remained the most loyal to the themes behind *I'll Take My Stand.* Davidson remained at Vanderbilt as an English professor until he retired in 1964, and as the South began to change he did not change with it. When discussions turned to integration, it became known in academic circles that Davidson was not only against its major goals but also a white supremacist. Until his death in 1968 Davidson maintained that the South would have been a better place had it won the Civil War.

THE BEST AND WORST OF TIMES

In some ways the 1930s were a nadir for Vanderbilt University. After the school received national recognition for the Fugitive literary movement, the next decade was by comparison quiet academically. Vanderbilt was in the fifth decade of Chancellor James Kirkland's tenure; in his departure speech a few years later, Kirkland was the first to admit that he stayed too long. Meanwhile, the university had not yet developed a fundraising arm. Since big foundations such as Carnegie and the GEB were giving less to colleges, Vanderbilt didn't have much money to build anything. In fact, the school couldn't even afford to tear down the shell that remained from the Wesley Hall fire of 1932.

Despite Vanderbilt's shortcomings, however, the school was an interesting place to be during the 1933-34 school year. Undergraduates were able to take classes from such scholars as Robert Penn Warren (English) and Denna Fleming (political science) and to watch a football team coached by the legendary Dan McGugin. Although the Great Depression was underway, students were about as isolated from it as anyone could be in America at that time. In spite of the fact that the clouds of war were beginning to build on the international horizon, students were not yet worried that they might have to go fight as their parents had. And Vanderbilt and Nashville were both such small places that the school and the city had a cozy feel that they would never have again. The school was so small that most students knew each other and almost all of the faculty; so self-important that most of the people there felt as if it were one of the best places to be in the South.

Perhaps there is no better summary of the curious world of Vanderbilt University at the height of the Great Depression than the following contrast: In February 1934, when legendary Kentucky basketball coach Adolph Rupp came to town, the Wildcats played Vanderbilt at the East High School Gymnasium (which seated more than the Vanderbilt gym). On the other hand, routine Vanderbilt events, such as dances and lectures, were regularly broadcast to a national audience on clear channel radio station WSM.

During the 1933-34 school year campus life was completely dominated by fraternities and sororities. About three-fourths of the students were members of such organizations — believed the largest percentage of Greek membership of any school in the South. The Greek system was so dominant that fraternity presidents met before class elections to decide who would be elected class president (in the fall of 1933, the torch of leadership went to Sigma Alpha Epsilon, which dominated class elections that year). This tradition was considered so hypocritical that some students proposed that class elections be discontinued.

The Delta Gamma chapter of the Delta Delta Delta sorority in 1931
Photographic Archives, Vanderbilt University

The practice of fraternity hazing was quite unregulated, but strangely public. One photograph published in *The Hustler* showed a row of Delta Kappa Epsilon freshmen on their hands and knees, pushing pecans with their noses. Standing over them were upperclassmen, holding paddles to punish the freshmen who fell behind in the race.

Among the clearest signs of the harsh economic times was the pay cut that faculty took the previous year. Among the more subtle was the administration's decision to close the school library on Sunday afternoons to save sixty dollars per semester.

In an era when commercial radio station owners believed their audience to be quite sophisticated, Vanderbilt got a lot of free media coverage from locally owned radio stations. WSM, which was owned by the National Life & Accident Insurance Co., broadcast a weekly show about Vanderbilt on Tuesday nights. The shows featured everything from live dances to a special show about the school's history. WLAC, which was owned by the Nashville-based Life & Casualty Insurance Co., frequently featured Vanderbilt professors discussing the issues of the day. One such faculty member was economics professor Roy Garis, who went on WLAC in December 1933 to talk about his opposition to President Franklin Roosevelt's move away from the gold standard.

There were increasing signs that war might again be on the world's horizon, although the campus view on international events was hardly uniform. In October 1933 when Germany broke with the League of Nations, three Vanderbilt professors were quoted as international experts by the *Nashville Tennessean.* Two of the three defended Germany. "Contrary to public opinion here, the masses of the people are for Hitler, because his rule brings relief to the poor and creates order," German professor John Frank said. "Probably, nothing is further from Hitler's mind than to wage war." Another Vanderbilt faculty member, philosophy professor Herbert Sanborn, described the League of Nations as a "mask for carrying out the sinister purpose of international bankers to consolidate their ill-gotten gains." The only Vanderbilt faculty member who was quoted in the article as criticizing Germany was political scientist Denna Fleming, who said that "no European can forget that a little different turn of events would have left the continent in the control of a triumphant, military Germany."

A few months later a visiting professor gave a talk on Japan that made a distinct impression on a *Hustler* reporter. "They (the Japanese) are a people medieval and mystical-minded, still bowing to an emperor who to them is God on earth – yet in power, industry and organization they have suddenly become ultra-modern," the article about the speech said. "Because of this most peculiar combination they are the most dangerous and unpredictable element in the world today."

In the fall of 1933, to ensure that students attended mandatory chapel, the administration started a system where students had to pick up a card at the beginning of chapel and have it signed as they left. "The new system will do away with the practice of leaving before the exercises are over," a short *Hustler* article about the change said. Mandatory chapel remained a frequent source of complaining on campus. "On all sides, we hear groans arising from the ordeal of chapel attendance," one editorial stated.

During the school year the most frequent advertisers in *The Hustler* were cigarette companies Chesterfield, Lucky Strike, and Camel. "For successful billiard play, watch your nerves!" stated one large Camel ad, featuring a nationally famous pool player. "I've smoked Camels for years. They are milder. They never upset my nervous system. And believe me, I smoke plenty!"

The week of the Vanderbilt-Tennessee football game, *The Hustler* did everything it could to encourage students to make the trip to Knoxville to see the game. One article previewing the weekend's events pointed out that there would be a dance on Friday night, a parade featuring the Vanderbilt band through downtown Knoxville on Saturday morning, and another dance on Saturday night. Just to make sure no one got lost on the way, *The Hustler* even had an article about how to get there, pointing the way through Lebanon, Carthage, Cookeville, Monterey, Crossville, Rockwood, and Kingston. Get there "by automobile, bus, train, hitch-hiking and tiddy-bumming," one story implored. Students who made the trip were unhappy when Tennessee won easily 33-6. The game was so disappointing that Nashville newspapers criticized the team for its performance.

"Vanderbilt not only was outplayed, outmaneuvered, outwitted and outcharged, but they were outclassed," huffed the *Tennessean. The Hustler* came to the school's defense. "Vanderbilt has never maintained a fund for the subsidation of football, holding rather to the original purpose of the university," the school paper opined. "We applaud the administration for that stand and defend it against the attacks of all so unbalanced as to not be able to recognize the significance of a victory or defeat in college football."

In February 1934 twenty-four new members of the junior class honor society known as the Owl Club were arrested for marching through streetcars and downtown movie theaters hooting as a part of a club initiation. The students spent three hours in jail before they were released to *Hustler* editor and senior class president Ben West. West, who later became the mayor of Nashville, convinced Nashville Judge Guild Smith to dismiss the charges. "The police had to arrest everyone, but once they got all those kids in jail and they were hootin' and hollerin' and shaking the bars and causing all sorts of commotion, they wanted to get rid of them," Andrew Benedict, the president of the junior class and a member of the Owl Club, said seven decades later. "Ben West helped get them out because he already knew a lot of people down at the courthouse because he had worked at the *Banner.* He was a politician from the time he got out of his cradle."

In the 1933-34 school year the most controversial incident on campus was a *Hustler* editorial (apparently written by West) attacking the school's faculty and intellectual atmosphere. "The once hallowed tradition of culture and learning peculiar to Vanderbilt is about as alive as the Commodore's statue in front of College Hall," the editorial in the March 30, 1934, *Hustler* said. "You recall the persona of such great men as Dr. Barnard and Dean Tolman, but you forget that these men are dead and their age is dead with them." The editorial lambasted what it called as the "present pseudo-intellectual passivity" on the campus, and finished by using the word "Panderbilt" to describe the school. (West later claimed that the use of the word Panderbilt was a typographical error.) Two weeks later, Kirkland wrote a long response, calling the editorial "slanderous" and lamenting the attention it had received from newspapers outside Nashville "to the joy of our enemies and the mortification of our friends."

Referring to the anonymous author of the editorial, Kirkland sarcastically pointed out, "I ought to be grateful that we have produced one young man with enough intelligence to value 226 courses of instruction in 17 different departments by 80 individuals who knows that they are all inane."

A LIBRARY FOR FOUR SCHOOLS

When Vanderbilt University opened a two million dollar library in 1941, it turned a major weakness into one of its strengths, and did so with the generous support of one of the nation's largest foundations. The university also laid the base for what would eventually be the most significant merger in its history.

During its first sixty-five years Vanderbilt had no library building and kept its book collection in a large room of the Main Building. When that structure was destroyed by fire in 1905, virtually all the library books were burned and the university had to start its collection anew.

Vanderbilt's lack of a library building was a notable deficiency, and was a cause of complaints among students for decades. "The most urgent need at present is for a library," *The Hustler* editorialized in 1905. Not only did it keep the university from having virtually any doctoral programs, it damaged the institution's national image. By the late 1920s both Duke University and the University of Texas had library collections almost twice as large as Vanderbilt's.

Chancellor Kirkland made the construction of a library the last major goal in his administration. In an era before Vanderbilt had an alumni fundraising organization strong enough to pay for a large capital project internally (other than a football stadium), Kirkland knew where he had to turn for help. During the 1920s the John Rockefeller-backed General Education Board (GEB) and the Rockefeller family made several major donations to Vanderbilt, funding construction of the Vanderbilt Medical School and a classroom building (named after GEB secretary Wallace Buttrick). Kirkland asked the GEB to contribute $500,000 toward a new Vanderbilt library that he at first believed would cost about a million dollars.

By coincidence, George Peabody College for Teachers asked the GEB to contribute to a new library there about the time Vanderbilt did. The GEB responded to both institutions by saying it would not contribute to separate library buildings so close to each other, but would give money for a joint library of Vanderbilt and Peabody that could also be used by Scarritt College and the YMCA College. But it left the plan for joint ownership and operation of that library up to the schools.

It took Vanderbilt and Peabody several years to meet the GEB's criteria. Eventually, that plan not only addressed the joint operation of a library, but reorganized the two institutions to work together to avoid overlapping functions and reduce inefficiencies. The key person in making this arrangement was Fredrick Kuhlman, who in came to Nashville in 1935 from the University of Chicago to work on the library concept.

Under the new Vanderbilt-Peabody arrangement, the two schools agreed on a mutual calendar and to recognize course work taken by students at either institution. They vowed to eliminate 280 quarter hours of duplicating work. The agreement also called for Vanderbilt to teach all content classes, with all education, fine arts, and practical courses left to Peabody.

The YMCA College went out of business in the mid-1930s, leaving Vanderbilt, Peabody, and Scarritt officials to work out details on how they would all share a common library. Under the agreement finalized in 1938, the universities set up a board consisting of faculty members from all three institutions. The three schools agreed to contribute financially to a facility that would be known as the Joint University Library. It would be built on the part of Vanderbilt's main campus closest to Peabody and Scarritt (a shift from Vanderbilt's previous plan, which had called for a central library in the middle of campus).

With this new working relationship between Vanderbilt and Peabody, the GEB agreed to contribute half of the money needed for the construction and endowment of the JUL facility, which by now was estimated to cost about two million dollars. The Carnegie Foundation pitched in $250,000. That left Vanderbilt, Peabody, and Scarritt in need of $750,000.

Nashville Banner publisher and Vanderbilt alumnus James Stahlman headed the library's fundraising campaign. He and other campaign leaders appealed hard to Nashville's sense of spirit, pointing out that it would be a black mark on the city if the three institutions could not raise enough money to take advantage of the GEB's donation. "Nashville is facing grave embarrassment which if not relieved will seriously impact the city's standing and future growth in the educational world," one article in Stahlman's *Banner* said. "As pointed out publicly by visiting educators in the recent symposium of higher education in the South, the library facilities of Nashville's leading educational institutions are wholly inadequate to support their purpose and opportunities." During a two-week period in the fall of 1938 school officials and boosters spoke at separate luncheons sponsored by the Nashville Chamber of Commerce, the Rotary Club, the Exchange Club, the Centennial Club, the Lions Club, and the Kiwanis Club.

The Joint University Library - circa 1941
The Banner Collection, Nashville Public Library, The Nashville Room

The fund drive never quite reached its goal, but it did raise more than $600,000. Over $104,000 of that amount was raised from Vanderbilt faculty, staff, and students, with most of the rest coming from Nashville's business leaders and Vanderbilt alumni living locally. The Vanderbilt Board of Trust allocated the remaining $150,000 from university reserves to put the library project over the top. By this time Kuhlman had been named director of the JUL.

Vanderbilt hired Nashville resident Henry Hibbs, who had previously designed the YMCA College building and Buttrick Hall, to be the library's architect. Hibbs designed a four-story collegiate gothic structure with beautiful reading and reserve rooms, a Treasure Room for rare collections, and special study rooms for professors engaged in research. It had space for half a million volumes, making it the fifth largest university library in the South at that time. Hibbs paid so much attention to detail that rubber tile was used throughout the building to make its interior as quiet as possible.

One of the big questions in planning the library building was whether it should contain central air conditioning. At the time, there were no buildings on the Vanderbilt campus equipped with central air. However, many theaters, restaurants, and stores in Nashville were beginning to install it. Eventually, library planners concluded that air conditioning was needed for two reasons: because most Peabody students attended school in the summer, and out of concern about the long-term impact of excessive heat on the library's book collection.

Another issue was whether to let students have direct access to most of the books. In the late 1930s the decision was made not to do so, which is why for many years students had to write down what books they wanted and give the note to a librarian, who would retrieve the book from the stacks. This policy changed two decades later, when the stacks were opened to undergraduates and a turnstile and guard were posted at the front door. At the time, students didn't think much of the added security. "Every time I go through the turnstile, I get my dress caught," one female student complained.

The Joint University Library was completed in the fall of 1941, and its dedication took place on December 5 and 6, 1941. The next day, Japan bombed Pearl Harbor.

The other, equally controversial Hustler

The Hustler is one of the oldest newspapers in Tennessee and was first published on October 20, 1888. Unfortunately, Vanderbilt University's Special Collections department has been unable to locate a single copy of the school paper from its initial three years; the oldest *Hustler* on microfilm is dated September 24, 1891. The only article believed to still exist from the first *Hustler* is an editorial, clipped by unofficial Vanderbilt historian Stella Vaughn, in which the new paper stated its creed. "It shall always be our purpose to furnish our readers with every item of news in connection with the campus," the editorial said. "To stand up for the right and condemn the wrong; to discuss impartially all questions concerning the interests of Vanderbilt . . . it has no wrongs to avenge, no axe to grind, no favors to ask." The editor of that first volume of *The Hustler* was Claude Waller, whose son founded the Nashville law firm Waller Lansden Dortch and Davis.

From its inception until the 1930s *The Hustler* put far more emphasis on sports than it would in later years. Virtually every football game, basketball game, baseball game, and track meet for six decades made the front page of the student newspaper. In fact, there were years when there was almost nothing except sports coverage in *The Hustler.*

James Stahlman, who would go on to become publisher of the *Nashville Banner* and a Vanderbilt trustee, apparently took part in one of the greatest pranks ever undertaken by a *Hustler* staffer. One night in February 1913, the sound of gunshots rang out on the Vanderbilt campus. A few seconds later, Vanderbilt students (and *Hustler* reporters) Stahlman and Fred Woodward came running into Kissam Hall in a panic, saying that they had been held up by a robber who fired shots at them as they ran away. "I surely was scared to death," Stahlman said in a *Hustler* article about the incident published that week. Three decades later, a *Hustler* article claimed that the Stahlman/Woodward holdup was a hoax perpetuated by Stahlman as a way to generate copy during a slow news week. The 1943 article about the incident – which cited no source – said that the police investigated the so-called crime with bloodhounds, and that the only scent that the dogs could find led them to the school newspaper office.

Prior to the Civil Rights Movement of the 1960s Vanderbilt student publications reflected a racial attitude prevalent in the Old South. A short editorial in a 1914 *Hustler* perhaps best demonstrates this. "A 'bunch of niggers' has been loafing around the gymnasium for years," the editorial said. "The most of them are 'no account parasites' that live off the students. It is all right for the pressing club to be maintained, but this shiftless crowd of 'nigger' loafers should be run off the campus." Usually, the student newspaper maintained more formal language. Four years later, *The Hustler* editorialized: "We are of a race that refuses to accept an inferior race as social equals. We have been told by some of our saintly critics that we are not Christian in our treatment of the Negro because we insist upon his submission to our superiority but our prejudice against accepting him as a social equal is too strong to be influenced by criticism from any source." The editorial concluded that the best course for the South is to educate both blacks and whites, in hopes that "the Negro may be less likely to commit crimes and so that white people may be less likely to defeat the purpose of the courts by taking the law into their own hands."

One of the most outstanding journalists ever to write for *The Hustler* was Ralph McGill, who attended Vanderbilt in the early 1920s and went on to be the editor of the *Atlanta Journal-Constitution.* Later in his life McGill had wonderful things to say about his college years. "Vanderbilt University was, for me, a sort of Tibet, high above all other plateaus I have known. The air was heady with excitement. I would not have traded my dark, bleak room in shabby old Kissam Hall for a castle in Camelot." Unfortunately, McGill did not graduate from Vanderbilt. Chancellor Kirkland suspended him in the spring of 1922 for a fraternity prank (the details of which are not known) and a controversial column in *The Hustler* (which this author read about, but could not locate).

No *Hustler* reporter has ever likely gone to greater lengths to get a story than Fred Boswell. In 1934 Boswell entered a walkathon/danceathon at Nashville's Hippodrome Theater with a young lady named Imogene Sherman. The pair stayed on their feet for more than twelve hours, all so that the freshman would have a good story for his school paper.

Prior to the 1960s the most consistent advertisers in *The Hustler* were tobacco companies. In the March 28, 1952, issue alone, *The Hustler* had a half-page ad for Lucky Strike, a quarter-page ad for Kentucky Club pipe tobacco, a one-third page ad for Camel, a one-third-page ad for Philip Morris, and a half-page ad for Chesterfield. That same issue contained a story announcing that the following Monday, an unknown Chesterfield representative would be walking on campus giving away freebies to nicotine-addicted students. "Any student carrying a pack of Chesterfield cigarettes will receive one pack free and any student actually smoking a Chesterfield will receive two free packs," the ad said.

Students in the 1950s were notably apolitical. Perhaps there is no better indication of this feeling than the reaction, or lack thereof, to an editorial written by a student named Doug Lipton in 1954. At a time when President Dwight Eisenhower had endorsed the idea of reducing the voting age from twenty-one to eighteen, Lipton wrote a long article about how he thought it was a bad idea. "Young people eighteen to twenty-one years of age lack the necessary maturity of judgment which a voter should have," the article said. "In this period of late adolescence, the youth is not settled. He is subjected to emotional and vocational problems . . . The growing young man and girl are surrounded by parents who influence and, in fact, often dominate their thoughts. They should not share in the heavy responsibility of voting until they are ready to make their own decisions." During the next month, *The Hustler* did not publish a single letter of opposition to Lipton's article.

One of the most controversial items to ever appear in *The Hustler* was published on November 8, 1963. In a column, student Tom Quinn lambasted the *Nashville Banner* for running excerpts from a book that harshly criticized President John Kennedy. "The *Banner* tries to counteract its constipation with journalistic diarrhea," Quinn wrote, in an article in which he referred to *Banner* publisher and

Vanderbilt trustee James Stahlman as a "journalistic junkie." The student-dominated Student Publications Board officially censured Quinn for "violations of good taste" and ordered the student to write an apology, which appeared in the paper. When Kennedy was murdered two weeks later, *The Hustler* story about campus reaction to the assassination (by reporter Frank Sutherland, who later became editor of *The Tennessean*) ran on the bottom of the front page.

Though Alexander Heard's chancellorship encompassed the wild 1960s, he rarely censored *The Hustler*. But in December 1967, two students named John York and Win Anderson wrote a story about the experience of finding and paying a prostitute in Nashville. "Bring along 20 or 30 dollars and your libido," the article began. "Yes, you – frustrated Vanderbilt male. Go see your friendly corner prostitute." The next month, the Student Association Public Relations Committee sent five hundred copies of the school newspaper to incoming freshmen. Instead of including the article about hookers, the committee deleted pages seven and eight from the mailouts. "It was inviting trouble if sent out to prospective students," said David Wood, dean of admissions.

Chuck Offenburger may have been the most committed, but the most shortsighted, *Hustler* editor of all time. In the fall of 1968 Offenburger was so passionate about his newspaper's endorsement of black activist Dick Gregory for president of the United States that he spent the money his mother had set aside for room and board to bring Gregory to campus. With nowhere to live, Offenburger (clandestinely) slept on a canvas cot in *The Hustler* office in Alumni Hall the entire semester. "I didn't have many clothes, and what few I had I kept in a filing cabinet in the office," Offenburger said years later. "Every day, I'd wake up, sling a towel over my shoulder and walk to a nearby dorm such as McGill Hall to take a shower." *The Hustler* was especially interesting that semester, and played a key role in the many changes that were taking place on campus such as the loosening of dress codes and curfews. However, Offenburger spent so much time editing and writing it that he failed three courses and was removed as editor in January 1969.

In addition to the long-standing *Hustler*, well over a dozen student publications have come and gone at Vanderbilt, with names such as *The Observer*, *Jade*, *The Masquerader*, *The Chase*, and, of course, *The Fugitive*. For the most part, these other publications were literary or humorous in nature and not newspapers. But when it was first started in December 1968, *Versus* was a full-sized weekly newspaper with a decidedly more conservative voice than *The Hustler*. In its first two years *Versus* took a skeptical view of the protests that were taking place at Vanderbilt. The *Versus* staff also had to work a lot harder than *The Hustler* staff because the publication initially received no money from the student activity fund to subsidize operations. However, *Versus* got in trouble with Chancellor Alexander Heard in September 1971 for running advertisements for a mail-order condom company. The controversy hurt the new publication and indirectly caused it to be changed to a literary magazine and opinion journal, which it remained through the rest of the century. The condom ad controversy also resulted in the school's hiring of a full-time person to "oversee" student publications.

One of the greatest reporters to ever take classes at Vanderbilt never wrote a word for *The Hustler*. In the late 1960s a middle-aged *Tennessean* reporter named Nat Caldwell took classes at Vanderbilt to finish his degree. Caldwell and fellow reporter Gene Graham had won a 1962 Pulitzer Prize for their coverage of labor leader John Lewis' financial dealings. Profiled by *The Hustler* in March 1969, student Caldwell had a strong opinion about trends underway in academia. "The universities have fallen into a 'star' system in the way they handle their faculty members," he said. "They put too much emphasis on how famous a professor is in the field and not enough emphasis on how well he teaches."

Throughout most of its history *The Hustler's* staff made an effort to try to write articles about school history. This tradition inexplicably vanished about 1970, after which there appeared only a smattering of historical articles. Many of these were grossly inaccurate, such as a tale repeated numerous times by student reporters and campus tour guides that Furman Hall's design is unusual because its architectural plans were mixed up with that of another building, and the real plans were sent by accident to the Furman University. Perhaps there is no better example of *The Hustler's* lack of interest in the school's history than the fact that in October 1975, when the school celebrated its centennial, the only historical article concerned the role of women in the school's history.

Finally, the fact that Vanderbilt's school newspaper happened to have the same name as a pornographic magazine was a source of amusement in the latter part of the twentieth century. But as early as 1908, some students didn't like the name "Hustler" for other reasons. "There is perhaps in the English language no one word which . . . more richly deserves the epithet vulgar than the word hustler," a student named H.Z. Kip wrote. "A hustler is a man who is . . . unrefined, shallow and offensive."

Part Four

Mr. Branscomb's School

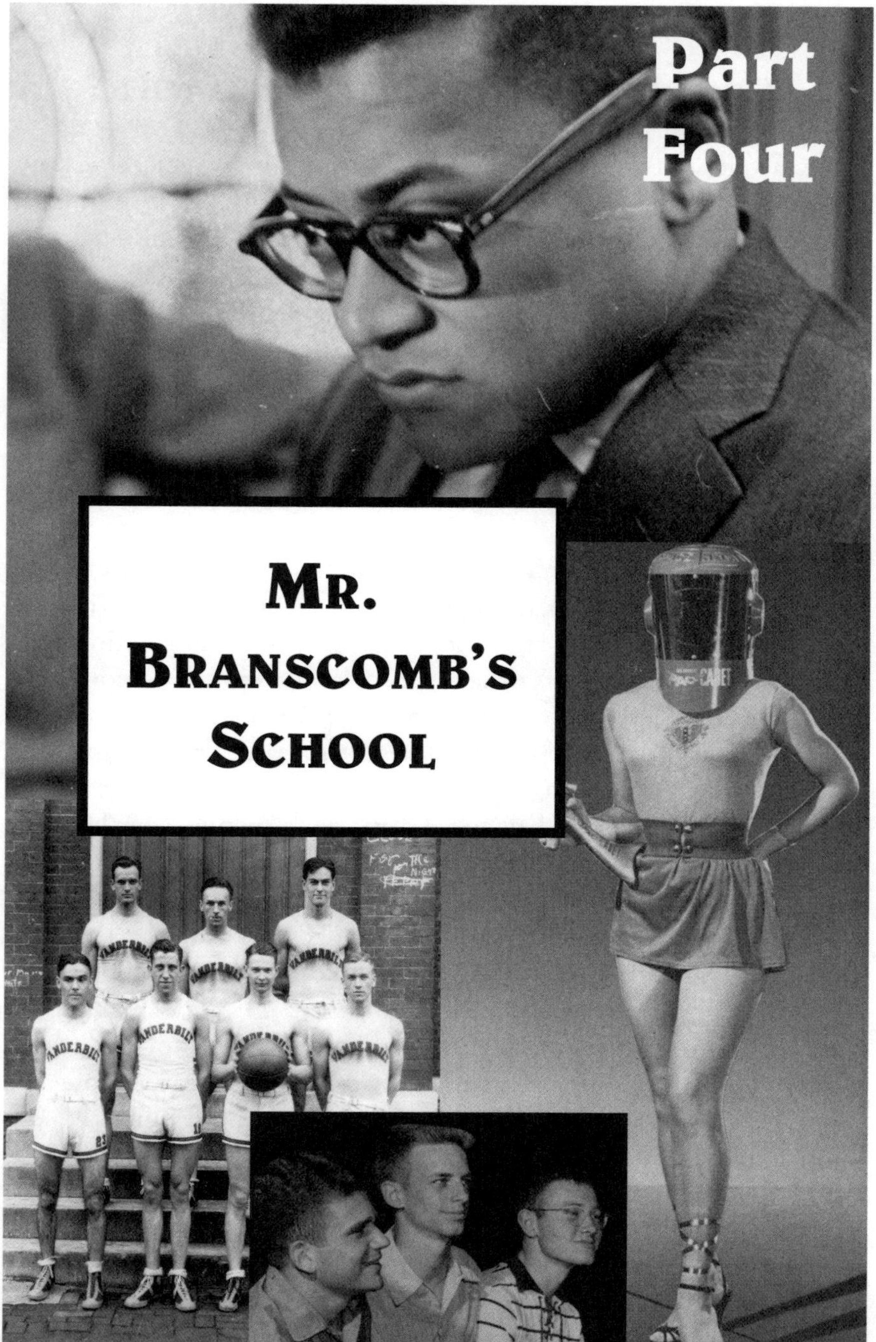

CIGARETTES WITH LIPSTICK ON THEM

It was one of the most important moments in American history, and a Vanderbilt student named John Akers captured it well. Early in the morning on December 8, 1941, Akers was in Alumni Hall with about a hundred of his fellow students, listening to the "Day of Infamy" speech by President Franklin Roosevelt. "Horror was written on the countenances of many," Akers wrote in *The Hustler.* "Tears glistened in a few girls' eyes; others knitted calmly. Cigarette smoke was heavy in the air and there was an air of shocked incredulity as the immortal five hundred words were unfolded by the chief executive . . . from time to time solemn students slipped through the door and joined the silent group."

For the next several years life would not be the same on campus. There were many, many signs that there was a war on. To comply with federal wartime regulations, the school administration took steps to conserve energy. Virtually all social functions, including fraternity meetings, were shifted from night to day. Early morning classes were changed from 8:00 a.m. to 8:30 to ease Nashville's traffic. Spring break was canceled. Students were instructed to save or donate just about everything: old textbooks, women's nylons, coat hangers, scrap metal. They were also encouraged to walk or use mass transit whenever possible.

During the war male students headed off to war by the hundreds, leaving dormitory hallways and fraternity houses abnormally quiet. The biggest drop was during the 1942-43 school year, when hundreds of young men either enlisted in the middle of the school year or finished training programs and were sent overseas. Among the male clubs that completely shut down were the Owl Club, the Ace Club, and Calumet. The absence of males on campus peaked during the 1943-44 school year, when women outnumbered men two to one. "All the cigarettes in the ash tray have lipstick on them," *The Hustler,* then entirely staffed by women, reported in the spring of 1943.

As for cigarettes, they were another item in short supply during the war, which may have forced some students to go to extremes to satisfy their nicotine cravings. "If you have not already succumbed to the temptation of 'reefers' by resorting to opium cigarettes as a means of beating this cigarette shortage, let us offer you a bit of consolation," *The Hustler* said in a March 1945 feature about the "cigarette of tomorrow."

Not just students went to the war; professors were also being drafted or were volunteering. Among the Vanderbilt faculty members who joined the service were mathematics professor John Dyer-Bennet, registrar Robert Cunningham, psychology professor Meredith Crawford, and Henry Lee Swint of the history department. Hardest hit by the draft was the athletic department, which saw head football coach Red Sanders, assistant football coach Paul "Bear" Bryant, and head basketball coach Norman Cooper all leave to serve their country.

There were several special military training programs on campus, including programs that trained army air corps aviators, medical officers, foreign language specialists, and army engineers. Many programs came and went over the course of the war, making it difficult to keep up with them. One of the more interesting organizations was the U.S. Army Meteorological Training Detachment. Through that program about two hundred men came to Vanderbilt's campus in February 1943 for twelve months of training on how to be an officer and how to predict the weather. After a year of being awakened by reveille in McTyeire Hall, the young men were commissioned and sent overseas in the spring of 1944. With military trainees dominating McTyeire and Kissam Halls, students had to reside three or four to a room or live off campus.

The war put Chancellor Oliver Carmicheal in an awkward position. He had a patriotic duty to encourage as many students as possible to fight the war, but he didn't want every male student to enlist and leave his campus empty. What he generally advocated was for students to finish their degrees and enroll in one of the many officer-training programs that were available to them at the time. In an October 1942 speech Carmichael said that there were only two types of students he felt should immediately enlist. "The first was the boy who had come to school simply for pleasure," a *Hustler* account of his address said. "The second was the boy who would like to be a private because he did not want to take the responsibility of an officer."

Much as they had done in World War I, many Vanderbilt faculty members had to teach new material as a part of the war effort. This trend was most notable in the engineering department, where virtually every professor taught specialized courses for students or military personnel being trained on campus. A structural engineering professor taught a course on bomb shelters and air raid protection. Two chemical engineering instructors worked on methods for dehydrating food.

In another parallel with the First World War, the relationship between normal Vanderbilt students and army trainees was not always smooth. In the spring of 1943 a *Hustler* editorial complained about the amount of public affection (smooching, the article called it) that was taking place in full view on campus. "It may be that many people have no place to meet their wives and sweethearts, but in war time one must consider not only himself but also the school where he is accepted as a student," the article said. "Some action by the authori-

Members of the Vanderbilt class of 1945
The Banner Collection, Nashville Public Library, The Nashville Room

ties should be taken soon to remove this sight from the public gaze if Vanderbilt is to retain its reputation as a school of culture and learning." The article was perceived as one that insulted the military people on campus, leading a student to write a letter attacking the editorial. "Personally, I have never had the fortune or the misfortune of witnessing such a disgraceful scene; perhaps, though, I just did not recognize it as being disgraceful," Earl Isbell wrote.

With so much emphasis on the war effort, a little noticed event took place on April 12, 1943, when a sociologist named Charles Johnson spoke at Wesley Hall on "the place of the Negro in society today." What made the event so unusual is that Johnson was black – possibly the first African American to make a speech on the Vanderbilt campus since Booker T. Washington in 1909.

The shortage of fuel was such that it was not easy to bring in outside speakers or performers. Because of this Vanderbilt students often had to make do with local talent. In 1943 local orchestra director Francis Craig played at the senior prom, a bit of a disappointment because Craig had played on campus so many times. And in the spring of 1944 English professor Edwin Mims gave the commencement address.

With the departure of so many coaches and young men to fight the war, the board of trust in September 1943 voted to discontinue the awarding of football scholarships for two years. This move to "informal teams," as they were called, was heavily criticized at the time and even resulted in a protest letter from overseas. "Football is loved by every red blooded American boy," alumnus Ben Austin wrote. "If for no other reason, Vanderbilt should hold onto football because of the opportunity it gives the students to express their school spirit."

Most of the people who went off to fight came home, but some did not. After the war the alumni office calculated that more than one hundred Vanderbilt students and alumni died in the war. Among them were Sid Hicks and Willie Cornelius, editor and business manager of *The Hustler* during the 1940-41 school year.

The war effort on campus began to wind down before the conflict ended. By December 1944 the military had as many people as it needed and it began to phase out training programs on campuses such as Vanderbilt. In January 1945 students moved back into Kissam and McTyeire Halls. During the next few months there were increasing signs that life was getting back to normal – more social events, more dances, and a loosening of wartime restrictions on fuel usage. By the time the war ended, Vanderbilt officials were beginning to work on fundraising projects for the engineering department and the law school.

Six hundred first-year students showed up for classes that fall, a class so large that Vanderbilt had to build temporary housing for them. They were greeted with the surprising news that Chancellor Carmichael had accepted a job as president of the Carnegie Foundation for the Advancement of Teaching. While the board of trust was looking for his successor, Dean of Men Madison Sarratt became acting chancellor.

Despite the temporary housing and the temporary chancellor, things were getting back to normal in the 1945-46 school year. Fraternity and sorority rush was back in full swing. Men's organizations like the Owl Club were back on campus. Even head football coach Red Sanders came back from the war.

THE MAN WHO WROTE ABOUT WHAT HE SAW

The redheaded boy from Guthrie, Kentucky, made a distinct impression on everyone he met. One person, seeing him for the first time, described him as "the most remarkable looking boy I had ever laid eyes on. He was tall and thin, and when he walked across the room he made a sliding shuffle, as if his bones didn't belong to one another. He had a long quivering nose, large brown eyes and a long chin – all topped by curly red hair."

The awkward-looking lad was Robert Penn Warren, known as "Red" Warren to his friends. Warren was an impressionable and energetic young man with a photographic memory. He spent much of his childhood at the feet of his maternal grandfather Gabriel Penn, who fought for the Confederacy in the Civil War. One of the most dramatic events in Warren's childhood was a battle between small farmers and large tobacco companies over the price of tobacco. When some farmers began siding with the companies, others formed brigades of so-called "nightriders" which began burning barns as a form of intimidation.

Warren would eventually become one of the most treasured novelists in American history, but that wasn't his original plan. At the age of fifteen, he wanted to go to the naval academy. For a while he had an appointment lined up, but then his younger brother hit him in the eye with a piece of hot coal, rendering him unqualified for military service.

Taking his second choice, Warren headed to Vanderbilt in the fall of 1921 with the intention of majoring in chemistry. But when he got to school, Warren found that he hated that subject. Under the influence of English professors John Crowe Ransom and Donald Davidson and classmates Allen Tate and Ridley Wills, Warren began to focus on poetry. Rather than memorize seven hundred lines of verse, as the English department required students to do, Warren memorized three thousand. Warren was so extraordinarily talented that he was invited to join the Fugitives literary group.

While in college, Warren's world consisted of classes and long evenings with his fellow Fugitives or with many hard-drinking acquaintances he made at that time. Two local events during Warren's time at Vanderbilt found their way into his later work. Warren would eventually write a book called *At Heaven's Gate* that was loosely based on the story of Caldwell & Co., a Nashville-based municipal bond house that acquired banks, insurance companies, and manufacturers in the 1920s but collapsed during the Great Depression. Despite the artistic success of the novel, there is no evidence that Warren ever met Caldwell & Co. president Rogers Caldwell. Another of Warren's novels, *The Cave,* was loosely based upon an event that took place in early 1925 near Warren's boyhood home. In the tragedy, a man named Floyd Collins became trapped in a part of Mammoth Cave and died after 18 days. Warren stayed in Nashville during the entire Collins tragedy and the media hype that surrounded it.

The 1925 trial of John Scopes in Dayton, Tennessee, also took place during Warren's undergraduate days at Vanderbilt. And like the other eleven Southern scholars who contributed to the 1930 book *I'll Take My Stand* – which indirectly came about because of the trial and its aftermath – Warren didn't bother to go see the big event. "Be it to my everlasting shame that when the Scopes trial was going on a few miles from me, I didn't even bother to go," Warren said many years later. "My head was too full of (writers) John Ford and John Webster and William Blake and T.S. Eliot. If I had been thinking about writing novels about the South, I would have been camping out in Dayton, Tennessee – and would have gone about it like journalism."

The reason Warren didn't leave town very much between 1921 and 1925 is that he was completely devoted to poetry. Warren's writing first appeared in *The Fugitive* in the August-September 1923 issue. About that same time, five of Warren's poems were published in *Driftwood Flames*, a small book of verse released by the Poetry Guild.

Warren drank too much at college and, unlike some of his fellow Fugitives, was chronically unsuccessful with women. Both of these factors may have contributed to his state of mind when he tried to commit suicide in his dorm room in May 1924. After a summer resting at home, Warren resumed his writing; by the fall of that year, new poems of his were being published in regional magazines.

When he graduated from Vanderbilt in the summer of 1925, Warren accepted a teaching assistantship at Berkeley. Later in the decade he spent time at Yale and Oxford Universities. While at Yale he wrote his first novel, *John Brown: The Making of a Martyr*. While in England he wrote "The Briar Patch," an essay about southern race relations that was published as a part of *I'll Take My Stand*. Warren then came back to the South, teaching at Southwestern at Memphis for a year and then returning to Vanderbilt as an English teacher. Unfortunately, he didn't get along with English department head Edwin Mims, which is why Warren eventually left Vanderbilt for a job at Louisiana State University.

About this time Warren began devoting more of his creative energy to writing novels. About the time he moved to Louisiana, Warren set to work on a book about the night riders he saw as a child in Kentucky. *Night Rider* came out in March 1939, and earned him a Guggenheim Fellowship. During World War II Warren completed two more manuscripts. The first was *At Heaven's Gate*, a book replete with references to people, places, and experiences that reflected his time in Nashville in the early 1920s. The second book, *All the King's Men*, was based on the life of Huey Long, the powerful Louisiana governor who was assassinated in 1935 (and who Warren never met). It won the Pulitzer Prize, would eventually sell almost three million copies, and be regarded as one of the greatest American novels ever written.

Critics cited Warren's even-handed point of view, his colloquial style, and his technical mastery as the bases for his novels' impact. Warren approached his heroes, whether the abolitionist John Brown or the fictional Governor Willie Stark in *All the King's Men,* with an evenness that left the point of view in his novels up to interpretation. "People, you must remember, are awfully complex creatures," he said many years later. "You may be in for some real surprises if you divide the cast into heroes and villains." But Warren's most frequently cited strength was the voice with which he wrote, a colloquial, perceptive, gruff, and authentic style that many compared to William Faulkner's. "A very remarkable piece of novel-writing *All the King's Men* surely is," a *Nation* reviewer said. "For sheer virtuosity, for the sustained drive of

Robert Penn Warren teaching a class at Vanderbilt
The Banner Collection, Nashville Public Library, The Nashville Room

its prose, for the speed and evenness of its pacing, for its precision of language, its genius of colloquialism, I doubt indeed whether it can be matched in American fiction."

Warren went on to write many more novels during his lifetime, among them *The Cave* and *Band of Angels.* His final novel, the semi-biographical *A Place to Come To,* caused a stir in Nashville with its sometimes-scandalous references to the affluent suburb of Belle Meade and to Vanderbilt society. For the most part, however, Warren devoted his energies to poetry in his later career, winning the Pulitzer Prize in 1956 for a collection entitled *Promises, Poems* and two decades later for *Now and Then.*

Strangely enough, the native Kentuckian, Fugitive, and Agrarian spent his latter years in New England, saying the culture of the modern South was alien to him. "In much of the South you have a straight TV culture superimposed on a vacuum, or a new kind of money culture," he said in the 1970s. "If I had a farm there now, I'd have to get in my car and go somewhere to find someone to talk to. Nobody to just sit on the corner of the fence and pass the time of day with." However, Warren did have a fond attitude toward his alma mater, and made several trips to Vanderbilt for Fugitive reunions and speeches.

SNEAKING INTO THE TUNNELS

By the latter part of the twentieth century, mandatory chapel, the Glee Club, and the mass hazing of freshmen had gone the way of the dinosaur at Vanderbilt. But that's not to say that students couldn't come up with things that they could (more or less) call traditions. Among the examples:

The pressure of conformity has always cast a spell over Vanderbilt students, but perhaps never more than in the ultra-conservative 1950s. A 1954 *Hustler* poll showed that 96 percent of the male students had brought to college a striped tie; 91 percent had grey flannel pants; 75 percent had an Oxford cloth button down shirt; and 73 percent had argyle socks.

For many years one of the biggest events on the Vanderbilt

social calendar was a series of socials known as Charm Week. The highlight of Charm Week was the Coed Ball, at which a Charm Queen and a King Rex were chosen and honored.

Until the 1960s almost nothing took place on the Vanderbilt campus on Sunday because so many students went home on weekends. In 1952, when almost 40 percent of students were Nashville residents, the Joint University Library was closed on Sunday. A poll taken in March of that year showed that 57 percent of the student body wanted to keep it that way.

To say that Vanderbilt's radio station was started without much of a budget would be an understatement. WVU, as it was first called, was literally pieced together by two students, Raphael Smith and Ray Gill, who came up with the idea while attending summer school in 1952. It took Smith and Gill several months, a lot of technical ingenuity, and some free equipment donated by Nashville radio station WSM to piece together a station, but somehow they did it. On March 30, 1953, the station debuted at 600 on the AM radio dial. During its early years WVU had campus news and sports and featured a wide range of musical genres, from classical to easy listening to jazz. It even had a rock 'n' roll show called "Bandstand." But WVU didn't have many listeners in the 1950s. The thirty-watt station, which was based in Neely Auditorium, didn't even reach the fraternity and sorority houses then located off campus. WVU became FM station WRVU in 1971.

In the spring of 1960, when Nashville's sit-in movement against segregated lunch counters was making national news, one of the biggest debates at Vanderbilt was whether students should listen to jukebox music or WVU while relaxing in the new Commodore Room. After several *Hustler* editorials and a student senate debate on the matter, WVU prevailed.

It is hard to know exactly when Vanderbilt students became wealthy enough to start going to the beach for spring break. But in 1968 *The Hustler* reported that the three most popular destinations for spring break vacationers were Ft. Lauderdale, Daytona, and Nassau, Bahamas.

Prior to 1969 female Vanderbilt students were not allowed to wear pants or shorts on campus. The only exception to this rule was that they were allowed to wear shorts under a long raincoat if they were going directly from their dormitory to the tennis courts or directly from the tennis courts to their dormitory. Most male students hated the ban on shorts, which is why the girl featured in *The Hustler*'s "Coed of the Week" photograph in the early 1950s was almost always wearing shorts. But a majority of Vanderbilt females polled by *The Hustler* in 1958 said they didn't mind the ban.

A series of man-made tunnels runs under the Vanderbilt campus, delivering steam, power lines, and phone connections to classroom buildings and dormitories. For many years, students regularly sneaked into the tunnels to explore, study, or find a quiet, dark place to take their dates. In the late 1960s undergraduates were wandering through the tunnels when they found decades-old law books under Tolman Hall and some of Chancellor Garland's old astronomical equipment under McGill Hall. Some years later, several students said they got lost in the tunnels for hours. Finally, they groped their way through the dark, pushed through a vent and found themselves in the hospital morgue.

In the mid-1980s Plant Operations intentionally made the tunnels difficult for unauthorized people to reach. From that point on, bizarre rumors circulated about the tunnels. Perhaps the most amusing was the idea that the tunnels existed to transport school administrators to a bomb shelter in case of nuclear war. "I have heard that the chancellor has some sort of underground monorail bunker system to protect him in the event of a nuclear attack," one student said in 1995. "He rides from Kirkland Hall in his silver chariot all the way to 400 feet underneath Stevenson."

From the mid-1960s until the mid-1970s all freshmen males lived in Kissam Quadrangle, which had single rooms and no security, and all freshmen females lived in Branscomb Quadrangle, which had double rooms and was surrounded by a high brick wall. In the mid-1970s the school mixed it up, turning about half the dorms in each quadrangle over to each sex. A couple of years later, two male students wrote a story about how much better their freshman dorm, Hemingway Hall, looked and smelled with female occupants. Hemingway "is much more colorful than in past years," the story said. "The nameplates on the doors no longer hold the typed white cards that give the name and hometown of the occupant. Instead, note boards with felt tip pens give messages of phone calls received and visits missed." As for the stairs, they "appear much cleaner than in past years, when there was a combination of beer and vomit on the floors and walls."

One of the stranger Vanderbilt traditions was known as "Pig Run," where freshman girls learned which sorority has chosen them as a pledge. The girls would congregate in one spot and, after receiving their bids, run one at a time through a gauntlet of male students to their new sorority houses. The most memorable thing that happened most years during Pig Run is that a girl would slip and fall in the mud. But in 1978 one of the pledges was injured by a snowball and was taken to the hospital.

Students waiting on Sorority Bid Day (also known as the Pig Run) in the 1970s
Photographic Archives, Vanderbilt University

The only thing stranger than the Pig Run was Derby Week, when each new sorority class would compete in a series of games, events, and skits sponsored by the Sigma Chi fraternity. In one popular Derby Week event, sorority girls would compete against each other by jumping into a pit of mud in an attempt to be the first girl to rescue a Sigma Chi member's hat. Not surprisingly, Derby Week was frequently criticized by some students and faculty members as sexist from about 1980 on. "Offensive, disgusting, and filthy," one person wrote in *The Hustler* in 1981. Sigma Chi members would always defend the event by pointing out that it raised money for charity.

From available evidence it would appear that Vanderbilt students were interested in campus politics until the late 1960s. Then, after students fought for and won a voice in how the school was run, a tradition of apathy descended on student government organizations that never went away. In February 1974 no one applied to run for thirteen of the forty-four positions on student government committees. The jobs were only filled after the deadlines were extended and the school newspaper ran an editorial imploring people to volunteer for the positions.

It may very well be that Vanderbilt students have historically not done enough crazy things. However, student Tony Lanzillo set a world record in January 1976 by crawling 6.46 miles around the Vanderbilt track. Lanzillo started on a Saturday at 6:40 a.m. and crawled for nine and a half hours. "When I first thought about it, I thought it would be easy, but I now realize that crawling is a very unnatural act which requires the use of muscles that are not normally used," said Lanzillo, who did it to raise money for the Vanderbilt Children's Hospital.

Thanks to the school's so-called Honor System, under which students agree not to cheat on exams or plagiarize term papers, Vanderbilt students built up a general reputation as an honest group. However, that image has been occasionally tarnished by well-publicized campus scandals. One took place in 1981, when dozens of students, through the use of code numbers, cheated the telephone company out of about forty thousand dollars in long distance charges. (To the dismay of a *Hustler* editorial, the students were given complete amnesty.) Another occurred in April 1989, when twenty-five

Vanderbilt students or ex-Vanderbilt students were arrested for manufacturing false ID cards as part of a citywide crackdown.

For most of its history Vanderbilt seniors elected their most deserving male student to be the Bachelor of Ugliness and the most deserving female to be the Lady of the Bracelet. However, the awards were discontinued in 1982 because of lack of interest.

There have been some unusual organizations in Vanderbilt history, but perhaps the most bizarre of all time is a 1988-89 group called Students for the Immediate Installation of Condom Machines. SIICM, as it was abbreviated, launched a crusade to pressure Vanderbilt administrators to install condom machines in dormitory bathrooms. Chancellor Joe Wyatt at first balked at the idea, which led SIICM to circulate a petition in favor of condom machines that garnered 1,259 student signatures. Wyatt eventually submitted to the will of the students, and seventeen glorious condom machines were installed in late January 1989.

The Helpful Bridge Builder

Arthur J. Dyer made the most of his life. He started with little and ended up as one of the most important and influential business owners in Nashville history. Along the way, he built countless structures and had a hand in changing the city he loved, usually for the better. But it is not because of these things that Dyer merits a passage in a history of Vanderbilt. Dyer's experiences are unusually well-documented, and they are representative of those of thousands of people who attended Vanderbilt during its first few decades. In addition, he was one of the most helpful and active alumni in the history of the school.

Dyer was poor when he enrolled at Vanderbilt in 1887. According to an unpublished biography written in the 1950s, Dyer could barely afford the seventy-eight dollar per year tuition. The suitcase he brought with him to school held virtually all the possessions he had at that time: underwear, socks, a few shirts made by his mother, a Bible, and some crude engineering and surveying instruments. Like many other freshmen that year, Dyer shared a room in one of the buildings on West Side Row. In later years, he and a classmate rented a room from William J. Vaughn, a mathematics professor who lived on campus.

A few anecdotes paint a picture of Dyer's college years. While he was a student, the campus gathering spot was also the school's only source of water – a community pump where upperclassmen often dunked freshmen as a form of hazing. (Dyer remembered being dunked a few times during his first year of college.) The campus rage at the time was bicycling; Dyer actually won a cycling race that took place at Sulphur Dell park. Another thing that Dyer did in his spare time was visit the sister of a classmate who lived in Edgefield. Since he often could not afford the horse car fare, Dyer frequently walked across town to see her.

The most curious anecdote about Dyer's undergraduate years took place his sophomore year. On January 4, 1889, Wesley Hall caught on fire. According to the coverage of the event in the *Nashville American*, one of the first people on the scene to help extinguish the blaze was Arthur Dyer.

Dyer, like many other students in the 1880s, arrived on campus deficient in several subjects and had to take remedial classes. By the beginning of his second year Dyer was a full-fledged student in engineering, a department that was at that time run by Dean Olin Landreth. Landreth was a civil and mechanical engineer, and so it is not surprising that Dyer decided to specialize in civil engineering. During the summers Dyer found jobs in his chosen specialty, working one year as a draftsman for an engineering firm.

Arthur J. Dyer
Photo courtesy of A.J. Dyer III

At that time, engineering students were required to write a thesis to graduate. Dyer and his

THE GYM WITH THE BENCHES IN THE WRONG PLACE

The first year Vanderbilt fielded a basketball team was 1893, when nine Vanderbilt students played a team put together by the Nashville YMCA. It wasn't exactly a high-scoring affair, as Vanderbilt edged the YMCA team 9-6.

During the next few decades, basketball began to catch on at Vanderbilt. By about 1960 many students, alumni, and fans would get more excited about basketball than football. Among the notable points of Vanderbilt basketball history:

During the early days of college basketball there wasn't much standardization when it came to equipment. Some schools had wooden backboards; others had wire mesh backboards. When Vanderbilt played its first road game at Howard College in Birmingham, Howard had a ceiling so low that players had to bounce the ball off the ceiling to make a shot.

Vanderbilt's first basketball championship came in the 1919-20 season, when, by virtue of their conference record, the Commodores won the Southern Intercollegiate Athletic Association championship. The achievement was given almost no media coverage because at that time, there was little or no seating or attendance at basketball games. The captain and coach of that 1920 team was Thomas Zerfoss, who later became a physician and the director of the Vanderbilt Student Health Service.

During the first half of the twentieth century the task of coaching the basketball team fell to an assistant football coach. Norm Cooper, who coached the basketball team in the 1946-47 season, said that he and fellow football assistant coach Jim Scoggins flipped a coin to see who would coach the basketball team that year.

In 1947, after several years of being humiliated by Adolph Rupp's Kentucky teams (once by a final score of 98-29), Vanderbilt hired Georgia Tech alumnus Bob Polk to be its first full-time head basketball coach. Scholarship basketball players were rare at that time,

The Vanderbilt basketball team in 1908
The Banner Collection, Nashville Public Library, The Nashville Room

and at first Polk didn't have much to work with. "I would walk around the campus and ask every tall guy I saw if he could play basketball," Polk later told author Roy Neel. Polk remained the Vanderbilt coach for thirteen seasons. During that stretch Vanderbilt had the upper hand on every other Southeastern Conference opponent except Kentucky and Tennessee. Under Polk, Vanderbilt basketball became far more successful than Vanderbilt football, which is one reason Polk and football coach Art Guepe did not get along.

Polk's greatest victory as a coach came in March 1951, when Vanderbilt won the SEC tournament with a televised upset of Kentucky, 61-57. The next year the Kentucky basketball program was engulfed in a point shaving scandal, which led many people to wonder whether the Wildcats actually lost that game on purpose.

Prior to the opening of Memorial Gymnasium in the 1952-53 season the Vanderbilt basketball team didn't have a respectable home. The team started by playing its home games in the Old Gym, then moved to Nashville's Hippodrome Theater, and by the 1930s was playing some home games in the East High School Gymnasium. In the 1940s Vanderbilt played most home games at the Old Gym again, which at that time had a wing that stretched onto what later became Alumni Lawn. But the Commodores also played home games at the David Lipscomb College gymnasium and at the Navy Classification Center on Thompson Lane.

Memorial Gymnasium is one of the few arenas in the United States where the court is actually higher than the first several rows of seats. Why did architect Edwin Keeble design the building like this? Because it saved money. When he sketched the building in 1949, Keeble was told to design an arena that had ten thousand seats but only cost $1.5 million. (At the time, the University of Kentucky was spending $4.5 million to build an arena not much larger than that.) Keeble found that by cramming the first few rows of seats as low as possible that he was able to build a smaller, cheaper building.

Memorial Gymnasium's unusual design is the reason that during basketball games, the team benches are located behind the baskets instead of along the side of the court. Over the years, this unusual arrangement is one reason Memorial Gymnasium became a very difficult place for visiting basketball teams to win.

Vanderbilt football fans are generally a calm lot, but something happens to school supporters during basketball season. Nothing summarizes the seriousness with which Vanderbilt fans take their sport than a story in the student newspaper of the University of Tennessee in February 1968. "Then there is the ever present problem of playing at Vanderbilt Gym," the story said. "Crowd noise is to be expected at any opposing school's gym, and this is how it should be. However, crowd abuse is another matter. Booing opponents, telling them to go to hell, throwing things on the floor and being rude to visiting

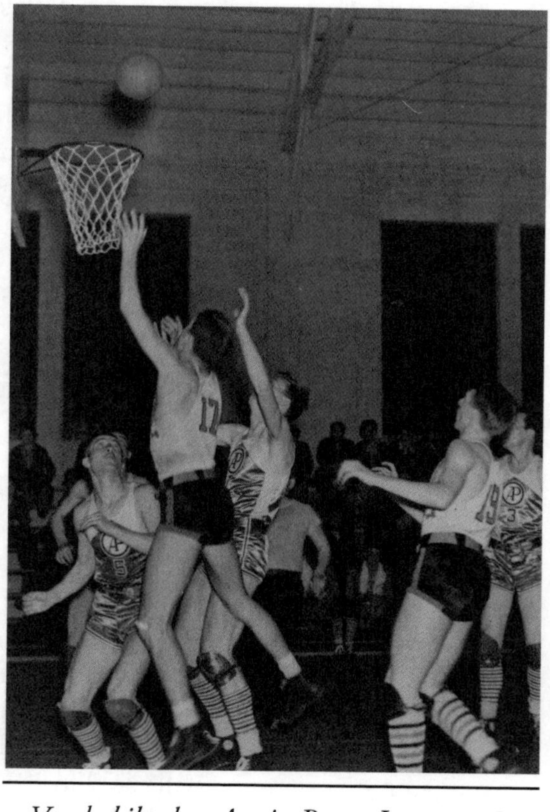

Vanderbilt plays Austin Peay - January 1938
Photographic Archives, Vanderbilt University

spectators is not only grossly unsportsmanlike, but also tends to intimidate the referees, causing them to call an uneven game. It is simply in bad taste and gives the school a bad reputation."

Roy Skinner replaced Polk in 1962 and over the course of his fifteen seasons won sixty-eight percent of his games, becoming the most successful basketball coach in Vanderbilt history. Skinner's most successful team was in 1964-65. Led by a six-foot-eight player named Clyde Lee, Vanderbilt won the SEC championship and barely lost to a heavily favored Michigan team 87-85 in a game that sent Michigan to the Final Four. That team did so well that after the season, Vanderbilt installed balconies in Memorial Gym to accommodate more fans.

Vanderbilt's all-time leading scorer is Phil Cox, who played from 1981 through 1985 and scored 1,725 points during that time. The school's top rebounder is Clyde Lee, who grabbed 1,223 rebounds from 1964 through 1966 (before freshmen were allowed to play varsity ball). However, many believe that Vanderbilt's greatest player ever was Jan van Breda Kolff, star of the 1973-74 SEC Champion Vanderbilt team. Van Breda Kolff later went onto a successful NBA career and a disappointing stint as Vanderbilt head basketball coach in the 1990s.

Vanderbilt fans will forever disagree about the greatest Commodore basketball team of all-time. The three teams that have made it furthest in NCAA tournaments were in 1965, 1988, and 1993. The 1988 team pulled one of the greatest comebacks in the history of the tournament, coming back from a six-point deficit in the final twenty seconds to beat Pittsburgh to advance to the final sixteen, where Vanderbilt lost to Kansas. The 1993 Vanderbilt team, led by three-point shooters such as Billy McCaffrey, Ronnie McMahan, and Kevin Anglin, won the Southeastern Conference regular season championship and then advanced to the final sixteen, losing to Temple.

A tennis ball once cost Vanderbilt the SEC basketball championship. In January 1989 Vanderbilt was leading Florida at Memorial Gymnasium 72-70 with two seconds to go in the game when someone threw a tennis ball at Florida player Dwayne Schintzius. (Schintzius, who had attacked a fellow Florida student with a tennis racket a few months earlier, was the object of scorn all over the conference that year.) The referee called a technical foul against Vanderbilt because of the thrown tennis ball. Schintzius calmly hit two free throws and sent the game into overtime, where the Gators prevailed 81-78. Florida won the conference with a 13-5 record that year, edging out 12-6 Vanderbilt.

Not that it compares with the NCAA tournament, but the 1990 Commodore basketball team won the NIT tournament with wins over Louisiana Tech, Tennessee, New Orleans, Penn State, and St. Louis.

Harvie versus the football team

Probably no chancellor has ever felt more ambivalent than Harvie Branscomb felt on Saturday, October 6, 1951. Because as Branscomb watched his football team pull a stunning upset of Alabama, he feared that the victory would do serious damage to his effort to reform the school's athletic program. And it did.

During the first four decades of the twentieth century Vanderbilt's football team was a glorious success on the field. Under legendary coach Dan McGugin, who coached the team from 1907 until 1934, the Commodores won 197 and lost 55 – one of the best records of that era. Vanderbilt was a national football powerhouse, comparable to Texas, Georgia Tech, and Michigan.

But after World War II college football evolved into a different sport. Crowds became larger and media attention to the games became more intense. Schools began actively recruiting, giving away sports scholarships and, in some cases, inventing majors such as physical education to accommodate students who wouldn't be admitted to college if it weren't for their athletic skill. Substitutions were legalized, resulting in more skill at each position and more players. There were even some well-publicized college sports scandals. In 1951 three Kentucky basketball players were arrested for allegedly taking bribes to shave points in a National Invitational Tournament game two years earlier. All of these factors increased the cost and political baggage of fielding a college football team and made it difficult for small, academically inclined private schools such as Vanderbilt to win on the field.

The first time these issues coalesced into a campus discussion appears to have been in the fall of 1939, when head coach Ray Morrison fielded a disappointing football team. As the season ended, *The Hustler* conducted an unscientific student survey about the athletic department. The survey claimed that 70 percent of Vanderbilt's students thought that the school should keep pace with the "professionalizing" of college football. An even greater percentage said Vanderbilt should stay in its conference and that it should make

The Vanderbilt football team celebrates a touchdown against Kentucky in 1955
Photographic Archives, Vanderbilt University

changes within the athletic program to improve the win-loss record of the football team. Less than one percent favored discontinuing intercollegiate sports.

A few weeks later Chancellor Oliver Carmichael took two steps to respond to the discontent among students and alumni. One was to fire Ray Morrison and replace him with Red Sanders. The other was to create an athletic director position, staffed by campus health director Thomas Zerfoss.

Thanks to the coaching of Sanders and his successor Bill Edwards, Vanderbilt fielded mostly winning teams in the 1940s. But because of the increasing costs of playing football, Vanderbilt's athletic department was running sizable financial deficits. In part because of the cost, Harvie Branscomb became convinced after he became chancellor in 1946 that Vanderbilt could no longer go along with the trends in Southeastern Conference football. "Football had become big business, with large professional staffs, astronomical budgets, and enormous public following," Branscomb wrote in his memoirs. "Unfortunately, the gladiators in these titanic struggles were college students who presumably had come to the institution to secure the education essential for their future careers."

During Branscomb's tenure he thrice tried to reform the system and failed each time. His first notion was to begin to build a rivalry between Vanderbilt and Ivy League schools in an attempt to change Vanderbilt's team into more of a low-budget program. In this effort Vanderbilt played a game against Yale in October 1948. However, it wasn't such a close contest. Vanderbilt trounced Yale 35-0, after which Yale said it no longer wanted to play Vanderbilt.

Two years later Branscomb, with the endorsement of the Vanderbilt Board of Trust, made a series of proposals to the presidents of the other Southeastern Conference schools. Among the suggestions were the elimination of bowl games, the discontinuation of spring practice, a ban on unlimited substitutions, and a severe reduction in the number of athletic scholarships.

Branscomb's suggestions met with mixed reviews among students and faculty, producing "a shower of onions and orchids around the campus," a *Hustler* columnist wrote that week. Many people probably reacted to the suggestions much like *Nashville Banner* columnist

Fred Russell. Russell, a Vanderbilt alum who probably attended more of the school's sporting events in the twentieth century than any other person, said he agreed with Branscomb on several points, such as the elimination of spring practice. But unlike Branscomb, Russell believed that the Vanderbilt athletic department could coexist with a Vanderbilt education. "There are at least 50,000 times more prep and high school football players today than there were available at the time Vanderbilt began playing football," Russell wrote. "Among that number certainly there must be, each year, 25 or 30 scholastically qualified boys of above-average athletic ability to whom a university of Vanderbilt's type appeals."

As it turns out, Branscomb couldn't have picked a worse time to be making the case that Vanderbilt couldn't compete in the SEC. Three days after the proposals were made public, Vanderbilt shocked Alabama 22-20. "The alumni forgot about the reforms and began dreaming about a possible bowl game," Branscomb wrote later. The chancellor's proposals, made in February 1952, were met with mild amusement by the presidents of the other SEC schools. The only suggestion that was accepted was a small reduction in scholarships, which was reversed years later.

Branscomb's final attempt to stem the tide of what he perceived to be the professionalization of college football was done in secret. In the late 1950s (the exact date is not given in Branscomb's memoirs), the Vanderbilt chancellor called a meeting of the presidents of six southern private universities – the other five being Georgia Tech, SMU, Rice, Duke, and probably Tulane. Branscomb suggested to the other college presidents that they form a new sports conference, so that they would no longer have to try to keep up with the big-time athletic programs of southern public schools.

However, the "Southern Ivy League" never got off the ground. Duke did not want to give up its rivalry with the University of North Carolina. Georgia Tech didn't want to jeopardize its game with Georgia. And SMU and Rice were not willing to give up their share of Cotton Bowl receipts.

By the time Branscomb resigned as chancellor in 1963, Vanderbilt's football team was no longer winning the way it had prior to World War II. Under Coach Art Guepe, who fielded a successful

8-3 team in 1955, the Commodores had three straight losing seasons in 1960, 1961, and 1962. Some alumni blamed this phenomenon on Branscomb, saying he was not supporting the team as he should. When Alexander Heard became chancellor, he hired a new athletic director and took many steps to support football. But the team did no better on the field.

In his retirement Branscomb believed that schools like Vanderbilt should set up sister "athletic schools to provide the semi-professional player" needed to compete with the Alabamas and Tennessees of the world. Better that, he said, than "suffer the humiliating weekend disasters which are the usual alternative."

Lust, Repression, and Good Clean Fun

In the early 1950s there were four men for every woman on the Vanderbilt campus. And although there were probably exceptions to the rule, as far as Vanderbilt boys were concerned the girls were to be admired, ogled, joked about, lusted after, and dreamed about, but not touched. At least not much. This repressed culture created some unusual student behavior.

At Vanderbilt, in the early 1950s, girls were generally either engaged, "pinned" (which meant "engaged to be engaged"), or free. From reading student publications in the 1950s, one gathers that there was considerable pressure for girls to be engaged or pinned. Many sororities kept up with the total number of its members in each category. And as *The Hustler* said in a 1952 feature about the nineteen coeds on campus who were about to get married, a bride "typifies the virtues of grace and dignity" and " represents the summit of all that is truly beautiful."

The formation of a new couple was quite an event. According to one article in *The Hustler*, an engagement or pinning resulted in the sorority sisters sending cigars to the fraternity and the fraternity brothers sending flowers to the sorority. "The pinning has its light side too, though, for it is usually followed by a ducking of the newly 'engaged to be engaged' pair in the lake at Centennial Park," the article went on to say.

Vanderbilt students, male and female, show off their legs in 1955
Photographic Archives, Vanderbilt University

And how did girls get engaged? Apparently by being nice and witty; by being smart (but not too smart); by being in a good sorority; by hanging out with pretty friends; by keeping themselves looking good; and by entering a lot of beauty contests. The 1950s was the era of the beauty pageant at Vanderbilt. By the middle of the decade two of the biggest events of the school year were the Miss Commodore contest (sponsored by *The Commodore* yearbook) and the Maid of Cotton contest (sponsored by *The Hustler).*

Brave girls went even further than that. In the late 1940s Vanderbilt students produced a humor magazine called *The Masquerader.* The publication contained inside jokes about faculty members and sororities, poems, and short stories. Starting around 1948, *The Masquerader* always had a pretty Vanderbilt girl on its cover. Then came the October 1949 issue. On its cover was a topless girl with her back to the camera, holding a towel across her chest. It was impossible to tell who the girl was, but *The Masquerader* implied that she was a Vanderbilt student. The publication even solicited guesses from its readers as to who the sexy cover girl might be.

Branscomb was not amused. Because of the suggestive cover, the student publications board banned *The Masquerader*. But the publication of sexy photos of girls continued. Within months students had started another humor publication called *The Chase*, which also had sexy covers and contained even more innuendo than its predecessor. (Not to be outdone by *The Hustler* and *The Commodore*, *The Chase* started its own beauty pageant called the Goddess of *The Chase*.) In 1952, *The Chase* contained a full-size calendar with a photograph of a Vanderbilt coed for each month.

Meanwhile, *The Hustler* began a weekly feature called the Coed of the Week — a photograph of an attractive, smiling coed, usually wearing shorts and a tight sweater and accompanied by a suggestive cutline. "Miss Virginia Kincannon, a junior from Memphis, is well liked for jumping up and down in front of the student body," reads a typical cutline. "She, distractingly, leads cheers, which is the reason most students go to basketball games." A few weeks later: "A gal who looks as if she had rather be doing something besides studying is Miss Shirley Moore, Atlanta junior who lives in the Kappa Alpha Theta house."

Of course, this was pretty lame stuff compared to things that would happen on the Vanderbilt campus after 1970. But in their time these were radical steps by the editors of such student publications and the girls who posed in them. Eventually the students would take it too far. In May 1954 *The Chase* published an entire issue in honor of Mother's Day. One page near the back showed four photographs with the words "Everyone Loves Mother" across the page. Three of the four photos had clear sexual implications; the fourth was the picture of a small girl with the words "Daughter loves mother (and wants to be one too)" written beneath it.

The feature, which was stranger than it was funny, caused Vanderbilt University a big headache. As it turns out, the young girl (whose picture the editors had apparently stumbled across somewhere) turned out to be the daughter of R.L. Langford, the minister of Nashville's Dalewood Methodist Church. Langford sued *The Chase*, editor Jim Gilliland, Vanderbilt University, and printer Benson Printing Co. for $180,000 in damages.

This time Branscomb came down harder than before. The school ordered *The Chase* to cease publication, allowing the magazine's office in Alumni Hall to become the new office of campus radio station WVU. A few months later, the student publications board published a list of new editorial standards that forbade sexual content in student newspapers and magazines. "No printed matter should deal with matters of sex in an obscene or vulgar manner or simply for the sake of dealing with sex," the new rule said. The policy conceded that there was legitimate sexual content in many books read in class. But the policy said "in the case of Shakespeare or in the case of Hemingway, sex is never an end in itself, but a part of the plot vehicle by means of which the artist is better able to develop his theme."

The Hustler objected to the new policy of censorship, and even went as far as reprinting the controversial *Chase* layout on its front page (for which the publications board fired *Hustler* editor Ormonde Plater). But this time, Branscomb meant business. Banning sex in student publications was only the first step. About that time, the chancellor wrote a letter to *The Tennessean*, assuring Nashville residents that, unlike other Southeastern Conference schools, Vanderbilt was not going to have scantily clad majorettes dancing at football games. (Branscomb's letter was chosen by the morning paper as the best letter of the week, and *The Tennessean* sent the chancellor a dollar as a prize.)

If Branscomb's intention was to make Vanderbilt students behave, his efforts failed. In 1952 students had begun taking part in the national fad known as the "panty raid." By the middle of the decade panty raids on the Vanderbilt campus began to get larger and even violent.

The panty raid of November 26, 1957, is one that few people involved will forget. It started as a pep rally, but before long hundreds of male students made their way to McTyeire Hall, where they damaged a lot of furniture. Next the crowd went to Cole Hall, and then Tolman Hall (both girls' dorms at that time). By the time the mob crossed Twenty-first Avenue on its way to the Peabody campus, the

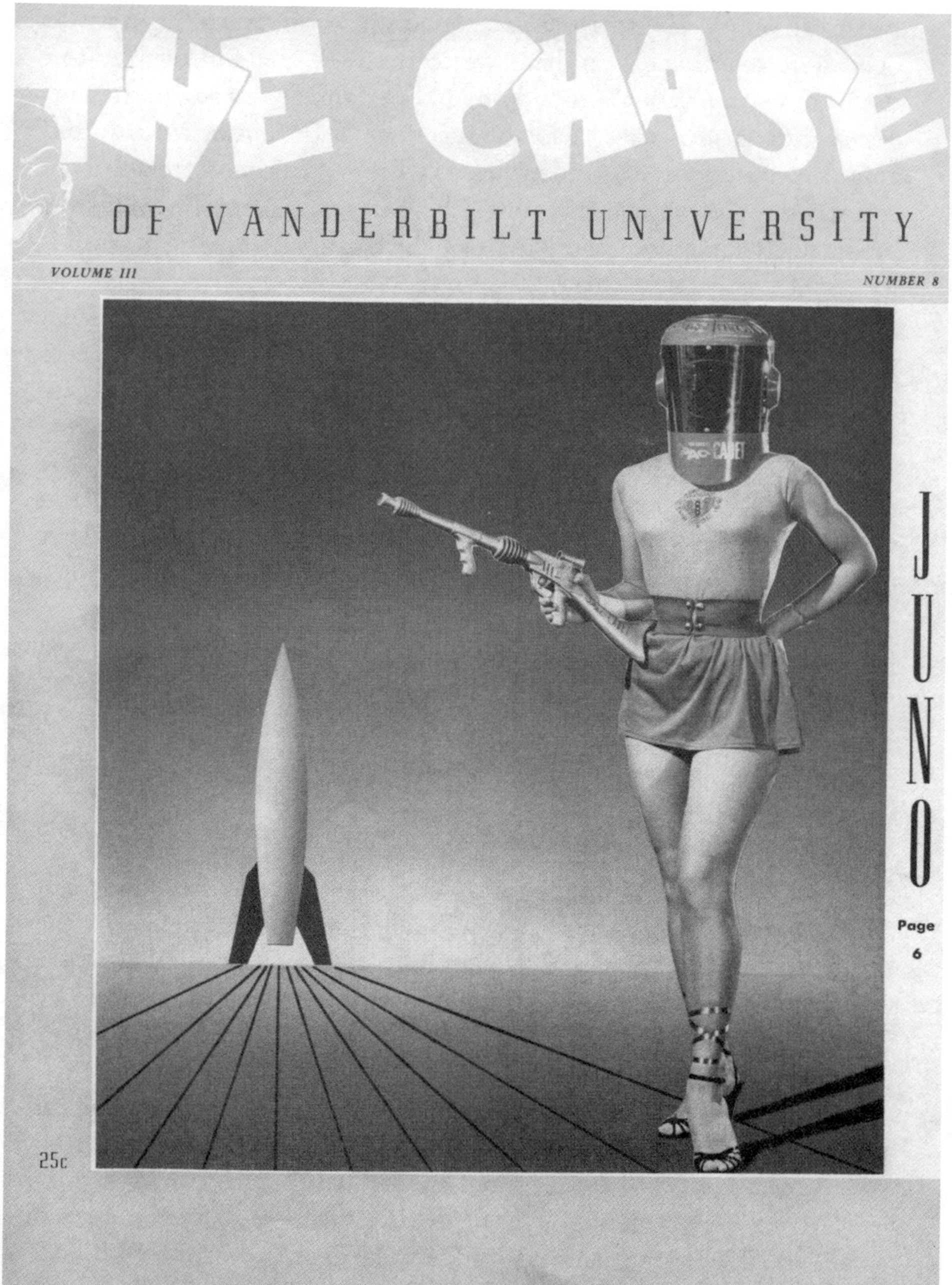

A typical cover of the campus publication "The Chase"
The Carey Collection

Nashville police department's riot squad was on its way. When it was over more than twenty students were arrested and about twelve hundred dollars in personal property had been damaged or stolen, including several slashed tires, a lot of furniture, a dumpster, and untold amounts of underwear. One professor who was visiting from a foreign country saw the debacle and said, "I have never seen anything like this before . . . To me I would say it looks like the top of American stupidity."

Branscomb, of course, was horrified. The next day he called a meeting of all students, demanding that everyone involved take responsibility for their actions. A few days later, the student senate wrote a letter of apology to the students at Peabody. "I remember it quite well," said John Hardcastle, a member of the student senate at the time. "I was late to the meeting, and as I walked in there was a round of applause and I was told that since I was late that I would get to write and deliver the letter to President Henry Hill of Peabody." The senate voted to assess a fifty-cent fine on all Vanderbilt students to to pay for the damage. Eventually, 265 students came forward and admitted to their roles in the great panty raid of 1957.

THE MEDICAL SCHOOL NEARLY GOES AWAY

There were two turning points in the history of the Vanderbilt Medical School. The first was in 1925, when the school left the south campus and moved to its new state-of-the-art hospital complex on Twenty-first Avenue, climaxing fifteen years of work by Chancellor James Kirkland. The second was in 1949, when the board of trust seriously considered shutting the school down.

During the two decades following the Vanderbilt Medical School's move to the main campus in 1925, Vanderbilt was the finest and best-equipped medical school in the South. Among its faculty were men who were giants in their fields. One of the most celebrated was Alfred Blalock, a surgeon who in the 1930s was credited with noting the connection between shock and blood loss, a link that saved the lives of countless patients. In 1944 Blalock became the first surgeon in the world to successfully conduct a "blue baby" operation, correcting a birth defect that restricted oxygen flow in babies. Another Vanderbilt medical pioneer was Ernest Goodpasture, a pathologist who in the late 1920s proved that chicken eggs could be used to breed viruses. Goodpasture's simple discovery was a milestone in the development of vaccines. "Thousands of soldiers in World War II and the Korean War survived long sieges in tropic swampland without a single case of yellow fever or typhus fever – thanks to the vaccine made possible through Dr. Goodpasture's discoveries," a story about Goodpasture said years later. "Smallpox vaccine was made so inexpensive by his method of producing it inside an egg that whole nations have been vaccinated by it."

However, Vanderbilt's hospital and medical school began having financial difficulties in the late 1930s, and the problems began to have a serious impact on the quality of instruction after World War II. In the late 1940s most of the private money that had supported medical training – including the General Education Board — evaporated. By the end of World War II the Vanderbilt hospital was reporting sizable deficits, eating away at endowment and eroding the medical school's ability to hire and retain the best professors.

Vanderbilt's financial problems forced the school to rethink its policy of treating patients for free. In 1948 Vanderbilt (officially, at least) eliminated the practice of giving free care for indigents, setting a policy that all patients had to pay a minimum daily charge of $8.50 to be treated. But in practice, the school couldn't actually force poor people to pay. Early attempts to get the government of Nashville or Davidson County to take care of the unpaid bills failed.

It was at this point that Goodpasture, by now the dean of the medical school, made a radical proposal: do away with the hospital and the medical school and convert both into a research facility. In hindsight, Goodpasture's suggestion seems like an extreme one. But there were those who took his idea seriously. In an era before almost anyone had private health insurance or was covered by government-sponsored programs such as Medicaid, it was extremely difficult for hospitals to make ends meet. And under Goodpasture's suggestion, it was not as if Vanderbilt would no longer be making a contribution to medical society. It would still be making medical discoveries and helping to train doctors under a post-MD program that Goodpasture

The Vanderbilt Medical Center in the early 1970s
The Banner Collection, Nashville Public Library, The Nashville Room

envisioned. It just wouldn't be treating patients anymore.

Despite Goodpasture's stature and some very good arguments, the board of trust rejected the dean's suggestion. (Goodpasture resigned shortly thereafter and was replaced as dean by John Youmans.) After extensive study, Vanderbilt then set off on a new course of strategy: to increase the flow of patients into the Vanderbilt hospital, thus improving the likelihood of operating the facility in the black.

At the time Nashville had two public hospitals: Nashville General Hospital downtown for white patients and Hubbard Hospital in north Nashville for black patients. Both, of course, were heavily subsidized by taxpayers. To increase patient flow, Vanderbilt first proposed that the city close General Hospital and build a new and more efficient public hospital next to the Vanderbilt campus, which the city could then pay Vanderbilt to run. The council rejected that proposal. Next, Vanderbilt suggested that it take over the operation of General Hospital and treat indigent patients there for a fee. After a nasty debate, full of accusations about the city "selling its sick" to Vanderbilt, the council agreed to the idea. In 1952 Vanderbilt took over the operation of General Hospital.

Running a long-neglected hospital didn't turn out to be a financial panacea. After two years of running both hospitals at about two-thirds capacity, plaster began falling from the ceiling at General Hospital in March 1954, giving further evidence of the gross inadequacy of the hospital building. A few months later Nashville Mayor Ben West appointed a five-person committee to come up with a recommendation on what to do with General. The group recommended the city close General Hospital and begin paying Vanderbilt an estimated $600,000 per year to care for all of the city's indigent white patients at its main facility on campus.

However, that proposal was also rejected by the council 13-7 after yet another ugly debate about Vanderbilt's intentions. "Vanderbilt is the most inhumane institution in Tennessee," a councilman named Charles Riley said during the proceedings. "It will not agree to any contract until it has robbed the city's treasury." Nashville's morning newspaper, which had supported the Vanderbilt deal, was disgusted with the council vote. "The city council has hit what is a new low even for that undistinguished assembly," *The Tennessean* said. Eventually the city repaired the General Hospital building, turned the operation of the facility over to an independent board, and negotiated a contract with Vanderbilt under which its doctors and medical students would help provide professional care there. The fate of General Hospital would remain a question mark through the mid-1990s, when, after a long debate, the old facility was finally shut down and its functions moved to the Hubbard building (which was renamed General Hospital after the move). Under the original blueprint, the new General Hospital would be run solely by Meharry Medical College. But in 1999 Vanderbilt and Meharry worked out an agreement under which the two medical schools would work together to run the new General Hospital and share some research and academic programs.

The other way Vanderbilt increased patient flow in the 1950s had to do with the treatment of veterans. Prior to that time Nashville's Veterans Administration hospital was located on White Bridge Road, where it went by the name Thayer VA Hospital. After World War II national VA director Paul Magnuson began co-locating VA hospitals with medical schools, thus making it easier, cheaper, and more efficient to get physicians to work there. In the early 1950s the VA and Vanderbilt worked out a plan under which the government would build a new hospital just south of the campus. At the last minute, however, Tennessee Congressman Joe Evins nearly canceled the plan to move the hospital because of the high cost of land near Vanderbilt. At that point officials at medical schools across the country criticized Evins' political meddling, pointing out that a VA hospital adjacent to Vanderbilt would provide better health care and run cheaper than one located on its own. Evins backed down, and the hospital broke ground in 1959.

Because of the increase of health insurance plans and the federal government's formation of Medicaid, the 1960s would be much easier years for hospitals than the previous decade. By the mid-1970s Vanderbilt felt good enough about its future that it broke ground on a $74 million new medical center just south of the existing structure – the largest construction project undertaken on the Vanderbilt campus to that point.

VISITS, BIZARRE AND FORTUITOUS

Not every important person who came to the Vanderbilt campus stayed long. Some stopped by only long enough to have an experience that they and others would never forget.

One person who didn't have this honor was Cornelius Vanderbilt, who never stepped foot on the campus named for him. But his son William Henry Vanderbilt visited the school briefly in September 1875, while the Main Building was under construction. The younger Vanderbilt, who was vice president of the New York, Central, and Hudson River Railroad at the time, walked into the Main Building while students were arranging the library. William Henry was so impressed that he offered $1,000 toward the purchase of more books. Only a few years later, William Henry contributed $150,000 toward the construction of the second large structure to be built on campus, Wesley Hall.

In 1907 President Theodore Roosevelt made a very short visit to Nashville and made only three stops before he got back on the train and left. The most memorable of those stops was to The Hermitage, where legend has it that he took a sip of Maxwell House coffee and said it was "Good to the Last Drop." (In fact, newspaper accounts of his visit report that Roosevelt took a sip of coffee and said, "That's the kind of stuff I like to drink, by George, when I hunt bears.") One of Roosevelt's other stops that day was to the south Nashville campus of the Peabody Normal School. A few years later Roosevelt and the other trustees of the Peabody Education Fund agreed to move the institution to a site near Vanderbilt and to transform it into a full-fledged teaching college.

The first black person to visit the campus in something other than a menial role was probably Booker T. Washington, who spoke at chapel in April 1909. Washington talked about the need to help the black race through better education and better understanding. He also complained about the media's coverage of the race issue. "If one Negro committed a crime the whole country knew all the particulars the next morning," Washington said. "But if each of one hundred

Negroes build a house, it would be known only in their immediate vicinity. Why is this true? The reason is apparent. The negro's crime and the white man's lynching is the sensational exception while this vast improvement that is going on all the time is the regular order of things."

Two of the most successful businessmen in Nashville history were Vanderbilt dropouts. One was James C. Bradford Sr., who founded the Nashville brokerage firm J.C. Bradford & Co. in 1927. The other was Rogers Caldwell, who started a Nashville-based municipal bond house and used it to build a financial empire consisting of insurance companies, real estate, manufacturers, newspapers, and even a minor league baseball team. Neither man was proud of the fact that he never graduated. Years after his empire had collapsed, Caldwell said that he wished he had acquired a better knowledge of economics before he went into business.

In 1921 General John Pershing visited the Vanderbilt campus and made a speech at College Hall. Attendance was optional, but one group of people that apparently showed up were young ladies, who, according to one account, "massed themselves on the front steps of college hall and attempted to make a hit with the young officers present in General Pershing's retinue."

Shortly after Harvie Branscomb became chancellor, he made a considerable effort to get Harold Stirling Vanderbilt, a trustee who had inherited much of what was left of Cornelius Vanderbilt's fortune, interested in the institution named for his family. At first the effort was fruitless. Then, Harold Vanderbilt's secretary called one day and said that her boss would be stopping by the school for a short visit in a few days. Branscomb got himself and the campus as ready as he could, hand-picking faculty and students that he wanted Mr. Vanderbilt to meet. To the chancellor's relief, the visit was a pleasant one. Vanderbilt was impressed with the campus and, according to Branscomb's memoirs, "seemed surprised that so many people would have given money to an institution named for his family." It was the beginning of a close relationship between Harold Stirling Vanderbilt and the school. He eventually became chairman of the board and left millions of dollars to the school when he died.

Vanderbilt's football coaches in the 1940s. Paul "Bear" Bryant is second from the left; Red Sanders is third from the left.
Photographic Archives, Vanderbilt University

Paul "Bear" Bryant, who coached the Alabama Crimson Tide to eight national championships in the 1960s and 1970s, was the line coach at Vanderbilt in 1940 and 1941 under head football coach Red Sanders. Bryant was Vanderbilt's acting head coach for one game, a contest against a heavily favored Kentucky team in October 1940 that ended in a 7-7 tie. "Acting Coach Bryant did a splendid job of shouldering his responsibilities and leading the Commodores to one of the nation's upsets," *The Hustler* reported that week. However, Bryant joined the Navy at the end of his second season and never came back to Vanderbilt's staff, getting a job as the head coach at Maryland after the war ended and a year later becoming the head coach at Kentucky. Almost immediately Bryant became a thorn in the side of his former employer. Kentucky, which had not outscored Vanderbilt since 1939, beat the Commodores 10-7 in 1946 and 14-0 in 1947.

Throughout the history of both institutions, Vanderbilt University and the Grand Ole Opry had little to do with each other. One of the rare exceptions was Joe Talbot, a Vanderbilt law student in the early 1950s who played guitar for Hank Snow and who said he got a lot of grief on campus for doing so. But in February 1955 the Grand Ole Opry was performed and filmed for several weeks at the Vanderbilt Theater Building on Garland Avenue (a structure that was built in 1948 and torn down in the 1970s). At that time the Opry was regularly performed at the Ryman Auditorium, which could not accommodate filming equipment.

Bronson Ingram, who became chairman of the Vanderbilt Board of Trust in the 1990s, wanted to attend Princeton University, but didn't study enough during his junior and senior years in high school and was not accepted into Princeton's freshman class. Ingram went to Vanderbilt instead, and half way through his freshman year asked Dean of Students Madison Sarratt whether he thought he should transfer to the school he had originally wanted to attend. Sarratt said that he definitely should, and Ingram finished his undergraduate education at Princeton in 1953.

Dr. Jonas Salk, developer of the polio vaccine, came to Vanderbilt in 1957 to inject students with his new serum. *Hustler* reporter Clinton Collins jumped in line, intending to interview Salk but not to get a shot. When he got to the front of the line, Salk was in no mood to give an interview, only to give out vaccine. With little time to waste, Salk said to the student, "Hey, is that Jayne Mansfield over there?" As the student looked away, Salk gave the reporter a shot.

The first American president to visit the "new" Peabody campus was Franklin Roosevelt in 1934. The first president to visit the main Vanderbilt campus was John Kennedy in 1963. By the end of the century presidential visits were almost routine matters. Among the future, standing, or former presidents who spoke at Vanderbilt in the latter part of the century were George Bush (1979), Gerald Ford (1986), Jimmy Carter (1986), and Bill Clinton (several times).

When black power activist Stokley Carmichael made his infamous visit to Vanderbilt in April 1967, a young reporter named Eldridge Cleaver covered the event for a magazine called *Ramparts.* While on campus, Cleaver met Carmichael's spokeswoman. The two eventually married.

In March 1972 a nationally known stripper named Heaven Lee came by the Vanderbilt campus and had dinner with the Alpha Tau Omega sorority. A few weeks later, *The* (Vanderbilt) *Hustler* contained a profile of Lee, illustrated with a nude photograph of her. "Why should anybody be ashamed of their naked body?" Lee said in the story. "After all, we are born without clothes."

Bill Parcells, who coached the New York Giants to two Super Bowl Championships in the 1990s, was the linebacker coach at Vanderbilt in 1974 and 1975 under head coach Steve Sloan.

In November 1974 a comedian named Steve Martin performed at the Different Drummer, a live club located in the basement of Carmichael Towers. At the time, Martin's main claim to fame was that he had been a writer for the "Sonny and Cher" variety show. After his show Martin and a group of students walked over to Krystal to get a bite to eat, and then they headed over to the office of WRVU so that Martin could make an impromptu appearance on what he jokingly called "Radio Free Vanderbilt." However, while they were crossing the campus, Martin and the students were stopped by Assistant Dean Steve Caldwell, who asked to see everyone's student ID card. "The mood of the group and of Martin changed in minutes from fun to disgust," student Randy Hodges wrote in a letter to the school newspaper the next week.

HARVIE VERSUS THE FRAT BOYS

It is undeniable that before there was a Greek system there wasn't much for a Vanderbilt student to do except eat, sleep, study, go to class, and attend chapel. During Vanderbilt University's first few years there were no intercollegiate or intramural athletics, no school publications, few clubs, and no girls (except for a few very popular professors' daughters). Neither Bishop Holland McTyeire nor Chancellor Landon Garland approved of Greek societies, and for years students were not allowed to form such organizations. Garland conceded in 1883, when he allowed students to openly join fraternities for the first time. By 1886 Vanderbilt University had eight such organizations.

In the 1890s fraternities were best described as literary societies that regularly held meetings in off-campus hotels and homes. But starting at about the turn of the century, they began leasing homes off campus. Boys being boys, these boarding-house communities inevitably became places where drinking and other vices would occasionally take place. By around 1905 Chancellor Kirkland blamed just about every off-campus student disturbance on fraternities. He set up a faculty committee, which came up with several regulations such as one that required all parties to end by midnight. But since the houses were located all over the place, it wasn't always easy to enforce the rules.

To find a better way for the Greek organizations to coexist with the school and the city, in 1918 Kirkland appointed a study committee of five faculty members, five alumni, and five students. Among the committee members were professors Edwin Mims and Gus Dyer and trustees Vance Alexander and Lee Loventhal. In May 1919 the committee recommended that all Greek houses be sold and that new

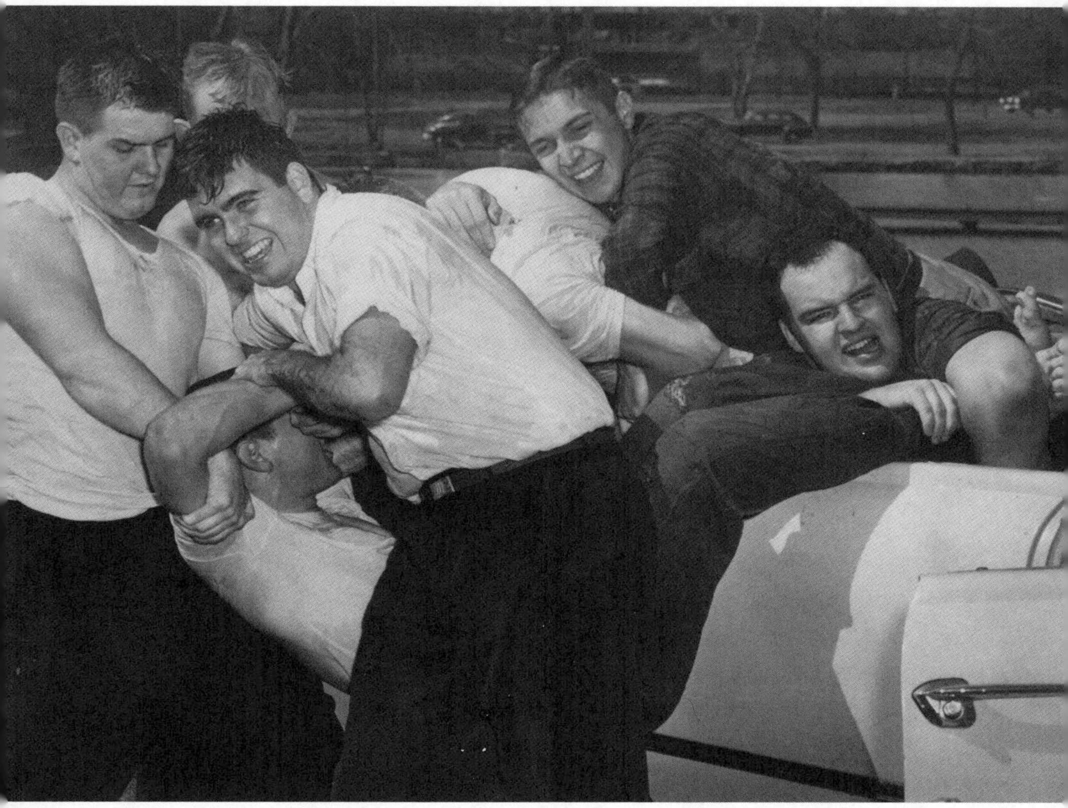

Fraternity boys throwing one of their own into the lake at Centennial Park - 1953
Photographic Archives, Vanderbilt University

dorms be built to house all students. As for the fraternities and sororities, the committee recommended that each of them build a new clubhouse, for activities but not boarding, in the area just west of the main Vanderbilt campus. To make this possible, the committee recommended that the school loan each fraternity and sorority fifty percent of the cost of building these new chapter houses. "The world expects college men to be leaders," the report concluded. "A student who goes through college confining his social life to 20 or 25 boys of his own stratum or group, not living and mixing with the general student body, may be able to say on graduation day that he has had four very delightful years and possibly profitable years, but in many ways they have not prepared him for leadership in this new world in which he is living."

Kirkland never moved ahead with the plan because it was too expensive. At the time of the recommendation Vanderbilt was trying to raise funds for a student center that included a gymnasium with an indoor pool. The project fell short of its financial goals, and the school ended up with a much smaller facility called Alumni Hall that had no gymnasium or pool. Had it succeeded, Kirkland's subsequent plan would have been to build new dormitories and new Greek clubhouses.

When Harvie Branscomb took over as chancellor two generations later, one of the first things he noticed was how much social life at Vanderbilt was dominated by the Greek system. In the late 1940s about three-fourths of the male students and four-fifths of the females were in fraternities or sororities. The members slept in their houses, ate meals in their houses, and brought dates to their houses. Incoming freshmen showed up for rush a week early each fall, so they were already wearing pledge pins and going through initiation rituals before they attended their first classes. Girls who were not accepted into a sorority, or the sorority of their choice, would often drop out of school. Fraternity presidents would meet and decide in secret who would win class elections and who would be elected editor of *The Hustler*. One year they might instruct their members to vote in a bloc for a member of Sigma Alpha Epsilon; the next year it might be Kappa Alpha's turn. Meanwhile, fraternity boys (but not sorority girls, curiously enough) consistently got grades below the school average.

Branscomb set as one of his major goals the de-emphasis of the Greek system at Vanderbilt. He would eventually succeed in doing so, changing the social life of the campus more than any of his predecessors and any of his successors (at least through the end of Chancellor Joe Wyatt's tenure). But the battle between Branscomb and the Greek system was a long and ugly one, and the chancellor made many mistakes along the way.

The first mistake Branscomb made was to try do too many things at once. In 1951, about the same time he was beginning to criticize fraternities, the chancellor went public with a high-minded (but unrealistic) effort to reform college football. This dual approach to "cleaning up" everything that distracted students from academic pursuits made Branscomb quite unpopular. One sarcastic column that ran in *The Hustler* predicted that if the chancellor had his way, life at Vanderbilt would consist of tea and crumpets, recitations, four-hour daily chapel exercises, and mandatory walks by the athletic director. "Oh, for the days when Harvey was only a big white rabbit," the article concluded, in reference to the Jimmy Stewart movie *Harvey*.

Branscomb's second blunder was to focus on rush before he moved on to the more important issue of housing. In the spring of 1952 Branscomb announced that starting in the fall of that year, fraternity and sorority rush would take place after midterm fall exams rather than at the beginning of the school year. Students reacted to this announcement as if the sky were falling. More than 600 of them signed a petition defending pre-school rush, a document that spoke volumes about the way Greek members viewed campus life at that time. In the petition, students said that fraternities and sororities gave "valuable training in the art of living." It also said that "by delaying pledging, the tensions and embarrassments which inevitably accompany rushing and pledging will be magnified and prolonged," a sentence that unwittingly conceded how badly many of the Greek organizations treated their pledges. For the rest of the decade, the (Greek dominated) school newspaper devoted far more column inches to the matter of delayed rush than it did to all other issues, such as the Cold War and the South's racial problems. Meanwhile, Branscomb's plan backfired because, in practice, Greek organizations began looking over and choosing their new pledges as soon as the school year started. "The tension and anxiety has been mounting for two months," one freshman girl said as official rush week neared in 1952.

The biggest mistake Branscomb made in his effort to de-emphasize the Greek system was to not be up front about his plans. Rumors began to fly that the chancellor was going to do something about Greek houses as early as 1952. However, on numerous occasions in the mid- and late 1950s, the administration emphatically denied that it had any intention of banning fraternity housing. In February 1956 Branscomb assured the Intra-Fraternity Council that "Greeks will not be forced into dorms" and said that rumors to that effect were "not only untrue, but unfair and harmful." But in fact, the chancellor had been thinking about a plan to move the Greek houses to campus. He didn't inform students or alumni about it until he was

Sorority girls playing a game with spoons and potatoes - circa 1949
Photographic Achives, Vanderbilt University

within days of presenting it to the board of trust.

If there was a turning point regarding Greek housing, it took place in October 1955. That month, the Phi Psi fraternity house, an old residence located east of the main campus, burned to the ground in five hours. No one was killed in the blaze, although one student was injured. The fire, which happened just as Vanderbilt was building six modern dormitories (later called Kissam Quadrangle), demonstrated the inherent danger of students living in old houses. "Most of the houses were built before our grandparents were born," *Hustler* columnist Chuck Nord wrote. "Most of the houses are archaic in one respect or many; some have never seen an inch of BX wiring; the heating systems are undependable; the stairways creak forebodingly; the exteriors would make the House of Usher look, by comparison, like the showplaces of Belle Meade." The fact that old buildings weren't as safe as new ones was further illustrated by an occasional national tragedy, such as the December 1958 fire that killed eighty-seven school children in Chicago. And as early as 1940, Vanderbilt health director Thomas Zerfoss did a survey of fraternity and sorority houses and found that the cleanliness and safety of each house was "much below a desirable standard."

In April 1959 (coincidentally, during the annual celebration on campus known as Greek Week), rumors about a dramatic plan to change Vanderbilt's fraternity and sorority system began to spread on campus. For several days, administrators dodged questions. By the time Branscomb announced the plan at Neely Auditorium on May 15, 1959, the fraternities and sororities were already whipped into a frenzy, having formed an entity called the United Greeks Organization to lobby against what they thought was coming. "You are good sports," Branscomb said as he began his presentation to students. "I had expected to dodge a tomato at this point."

Branscomb's plan was almost the same plan that a committee of students, alumni, and faculty had come up with forty years earlier. (Whether the chancellor knew about the 1919 Greek system report is not known; to the author's knowledge, there were no public references at the time to the fact that the 1959 plan coincided with the earlier plan.) Under Branscomb's blueprint, Vanderbilt would build another large series of dormitories, enough to house another 500 students. Once those dormitories were completed, in the fall of 1962, all students would be required to live on campus, except for those who still lived with their parents in Nashville. As for the fraternity and sorority houses, Vanderbilt would buy each of them. Each fraternity and sorority would then be able to build a much smaller "chapter house" in the small residential neighborhood between the main campus and Memorial Gymnasium. But unlike the old fraternity and sorority houses, students would not live in the chapter houses, the cost of which could not exceed $120,000. To make this possible, the school would help finance two-thirds of the cost of the chapter house for a period of thirty years.

Needless to say, many students were furious at the decision. With a board of trust meeting pending, the newly formed United Greeks Organization fired off twelve thousand letters to alumni, asking everyone who had ever pledged a fraternity or sorority at Vanderbilt to let Branscomb know that they were against the plan. The letters told alumni that Branscomb's plan would "mean the death of the fraternity and sorority system as you know it and as we know it." A month later, the chancellor said that he had received thirty-two letters from alumni complaining about the proposal (and ten letters from alumni supporting it).

A few days after Branscomb's announcement, several hundred students held a protest rally on Alumni Lawn, carrying banners that said things such as "United Greeks" and "Save our Frat Houses." The rally was believed to be the biggest protest of any kind since the school was organized. A few days later, two engineering students sabotaged Kirkland Hall's new carillon so that it would transmit a pre-recorded voice from campus radio station WVU rather than the sound of bells. At midnight on Sunday, May 17, everyone on or near the Vanderbilt campus heard a mysterious voice claiming to be the ghost of Kirkland Hall coming from the bell tower. For several minutes, until someone could disconnect it, the voice spoke out against Branscomb and the new fraternity policy. In perhaps another sign of student anger, twice during the next several days large groups of male students staged panty raids on female dorms.

Students went home a few weeks later. By the time they returned that fall, many of them had bitterly accepted the new policy (the fact that it would not affect them so much as it would future students may have been the main reason that the protest died down). In October, the board of trust voted to build the new dormitory complex and accept the new housing proposal with two minor changes. One is that four members of each Greek organization be allowed to live in each chapter house. The other is that the amount of money that each house could cost was reduced from $120,000 to $90,000.

During the next two years each fraternity and sorority quietly got to work on its plans for a chapter house. The first one to open, in the fall of 1960, was Kappa Sigma. "The house has regular maid service, built in dining room lights that can be dimmed for a candlelight buffet, a three-channel stereo donated by an alumnus and a black marble hearth," *The Hustler* said. It was the beginning of the end of Greek domination of campus social life. In the spring of 1962, Vanderbilt finished the new dormitory complex. Appropriately, it became known as Branscomb Quadrangle.

Vanderbilt Gets in Bed with Big Brother

A private, academically inclined school with more than a few rich kids, Vanderbilt has not always had peaceful relations with its neighbors. But no amount of fraternity antics, parking shortages, or disappointing football teams ever compared with the public relations problem that the university developed as a result of its geographic expansion during the urban renewal era. However, people who remember Vanderbilt's urban renewal controversy often forget two things. One is that Vanderbilt's was the fifth such plan carried out in Nashville. The other is how popular the concept of urban renewal was prior to Vanderbilt's involvement in it.

Before urban renewal, thousands of Nashville's poor inner-city residents lived in crowded shacks with no running water, no heat, and unsafe wiring. There were entire neighborhoods in which the plumbing system consisted of water spigots in the front yard and outhouses in back. These slums had abnormally high crime and low life-expectancy rates. Some neighborhoods also had high concentrations of vice, from open prostitution to cockfighting.

Behind the idea of urban renewal was a belief that if the government removed people from such places and put them in new, clean environments, it would not only improve their lives and their self-image, but their behavior. This idealistic philosophy became common in America by the end of World War I but didn't become a real force in government until Franklin Roosevelt's New Deal policies of the 1930s.

One of the most tangible signs of this philosophy in government was public housing, which was authorized by the National Housing Act of 1937 and resulted in the construction of four public housing complexes in Nashville by 1941. After World War II Congress passed a new housing act that stretched the limits of local government power. The law authorized cities to buy land using power of eminent domain, not just for civic projects such as roads and public housing, but for resale to private owners, who could put commercial, industrial, or residential developments on the site under master plans approved by the local planning commission. With the act, Congress committed to funding two-thirds of the cost of urban renewal projects, with local governments required to fund the remaining third.

This act established a legislative precedent for eminent domain that remained through the rest of the century. It not only set in motion massive urban renewal programs across the country; it also gave local governments the legal authority to help large employers acquire land for skyscrapers.

Nashville's leaders were ready. Before the 1949 act Nashville planning director Charles Hawkins met with representatives of Gov. Gordon Browning's administration to develop a plan for the blighted area on the north side of the State Capitol. That plan called for the clearance of ninety-seven acres. About half of the land would then be sold to the state and left undeveloped as green space around the Capitol. The rest would be redeveloped into a commercial corridor, eventually called James Robertson Parkway.

Nashville's Capitol Hill Redevelopment Project became the nation's first urban renewal project funded by Congress. Within a couple of years more than four hundred homes along roads such as Gay Street were assessed, acquired, and razed. All traces of the old streets

Tennessee Governor Frank Clement and Nashville Mayor Ben West admire a model of the Capitol Hill Redevelopment Plan
The Carey Collection

were removed, and James Robertson Parkway was laid out and paved. Resale of the land to private developers was delayed by a major lawsuit filed by Bijou Theater owner Alfred Starr and Nashville grocer H.G. Hill Jr. against the Nashville Housing Authority. In that lawsuit, Starr and Hill claimed that the purchase of their land through eminent domain for resale to other private owners violated their rights. But Starr and Hill lost their case before the U.S. Supreme Court, which opined that the practice was legitimate.

According to official documents, the Capitol Hill Redevelopment Project displaced 301 families and 196 single residents who previously lived in the area. Gerald Gimre, executive director of the Nashville Housing Authority at the time, once wrote in a trade journal that most of those residents were African American and "many went into low-rent public housing projects." Because Nashville's newspapers published few articles about the fate of poor blacks who were being moved, it is almost impossible to obtain more details about what happened to them.

However, in terms of downtown planning and beautification, there is little doubt that the project was a success. It alleviated traffic problems and provided state employees with needed parking. Property tax revenues from the area increased because of the sale and redevelopment of the land – a notable achievement considering so much of the acreage became tax-exempt state property. And for the first time in generations, Nashville residents could appreciate the beauty of their State Capitol, no longer flanked by slums. "Capitol Hill was two-thirds slums and dilapidated commercial structures and one-third littered streets and dismal alleyways," a *Tennessean* article declared in 1958. "Today it is a clean and graceful area of parkways, sloping lawns, new streets, and 40 acres of sorely needed desirable new downtown building sites."

In 1958 Mayor Ben West and the Nashville Housing Authority moved on to another big urban renewal project, this time on a 2,051-acre area of east Nashville. Unlike the Capitol Hill project, east Nashville was a "rehabilitation" area rather than a "slum clearance" area. What this meant was that the housing authority wouldn't buy and clear every piece of property, but handle each parcel on a case-by-case basis. Some houses would be torn down to make way for commercial or industrial use or a government project. Others would be allowed to remain, but only if the owner brought the building up to existing codes.

Nashville's City Council voted unanimously to ask the federal government to fund two-thirds of the cost of the $20 million East Nashville Urban Renewal Project. Among the proponents of the idea was council member Alfred Woodruff of east Nashville, who said urban renewal represented "the greatest opportunity ever offered to the city of Nashville and certainly the greatest thing ever offered to east Nashville." At least one person spoke out against the plan. H.P.

McCarver, who owned a sheet metal business at 801 Woodland St., called the proposal "the nearest thing to communism that has ever happened in Nashville." Four months later Congress agreed to fund it.

Throughout 1958 the Nashville Housing Authority executed its plan in east Nashville, ordering some properties torn down and others renovated. The authority had so much work that it hired five new inspectors. One of them was Richard Gordon, who usually dealt with houses in the so-called Crappy Chute black residential area north of Main Street in east Nashville. "I grew up in east Nashville in a house that was razed by urban renewal, and I can tell you that some of these places had unsafe wiring, leaky roofs, and outdoor privies," said Gordon, who remained a city employee through the 1990s. "What we did was for the betterment of the area."

A few people in east Nashville complained about urban renewal, such as a homeowner in the historic neighborhood of Edgefield who managed to save her home from demolition. But such dissension was rare and received little press at the time. The Nashville Housing Authority razed 1,069 structures in east Nashville because of urban renewal – far more structures than were destroyed by the legendary fire of 1916. East Nashville homeowners who managed to stave off their homes' destruction had to spend an average of $702 per household on "rehabilitation" costs. However, city leaders and government bureaucrats were pleased with an official report that claimed that urban renewal reduced the percentage of "substandard" housing units in the area from 48.2 to 10.1 percent.

One of President John Kennedy's first executive acts was to increase urban renewal spending, leading the Nashville Housing Authority to begin work on three more plans. One was a redevelopment area downtown that would eliminate Nashville's old Public Square and enable companies to acquire enough land to build large buildings if they chose. Another was a large urban renewal area in Edgehill, stretching from what later became the Music Row area south and east to Interstate 65. A third was the area immediately surrounding Vanderbilt University. On August 15, 1961, the council unanimously approved a measure asking the federal government to fund all three projects.

BRANSCOMB DECIDES TO STAY PUT

So why did the Nashville council approve an urban renewal program for the area near Vanderbilt? Not because the area was a slum, like parts of east Nashville and the area surrounding the State Capitol. It was because the school and chancellor Harvie Branscomb requested it.

Back in 1873, when Bishop Holland McTyeire acquired seventy-six acres for a Methodist college, it seemed like plenty of land. After all, Vanderbilt's medical school and law school were located in other parts of town. In its early decades the school didn't build dormitories because its trustees thought they would encourage sinful behavior, preferring for students to reside with families in the area.

But as the years went by the school got bigger and more crowded. By the time Harvie Branscomb became chancellor in 1946, he recognized that the combined impact of the post-World War II baby boom and the GI Bill meant enrollment would be going up. (Vanderbilt's enrollment was thirty-five hundred in 1950 and would be seventy-five hundred by 1972.) Branscomb also knew that the school needed to build more dorms, a new gymnasium, a center for the social sciences, and more buildings for the medical school. Since the campus was surrounded by other schools, businesses, and two major traffic arteries, he thought it might be time to move the university to a new campus in a rural area.

In his memoirs Branscomb wrote that he was serious about the idea of moving the campus. But he decided against the move for three reasons. One was that it would require the university to be separated from its medical school, undoing Chancellor James Kirkland's work to unite them. The second reason was that it would separate Vanderbilt from Peabody and Scarritt and thus violate the terms under which the Joint University Library had been built. Finally, Branscomb didn't want his term as chancellor to be dominated by logistical problems. Branscomb did not mention any architectural or historic reasons for his decision.

In any case Branscomb decided to expand the campus rather

Branscomb (second from right) in 1947
The Banner Collection, Nashville Public Library, The Nashville Room

than move it. Since the campus was bordered on the north by West End Avenue and the east by Twenty-first Avenue, the logical direction to go was southwest, in the direction of a residential area that had been developed between 1900 and 1930.

In the late 1940s Vanderbilt began quietly buying up property in the neighborhood as it came on the market. (It did so largely by spending money from a living trust fund that had been donated by trustee Harold Vanderbilt.) In an era before organized neighborhoods or activist newspaper reporting, it managed to do so quietly for a few years. But in the mid-1950s Branscomb realized that the plan wasn't working fast enough. He instructed vice chancellor Jack Stambaugh to speed it up and make unsolicited offers to property owners in key locations. Some owners sold and others refused, making it obvious that the university would have to pay a lot to buy all the land it wanted.

In 1958 the Vanderbilt chancellor approached Union University in Jackson, Tennessee, and asked it to lobby the Tennessee legislature for a law giving private schools the same power of eminent domain that the University of Tennessee possessed. (Vanderbilt itself did not lobby for the bill because Branscomb apparently believed that a small college located outside of Nashville would have more success with the General Assembly.) Cecil Sims, a prominent Nashville attorney who represented Vanderbilt at the time, told Branscomb that he thought the law was unconstitutional. The legislature passed the bill anyway.

Vanderbilt never actually used the state law, which remained in effect until the legislature repealed it in 1978. By the mid-1950s private universities throughout the country – the University of Chicago and the Massachusetts Institute of Technology are two examples – were hemmed in on all sides and had no room to expand their campuses. At the same time their enrollments were rising on a wave of baby boomers and students on the GI Bill. Some colleges were considering moving to the suburbs. Faced with a land shortage, many schools bonded together and asked Congress to give them some level of eminent domain power.

As a result of pressure from private universities, Congress passed a law in 1959 (known as Section 112 of the federal urban renewal program) that allowed local governments to partner with four-year colleges that needed land. The law said that local governments could acquire land on behalf of universities using the power of eminent domain – as long as that land was in an area that met the government's definition of a "slum." Once the university bought this land from the local housing authority, the money could be used to draw matching federal funds.

Mayor Ben West was so excited about this program that he immediately invited representatives of Nashville's universities to his office to discuss using urban renewal to expand. Several considered it. But Vanderbilt was the only university to move ahead with such a plan because it was the only one that could afford it.

The Internationalist and Revisionist

During the years immediately following World War I most Americans were happy to return to a policy of isolationism, believing that such an approach was the best way to avoid another war. After World War II most Americans supported the Cold War, believing that the best way to avoid World War III was to take a hard line against the Soviet Union. One of the most important critics of both policies was a Vanderbilt political science professor named Denna Frank Fleming.

There was nothing remarkable about D.F. Fleming's early life. He was born in rural Illinois in 1893. He attended Eastern Illinois University and the University of Illinois, then became an anti-aircraft machine gun operator during World War I. Like thousands of other veterans of that war, Fleming was exposed to mustard gas in Europe and had weak lungs for the rest of his life.

Fleming initially taught at Monmouth College, where he first received recognition in his field for his essays on the U.S. Senate's failure to join the League of Nations. Norman Davis, a Vanderbilt trustee and New York banker, was impressed by Fleming's work and recommended him for a job at Vanderbilt.

Fleming moved to Nashville in 1928 and would remain a full-time employee of Vanderbilt for thirty-three years. In 1932 he published *The United States and the League of Nations: 1918-1920*, a book that expanded his thoughts on why the U.S. Senate decided not to join the international body formed after World War I. Shortly thereafter he served as a member of an American delegation to the League of Nations, and later as a member of the League's Disarmament Conference. Because of these appointments, Fleming was frequently quoted in news articles as an international expert. By 1933 he was making occasional appearances on Nashville radio stations. In 1939 his talks became a regular feature on WSM, the Nashville-based station that could be heard all over the continental U.S. at that time. In an era before television, there is no way of knowing how many Americans were influenced by Fleming's opinions or impressed by the fact that he was a faculty member at Vanderbilt University.

In the 1930s Fleming would have been classified as an internationalist, who believed America could no longer shut out the outside world. Fleming believed that the American refusal to join the League of Nations was a tragic mistake. With the rise of Adolph Hitler and the outbreak of World War II, his opinion became more widely held among Americans.

As World War II neared its end, Fleming began to fear that America would return to the isolationist policies that had followed the First World War. Because of this he wrote and produced a series of radio speeches between November 1944 and February 1945 called "How can we make the victory stick?" The talks were transmitted on sixty-six radio stations. "If we are to learn anything from this second frightful world war it must be the simple lesson that the time to combat aggression is when it is young and that everybody must agree firmly in advance to do his part," Fleming said in one of the pieces. "Nor is this a lesson that we can afford to re-learn through a third World War. Our meteoric progress in inventing new engines of death forbids us that luxury. It is true that we have kept the bombers, robot bombs and rocket bombs away from our cities this time, but it should be clear to anyone that this is the last chance we shall ever have to prevent the devastation of this continent."

After the war Fleming worked briefly as a state department official before coming back to Vanderbilt. As the Cold War dominated American foreign policy over the next few years, Fleming developed a controversial theory that he explained fully in his two-volume work *The Cold War and its Origins: 1917-1960.* The United States, not the Soviet Union, he wrote, was primarily to blame for the Cold War. The policy of America and its allies in the 1930s helped isolate the Soviet Union and ensure the decimation of its population during World War II. After the war the Soviet Union's main goal was not to spread communism, but to defend itself against future invasions. America, in Fleming's opinion, overreacted to everything the Soviets did in a strange attempt to make up for the isolationist policies of the 1920s.

In an era in which American troops were deployed all over the globe against Soviet forces, Fleming's book was highly controversial.

"Whatever one's judgment of the author's premises or conclusions, one can only respect the devotion and courage with which D.F. Fleming . . . has written this massive treatise," the review of his book in *The New York Times* said. Some historians didn't buy a word of it. "It is idle to pretend that Soviet behavior between 1917 and 1934 did not make Western distrust natural and inevitable," a Stanford historian wrote in a *New York Times* review of one of Fleming's later books. Prominent historian Arthur Schlesinger Jr. was so angered by revisionism that he wrote several articles attacking it.

In the 1930s and 1940s Vanderbilt was unambiguously proud of Fleming. But as his revisionist theories became known in the 1950s and 1960s, Chancellor Branscomb became nervous about what trustees thought of Fleming. Branscomb, after all, was quite conservative. When Congress began conducting a national witch-hunt for "subversives on college campuses" in 1953, Branscomb told *The Hustler* that if they found any communists at Vanderbilt, he would be "surprised, disappointed, and grateful." About that time, in a letter to a trustee, the chancellor acknowledged that Fleming's Cold War views concerned him. But he pointed out that by that time, Fleming no longer taught lower-level courses, which meant that freshman and sophomores would not be exposed to his dangerous views.

A shy personality and a busy schedule of off-campus activities kept Fleming from being as great an influence on students as he might have been. But Fleming had a major impact on at least a couple of lives. One was political science major Jim Sasser, who remained friends with Fleming after he left Vanderbilt and who later became a U.S. senator and ambassador to China. Another was Walter Durham, who became a successful Gallatin businessman and the author of several Nashville history books. "I first heard him speak when I was 15 years old in 1939, and a few years later I went to Vanderbilt and signed up for as many of his classes as I could," said Durham, who became the Tennessee State Historian in 2002. "Many years later, he and I became good friends. He told me that since I was a member of the business community who hadn't sold his soul that he would like for me to be the person to settle his estate, and I was."

By the time Fleming retired from Vanderbilt in 1961, his views had become so offensive to conservatives that his presence on the

Vanderbilt campus was an embarrassment to Branscomb. Fleming's opinions were so controversial that an offer for a part-time retirement job at the University of South Florida was later withdrawn, a much-publicized episode in academic circles. None of this changed the political scientist's viewpoint. By the late 1960s he had developed another controversial opinion: that the American involvement in the Vietnam War was pointless, unethical, and a violation of international law. "If we can make the American dream come true in the United States then we won't need to worry about U.S. prestige, influence and power in the good sense," Fleming said in a 1965 *Hustler* interview. "If we do this, everyone will see it and admire it. This can accomplish more than all of our horrible weapons."

JAMES LAWSON REFUSES TO QUIT

Author's note: The Lawson affair is the subject of thirty-five pages in Paul Conkin's Vanderbilt history Gone with the Ivy; *forty-six pages in Dale Johnson's* Vanderbilt Divinity School: Education, Contest and Change; *and is a major topic of David Halberstam's* The Children. *It is thus the most documented event in Vanderbilt history. This section is not intended to retell every aspect of the story, but to summarize its major points. The author is indebted to Conkin, Johnson, and Halberstam for their work.*

The decision by Chancellor Harvie Branscomb to expel divinity student James Lawson for being a leader in Nashville's sit-in movement is one of the most controversial chapters in Vanderbilt history. In academic circles the Lawson affair was a turning point in the Civil Rights Movement. It also haunted Branscomb for most of the rest of his life, and had led many people affiliated with the school to the opinion that Branscomb was a great chancellor except for the way he handled the Lawson affair. However, there are aspects of the event that are overlooked. When Branscomb expelled Lawson, he had the support of the Vanderbilt Board of Trust, the student body, the elected leaders of the student body, most of the faculty, Nashville's mayor, at least one Nashville newspaper, and the majority of people who lived in Nashville.

From 1953 until 1962 Vanderbilt University had a policy related to admitting African Americans that seemed to Branscomb like a safe, middle-of the-road approach. In those days most Southern colleges admitted whites or blacks, but not both. Under Vanderbilt's policy, divisions of the university that were unique to the Nashville community (such as the divinity school and law school) would consider blacks for admission. However, programs that had counterparts at other local institutions (such as the medical and undergraduate schools) would not.

Under this policy, as explained by Branscomb in his memoirs, "Vanderbilt need not feel obligated to admit Negro students into degree programs already available to them, namely at Fisk, Tennessee State, and Meharry. Thus we would be able to say with some satisfaction that no Negro youth in our community had been denied because of his race or color an education for which he was qualified." To minimize the mixing of races, the Vanderbilt policy prohibited the few black students admitted under these terms from living in dormitories or eating in the cafeteria.

The first black person to attend one of Vanderbilt's schools was Joseph Johnson Jr., who was admitted to the divinity school in 1953 and graduated with his Bachelor of Divinity degree a year later. When Johnson was admitted, the Vanderbilt school newspaper endorsed the move, saying it was a "milestone" for which the board of trust should be congratulated. Three years after Johnson's admission the law school accepted two African Americans – Tennessee State graduate Edward Porter and Fisk alumnus Frederick Work.

In May 1958 an Ohio native and ordained Methodist minister named James Lawson applied to the Vanderbilt Divinity School. Lawson was thirty-one years old and had already had a rather interesting career. During the Korean War Lawson had been sentenced to three years in federal prison for refusing induction into the army (he served eleven months of that sentence). Lawson had also spent time in India, where he studied Mahatma Gandhi's methods of nonviolent protest. When Lawson came to Vanderbilt in the fall of 1958, he came with two purposes. One was to complete his B.D. degree. The other was to work as regional director of an activist civil rights organization called the Fellowship of Reconciliation.

From his base in Nashville Lawson conducted workshops on nonviolent protest. As a member of a group of black ministers called the Christian Leadership Council he also helped organize a group of African American students, mostly from Fisk and the American Baptist College, on the methods of nonviolent protest. Meanwhile, Lawson was a fine student who excelled academically and even participated in intramural sports (ignoring the policy that prohibited such activities). But Lawson didn't tell his Vanderbilt colleagues and professors much about his off-campus life. "I think that one of my errors in that period was that I did not more explicitly talk about the workshops," Lawson said years later.

In early February 1960 well-publicized and well-organized sit-ins at lunch counters took place in Greensboro, North Carolina. Lawson and other Nashville organizers, who had been training and

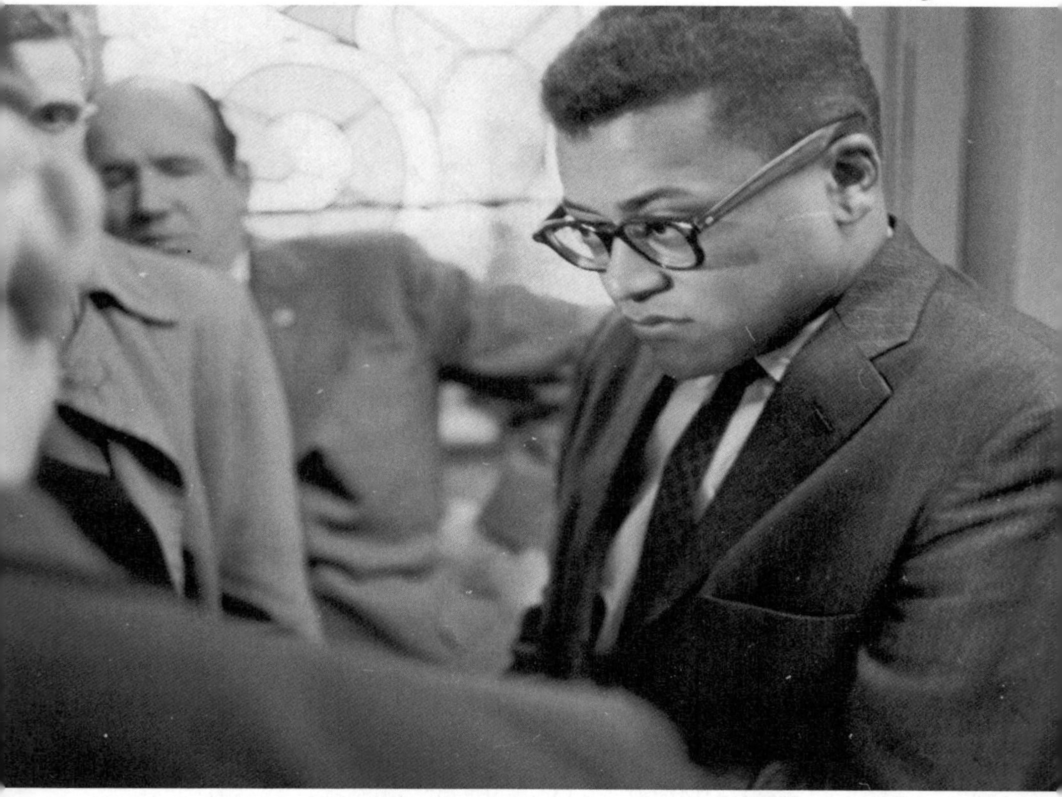

James Lawson after his arrest for taking part in the sit-in movement
The Banner Collection, Nashville Public Library, The Nashville Room

waiting for months, decided it was time to act. On Saturday, February 13, 1960, about a hundred students staged sit-ins at several variety stores in downtown Nashville's Fifth Avenue shopping district, such as Woolworth's, McClellan's, and Walgreen's. The event came off without any reported acts of violence.

Two weeks later came the day referred to by many as "Big Saturday." On February 27, eighty-one students – seventy-six of whom were black – were arrested as they staged sit-ins at several segregated lunch counters. For hours the students sat passively at the lunch counters while many white bystanders taunted them and, in at least four cases, physically attacked them. "A group of white boys attacked two Negro demonstrators at Woolworth's after receiving no response from comments such as 'Go home, nigger' and 'What's the matter, you chicken?' " *The Tennessean* reported. "A third Negro was pushed down the stairs in the accompanying confusion."

One of the demonstrators who was attacked was Paul LaPrad, a white student from Fisk. "He (LaPrad) was sitting at the counter with two black students, Maxine Walker on one side and Peggy Alexander on the other, when someone came up from behind him and yanked him off the stool," an account of the events in David Halberstam's *The Children* said. "Down he went. People were swinging at him and when he was down he felt someone kicking him. The kicks were sharp, the pain the kind he imagined would come with being stabbed. He moved into the fetal position, trying to protect himself, as they had all been taught to do." When the police began arresting students, most bystanders cheered.

During the next few days both the *Nashville Banner* and *Tennessean* published editorials against the protests. The *Banner* compared the leaders of the sit-in movement to John Kasper, a segregationist who helped provoke a near-riot when Nashville began integrating its public schools in 1957. *The Tennessean*, under the editorship of Edward Ball, said that "the inviting of disturbances is no way to settle problems or illuminate opinion. The upholding of law and order transcends all other issues, for without this there is mob rule and chaos." During subsequent weeks *The Tennessean* would change its stance and come to support the demonstrators, partly under the influence of young, idealistic reporters such as Halberstam. The *Banner* did no such thing. Everything about Nashville's afternoon newspaper reflected the personality of Vanderbilt alum James Stahlman. "People down here just don't believe in social mixing of the races," Stahman told a national news magazine in 1956. "There are a lot of us who don't want any social integration in any particular, and a lot of us are determined that it isn't going to happen so long as we can do anything about it, legally." The *Banner* editorialized against the sit-in movement, and the entire Civil Rights Movement, through the rest of the 1960s.

On Monday, February 29, a Nashville judge fined three students for disorderly conduct for their roles in the lunch counter demonstrations. During the hearing about two thousand black people stood outside the municipal safety building, which housed the city court at that time. That same day Nashville Mayor Ben West met with a group of over one hundred black ministers, most of whom were furious over the police's actions at the sit-ins two days earlier. Through coverage of that meeting, it first became publicly known that Vanderbilt student James Lawson was a leader in Nashville's sit-in movement.

Lawson's role in planning the sit-in movement immediately became the subject of stories and editorials in the *Tennessean* and *Banner*. "To plead his (Lawson's) cause in the name of 'Christian reconciliation' as a 'Christian missionary' is so much hogwash," the *Banner* said. "And his use of the Divinity School of Vanderbilt University as a base and screen for his nefarious operations is as detestable as his effort to cloak his racial deviltry in clerical garb."

By this time Branscomb was torn about what to do about Lawson's situation. He knew that according to local ordinances of that era, white storeowners did not have to serve black customers if they didn't want to. He frequently told friends, alumni, and trustees that the concept of full social integration was a troubling one for him to accept, and he knew that social integration was not popular with most alumni. Nevertheless, Branscomb would later claim in his memoirs that by 1960, he had every intention of integrating by policy all divisions of the school before his retirement.

Branscomb asked Divinity School Dean Robert Nelson to talk to Lawson and find out whether the newspaper accounts of his involvement were accurate. Lawson responded that the stories were inaccurate on one major point: he was one of the leaders of the sit-in movement; not the sole leader as local papers had claimed. And he said that he would continue to support and participate in the movement.

As fate would have it the executive committee of the board of trust already had a meeting scheduled the next day, March 3. The seven people who took part in that gathering were Branscomb, Nelson (summoned to answer questions about Lawson), Stahlman, Third National Bank president Sam Fleming, Nashville attorneys Cecil Sims and William Waller, Cain-Sloan department store president John Sloan, and National Life & Accident Insurance Co. executive Jesse Wills. Nelson read a long letter that Lawson had written to the board in which he flattered the university but defended his right to fight against laws that he considered unjust. The committee voted unanimously to give Lawson a choice: Quit school or be expelled.

Nelson delivered the message to Lawson. After talking to his wife Dorothy and to his friend and white civil rights activist Will Campbell, Lawson decided not to quit.

Branscomb Gets It From the Left

When James Lawson was expelled for his role in Nashville's sit-in movement, most white Nashville residents and Vanderbilt students applauded. The week after Lawson was dismissed the undergraduate student senate – which included a young man named Lamar Alexander – unanimously backed the board of trust's decision. *The Hustler* agreed, saying students who had been expelled for their involvement in recent panty raids on campus hadn't done anything nearly as bad as Lawson. "The 'sitdown' affair, in which Mr. Lawson has admitted a part, is of a far more serious nature (than the panty raids)," *The Hustler* said. However, Vanderbilt would eventually lose the public relations war over the Lawson affair.

The day after Lawson was expelled eleven of the sixteen faculty members at the Divinity School said in a joint statement that they saw no justification for his expulsion. Meanwhile, about fifteen people – mostly divinity students and faculty – picketed in front of

Kirkland Hall.

The situation then took an unexpected turn. On March 4 police arrested Lawson while he attended a meeting at the First Baptist Church on Eighth Avenue on charges of conspiracy to violate the state's trade and commerce laws. (A photograph of Lawson being dragged out of the church made the front page of *The Tennessean* the next day.) Hours after his arrest four Vanderbilt divinity school faculty members – Nelson, Langdon Gilkey, Everett Tilson, and Gordon Kaufman – posted Lawson's $500 bail and got him released. "The faculty wants to show it is horrified," said Gilkey, a former prisoner of war in World War II. "We feel the city has made a very serious mistake in arresting Lawson and we want to protest it as vigorously as we can."

A few days later 111 Vanderbilt faculty members published a statement supporting Lawson. Weeks later the divinity faculty officially asked trustees to reconsider their decision.

Divinity faculty members were opposed to the handling of the Lawson affair for several reasons. Many were in full agreement with the rationale and tactics of the sit-in movement, and regarded its participants as heroes. Some professors had other reasons. By hastily expelling Lawson, the board of trust, under pressure from a Nashville newspaper, completely bypassed anything resembling a chain of command (a curious parallel with board of trust chairman Whitefoord Cole's 1919 decision to suspend part-time faculty member Russell Scott for speaking at a socialist rally). The decision to expel Lawson was also unfair on other grounds. Since charges were eventually dropped against him, Vanderbilt expelled Lawson for something for which he was never convicted.

As fate would have it the Lawson controversy peaked at the same moment the Divinity School was opening its shiny new quadrangle, ending three decades in which the school had been housed in an aging, ill-equipped building across Twenty-first Avenue. Several of the speakers at the opening ceremonies made critical references to the university's expulsion of Lawson, references that were applauded by many of the alumni in attendance.

Through March, April, and May, there was increasing pressure on Branscomb from divinity professors, from a few other faculty members, and from national media to reverse Lawson's expulsion. On the other hand, many professors supported the decision to expel Lawson; in late March a petition supporting Branscomb's decision garnered almost a hundred names. Stahlman used the *Banner* to exert as much pressure on Branscomb and on other trustees to keep Lawson expelled. Official and personal documents that remain from the period indicate that only one trustee, Hugh Morgan, supported the idea of readmitting Lawson.

While Vanderbilt fretted with its internal controversy, Nashville's sit-in movement succeeded faster than anyone could have predicted. A few days after eighty-one students were arrested in the sit-in movement, Mayor Ben West appointed a multi-racial citizens committee headed by former Vanderbilt Dean of Students Madison Sarratt to seek a solution to the racial problem. That committee suggested distinct segregated and desegregated sections of every dining area. Unhappy with the recommendation, demonstrators resumed sit-ins and even instituted a boycott of downtown retailers. For a while, it looked like Nashville was in for a long, protracted stalemate on the lunch counter issue.

Then, on April 19, someone threw a bomb through the window of the home of Z. Alexander Looby, one of Nashville's most prominent black lawyers. That day an estimated three thousand people marched from Tennessee State University to the courthouse. The crowd's leaders spoke with Mayor Ben West on the steps of the courthouse. A Fisk student named Diane Nash asked the mayor if he would use his authority to end lunch counter segregation. The mayor said yes. "Integrate counters – Mayor" read *The Tennessean's* front page headline the next day. Within a couple of weeks, seven stores opened their lunch counters to all races. Nashville's sit-ins had achieved their goals so peacefully that Martin Luther King Jr. later referred to it as a model movement.

With the sit-ins successful and charges against Lawson dropped, divinity school faculty members made a subtle change in their approach. Rather than ask that Lawson's expulsion be reversed, the faculty requested that Lawson be readmitted to Vanderbilt for the summer semester. To that end, Lawson quickly filled out an admissions application and got a new round of letters of recommendation.

After all, Lawson was no longer a lawbreaker; he had been a leader in a peaceful movement to change a law that even Mayor Ben West had now come out against. Surely, Lawson's supporters thought, Branscomb would let Lawson back into Vanderbilt.

But he didn't. On Monday, May 30, Branscomb told the divinity school admissions committee that he had denied the proposal to readmit Lawson. As a result, the Lawson affair reached a higher level of intensity. Within a few hours of Branscomb's announcement, Dean Nelson, nine divinity professors, and four medical school professors said they planned to resign from Vanderbilt. The resignations represented two-thirds of the divinity faculty and several professors who were involved in an expensive, federally supported cancer research program at the medical school.

During the next few weeks several of the protesting faculty members regularly met in an ongoing attempt to resolve the Lawson matter. Two of them, divinity school professor Langdon Gilkey and medical school professor Rollow Park, even visited three board members at a Belle Meade home in hopes of changing their minds. "Park did all the talking," Gilkey said in an oral account of those visits thirty-eight years later. "He said, 'We hope that you realize that with this, Vanderbilt ceases to be a major university in America. You will not be able to get an appointment from anybody from MIT or Cal Tech or the University of Chicago or any other place. No one will consider coming here, and you will become a southern finishing school.' He said this to all three of them. And all three of them replied, 'Well, sir, we'll take the southern finishing school.' "

Over the following weeks Vanderbilt received more negative national press than at any other time in its history. "This is what comes of allowing Christian doctrine to be taught in such places (as Vanderbilt)," a *Washington Post* editorial on June 1, 1960, said. "It is hardly surprising that students who have been allowed to read the Sermon on the Mount and listen to a lot of talk about the brotherhood of man should have their heads filled with ideals about equality and justice and should begin carrying these ideals into their daily lives. Vanderbilt University's trustees seem to have decided that they are not going to tolerate any more of this sort of morality in their divinity school."

Meanwhile, Branscomb made ambivalent statements, depending on the hour and date. When first told about the divinity school resignations, the chancellor threatened to turn the new divinity quadrangle over to the law school. Other times he told people that he was seriously considering resigning.

Despite the tense situation, Vanderbilt, its chancellor, and its divinity school somehow survived the Lawson affair. Negotiations between the divinity school faculty continued. Finally, the board of trust executive committee agreed to award Lawson his Bachelor of Divinity degree either by transfer of credit or by written examinations, but without readmission. Lawson chose not to do so, completing his degree at Boston University.

In the end, all but one of the faculty members who had announced their resignations in protest of the Lawson affair decided not to leave Vanderbilt after all (the one who left was Bard Thompson, who had already announced his departure months earlier). Each faculty member had his own reasons for doing so. Some said that they regarded the eventual offer by the board of trust executive committee to award Lawson his degree without readmission as enough of a concession. The only Vanderbilt employee actually dismissed over the Lawson affair was Dean Robert Nelson, whose handling of the affair has been criticized in accounts of it.

So much has been written about the Lawson affair that it is hard to gauge its significance. However, there is little question that by expelling Lawson, Vanderbilt drew more attention to the Nashville sit-in movement that it otherwise would have received, at least in higher education circles. Its decision to expel Lawson hurt Vanderbilt's reputation for several years among racial progressives. Vanderbilt's treatment of Lawson also helped galvanize the national academic community regarding racial issues.

The Lawson affair has a happy postscript. James Lawson became the director of nonviolent education for the Southern Christian Leadership Conference, and thus one of the most important civil rights leaders in America in the 1960s. He didn't hate Vanderbilt for what had taken place. In fact, Lawson returned to campus in 1970 to do some graduate work (Chancellor Alexander Heard made certain that Lawson was readmitted this time). He later became the pastor of Los Angeles' Holman Methodist Church, a large, integrated, and mostly middle-class congregation.

Concern that the Lawson affair would taint his legacy haunted Branscomb. In 1985 when Conkin's *Gone with the Ivy* was released, the Vanderbilt administration did not embrace the book largely because of Branscomb's feeling that it didn't treat him fairly concerning the Lawson affair. For years, Branscomb talked about writing his own lengthy account of the incident. It was one of the few things he talked about but never did.

On October 24, 1996, a divinity school professor named Joseph Hough arranged a meeting between Lawson and the 102-year-old Branscomb. The two men had a pleasant conversation. According to Hough, Branscomb expressed deep regret for all that had happened thirty-eight years earlier. "After a few minutes of conversation, Harvie said something like this," Hough said. " 'Dr. Lawson, I want you to know that I now regret the decision I made in 1960, and I think it was a mistake. I want you to know that, and I should like your forgiveness for any harm that came to you as a result of the decision.' " Lawson said that he had long ago forgiven Branscomb for any perceived wrong and that, "I never thought you were anything less than a Christian man who was trying to do the right thing in a very difficult situation." The next day Branscomb was in attendance when Lawson became the first person to be honored as a Vanderbilt Divinity School Distinguished Alumnus.

Part Five

Breaking with the Past

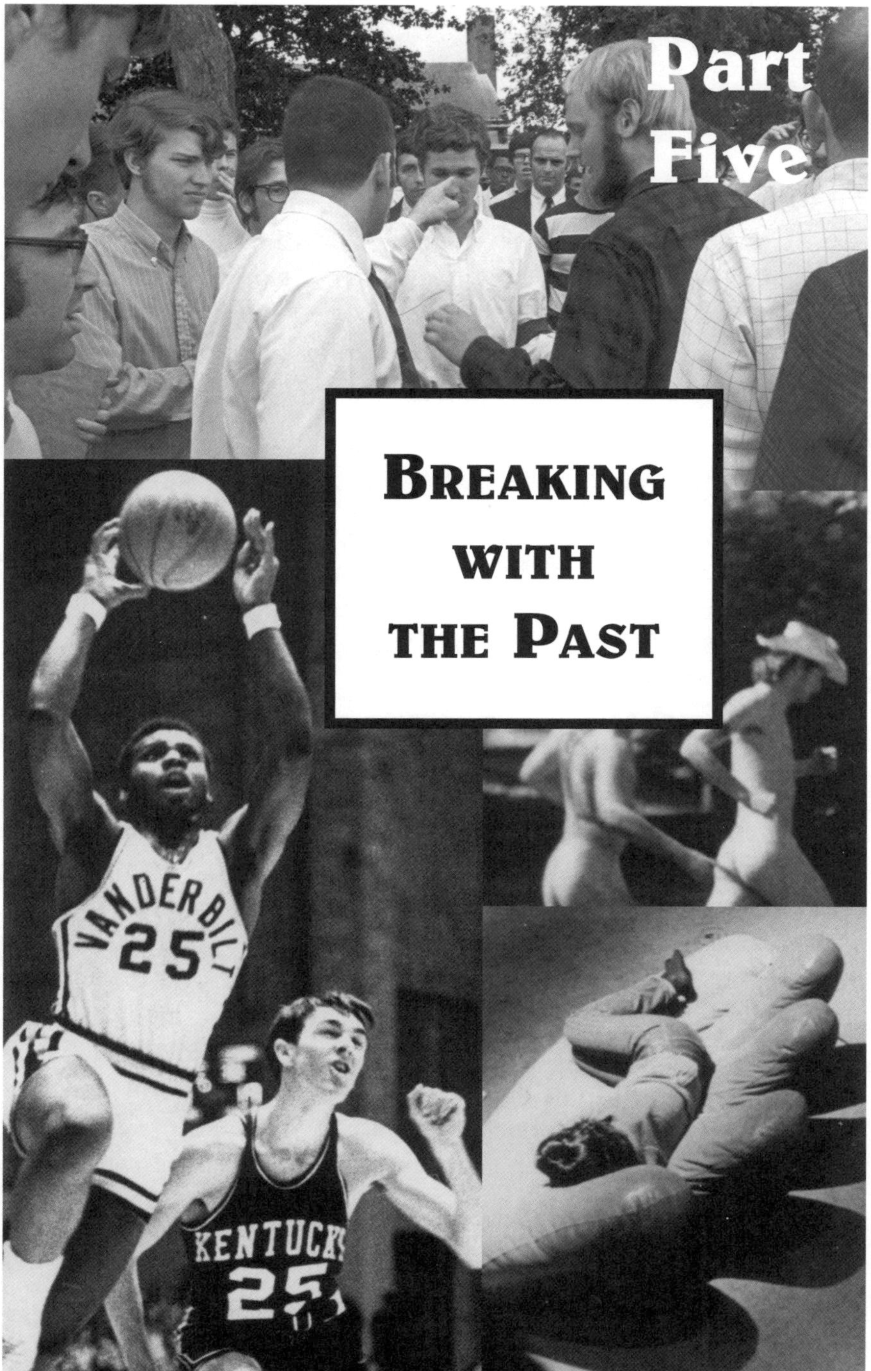

THE CHANCELLOR, THE FUTURE GOVERNOR, AND THE REFERENDUM

In March 1962 a Vanderbilt senior received an unexpected call from Chancellor Harvie Branscomb's office. The chancellor would like to see you, the secretary said. But I'm on my way home, the student said. It won't take long, she said. But I'm wearing blue jeans, he said. He won't mind, she said. Just come the way you are.

The student walked to Kirkland Hall and into the chancellor's office, where two men were waiting to see him. One was Branscomb, whom the Vanderbilt senior had met before. The other was a tall, distinguished-looking man he had never met. "I would like you to meet Mr. Harold Stirling Vanderbilt," Branscomb said to the student. "He is the chairman of the board of trust. I want you to tell him about the idea of integration on campus and how students might react to it, because I think he needs to know."

The student was a young man from Maryville, Tennessee, named Lamar Alexander. At that time he was the editor of *The Hustler*.

During his tenure as Vanderbilt chancellor, Branscomb took several steps to transform Vanderbilt from a regional to a national university. Among them were building more dormitories, moving fraternities and sororities onto campus, and improving the school's graduate programs. Integrating every division of the school was also something Branscomb wanted to do, but he did not want to do it badly enough or quickly enough to disrupt the peace of the campus or alienate alumni, most of whom wanted the university to remain all white. However, Branscomb did not want the Lawson affair to be his sole legacy related to race relations. He also knew he would retire the next year, and he did not want his successor to have to deal with the board of trust over the issue of integration. Meanwhile, other schools in the South had begun admitting blacks into the general student population.

In the January 5, 1962, issue of *The Hustler*, editor Alexander wrote in his weekly column that racial integration was something that the school needed to deal with. Calling the current policy of admitting blacks into only certain parts of the school "cowardly," he wrote that it would be "a blot on the university's reputation if the administration continues to avoid this subject." At about the same time a student senator named John Sergent proposed a measure to the student senate that called on the board of trust to initiate a program of integrating the undergraduate schools. (Whether Alexander's column or Sergent's proposal came first is difficult to determine.) "Vanderbilt should realize that the world is in a state of change," Sergent said at the time. "Thirty years from now, it will look back in shame (at its segregationist policy)."

Forty years later Sergent said that neither Alexander, Branscomb, nor anyone else asked him to make the proposal or talked him into it. He also said he had no idea at the time how significant an

Harold Stirling Vanderbilt and Harvie Branscomb at the grand opening of Rand Hall in 1953
Photographic Archives, Vanderbilt University

action he had taken. "That may sound strange today, but keep in mind that times were different. We were generally an apathetic student body when it came to most things and I didn't realize what a big deal it was."

In the next issue of *The Hustler,* news editor Roy Blount Jr. praised Sergent's proposal and encouraged it to be passed. Using the wit that would later make him a famous humorist, he made fun of the background of many Vanderbilt students. "The majority of the people here come from people who have tried to make Negro field hands work, have seen many Negroes and not many white men in knife fights, have given extra money to the yard man because he has spent all the rent money on something he shouldn't and his children are hungry, and who remembers fondly the old colored folks at home who are angered by Martin Luther King," Blount wrote. He concluded that the American black man "has a right to become a member of the family" and that "white supremacy is an outmoded doctrine that deserves to be cast aside."

Not everyone agreed. At the February 7, 1962, meeting of the student senate in Alumni Hall, Sergent's measure was rejected 14-13 after a three-hour debate. "The room was not the only thing hot on a sticky Wednesday night," an account of the meeting said. "Several times during the debate, tempers flared." However, the senate also passed a measure that put Sergent's proposal before a campuswide referendum.

One week later, on February 14, 1962, Vanderbilt students voted 862 to 661 to reject Sergent's proposal and not recommend a policy of integration to the board. The turnout – more than sixty percent of students – was high given the short notice of the election. Students in Arts and Sciences voted in favor of integration. But by a vote of 239 to 93, engineering students voted against it.

The Hustler lamented the results of the referendum, saying students had taken the position that admission should be more about "social standards" than "academic standards." Another person upset over the result was a student senator named Lionel Barrett, who voted for the integration proposal and was quoted as saying, "I'm afraid people just couldn't put aside their personal prejudices." Sergent, meanwhile, said the matter was not dead. "(Integration) will become an increasingly uncomfortable thorn in the flesh of the board members until Vanderbilt's unfair admissions policy is declared incompatible with the institution's expressed devotion to academic excellence," he said.

Students who voted against the measure cited several reasons for doing so. One was a feeling that its passage would disrupt a major fundraising drive then underway. "This bill will have an effect on alumni giving and I personally am morally in favor of it but I am practically against it," said student senator Judy Wimberly, who had the honor, or the curse, of having to cast the twenty-seventh and decisive vote in the senate. Some students had other reasons. "I voted against it because I'm a nonconformist," one student said. "I mean, it's just the fad to integrate everywhere else." Another student, identified only as a freshman, gave a quote that may have summarized the attitudes of thousands of Southern whites at that time. "Oh, I'm for integration all right," the person said. "I just don't want to go to school with them [blacks]."

Many students who voted against integration came to regret doing so, and one such person was a student senator named Martha (Cissy) Kerkow. "Few of us would relish being asked to explain or defend what we did in college forty years ago," Kerkow, whose married name was Martha Daughtrey, said many years later. "It would be nice to think that, at that time, we were all as progressive and forward-thinking as Johnny Sergent or Lamar Alexander and that we could have grasped the moral issue and taken the high ground.

"The truth is that we were, most of us, mere post-adolescents who were playing at campus politics and, in the end, were the product of our times. I suspect that everyone who voted against the resolution, thinking that we were acting in the university's best interest, would have taken exactly the contrary position had we been asked to vote again five years later."

With the 1962 referendum students made it clear that they didn't want black classmates. But they didn't mind being exposed to black culture in other ways. Only two weeks after the vote was held, a story about the black Isley Brothers band was the lead item in *The Hustler.* The band's appearance was to be the highlight of the annual Greek Week festival.

At first glance it would appear as if the race referendum had thwarted the idea of integrating the campus, but the opposite was actually true. The referendum had gotten the debate going, and there was no turning back. A few weeks after the referendum the graduate student council voted 16-0 to recommend open admissions to all divisions of the graduate school. A few weeks later the faculty voted 79-27 to recommend a policy of racial integration.

On May 6, 1962, a proposal to allow qualified African Americans into all aspects of the university came before the Vanderbilt Board of Trust. It was officially proposed by trustee William S. Vaughn and seconded by trustee Cecil Sims. The measure was approved, with six of the thirty-four trustees recording negative votes. Branscomb announced his retirement a few months later. By the fall of 1964, when nine African American undergraduates entered the school, Vanderbilt had a new chancellor named Alexander Heard.

Many of the students who played an active role in the race referendum of 1962 went on to prominent careers. John Sergent became the chief medical officer at the Vanderbilt Medical Center. Roy Blount was a nationally prominent author and humorist. Lionel Barrett became one of Nashville's most prominent criminal defense attorneys. Martha Daughtrey became a federal judge in the Sixth Circuit of the U.S. Court of Appeals. And Lamar Alexander served as governor of Tennessee from 1978 until 1986, U.S. Secretary of Education from 1991 until 1993, and was elected to the U.S. Senate in 2002.

A SPLIT-LEVEL HOUSE FOR A BASSET HOUND

It was, in the opinion of many who saw it, one of the most glorious moments in Vanderbilt sports history. On November 28, 1964, during the Vanderbilt-Tennessee football game at Dudley Field, a dog named George didn't like the looks of the walking horse that at that time served as the UT mascot. In the middle of the game George took off after the horse, charging it with all the intimidating noise and perpetual motion that a basset hound can muster. The walking horse did what all well-bred walking horses would do. It ran clear out of the stadium, to the delight of the Vanderbilt fans in attendance that day.

That afternoon, Vanderbilt defeated Tennessee 7-0.

"I don't really know what George was thinking," said Toby Wilt, the Vanderbilt halfback and George's master, whose forty-yard run set up the winning touchdown that day. "My guess is that he had never seen a horse before and thought it was a big dog."

It was the defining moment in the life of George. A few weeks later a student booster organization elected George the school's official mascot in honor of his courageous charge. For the next two years George was the most revered animal on campus, loved by all and fed by many.

The story of George the mascot began in the fall of 1961, when Wilt arrived at Vanderbilt. The youngest of four children, Wilt was the last to go to college. After the last bird flew the nest, Wilt's parents weren't enamored with the idea of having to take care of the family pet anymore. "So I took him with me," said Wilt.

During his first years at Vanderbilt George lived in the Sigma Chi house and attended most football practices. By September 1964 he had become such a ubiquitous presence that he was the subject of a *Hustler* article. Wilt's girlfriend brought George to home Vanderbilt games that fall. After he chased the UT walking horse out of the stadium, he became a VIP of the athletic department, with a ringside seat for every football and basketball game.

A few months later the Metropolitan Health Department inspected the Sigma Chi house and didn't approve of George's presence there. (In an interview thirty-six years later, Wilt insisted that his dog was unfairly blamed for the unsanitary condition of the house.) George had to live somewhere else. The idea of a homeless mascot didn't sit well with the Vanderbilt student body. So in the spring of 1965 the Council of Student Athletic Activities voted to build George a doghouse. Thus began one of the great Vanderbilt campus controversies of the mid-1960s.

The debate was not over whether to build George a house, but how nice a house to build him. By the time George's house made it to blueprint, it had become a split-level structure (after all, it was the 1960s) containing wall-to-wall carpet and a central heating system. The doghouse was to be located on the north side of Rand Hall, where students could see and pet him every day. It would also serve as a stand for cheerleaders and a rallying place for pep meetings. Estimated cost: $2,000. "This is not just a doghouse," said student Joe Brewer, who headed up the George Doghouse Committee. "School spirit is lagging and lagging badly. We need a boost that will be long lasting; the doghouse can do it."

During the next few months the Intra-fraternity Council obtained pledges of about $1,000 toward George's house. Another $600 was raised through special events and the sale of so-called "paw graphs." In the excitement of the moment some suggested a permanent lineage of horse-chasing mascots. "Toby Wilt, George's master, has been investigating the possibility of breeding the basset hound so that Vanderbilt will always have a direct descendant of George as a mascot," the Nov. 5, 1965 *Hustler* reported.

But the opulence of George's house, coming at a time when students were beginning to notice such things as the Civil Rights Movement and the Vietnam War, didn't sit well with the school newspaper. "*The Hustler* is not anti-George," it said, in one of many articles that reported different prices for the doghouse. "We're not even anti-George doghouse. It's just that $1,500 is far too much to spend on such a project."

With many on campus criticizing the expense of George's planned abode, Nashville general contractor Robert Mathews agreed to provide the labor for George's doghouse, bringing the actual price of the house down to a far more manageable $300. But the enthusiasm for building George an expensive home faded in the summer and fall of 1966. One reason was that George stopped bringing luck; the Vanderbilt football team went 2-7-1 in 1965 and 1-9 in 1966. The other reason was George's own apathy. For some reason, the animal began losing interest in Vanderbilt sports. "He's been hard to find," *The Hustler* reported in February 1966. Finally, an anonymous trustee donated a standard-issue wooden doghouse for George to sleep in.

In early November 1966 George was wandering across campus when he spotted an ice delivery truck heading toward Kirkland Hall. It was the last thing he ever chased. The hound received a hero's funeral; he was embalmed and given a coffin by a local funeral home. George was buried in a small plot just north of Dudley Field, where he apparently still lay at the end of the twentieth century.

After George's death students tried to replace George with a female basset named Samantha. Samantha remained on campus until January 1970, filling the ubiquitous role that George had maintained. But somehow it just wasn't the same; Samantha was happy enough, but didn't have George's mean, unpredictable streak that made the dog a good role model for the football team. Eventually Vanderbilt fans gave up on the idea of a hound mascot.

Tolerance and Rap from the 11th Floor

Despite the Lawson affair and the race referendum of 1962, not much changed around the Vanderbilt campus during the early and mid-1960s. Most students were apparently still satisfied with the world around them. The school newspaper didn't write about much more than sports and the Greek system. Protest and dissent were things that happened on other campuses. But things changed fast between 1963 and 1970. The first big change took place at the top.

When Alexander Heard replaced Harvie Branscomb, the philosophy behind the chancellor's office changed dramatically. Branscomb was uncomfortable with integration, even though his professional responsibilities forced him to move Vanderbilt in that direction in the 1950s. Heard was a New South liberal who truly believed in an integrated society. "The presence of both races creates a more useful educational environment for the whole campus," he said after he became chancellor in 1963. "The college-age people of today will be living in the future in a world that is desegregated. It is the function of the university to prepare them to be a part of that."

Branscomb worried about how trustees felt about people he perceived to be upstart faculty members. In Branscomb's mind, someone like Cold War revisionist Denna Fleming was a radical. Heard allowed revolutionaries to speak on campus.

Branscomb believed in a top-down administrative structure, which is why he was so angry about the faculty rebellion that followed the Lawson affair. Heard preferred a more open and democratic system. In Heard's opinion, if faculty or students wanted something changed, then maybe it should be changed.

Branscomb was a formal person whom students didn't often see. Heard went out of his way to let students know he was available and even interested in seeing them. During his tenure as chancellor Heard would sometimes walk out onto Alumni Lawn and throw a football with a student or with a fellow administrator. If invited, he would have dinner with students.

These changes weren't apparent when Heard became chancellor, but the first example of what was to come took place in the fall of 1963. At that time one of the more popular off-campus hangouts was a restaurant on Twenty-first Avenue called the Campus Grill. In October 1963 a small group of Vanderbilt students began protesting the fact that the Campus Grill refused to serve blacks. "The Campus Grill no longer serves the students of this (university) center," a divinity student named Kendrick Grobel wrote at the time. "It serves some students, but not others. Every student who eats there now repudiates certain of his fellow students . . . whose complexion is of an ancestral legacy from one particular continent."

The Hustler, under the editorship of Dick McCord, gave the protest considerable coverage but little sympathy. "The whole affair shapes up as one of self righteousness, expediency, dullness, hasty action, a desire to cause trouble for the sake of causing trouble, and an urge to jump on the national bandwagon," the paper said. "Personally, we feel that the girl who is barred from sorority membership because of an ugly face goes through a much more serious and harmful experience than the Negro who cannot buy a hot dog at the Campus Grill."

Heard's reaction to the Campus Grill protests took a lot of people by surprise. Only three years earlier Branscomb had expelled James Lawson for being a leader in downtown Nashville's sit-in movement. But in 1963, with students picketing the Campus Grill, Alexander Heard reacted by citing newly written university policy that defended students' right to "assemble peacefully for the sake of redress of grievances."

Despite the school's tolerance for the protesters, it would be about two more years before liberal activism rose to another level on the Vanderbilt campus. In March 1965 a group of undergraduates led by Lee Frissell and Winston Grizzard start a local chapter of the left-wing student group Students for a Democratic Society (SDS). Vanderbilt's SDS chapter didn't last long; it actually ceased functioning that fall because its organizers were unable to devote enough time to the organization. But while it existed it laid the groundwork for the protest movements that would later take place on campus. When Alabama Governor George Wallace spoke at the 1965 Impact lecture series, Vanderbilt's SDS group generated about four hundred signatures protesting his appearance on campus. (SDS members later claimed that they were called "communists" and "nigger lovers" during that petition drive.) The SDS also sponsored two so-called "teach-ins" on the Vietnam War, in one of the first attempts to bring awareness of the war to campus.

Liberal activists were beginning to get so much notice in newspapers that the school saw its first counterprotest. In December 1965 a group of students led by Benny Waggoner organized a group called Students for Support of Soldiers in Vietnam. The group sponsored a blood drive that collected 186 pints, circulated a pro-military petition that got two thousand signatures, and held a big rally on Rand Terrace. Waggoner's group even produced a pro-American audiotape featuring students, Nashville politicians, and country music stars to be played to American troops over armed forces radio.

The next year national debates over the Vietnam War, the Civil Rights Movement, and the general culture of dissidence became more visible. In February national anti-war activist Tom Hayden spoke to about four hundred people on campus. That same week, St. Louis native and First Lieutenant William Settlemire became the first known Vanderbilt alumnus to die in the Vietnam War. By this time *The Hustler* was devoting less space to campus social events such as Charm Week and more space to national issues. In March the school newspaper profiled James Cashwell, an Army ROTC instructor and Vietnam veteran who criticized the media's coverage of the war. "Sometimes I'm disappointed looking in the newspapers seeing pictures of dead Vietcong tied behind an American tank or a dead mother and her baby crying," Cashwell said. "If they're going to show atrocities they ought to show those of the communists as completely as those they judge to be the fault of the U.S." In April student organizations sponsored a debate on the war.

That fall the university took another major step toward tolerating, even encouraging, a culture of dissidence with the hiring of Beverly Asbury as the school's first chaplain. Within months of his arrival Asbury began delivering sermons in which he praised civil rights leaders and called the Vietnam War unpatriotic. He also became a regular fixture at all political protest meetings, and would remain so until his retirement in the 1990s.

By 1967 the Vanderbilt campus was beginning to look much different than it had only a few years earlier. Male students, who had worn nice slacks, well-pressed shirts, and monogrammed sweaters in the 1950s and early 1960s, began wearing blue jeans and T-shirts. Female students, who were forbidden under school policy from wearing pants and shorts on campus, complained about their dress code. The school eased dormitory visitation policy. The number of freshmen who pledged fraternities and sororities began to decline (from 63 percent in 1965 to 54 percent in 1967). The number of campus speakers increased notably. Meanwhile, students seemed to have stronger opinions about everything from national politics to race relations to sex.

The Hustler couldn't contain them all. Between 1966 and 1968 the school saw a proliferation of "underground" student publications. The most radical of them was called *Dirty We'jun.* At a time when many Southerners were uncomfortable with the idea of interracial dating, its October 1967 issue contained a centerfold photograph of a shirtless black man standing over an attractive young woman wearing a towel.

Suggestive centerfolds weren't the only way in which the black presence was becoming more noticeable on campus. In the fall of 1967 the school's first two black athletes – basketball players Perry Wallace and Godfrey Dillard – began dressing out with the varsity team. Meanwhile, a group of students led by Bob Moore organized the first Afro-American Student Association. One of the first items on the organization's agenda was to lobby for academic courses in black studies, a request that would come to fruition in only two years. Soon black students Wesly Bradby and Ilene Carpenter were co-editing *Rap from the 11th Floor*, an underground publication containing poems and essays about black culture.

In October 1967 *The Hustler* ran a series of articles about the cultural barriers faced by Vanderbilt's black students. Among the anonymous quotes: "White students are friendly to me in the dorm, but outside on the street it's a different thing: I cannot speak to them, they have to speak to me. They wonder if they can speak to me without being embarrassed." Not everyone appreciated the articles. One subscriber from Jacksonville, Florida, wrote that "when my son enrolled at Vanderbilt several weeks ago, I subscribed to *The Hustler* with the thought of being able to know more about the college and its activities. So far I have received three copies and each one has an article about the poor, mistreated, misunderstood nigger."

By this time the culture of the 1960s was even affecting apolitical sorority girls and football fans. Before the Georgia Tech football game in the fall of 1967, students replaced the weekly pep rally with what was called a "Sing Out, Love In" on Rand Terrace. The cheerleaders, some of whom had flowers painted on their legs, performed in sunglasses and boots. Girls from the Kappa Delta sorority tossed flowers in the air. After the pep rally the football boosters went over to the stadium in an attempt to give the team good vibes. Unfortunately, the new approach didn't help, as Vanderbilt lost that week 17-10.

Games, Tragedies and Embarrassments

Every Vanderbilt fan has memories of the games and the seasons they saw. Among the more interesting curiosities of Vanderbilt football in the last half of the twentieth century:

Vanderbilt has only won one bowl game in its history. In 1955 the 7-3 Commodores entered the Gator Bowl a touchdown underdog to 8-1-1 Auburn, which was led by an All-American running back (and future Alabama governor) named Fob James. Auburn should have let James carry the ball the whole time; another Tiger running back named Howell Tubbs fumbled four times and gave Vanderbilt all the chances it needed to win the game 25-13. Vanderbilt quarterback Don Orr ran for two touchdowns and threw for another and was selected the game's Most Valuable Player.

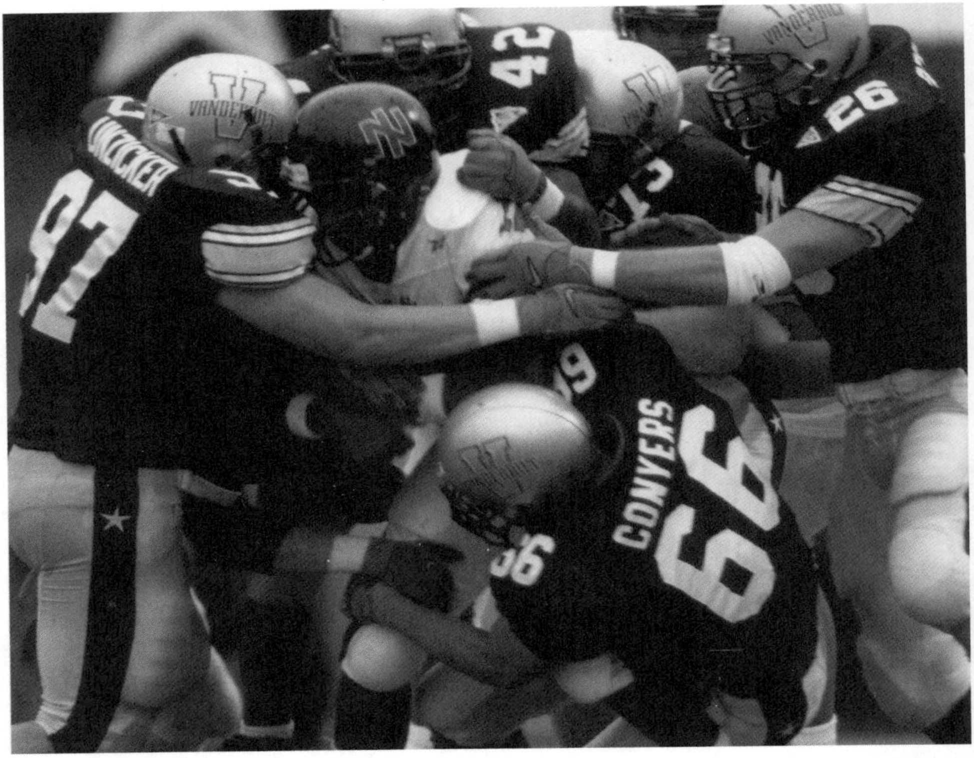

The Vanderbilt defense gangs up on an opposing running back in the late 1990s
Vanderbilt News and Public Affairs

In November 1958, after the University of Tennessee defeated Vanderbilt 10-6, hundreds of UT fans ran onto the field and tore down the goalposts, the first time such a thing had ever happened at Dudley Field. A group of courageous Vanderbilt students tried to stop them — after all, they were the goalposts used during the McGugin years. A few days later a Vanderbilt official was asked whether he objected to the Vanderbilt students who tried to stand up to the mob. "I am delighted, overjoyed that Vanderbilt students finally are trying to protect something that is their own," he said.

One of the most regrettable sporting events Vanderbilt ever played was a game the Commodores won 31-0. On November 23, 1963 – the day after President John Kennedy was assassinated — Chancellor Alexander Heard chose not to cancel a game against George Washington University. Student John Dobrin was disgusted. "The university community demands decorum and proper behavior from its students, but allows a game to be played on Saturday the twenty-third," Dobrin wrote in a letter to *The Hustler* the next week. "By this action, the university has placed itself beyond the bounds of good taste, thus demonstrating either gross misjudgment or an incredible lack of morality."

Vanderbilt didn't have many glorious wins on the football field during the latter part of the twentieth century. One of the few took place on October 11, 1969, when the home Commodores, led by a quarterback named Watson Brown, upset Alabama 14-10. "They outgained us, outhit us, outran us, outpassed us, and outcaught us," Alabama head coach Paul "Bear" Bryant said after the loss. "Alabama football kind of reached the bottom, or to put it another way, Vanderbilt put us on the bottom." Bryant never lost to Vanderbilt again, whipping the Commodores in the 1970s by scores such as 42-0, 48-21, 44-0, 40-7, 42-14, 51-28, and 66-3.

In the summer of 1970 Vanderbilt went along with a national trend and placed artificial turf on Dudley Field at the cost of $250,000. The price of installation was largely offset by the sale of an airplane that had been donated to the school. At the time athletic director Jess Neely believed that playing on a carpet would help attract better recruits. Three decades later Vanderbilt became the last Southeastern Conference team to replant a grass field.

Lights were added to Dudley Field in 1960. For the next fourteen years Vanderbilt played almost every one of its home games at night. In 1974 Vanderbilt moved its home games to the afternoon. The stated reason: the energy crisis. "The energy shortage was given as the official reason for the scrapping of night games," *The Hustler* pointed out, "but Vanderbilt fans are hoping that officials were referring to the power and not an energy shortage on the field."

For a while it looked as if Vanderbilt might abandon Dudley Field. In 1978 a citizens committee appointed by Mayor Richard Fulton recommended that Nashville build a fifty-thousand seat football stadium in Sulphur Dell, the area that later became the site of the Bicentennial Mall. Under the plan both Vanderbilt and Tennessee State University would use the stadium, which would be developed with a convention center in time for Nashville's bicentennial. The committee also recommended that Vanderbilt contribute ten million dollars toward the facility. The downtown stadium plan fizzled after Vanderbilt did not go along with the plan, choosing to add seats to Dudley Field instead.

Since Vanderbilt did not usually field winning football teams in the latter part of the twentieth century, fans had to make the most of near-upsets. Two stand out. In 1977 Vanderbilt was a thirty-one-point underdog playing at top-ranked Oklahoma, but lost only 25-23 after having a field goal blocked on the game's last play. Then, in 1996, the Commodores were forty-three-point underdogs to a Florida team that was ranked number one in the country and had already destroyed ranked opponents such as Georgia and Auburn. Florida head coach Steve Spurrier was so certain that his team would humiliate Vanderbilt that he said before the game that if Vanderbilt fans booed in the fourth quarter that he would punish them by running up the score. However, the Gators struggled that Saturday, building up a 21-3 lead and holding on to win 28-21. Spurrier was pelted with cups and other debris as he left the field, a rare instance of Vanderbilt fans behaving in such a manner.

In November 1985 a Nashville radio station gave kazoos to every person who attended the Vanderbilt-Virginia Tech football game at Dudley Field. At halftime all thirty-five thousand fans played their kazoos at the same time to the tune of the Oak Ridge Boys song "Elvira," setting a world record for the largest kazoo band of all time. The kazoos did not inspire the home team, as Tech won 38-24. "Do those kazoos play taps?" *The Hustler* headline asked the next week.

Perhaps the most heartbreaking loss Vanderbilt ever had to Tennessee was in 1987. Playing in Knoxville, the Commodores built a 28-3 second quarter lead, confusing Tennessee by mixing up the wishbone and spread formations. Tennessee came back and won, 38-36.

A Vanderbilt Guest Starts a Riot

Vanderbilt's 1967 Impact program featured Martin Luther King Jr., poet Allen Ginsberg, and South Carolina senator Strom Thurmond. But few people remember anything King, Ginsberg, or Thurmond said. What they remember is that Stokely Carmichael came and was accused of starting the worst Nashville riot since the Civil War.

In sharp contrast to Martin Luther King's philosophy of non-violent protest, Carmichael was a black power activist who made inflammatory speeches in which he derided the very notion of nonviolent protest and called on blacks to take up arms against "oppressive" whites. Vanderbilt's student-run Impact program extended Carmichael an invitation in the fall of 1966, but Carmichael didn't accept until about three weeks before he was to speak.

Immediately after it was announced that Carmichael was coming, the *Nashville Banner* harshly criticized the decision to invite the black activist. The *Banner* pointed out in front page stories that Carmichael had denounced the Vietnam War as "racist" and called black people who went to fight the war "white mercenaries." Carmichael also said that black people need not obey laws passed by white people. Two days before his appearance in Nashville a student in Birmingham asked Carmichael what black people should do when whites mistreat them. "If a white man tries to walk over you, kill him," Carmichael said.

A few days before the symposium the Tennessee State Senate passed a resolution calling Carmichael a "dangerously unprincipled demagogue" and condemning Carmichael's appearance at Vanderbilt. But despite the resolution, complaints from the *Banner*, calls from concerned trustees such as James Stahlman, Sam Fleming, and Harold Stirling Vanderbilt, and hundreds of letters from alumni protesting Carmichael's invitation, Chancellor Alexander Heard did not cancel the speech. When asked about the students' right to invite Carmichael, Heard frequently referred to a speech he had made in September 1965 in which he said, "It is the business of the university to maintain an open forum. In an open forum, if it is an effective one, conflicting points of view will inevitably be expressed . . . Think of the campus platform in the same terms as the library. No one to my knowledge has claimed that Vanderbilt dignifies and endorses the views expressed in the books it works so hard to acquire."

While in Nashville Carmichael made several public appearances (although Vanderbilt's was the only speech for which he was paid). The first was at Fisk University. There, Carmichael touched on everything from the Vietnam War to the importance of education to the need for black people to take more pride in their accomplishments. "White people should have the gall to call us lazy when they came to Africa to bring us over here to do the work they were too lazy to do themselves," he said. "Our sweat built this country. White people are lazy."

The next day Carmichael made a more inflammatory speech at Tennessee State University. "You ought to organize and take over this city," he said, "but you won't because you don't want power." *The Tennessean* estimated the TSU crowd at four thousand. The *Banner* put the number at twelve hundred.

Saturday, April 9, 1967, was a day few Nashvillians will ever forget. At three in the afternoon Carmichael finally made his Impact appearance, giving what was by his standards a mild speech. In front of an estimated four thousand people, Carmichael talked about how the black community needed to organize itself. "Our Negro communities can become either concentration camps filled with miserable people who have only the power to destroy, or they can become organized communities that make

Stokely Carmichael and Allen Ginsberg answer questions from a student reporter during their visit to Vanderbilt in 1967
The Banner Collection, Nashville Public Library, The Nashville Room

a meaningful contribution to the nation," he said. Carmichael went on to criticize the current crop of black leaders, calling them "vote deliverers" for white politicians. About two-thirds of the audience gave him a standing ovation.

Tennessean reporter (and Vanderbilt student) Frank Sutherland was quick to point out the difference between Carmichael's message and King's speech delivered the night before. "King said massive action programs must be undertaken to lift the economic standards of the Negro community," *The Tennessean* reported. "He favored integration of whites and Negroes to help the Negro to compete in economic society. He emphasized that nonviolence was the only way to achieve this."

The events of that night will forever remain in dispute. The trouble apparently started when the owner of a Jefferson Street restaurant called the police, asking that a student be ejected from the building. Once ejected, the student organized picketers, who began harassing occupants of the restaurant. Police were called back to the scene. Then students began throwing rocks at the police and at passing cars. The students barricaded behind the rock wall surrounding Fisk. More police came, and they charged the wall. The students dispersed into smaller groups. And the riot was on.

The next morning readers of Nashville's morning newspaper were greeted with the headline "RIOT FLARES IN FISK AREA." No one had been killed. But at least fourteen people had been hospitalized, including an eighteen-year-old man who had been shot in the leg. "It was scary," said Sutherland, who covered the riot. "I remember that there was a phone booth about thirty feet from the intersection of Seventeenth Avenue and Jefferson Street. I'd run back and forth from that phone booth, calling in my story every time something happened." Sutherland said that he was hit by rocks about eight times.

The rioting moved to Tennessee State University the next night. The violence took place throughout the night and early morning. Molotov cocktails were thrown through the windows of several small businesses, including a barbershop, a gas station, and a liquor store. Again, no one was killed. But again, dozens were injured, including a TSU student who was shot in the neck. Police arrested about forty people, including an Atlanta resident who was a key member of Carmichael's organization, ironically called the Student Non-Violent Coordinating Committee (SNCC).

On Monday Nashville Mayor Beverly Briley, both newspapers, clergymen from all races, and black leaders called for an end to the violence. Just about everyone was quick to lay the blame for the incident on the man Vanderbilt University had brought to town. A reporter asked Briley if he thought Stokely Carmichael was responsible for the rioting. Briley's response: "Yes. He and his aides are responsible." Avon Williams, an attorney and a leader in Nashville's black community, called the riots "the design of Stokely Carmichael" and said that "it is my conviction that Stokely Carmichael should stay out of here and our people and our community will be better off."

No one was more eager to point the finger at the black power activist than the *Banner*, which had warned Nashville residents that something like this might happen if Carmichael came. In a front-page editorial that came out the afternoon after the second day of riots, the *Banner* castigated Vanderbilt's administration for inviting Carmichael. "The stupidity of a campus group's explanation that he was brought here as a part of a 'search for truth' was more than matched . . . by Vanderbilt administrative officers who so far disregarded a duty to the campus, the institution and the community itself," the editorial said. "The Pandora's box of violent contents was opened by academic hands . . . in the final analysis, the ultimate responsibility for what occurred lies at the door of the Chancellor."

The Impact series and the riots that followed it tested Heard's philosophy of campus openness. During the three weeks following the events there were frequent rumors that Heard would be fired. They were fueled by an April 21 *Time* magazine article that said *Banner* publisher and Vanderbilt trustee James Stahlman was exerting so much pressure on Heard that the chancellor would resign if he did not get a vote of confidence at the next board of trust meeting. Stahlman denied this report.

Fortunately for the chancellor he received moral support from a few newspaper columnists. *Chattanooga Times* writer Fred Travis called Heard "one of the South's most eloquent spokesmen on behalf of academic freedom." He openly speculated that Heard might be ousted for the incident and warned that if such a thing took place that it would have dire consequences for higher education in Tennessee. Another southern journalist, Vanderbilt alum Roy Blount, penned an article in the *Atlanta Journal-Constitution* in which he said that "a great deal of credit for the trouble must go to local racial festering and to the *Banner's* week-long frenzy" that preceded Carmichael's speech.

Stahlman was probably the angriest trustee. But it has never been fully understood whether Stahlman's intention was to oust Heard or to simply get the university to admit that the Carmichael invitation was a mistake. In any case, Stahlman did not succeed on either count. Despite intense criticism, Heard convinced most of the trustees that the Carmichael incident, though regretful, did not justify a reversal of the school's direction. At the May 5 board of trust meeting there was considerable talk about the Carmichael speech from both Stahlman and Heard. But there was no vote to dismiss the chancellor.

HEARD GETS IT FROM THE RIGHT

Nashville Banner publisher James Stahlman is cited so often as the most conservative member of the Vanderbilt Board of Trust in the 1960s that people forget about the time he stomped out a right-wing rebellion against Alexander Heard.

Alumni feel a certain amount of ownership in their school, and so it is not surprising that the changes taking place in the mid-1960s did not sit well with everyone. The loudest dissenter was a 1938 graduate and the owner of a chain of farm magazines named Thomas Anderson.

Anderson was a member of an old Vanderbilt family; his father graduated in 1905 and coached the track team for four decades, and his sister Jane was married to Vanderbilt trustee Guilford Dudley Jr. Like many other alumni from his era, Anderson did not appreciate the way Vanderbilt was changing in the 1960s. He didn't believe the university should be pursuing national foundation money, didn't believe it should admit black students, and didn't believe it should host leftist speakers. "Communism isn't our real enemy," he said. "It's liberalism. Every country that has gone communist has been delivered by the liberals."

In June 1967 Anderson, alumnus Horton Early, and Anderson's son-in-law Thomas Kinney (a star Vanderbilt football player in the early 1960s), sent letters to every alumni whose address they could obtain. (Since the university wouldn't give them a complete list of graduates, it is impossible to know how many letters they actually sent out.) The letter cited the April 1967 campus appearances of poet Allen Ginsburg and activist Stokely Carmichael as proof that communism and sexual promiscuity were being taught at Vanderbilt. "Religion, morality, honor, patriotism, marriage, faith and truth are being deliberately downgraded and destroyed," the letter said. "This is not only happening at Berkeley, it's happening right here, right now, at Vanderbilt . . . Communism, like rape, is not a moot question which deserves pro and con treatment. Communism is not an ideology or political party, but a criminal conspiracy to enslave the world. Communism should not be heard (no pun intended) but imprisoned." The letter asked recipients to either write *Banner* publisher James Stahlman (whom the letter described as "the only trustee who hadn't sold out") or to a committee called Vanderbilt Today for more information. Its authors enclosed an editorial written by Stahlman that excoriated the school for hosting Carmichael.

The media coverage of the letters gave Anderson a chance to better explain his viewpoint. Through this coverage Anderson professed to being a white supremacist who had renounced the Methodist Church for its increasing liberalism. Among the quotes he also gave a *Hustler* reporter:

"There is no question that Vanderbilt has gone far to the left. It has been seduced by the foundations. To get the loans and grants, it has to subscribe to foundation regulations about teaching and curriculum. The board of trust has sold out to these foundations."

"Harold Vanderbilt brought Heard, who is a liberally oriented opportunist politician, here and stands behind him. I don't know why, except maybe it's a guilt complex he has for making so much money and not having earned any of it. Of course, the board won't buck Harold Vanderbilt. He's going to give the school $55 million when he dies, and they'd do anything for a buck."

"What you need for a good education is a good teacher under a tree. It doesn't take escalators. What we need is a search for the truth, honesty and integrity. Education should restore morality, which has been in decadence."

"The amount of money spent on education today is pathetic; we've gone overboard on education. I could really care less if a person working for me has a college diploma, because so many graduates don't begin to have an education."

Anderson said that he received about fifty letters in response, all but one of which was in agreement with him. But Anderson's cause was undermined when he was denounced by his patron saint. After the letters were sent out, Stahlman published an editorial in which he denied any affiliation with the Vanderbilt Today group and distanced himself from Anderson. "I say to any man who may receive copies of the letter under discussion, please do me the courtesy to ignore any suggestion that I become the repository for your letters of protest," the *Banner* editorial stated. "I want no part in the unwise maneuver and I reiterate my bitter resentment and total rejection of any effort to make me a spokesman for any group."

In any case, it does not appear as if Anderson's letter shook the foundation of Kirkland Hall. Anderson got a lot of publicity because of the letters, and he actually spoke in front of about three hundred students at his alma mater in February 1969. But no trustee publicly supported Anderson or his right-wing group. As for Heard's effectiveness with alumni, the chancellor was in the early stages of what turned out to be a successful $55 million fund drive.

DINAH, DICKEY, AND THE PRESIDENT OF PANAMA

Far too many important people have graduated from Vanderbilt to detail in this volume. But there are some interesting alumni that the school often makes reference to, and a few outstanding ones that have long been forgotten.

For instance, a Vanderbilt alumnus was once the president of

Panama. In 1955 Jose Guizado, a 1920 graduate of the Vanderbilt School of Engineering, became president of Panama after the assassination of President Remon. After his ascendancy a college friend of Guizado's named Raymond Denney recalled that Guizado's nickname in college was Cannobe, because of his habit of saying the words "can no be." Guizado only stayed in office for about three months.

A few American politicians have gone to Vanderbilt as well. Among the more prominent are Vice President Al Gore, U.S. Senators Jim Sasser, Bill Frist, and Lamar Alexander, and Atlanta mayor Bill Campbell.

It wasn't something that the school was proud of at the time, but first person who probably ever played country music on radio station WSM was a Vanderbilt graduate. In October 1925 – weeks before the spontaneous start of a music show called the Grand Ole Opry – WSM station manager George Hay began featuring a hillbilly band called the Castalian Springs Barn Dance Orchestra. The leader of the band, later known as the Possum Hunters, was a graduate of the Vanderbilt Medical School named Humphrey Bate.

There has been so much emphasis on the Fugitives in Vanderbilt's history that other important writers the school helped produce have often been overlooked. Author Peter Taylor, who wrote several novels including *A Summons to Memphis*, graduated in 1940. Poet and *Deliverance* author James Dickey graduated with a major in philosophy and a minor in astrophysics in 1950. Many years later Dickey said that he didn't do much as a student other than go to class and hang out at the library. "I was just a veteran, going around campus in a ragged sheepskin flying jacket," he said. "I really sort of conducted two separate educations. One was the course work, where you had to hand in papers and turn in things. But then I had a private education, and that was really the more important. But they were both good – there ain't nobody that says you can't have it both ways. And I read – I remember reading the whole rack of anthropology one summer, and it was the most interesting stuff I'd ever read in my whole life. Nobody could have driven me out [of the library]."

James McReynolds, a graduate of Vanderbilt in the 1890s, was appointed to the U.S. Supreme Court by Woodrow Wilson and remained on the high court for twenty-six years. In 1927 there were

The Vanderbilt Board of Trust in the mid 1930s. Chancellor James Kirkland and board chairman Frank Rand are on the front row, fourth and fifth from the left. James Stahlman is on the back row, far left.
The Banner Collection, Nashville Public Library, The Nashville Room

even rumblings in the Democratic Party about nominating him to run for president. McReynolds was a prominent critic of Franklin Roosevelt's New Deal in the 1930s.

One of the most famous Vanderbilt graduates of all time was Fanny Rose Shore, a member of the Alpha Epsilon Phi sorority and a sociology major from the class of 1938. The career of Dinah Shore, as she later called herself, took off immediately after she graduated. By 1941 the singer and radio personality was earning $26,000 a year. "This only ain't hay," *The Hustler* pointed out, "but it is more than the chancellor, plus coach, plus a couple of professors are making."

Another remarkable female Vanderbilt graduate was Martha Ragland, who got her undergraduate degree in 1927 and her masters in 1928. At a time when few women were involved in politics, Ragland was extremely active in women's political causes and was a leader in

Estes Kefauver's bid for the U.S. Senate in 1948.

Delbert Mann, an alumnus from the class of 1941, went on to be a Hollywood film director who won an Academy Award for directing the 1954 movie *Marty*. His other film credits included *All Quiet on the Western Front* and *The Man without a Country*. Mann majored in political science; when he was a student, Vanderbilt had no theater course of any kind, but he participated in the Nashville Community Playhouse. "I majored in having a good time," he later said. "I don't know how I ever got out of school."

As might be expected, Vanderbilt graduates dominate the ranks of Nashville's business leaders in the twentieth century. Among the more prominent local businessmen who graduated from Vanderbilt were Third National Bank's Sam Fleming; First American National Bank's Andrew Benedict; Life & Casualty Insurance Co.'s Guilford Dudley Jr.; National Life and Accident Insurance Co.'s Edwin Craig; H. G. Hill Co.'s H. G. Hill Jr.; Equitable Securities' Brownlee Currey Sr.; and Hospital Corporation of America's Thomas Frist Jr. (The two most important businessmen in Nashville in the twentieth century who didn't go to Vanderbilt were Genesco's Maxey Jarman and Kentucky Fried Chicken executive and HCA co-founder Jack Massey.)

There was a time when Vanderbilt alumni apparently felt it was their duty to serve in the state legislature. In 1928 there were seven Vanderbilt alumni in the state house and seven others in the state senate. However, this tradition waned by the end of the twentieth century. In 2003 there were no Vanderbilt graduates in the house and only three in the senate – Douglas Henry, Steve Cohen, and Roy Herron.

Changing the Game

By 1966 Vanderbilt had a handful of black students in its freshman, sophomore, and junior classes. But the school's athletic program was still all white.

It wasn't that the coaches didn't want black players. Starting in 1964 head basketball coach Roy Skinner began trying to recruit black athletes from as far away as Michigan and Illinois. He did so with the support of Chancellor Alexander Heard but the expressed displeasure of many fans. "I remember getting petitions against the idea of my recruiting black players with a lot of signatures on them," said Skinner, Vanderbilt's head coach from 1961 until 1976. In an era of racial problems in the South, Skinner had a hard time finding a black high school student who would commit to Vanderbilt.

In the winter of 1965 Skinner began scouting an extremely talented player named Perry Wallace Jr. Wallace grew up in the heart of black Nashville, near the corner of Jefferson Street and Twenty-sixth Avenue. As a senior at Pearl High School, Wallace led his undefeated state champion basketball team in scoring and rebounding. He was also the valedictorian of his graduating class.

Wallace was recruited by just about every major university in the country. But the idea of going to Vanderbilt and becoming the first black basketball player in the Southeastern Conference appealed to him. "I wanted to go to a major university and major in engineering and play big-time basketball," said Wallace, later a professor at the Washington College of Law at American University. "I had a good feeling about going to Vanderbilt, even though the South was a different place then and I knew that I would be the first black to play there. And I knew that my parents could come across town and see me play and that they would be treated with respect by white people, which I knew would be a huge triumph for them."

In May 1966 Wallace announced he would come to Vanderbilt. When he started school that fall, he was one of two African American freshmen recruited to play ball. The other was his roommate, a young man from Detroit, Michigan, named Godfrey Dillard.

In those days freshmen were not allowed to play varsity sports, and so Wallace and Dillard didn't begin playing big-time college basketball until the fall of 1967. As if being the first black player in the conference weren't enough, the NCAA outlawed dunking that year, making it even tougher for Wallace. "That was the worst thing that ever happened to Perry's game, because in high school that was the only shot that he could make," said Skinner.

For the next three seasons Wallace and his white teammates

suffered the abuse of opposing fans. "Sometimes, things would get ugly," Wallace said. "People would yell things, people would taunt me. Sometimes the cheerleaders at the other schools would lead cheers against me. Things were worst at the two Mississippi schools and at Auburn. I was made very aware of the fact that they weren't used to seeing black players, and that they didn't like black players."

Years later Roy Skinner said that Wallace's poise on the road trips was remarkable. "It was as bad as it could be," Skinner said. "The crowd made remarks to and about Perry that were ridiculous. I think some of them should have been arrested for some of the things that they were saying. I felt real sorry for Perry for having to go through that."

Perhaps the most difficult experience for Wallace took place in Oxford, Mississippi, on February 10, 1968. According to both Skinner and Wallace, some of the fans at that year's Vandy-Ole Miss game mercilessly taunted Wallace, using racial epithets to distract his concentration and try to turn him against his teammates. On top of that, Wallace perceived that some of the Mississippi players were going out of their way to rough him up. "First I got poked directly in the eye after I got a rebound," Wallace said. "And then I drove in and someone hit me harder than anyone had ever hit me before. It was like a full body slam."

The taunting and the rough play backfired. "That was the only time I saw him really get upset," Skinner said. "And he became a man possessed. He began grabbing every rebound and just controlling the game." Vandy won, 90-72.

The atmosphere at the games and on campus was too much for Dillard. After suffering a season-ending injury at the beginning of his sophomore year, Dillard tried to come back his junior year but didn't make the team. Years later Dillard said he didn't make the team because of things that happened off the court. "By the time I came back, I had gotten involved in a lot of political activity and I was very vocal about the racism that I was encountering on campus," said Dillard, who later became an attorney. "Athletes weren't supposed to do that." Skinner maintained that Dillard was cut because he wasn't as good a player as he was before his knee injury.

The Vanderbilt basketball team had a disappointing season in

Perry Wallace goes up for a shot against Kentucky in 1970
Photographic Archives, Vanderbilt University

1969-70, fielding its first losing season in twenty years. Senior and team captain Perry Wallace was the bright spot, leading the team in rebounding and scoring.

Wallace also saved his best game for last. On March 7, 1970, Wallace scored twenty-nine points and grabbed twenty-seven rebounds as Vanderbilt defeated Mississippi State in Memorial Gymnasium 78-72. The game was such a triumph for Wallace that he even concluded it with a dunk, an illegal move that the referees inexplicably ignored. The 13,855 Vanderbilt fans were so happy for Wallace that they gave three standing ovations.

What Wallace did the next day angered many people. Only a few hours after his victorious final game the Vanderbilt senior had a long interview with *Tennessean* reporter Frank Sutherland and spilled his guts about what it had been like to be a black man on the Vanderbilt campus during the previous four years. "I have been a very lonely person at Vanderbilt," Wallace said. "Things have gotten a lot better over the years, but it has been a lonesome thing."

In the front-page *Tennessean* article, Wallace said he appreciated the value of the education he had received at Vanderbilt. But he said that he had been shut out of almost every aspect of social life at the school, from fraternities to area churches to dorm life. "On the dormitory halls I got to know some people but there were others who condescended, people who were used to blacks who cut the grass and who swept floors," he said. "They respected my basketball ability but they still considered me as a person who sweeps floors ... It sort of ended up there wasn't a lot to do. I existed as a very lonely person."

Wallace said that the one place at the school where he had always been treated well was Memorial Gymnasium. "The fans have really been good," he said. "That was what really impressed me about Vanderbilt. They really stick with you."

Years later Wallace said that he didn't regret the things he said in the interview. "If Daniel Boone and Davy Crockett had come east in the old days and told people in the big cities that the west was a wonderful country and that there was no danger and no bad weather and that the natives were friendly, then think what would have happened," said Wallace. "I know that a lot of people were upset at the time. But I really thought it was my duty to paint an accurate picture of what it was like."

One person upset about the interview was Coach Roy Skinner. Thirty-two years later, Skinner said he had changed his mind. "When I first read it, I was really surprised and thought that it was a real ugly thing to do because he had been treated so nicely by so many people," he said. "But it also woke me up. He talked about some things that were going on at the time that I hadn't really thought about. After it had sunk in, I admired him for it."

Wallace got his degree in electrical engineering and engineering mathematics, becoming the first African American athlete to graduate from a school in the Southeastern Conference. By the time he graduated, Auburn had a black basketball player on its varsity team. By the early 1980s some of the schools whose fans had taunted Wallace were cheering for predominantly black teams. "When I see games on television now with so many black players, it is just unbelievable to me," said Wallace. "It doesn't feel like it's been that long since my experience."

Most people who attended Vanderbilt in the late 1960s or lived in Nashville at that time remembered Perry Wallace. However, most students who came in later years had never heard of the man, something that some of Wallace's former peers said was a travesty. "I don't think he has ever been fully thanked for what he did," Jerry Southwood, a former teammate and roommate of Wallace's at Vanderbilt, said in 2001. "If you asked players in the conference today who the first black player was, then I'm sure no one would have heard of him. And yet he helped set into motion a process to allow hundreds of young people to go to college and get a degree."

SARRATT AND THE QUIET LOUNGE

It is hard to imagine the Vanderbilt campus without Sarratt Student Center and its many places to eat, its concrete walkways, brick walls, bookstore, post office, and of course its "tunnel." However, the student center complex has a very curious architectural design because it has because it has been changed and been added to more than any other structure on campus.

The first phase of the student center's construction began in 1952, when the university tore down the Barnard Observatory and built a complex that included a cafeteria, post office, and bookstore. The $1.2 million building was named for Frank Rand, former president of the International Shoe Co. and the chairman of the Vanderbilt Board of Trust from 1935 to 1949. It was partially funded with a $500,000 gift from Fredrick W. Vanderbilt. Like many other structures that were designed during that era, Rand Hall was long, low, and modern. Among the unique features of its cafeteria were hidden serving lines and fireplaces at both ends of its dining room.

Rand was a huge step forward for students. Prior to that most of them ate in a dining room in the basement of aging Kissam Hall. Unlike Kissam, Rand was air conditioned and convenient. As one *Hustler* reporter wrote, "the food is good, and they have those cute little gadgets to send trays back on." The best part of the new building was the Commodore Room, which in the 1950s contained a jukebox and piano. But despite the amenities, Rand wasn't exactly a student center. In the 1960s the closest thing to a student center on campus was Alumni Hall, where student meetings were held and where the offices for *The Hustler* and *The Commodore* were located. The school had no movie theater and almost no areas set aside for student organizations to meet.

When Alexander Heard took over as Vanderbilt chancellor in 1963, he knew the university needed a new student center. But the campus had other needs that came first. One was a new center for the physics, chemistry, and mathematics departments, a need that led to the expansion of Stevenson Center. Another was dormitory space, which led to the development of Carmichael Towers. "We had to build dorms as fast as we could, because the baby boomers were beginning to arrive on campus," Heard said years later. "In those days, you couldn't have a conversation without the phrase 'baby boom' popping up."

Vanderbilt began planning and raising money for a student center in the mid-1960s. A private consulting firm came up with a recommendation for it to be located at the corner of Garland and Twenty-fifth Avenues (about where the University Club parking lot was later placed). In its design it was huge and contained many facili-

Madison Sarratt speaking at the dedication of Sarratt Student Center
The Banner Collection, Nashville Public Library, The Nashville Room

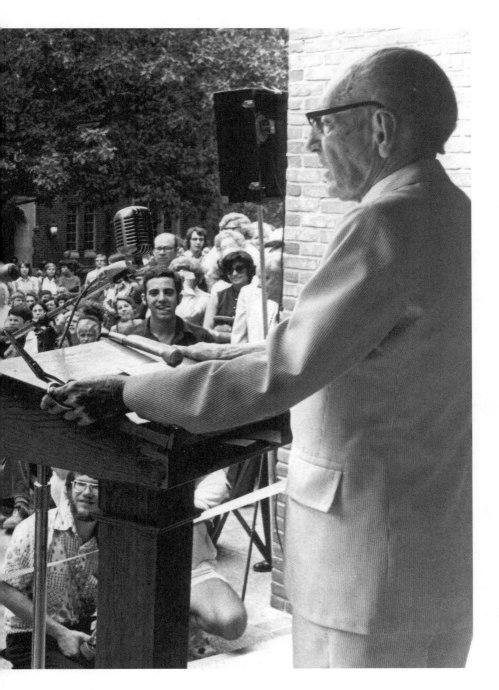

ties that were commonly built in student centers on other campuses of that era, such as a bowling alley and an ice skating rink.

Heard and Dean of Student Affairs Sidney Boutwell wanted student input regarding the student center. And as it turned out, students didn't think much of the plan. "Many students didn't see the need for all the things that were in the original student center plan," said Jim Sandlin, Vanderbilt's associate dean of men at the time. "They also said that diversity was important to them and the little subgroups of campus life were important to them – not necessarily big open spaces in which everyone could gather."

In part because of student opinion, the student center plans were changed. Meanwhile, the decision was made to put the facility between Rand Hall and Old Science (later Benson Hall). This created a new problem: Only a couple of years earlier, the idea of putting a social sciences center in that same area had produced rigorous opposition from students, who were opposed to the idea of tearing down trees and eliminating all the open space on campus. Eventually, the idea began to emerge that the student center could be placed north and west of Rand Hall and linked with that structure. The university asked Nashville architect Bob Street, who had designed many projects on campus, to work on such a plan.

Street's job was not easy. He was tasked with designing a structure that was limited in size but contained meeting places, clubrooms, a crafts workshop, a games area, a movie theater, a place for art exhibits, and a restaurant. Meanwhile, the building had to link with Rand Hall and blend in with nearby structures such as Cole Hall.

One way Street accomplished this was to convert an area that had been used as a storeroom for the university and a washroom for Rand Hall into a passageway connecting student organizations such as *The Hustler*, *The Commodore,* and WRVU. Years later, that passageway became referred to as the "tunnel," and students that worked for university publications and the station became known as "tunnel rats."

Another thing Street did was create a handsome stairway entrance to the student center from the west. "I can't remember how many bricks we used, but it was some huge number," said Street, who later designed the Blair School of Music. The liberal use of bricks is a recurring motif with Street. When he designed the renovation of

Kirkland Hall in the mid-1980s, he covered the interior hallway walls with brick. "I like brick," said Street. "Brick gives off a very warm feeling." Street also influenced the decision by campus planners to start building sidewalks out of brick, a trend that was later reversed because brick sidewalks become slippery when wet.

Street's plans were released in the fall of 1971, but the student center was not completed until three years later. Prior to that time the board of trust voted to name it for longtime Dean of Students Madison Sarratt.

Street received national recognition for the Sarratt design. The project blended in so wonderfully with existing construction that future generations of students would not be able to tell where the old Rand complex ended and Sarratt Student Center began.

In 1986 a second floor was added to the bookstore and the dining room. Then, in a renovation that was completed in the mid-1990s, parts of the Sarratt tunnel and plaza were altered to add more

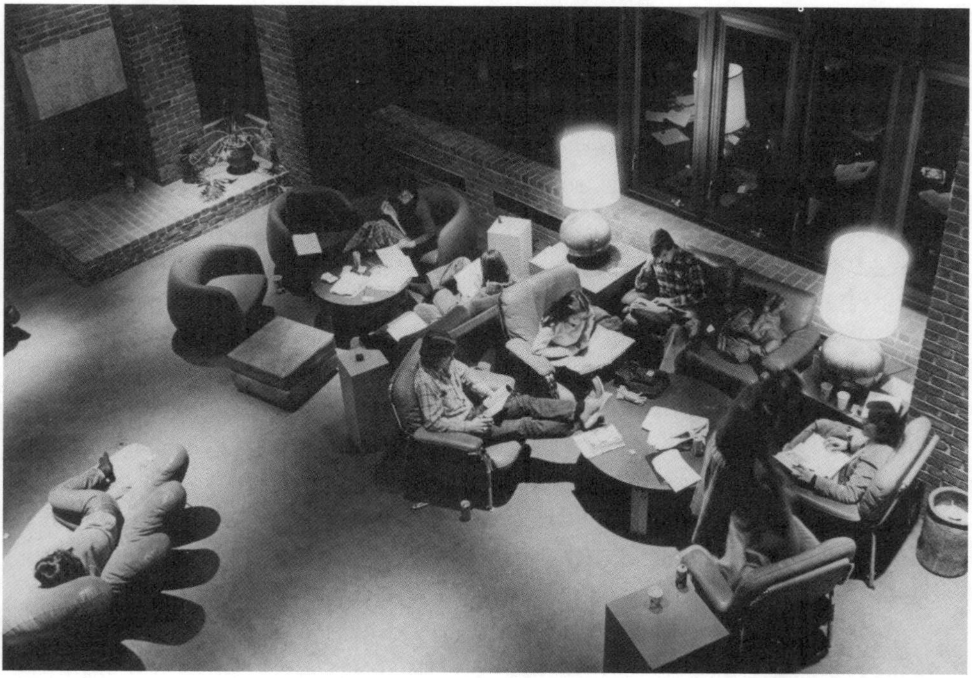

Sarratt Student Center's Baseball Glove Lounge, originally envisioned as the "loud" lounge
Photographic Archives, Vanderbilt University

food service, retail space, offices, and student meeting areas.

On a visit in 2002 to the student center he helped create, Street said he couldn't remember many of the original ideas behind Sarratt's design because the building has been altered so much since then. However, one thing Street did remember was the idea behind the study lounge known as the "Baseball Glove."

"It was called the 'loud lounge' in the drawings," said Street. "The idea was that students already had enough places to study, but what they needed was a place to get together and socialize that was not located in a dorm." Within a couple of years of Sarratt's opening, students had turned the loud lounge into a study hall. "I remember at one point I walked through it and got shushed," Street said. "So much for the loud lounge."

PROTESTING EVERYTHING

Vanderbilt was a strange and exciting place to be in the late 1960s. It was a place where the Old South was turning into to the New South, where a tradition of segregation was giving way to unexpected complaints about racial insensitivity, where allegiance to country was being confronted by war protesters. On a campus where almost nothing had changed in decades, it seemed as if old traditions – good, bad, and harmless – were being discarded monthly.

At the beginning of the 1960s students who demonstrated ran the risk of being expelled. By the end of the 1960s students were almost expected to protest.

Several decades later it is tempting to downplay the many causes students supported in the late 1960s. But the Vanderbilt students who organized, demonstrated, wrote letters, and believed in their causes probably did more than detractors gave them credit for. By the time it was over, students had more rights, more freedom, and more input about what happened on campus. And most people who took part in the process will tell you that they had a lot of fun along the way. "It was a great time to go to school and a fantastic time to go to Vanderbilt," said Chuck Offenburger, a member of the class of 1969 and the editor of *The Hustler*. "Not only did we as students change while we were there, but the university changed while we were there. Back then, we felt as if it was our duty and our right to be informed about everything and to be active regarding everything. And when I think about the speakers that came to campus and the entertainers that came to campus during my tenure, I can't get over what a great liberal arts education I had."

So much happened between the fall of 1967 and the spring of 1970 that a chronology is helpful.

November 1967

— A campus-wide poll reveals that 77 percent of the students (but only 37 percent of faculty) favor "the complete American defeat of the communist forces in South Vietnam" over other alternatives, such as "negotiated cease fire" and "let the United Nations deal with it."

— A handful of students picket the Navy ROTC Fall Review, in what is believed to be the first protest of such an event in campus history. "We want to get it across to the students in ROTC that they're making a big mistake putting themselves in the armed forces," says student Stephen Parker. The next week, a group of students rent a coffin from a local funeral home and stage a protest over a recruiting visit by Dow Chemical Co., producer of napalm.

January 1968

— The Vanderbilt Vietnam Action Committee, started by physics professor David Kotelchuck, sponsors a series of lectures on the war. Among the lecture topics are how to protest the war and how to avoid the draft.

February 1968

— About a thousand students turn out to hear a speech by William Coffin, the Yale University chaplain who had recently been indicted for counseling students on how to resist the draft.

—- Campus Crusade for Christ founder Bill Bright speaks on campus. *The Hustler*, under the editorship of student Greg Tucker, criticizes Bright and his organization. "The campus crusade is dangerous," *The Hustler* says. "It preys upon the elements of insecurity which exist in the modern college world and breeds in its adherents a false, misleading sense of just assurance."

— Chancellor Heard suspends four students and places on probation thirty-eight others for use or possession of marijuana, and then sends out a press release to Nashville's newspapers about the crackdown. "I want what has been done to be accurately understood on the campus and elsewhere," he says.

April 1968

— Junior football player Terry Thomas says he is quitting the team because he says he was pressured to do so by head coach Bill Pace after he signed an antiwar petition. Thomas, who is white, also says coaches told him he couldn't bring a black date to a football awards banquet to be held at Hillwood Country Club. The "Thomas incident," as it becomes known, results in a campus debate about the isolated "jock cult" of big-time college sports. Eventually, five hundred students and faculty sign a petition (published in the school paper) protesting the school's shortage of black athletes and the way Thomas was treated.

— Vanderbilt prepares for another Impact symposium, booking such speakers as presidential candidate Robert Kennedy, civil rights activist Julian Bond, *National Review* founder William Buckley, and New York Mayor John Lindsay. The night before the event Martin Luther King Jr. is assassinated in Memphis. Because of riots in New York, Lindsay has to cancel his appearance. The speakers who do come to the program comment on what the King assassination means. "Nonviolence died last night in Memphis," says Bond, in a comment that he later says is taken out of context. Chancellor Heard calls off classes for a day after the King assassination, infuriating some students. "If people want to eulogize this martyr that is fine with me," student Richard Ranson writes *The Hustler*. "But if I am paying $4,000 a year for the 'honor' of attending this university, then I'll be damned if I expect Vanderbilt officials to call off classes as a tribute to some damned riot-rouser."

September 1968

— The big controversy on campus is the passage by the Metro Council of a mandatory $15 tax for out-of-town cars parked in

Nashville's streets. About five hundred students show up at an anti-tax rally in front of Rand Hall. "Mr. [Beverly] Briley, I'm going to cheat you and not pay that tax," one student says at the rally. "My green '64 Rambler is worth about $50 on the market right now." Another student named Marshall Chapman plays her guitar at the rally and sings a tune called "You Dirty Egg Sucking Dawg," dedicated to Nashville's mayor.

— *The Hustler*, under the leadership of new editor Chuck Offenburger, takes the bizarre step of endorsing Dick Gregory, a black activist and comedian who has not been nominated by any party, for president of the United States. The endorsement reflects the disgust that many students have for the fact that the choices on the ballot are Democrat Hubert Humphrey (Lyndon Johnson's vice president), Republican Richard Nixon, and Independent George Wallace. However, the endorsement doesn't sit too well with many students and alumni. Two of *The Hustler's* wooden distribution stands are inexplicably set afire that week. Meanwhile, Chancellor Heard receives a letter from an alumnus, enclosed with a check that has been torn to bits. The alumnus informs Heard that he was going to make a donation to the university but changed his mind when he saw *The Hustler's* endorsement.

— About a dozen students wander through fraternity and sorority row during rush handing out anti-Greek pamphlets. The literature asks rushees to question whether "they (the frats) like you as a unique person or an advertising prop?"

— Larry Moore becomes the first black member of a Vanderbilt fraternity when he is pledged by Alpha Epsilon Pi. A few months later the Intra-fraternity Council votes not use a recreation center in Nashville that doesn't allow black people to use the facility.

October 1968

— At a student-sponsored series of lectures on drug use, Dr. Joseph Schooler of the Baylor University Medical School says marijuana is not a narcotic, does not induce increased dosage, is not physically addictive, and does not cause violent crime. But he says it is harmful. "Even its casual use should make the user stop and figure out why he is using it."

— *Hustler* film critic Mary Brabston writes an article about how mortified she is that so many Vanderbilt boys go to independent films just to see nude women. "When the lights were turned out, howling started, and mooing," she writes. "I never knew so many Vanderbilt males could imitate cows so well." A few weeks later, *The Hustler* points out that X-rated films at the nearby Belcourt Theater are always packed with male Vanderbilt students. In a review of one X-rated flick, *The Hustler* claims that "whatever anybody's response to the film might be, it will be at the Belcourt for some time due to its magical X-rating, a virtual assurance of packed houses hungry for forbidden fruit." By the end of the year, an X-rated movie theater in Nashville's Lower Broad area becomes one of *The Hustler's* most loyal advertisers.

November 1968

— In a campus poll, 57 percent of students prefer Nixon to 24 percent who prefer Humphrey.

— A student group books Black Panther Eldridge Cleaver to speak on campus. At the last minute Cleaver cancels his appearance because of a gunfight between Black Panthers and the San Francisco police. "The primary disappointment was that we students are not going to have the opportunity to hear a man with such relevant and important ideas who leads an important force in our society today," SGA president Al Hubbard says.

— About 200 female students officially ask an administrative body to get rid of curfews for female students. The administration reacts by doing away with curfews for senior women, while saying it will poll parents to see how they feel about doing away with curfews for sophomore and junior women.

December 1968

— Mike Davis, a young man who had earlier transferred from Vanderbilt to the University of Tennessee, says in a *Hustler* article that he and other Army ROTC cadets were trained to hit people with rifle butts and march over them in case of protests. Army ROTC Commanding Officer Col. Robert Crouch says Davis is lying. "If any cadet took an action like this . . . it would be completely out of line," Crouch says. "We have no authority to control a crowd of any kind, student or otherwise." True or not, Davis' statements lead to a *Hustler* editorial that says the paper "opposes in principal the presence of ROTC programs on this campus."

— The student-led protest on women's curfew gains strength. At one campus rally a student named Julia Malone speaks out against the many rules that apply to women on campus, including the "popular convention" that women wear skirts rather than pants.

— A group of students starts a broadsheet weekly newspaper called *Versus.* From its inception *Versus* takes a more conservative editorial slant on campus and national political events than *The Hustler.* "We thought *The Hustler* was a pretty pale imitation of 1960s campus revolutionism," Michael Franks, the first editor of *Versus,* said many years later. "We came up with the name *Versus* because we were against *The Hustler.*" Although *Versus* is more conservative in its politics, its staff takes the rebellious step of refusing to join the student publications board, making it completely independent in operation. Since *Versus* has no financial support from student funds, its staff has to sell more ads than *The Hustler* to get by, which it does.

January 1969

— The refusal of two undergraduates, Mike Kiernan and Stonewall Breyer, to take mandatory physical education courses becomes well known on campus. Their stance is one of many reasons that the administration appoints a faculty group to consider the idea of doing away with the P.E. requirement. While the issue is being debated, Kiernan says he'd be glad to take courses in sex to fulfill the requirement. "Lovemaking, after all, is the most creative form of exercise," he says.

— The Student Affairs Committee removes Chuck Offenburger as *Hustler* editor because he failed three classes the previous semester. "I was working crazy hours, driving to and from Murfreesboro twice a week to lay out the newspaper, and I just completely forgot about my grades," Offenburger said three decades later. The dismissal results in the inevitable *Hustler* editorial complaining about Offenburger's removal. "The university decided to deny him the right to do what he does best – edit a newspaper," the article states. "As long as the university remains a parent/punitive kind of institution, it should be no surprise that girls are locked up at midnight and 21 year olds are denied their right to determine their own direction within the university."

February 1969

— Chancellor Heard announces plans to tear down Old Science and Old Central and put a social sciences complex on the site that includes two eight-story towers and two six-story towers. Student Mark McCrackin helps form a protest group called Save Open Space (SOS) to protest the plans. "The Vanderbilt campus is already congested . . . the social sciences center would carry congestion to strangulation and would set a dangerous precedent for future development of the campus." Not everyone agrees with SOS. A letter favoring the social sciences center, student Ssu-ma Ch'in argues that "Old Science has no historical significance. It is an example of Tennessee bastard eclectic architecture . . . I suppose I am willing to let Old Central stand as a concession to the Fugitive syndrome at Vanderbilt, but that is something that this university will have to get over sooner or later, and it might as well be right now."

— One week after the University of Tennessee administration does away with upperclass women's curfews on that campus, more than a thousand students take part in a protest meeting at Vanderbilt. Among the women who speak at the rally are Vanderbilt students Martha Leatherman, Pam Owens, and Cheryl Mitchell and UT student Mary Ann Flemm. Flemm tells the crowd that peaceful protest has become so popular on her campus that "at UT this quarter, we have lost interest in sports." Flemm impresses many of the Vanderbilt men in the crowd. "(She) stole the show with her poise, remarks and, to be realistic, her just plain good looks," a *Versus* article about the event said. A week later the Vanderbilt administration officially does away with curfews for sophomore and junior women.

— Imitating a program at a California college, Vanderbilt students form a so-called "Free University," a student-run program where students and the general public can sign up for free classes taught by students and faculty in everything from racial sensitivity to journalism to self-defense. FUN, as it was abbreviated, would remain in existence until at least 1976, when its courses included amateur radio, bicycle

repair, vegetarian cooking, and painting.
— To help raise money for the elusive student center, several faculty members agree to "auction off" items or time. Philosophy professor John Lachs agrees to auction off "as much bourbon as one can drink in five minutes followed by a philosophical discussion."

April 1969
— Twenty-nine college newspaper editors across the country (not including Vanderbilt's) condemn the institution of ROTC on college campuses. A few weeks later Vanderbilt Provost Nicholas Hobbs appoints a committee of seven faculty and six students to make recommendations regarding the future of Army and Navy ROTC at Vanderbilt.
— With guests such as Maine Senator Edmund Muskie and foreign policy expert McGeorge Bundy, the fifth annual Impact series captivates few. Nevertheless, the series has made such an impression in the academic world that it is being imitated all over the South, with copycats such as the University of Alabama's "Emphasis" series and Southwestern at Memphis's "Dilemma" series.
— *Versus*, the weekly student newspaper started a year earlier, is given official financial support by student publications and becomes a permanent addition to Vanderbilt culture.

May 1969
— A group of left-wing students led by Paul Menzel and Joel Smith tries to "wash" an American flag in a large tub next to the Navy ROTC Spring Review in an attempt to symbolically "cleanse" it of Vietnamese blood. The students are confronted by a larger group of counterprotesters, one of whom shoves Smith to the ground and breaks his glasses. "Washing the flag in that context is desecration," counter-protester Don Dickinson says. As tensions mount, Assistant Dean of Men K.C. Potter intervenes, informing the counter-protesters that the protesters have a legal right to carry out their ritual. To prevent further trouble, the protesters agree to sprinkle the flag with water rather than dip it in the tub.
— Giving in to the students and alumni who don't like the idea of a social sciences complex in the middle of the old campus, Heard asks

campus planners to "restudy" plans for the new development. Within six months, the university announces plans to build the complex in an expanded Stevenson Center, complete with a new math building, molecular biology facility, and science library.

June 1969

— The school agrees to award degrees to students Mike Kiernan and Stonewall Breyer, so long as they meet their physical education requirement by undergoing a P.E. regimen over the summer that includes bowling, archery, and horseback riding.

September 1969

— For the first time incoming freshmen are briefed about alternatives to ROTC as a part of their indoctrination to campus life. Among the options are Officer Candidate School, enlistment, resistance, and con-

With trademark pipe intact, Dean K.C. Potter tries to prevent a brawl between protesters and counterprotesters on Alumni Lawn in May 1969
The Banner Collection, Nashville Public Library, The Nashville Room

scientious objection.
— About a dozen students drive to Somerville, Tennessee, to take part in a large civil rights march there. Eight return to campus with the proud news that they were arrested.
— Student (and future state senator) Steve Cohen, who has been chosen as school mascot "Mr. Commodore," has to go to great lengths to fund the purchase of his $125 costume. The athletic department refuses to pitch in, but the student association comes through with $50 and Dean Sidney Boutwell contributes the rest of the money "so that this year's edition of Mr. Commodore would not go naked," a school newspaper explains.

October 1969
— The Vanderbilt football team upsets Alabama 14-10. Five days later thousands of students and faculty take part in the national Vietnam War "moratorium." As a part of the event many students skip class, go to special talks on the war, and hand out anti-war leaflets in Nashville neighborhoods.

November 1969
— The administration appoints a committee to study the creation of coed dorms on campus.
— The university announces plans for a new chemical engineering complex, which eventually becomes Olin Hall.

February 1970
— A faculty/student committee recommends Army and Navy ROTC be retained. But it also suggests several steps toward de-emphasizing ROTC, such as the idea that credit no longer be given for courses in military and naval science. The study also contains a lot of language reflecting opposition to the Vietnam War. "At present, our nation finds it necessary to support a large military organization," it says. "We reject this situation as a satisfactory or a permanent state of affairs. While working to diminish the need for large armed forces, we must increase our efforts to the end that our officers be humane, balanced individuals. In this effort colleges and universities must be involved." Eventually, most of the recommendations are implement-

ed.

— *The Hustler* comes out with a special section about drug use on campus. A few days later a student named Howard (Hap) Kelley commits suicide by jumping out of the tenth floor of Carmichael Tower Number One. In the wake of Kelley's death it is revealed that the young man was high when he killed himself, prompting a former friend of his to write an embittered (and anonymous) letter to *The Hustler* about the school community's casual attitude about drugs. "To the best of my knowledge, Hap was not using drugs when he came to Vanderbilt," the letter said. "He spent three years at a school whose administration, organizations and newspaper hinted at permissiveness and seldom, if ever, even suggested that drugs were harmful, but instead urged us to be careful and not get caught. This attitude was supposedly representative of the new, progressive, liberal Vanderbilt. Drug freedom and the like were going to make us a great university. If a university is a machine that confuses young people, then subtly suggests that blowing one's mind is a good way to escape the pressure, then I want no part of it."

April 1970

— A faculty committee recommends the elimination of the physical education requirement for graduation. The recommendation is later approved.

May 1970

— After President Nixon sends American troops into Cambodia, several students take petitions protesting the move through Nashville neighborhoods. Eventually about a thousand students and about twenty-five hundred residents sign petitions, although many outsiders don't treat the solicitors kindly. One man, asked to sign a petition in a mall parking lot, says, "Hell no, I won't sign your petition, but I'd sign a petition to get your ass over there!" Meanwhile, frequent *Hustler* contributor Hunter Kay pens a long letter defending Nixon. Kay says that one of the reasons he is not worried about the invasion is Nixon's honesty. "Now I'm not saying he's honest because he's naturally that way," Kay says, "but because a smart politician must be careful lest his promises come back to haunt him."

VANDERBILT GETS ITS SLUM

While students were actively protesting everything from the Vietnam War to mandatory P.E., Vanderbilt's geographic expansion to the south became a charged controversy as well. The protests were started by a few angry residents, who had compelling moral and practical arguments against the governmental and academic bureaucracies they were fighting. They would eventually win the public relations battle, but lose the war over their homes.

When the Nashville City Council authorized an urban renewal plan for the Vanderbilt area in August 1961, the Nashville Housing Authority had a problem. Despite the council vote, the 110-acre neighborhood adjacent to the campus had to meet the government's official definition of "slum" to draw federal dollars. This was not an easy task. "The land the university was to acquire lay in the heart of an exclusively white, predominantly middle-class neighborhood which bore little resemblance to the conventional image of a slum," an article in the May 1974 *Vanderbilt Law Review* said. According to a 1960 housing census only twenty-one percent of the homes in the area were considered substandard by government standards. In the other two residential areas of the city that received urban renewal treatment, over half of the houses were considered substandard.

In early 1962 the federal government approved Nashville's other urban renewal programs, but told the Nashville Housing Authority it could not fund the program in the Vanderbilt area until it proved that the area was, in fact, a slum. To do this, the housing authority ordered another housing inspection. Rather than use its own inspectors, the authority hired a New York consulting firm called Clarke and Rapuano.

Legal attacks on Vanderbilt's urban renewal plan would later point out that Clarke and Rapuano had already come up with a master plan for the university, giving the firm an enormous incentive to conclude that the neighborhood was a slum by government standards. However, the Housing Authority defended its decision to use Clarke and Rapuano, pointing out that the firm had planned Nashville's

Capitol Hill Redevelopment Project a decade earlier and was one of the best urban planning businesses in the country.

In 1962 Clarke and Rapuano's inspectors descended on the Vanderbilt neighborhood. The nature of these inspections remained in dispute through the end of the century. Inspectors said they acted in an evenhanded manner. However, some neighborhood residents claimed that the official conclusion by the inspectors – that the area was a slum by government standards – was absurd. For example, the very act of a house being used as rental property was often cited as criteria for the house being classified as blighted. Houses that had working plumbing, but not modern plumbing in the opinions of the inspectors, were also classified as blighted.

Vanderbilt's position was made all the more awkward by the fact that, as a result of Chancellor Harvie Branscomb's earlier policy of buying land as it came available, the university owned about one hundred tracts of land in the neighborhood by the time of the inspections. Many residents, such as neighborhood activist Joe Johnston, later accused the university of neglecting those homes to further its long-term goal of destroying the neighborhood. "By the time the inspections were made, the university made certain that the houses it owned were poorly maintained," said Johnston, a descendant of Confederate General Joseph Johnston and whose grandparents built a house in the neighborhood in 1936. "Then the inspectors came in and applied all sorts of strange rules, such as the fact that if your house was next to a blighted house, then it too would be classified as a blighted house. Using the standards that the inspectors used, they could have had Belle Meade declared a slum."

After Clarke and Rapuano's 1963 report concluded that the Vanderbilt-area neighborhood did, in fact, meet the government's definition of slum, not much happened for about four years. The main reason for this was that Nashville was busy completing the east Nashville, Edgehill, and downtown urban renewal projects and because Nashville and Davidson County were reorganizing under a metropolitan form of government.

Meanwhile, there was little coverage of the Vanderbilt area urban renewal plan in Nashville's newspapers. Many of the people who lived in the area were confused about whether the urban renewal plan would result in the destruction of some homes (as the East Nashville Urban Renewal Project had done) or the destruction of all homes (as the Capitol Hill Redevelopment Project had done). Others doubted it would ever take place at all.

Finally, in 1967, the federal government told the Nashville Housing Authority that it had to either move ahead with the Vanderbilt-area urban renewal plan or it would lose money for the project. City officials met with school officials, came up with the final plan for the area, and presented it at a public meeting that took place at Eakin School in April of that year.

According to the account in *The Tennessean*, about five hundred residents attended that meeting, and most of them were hostile to the plan. Many of those residents attended a Metro Council meeting two weeks later and spoke against the plan there also. But it was to no avail. "Each speaker who wished to address the meeting was limited to five minutes of speaking time," the *Vanderbilt Law Review* article said. "Five minutes represented a brief opportunity to develop a concerted or detailed series of criticisms of a plan that had taken seven years to draft." During the next week a petition condemning the

Chancellor Heard at a public meeting about Vanderbilt's urban renewal plans - 1973
The Banner Collection, Nashville Public Library, The Nashville Room

urban renewal project was signed by 727 residents of the area.

The protests were too little and too late. On August 15, 1967, with the blessing of Mayor Beverly Briley and both Nashville newspapers, the Metro Council voted 30-4 to move ahead with what was called the University Center Redevelopment Project.

Under the original terms of the plan, property owners were given a certain amount of time to sell to Vanderbilt. If they refused, the Nashville Housing Authority would take the land under eminent domain. Most of the property owners did so without a fight, which is why the university was able to purchase about two hundred additional parcels in the area between 1967 and 1973. Some did not. Two organizations, the University Neighborhood Association and the Committee for the Protection of Private Property, were involved in numerous attempts to thwart the Vanderbilt-area urban renewal plan in the courts and in the Metro Council. Those attempts failed to stop Vanderbilt's land acquisitions, but succeeded in slowing them down and in embarrassing the university. The best example of the latter took place on October 11, 1971, when a *Newsweek* article painted a picture of Vanderbilt as an insensitive and greedy neighbor. "This isn't a slum, never was a slum," the article quoted resident Robert Gardner saying. "It's nothing but a free land grab."

In 1972 residents of the area scored a small victory. Under the original master plan for the acquired area, Natchez Trace Road would be cut off from public use. Area residents asked the council to delete the Natchez Trace closure from the plan at a televised meeting of the Metro Council in January 1972. The council did so, which is why Natchez Trace remained a thoroughfare.

The next year residents appeared to have won a larger victory. In July 1973 Vanderbilt-area Councilman James Hamilton proposed a measure to remove the remaining sixty-eight lots in the neighborhood still owned by private individuals from the urban renewal plan, effectively blocking Vanderbilt's ability to acquire all the land it wanted. The council, acting on the reversal in public opinion toward urban renewal since 1967, approved Hamilton's measure 19-14.

However, the university then mounted a major lobbying effort of its own. Using its own lawyers and independent lobbyists such as former Lieutenant Governor Frank Gorrell, Vanderbilt showed the council that it had already spent millions of dollars to acquire land under agreements with the city that were ratified by council votes in 1961 and 1967. In November 1973 the council rescinded the Hamilton amendment by a vote of 26-10. The long debate over Vanderbilt's urban renewal policy was finally over, as far as the council was concerned.

There was still one aspect of the controversy left, however, and that was the one that took place in court. In 1970 area residents Charles and June Adair and Robert and Ruth Gardner had filed a lawsuit against the Nashville Housing Authority and the university, claiming that the area did not meet federal guidelines as an urban renewal area. The lawsuit was dismissed by local courts and finished for good in November 1975, when the U.S. Supreme Court declined to hear the case.

During the next decade Vanderbilt acquired the remaining parcels one by one. It was an ugly process, often played out in the local media. The acts of defiance by residents who were removed were later regarded as legendary. One elderly woman simply moved away, leaving Vanderbilt to deal with her possessions. Because of a court settlement between residents and Vanderbilt, Johnston stayed in his house at 3013 Vanderbilt Place until 1984. When the university finally acquired his property, he moved the house, piece by piece, to 2815 Belmont Blvd. A couple of years later Mr. Gardner died and became the last resident of the neighborhood to leave. By that time the Metro Council had named a park across Blakemore Avenue from the former site of the neighborhood after Fannie Mae Dees, an elderly, eccentric lady who would frequently sit outside the office of the Nashville Housing Authority for hours in silent protest of the urban renewal project.

The irony of Vanderbilt's urban renewal process is that it took so long to acquire the properties that the university never carried out the plan for which it wanted the property. Rather than build dorms and classroom buildings all the way to Blakemore (as the plan envisioned), the school built larger dorms and new classroom buildings on its older campus area (most notably, the four Carmichael Towers dormitories). Most of the land acquired through urban renewal was either used for parking, athletic fields, or expansion of the medical center.

Regardless of how the land was used, it took years for the university to patch things up with its neighbors. To aid revitalization of the neighborhoods surrounding it, the university initiated a loan program to encourage its faculty and staff to move into areas bordering the university. That program, which didn't receive much publicity, was one reason property values in the Belmont and Hillsboro neighborhoods began to rebound in the 1970s. "The [urban renewal] project left a fairly high level of distrust in the neighborhood toward Vanderbilt, and we spent a lot of effort trying to rebuild that relationship," said Jeff Carr, Vanderbilt's legal counsel and later vice chancellor for university relations. "But it is very clear in my mind that the university did what it had to do. I don't know what we would have done over the years to meet the needs of the school had we not acquired that land."

Perhaps the most important consequence of urban renewal was that it served as a catalyst for neighborhoods to organize. In 1970 fear of urban renewal led to the formation of the Belmont-Hillsboro Neighbors, one of Nashville's first neighborhood organizations. "People fully expected urban renewal to spread out and go further, and a lot of people were afraid of losing their homes," said Eugene TeSelle, a Vanderbilt divinity professor and one of the neighborhood group's organizers. By the year 2000 there were about a hundred such neighborhood groups in Davidson County.

Betty Nixon, who represented Vanderbilt in the Metro Council from 1975 until 1987 and ran unsuccessfully for mayor against Phil Bredesen in 1991, said that her experience as an activist against Vanderbilt is what caused her to go into politics in the first place. "My mother-in-law used to own an antique shop about where the Vanderbilt track is located now, and it seemed like a terrible thing for the university to move out that old neighborhood," said Nixon, who later became Vanderbilt's Director of Community, Neighborhood and Government Relations.

Nixon said the Vanderbilt urban renewal project was a turning point for Nashville's balance of civic power. "At that time, Nashville was a leadership-driven city," she said. "You had a few people who decided what was best for us and there wasn't a grassroots movement at all to speak of. Not any more."

The Tire Showroom on West Side Row

Not everyone at Vanderbilt spent all of his or her time protesting during the late 1960s. If there was a "counter-counter culture" on campus, it was best personified by a young man named John Mayo.

During the fall of his freshman year in 1968 one of Mayo's colleagues drove him across town to visit a tire warehouse called Gates Tire Factory. Mayo knew a little about the tire business because his father sold tires in Birmingham. Seeing an entrepreneurial opportunity, Mayo purchased about half a dozen tires and brought them back to campus. He set them up in the lounge of his dormitory, and printed a series of crude promotional brochures. He left these under the windshield wipers of cars on campus that he thought needed new tires.

"There were something like seven thousand cars that came and went on the campus in those days," Mayo said years later. "And I could sell tires cheap because the business I was running had almost no expenses."

The Mayo Tire Company, as the business eventually became known, did well from the start. The way the business worked, Vanderbilt students, faculty, and staff would be lured into the showroom at the dormitory by the promotional leaflets. With Mayo's help, they would then pick out a type of tire. Mayo would then call the Gates Tire Factory and order the set, which would be delivered to campus by taxi. "I didn't have a car at that time," Mayo explained. A local gas station would usually install the new tires.

By the end of his freshman year Mayo had several fellow students working for him. However, someone complained about the use of the dormitory lounge as a showroom, so Mayo was summoned to see Dean of Housing K. C. Potter. Potter, who was accustomed to disciplining students for things like drunkenness and vandalism, couldn't find it in his heart to shut down Mayo's tire business. Instead, he told Mayo that he could store tires in the basement of the West Side Row building in which Potter lived.

Before Potter knew it, his basement had been cleaned out,

carpeted, and completely refurbished as the new showroom of the Mayo Tire Co. "I know I should have stopped him," Potter said many years later, "but I just let it slide because he was such a fine young man." Mayo hired even more students as employees, and they began manning a Mayo Tire booth at Rand Hall. "I have to admit that I was quite a strange duck, walking around with my briefcase and my stack of tires," Mayo said. "I was definitely out of touch with the mainstream of the student protest movement."

Mayo Tire was growing fast, but things got a little sticky when Mayo sought insurance for his business. He was summoned to see Chancellor Alexander Heard, who told him that the business could no longer operate its headquarters on campus because it might endanger the school's not-for-profit status. Mayo asked if he could appeal the decision. Heard said he could, but said that the next appeal would have to be to the board of trust.

"So I took my case to the board of trust," Mayo said. "I explained the whole situation and made my pitch to Harold Vanderbilt and Sam Fleming and all the rest of them. They were very nice and said that they loved what I was doing, but they too told me that I would have to move the business off campus. But in retrospect it was a great thing for the business. After all, what better way to have met all those people?"

Mayo then found some vacant commercial property at 1805 Church Street and opened a business there. At first it was only open from noon until six p.m. "I would go to class in the morning and then go by and run the business in the afternoon," said Mayo, who graduated in 1972 with an interdepartmental major in economics, psychology, and sociology. By the end of Mayo's junior year his business had three offices in Nashville and about twenty employees, most of whom were Vanderbilt students. "I spent a year working for John as the manager of the Church Street showroom," said Steve Baker, a 1971 graduate who later became an attorney in Nashville. "I worked really hard and remember that I was making more money at that time than I made during the first few years after I graduated from law school. And it was all very strange, really. There I was, twenty-one years old, managing a tire store, and my boss was younger than I was."

By the end of Mayo's senior year the company had sold over

a million dollars worth of tires. The business continued to grow in the 1970s and continued to market itself to Vanderbilt students (it frequently purchased an ad on the back page of the Vanderbilt phone book). Mayo sold his firm in 1990 and moved to Hawaii, starting a tire business there as well. It was while he was living in Hawaii that Mayo finally repaid a long-standing debt, sending Dean Potter a complimentary airline ticket to Hawaii. "It was the least that I could do for what he did for me," Mayo said.

STREAKERS AND COED DORMS

The great coed dorm controversy of 1974 probably started on February 25, 1974, when two fraternity boys tossed aside their trenchcoats and scaled the brick wall surrounding Branscomb Quadrangle. Wearing nothing but tennis shoes, the young men ran and danced around, attracting as much attention as they could before they jumped back over the fence and disappeared into the night. "We did it just to do it, to be first," one of the young men (whose identity was not revealed) said to a *Hustler* reporter a few days later. "I mean, we had heard of it, but it wasn't in all the papers around here yet, so it seemed like less of an old idea. Besides we were pretty drunk."

During the next several weeks, there were at least six reports of other streakers on the Vanderbilt campus. On March 12 the school newspaper ran a front-page photograph of three male students running naked down West End Avenue (taken from behind the students, of course).

Of course, streaking wasn't the only thing happening on the Vanderbilt campus that many parents and older Nashville residents objected to. Ever since the mid-1960s, when college campuses across the country became hotbeds of discontent and social revolution, it seemed like there was one story after another related to the sexual revolution on college campuses, even relatively conservative ones like Vanderbilt. In October 1971 the Vanderbilt publication *Versus* contained ads for condoms. "Making love is great," the ads said. "Making her pregnant isn't." The ads, which actually violated state law, resulted in angry fliers calling the publication "vulgar smut" and loud com-

Streakers during a Navy ROTC Spring Review in the mid 1970s
Photographic Archives, Vanderbilt University

plaints from trustee John Sloan. "I just can't understand the morals of young people today," Sloan said. "When I was in college, those things were the subject of outhouse discussion only."

Nowhere were people less amused about the "new morality" than at the state legislature, whose members had a hard time relating to post-1960s college students. Although its members had other things to worry about at the time, lawmakers decided to do something about sexual promiscuity among the younger generation. They honed in on coed dormitories.

On March 12, 1974, the state senate passed a bill 21-6 that would ban coed dorms at public and private colleges and universities in Tennessee. Four days later the state house passed a similar version of the bill 61-17, with sponsor Rep. Marvin Hopper of Nashville saying it would stop "the immoral and un-Christian acts" taking place on college campuses. Among those who opposed the measure in the House was Rep. Doy Daniels, who called the bill "a farce, a sham, a public disgrace, an absurdity and an insult to the intelligence of the students." Daniels told a reporter that in his opinion, the streaking fad is what actually brought the bill to the forefront. "Many of these people believe exactly what they read in the papers . . . it [streaking] persuaded many people that there is a real lack of moral fiber on college campuses." During the many debates over the bill several other opinions were put forth, including that of Sen. J. H. White. "I personally don't mind the boys visiting the girls rooms as long as they stand up for the 'Star Spangled Banner," he said.

At the time Vanderbilt had several dorms that met the state's definition of coed, including three of the Carmichael Towers, McGill Hall, McTyeire Hall, and Landon House. School officials were completely blind-sided by the measure, which carried a sentence of up to two months in jail for noncompliance. Among those who spoke out against the bill was Vanderbilt Dean of Housing K. C. Potter, who said that, if anything, coed dorms appeared to have less disciplinary problems than male dorms. "One man said that it [coed dormitories] was a result of communism," Potter said. "Hell, I voted for [Barry] Goldwater; I'm no communist . . . I happen to think the moral climate on this campus is damn good." Potter began working on a contingency plan in case the measure became law.

With the bill awaiting the signature of Governor Winfield Dunn, Vanderbilt students finally began getting involved. One student wrote a letter to *The Hustler* asking his colleagues to boycott Hopper's restaurants because of the bill. (At the time, Hopper was the Nashville franchisee for Kentucky Fried Chicken.) *The Hustler* came out with its obligatory sarcastic editorial. "Dozens of upstanding Christian students . . . have complained about the futility of attempting to walk along Rand Terrace without being dragged bodily into McGill Hall and compelled to view or participate in the daily orgies of that bawdy house," the school paper said.

The head activist was a freshman student named Teri Hasenour. During the next few days Hasenour collected about fifteen hundred signatures on a petition opposing the bill, which she and some of her colleagues tried to hand deliver to Governor Dunn. "I remember that we actually sat in his office down at the capitol for a long time waiting to see him and he wouldn't see us, so we had to just leave the petition for him to see later," said Hasenour. "The reason I remember this is because a picture of us appeared in *The Tennessean*, and someone sent a copy of the picture to my father. He was not happy."

Hasenour said many years later that she initiated the petition because if the law had passed, she wouldn't have been able to live on campus her sophomore year. "When we heard about this, everyone was up in arms," said Hasenour, whose married name became Teri Gordon. "I even remember someone called me from the law school and said that if the bill became law, they would help me sue the state. I was ready to be the plaintiff."

Dunn vetoed the coed dorm bill on April 2. In the letter to the legislature explaining his actions, the Republican governor made it clear that he did not "condone immorality or promiscuous actions on or off the campus," but could find no information to suggest that such promiscuity is related to the existence of coed dorms.

A quarter of a century later Dunn said he remembered the coed dorm bill and the controversy it created. "I seem to remember that in addition to individual legislators, there were a lot of people in Murfreesboro who were calling my office asking for the bill to be passed because something had happened at Middle Tennessee State that had really offended people, but I don't remember what that was," Dunn said. "But I also remember having a long talk with Alexander Heard about the bill. It was a terrible piece of legislation."

But the measure wasn't dead yet. In Tennessee only a simple majority of both chambers is needed to override a veto. In late April the sponsors of the measure let it be known that they were about to call for a veto override.

Finally, Vanderbilt students began migrating to the State Capitol to lobby against the bill. At first most of them were male. But after a couple of days it became clear that the students weren't getting their message across. In an act of desperation, SGA President Brad Millsap made an appeal on WRVU for female students to lobby. At that point about sixty female students showed up at the capitol. On April 23 the veto override failed by two votes in the Senate. State Senator Carl Koella, who voted against the veto override, said the girls made better lobbyists than the boys. "When a pretty girl asks 'why are you calling me immoral?' that's pretty effective," Koella said.

Part Six

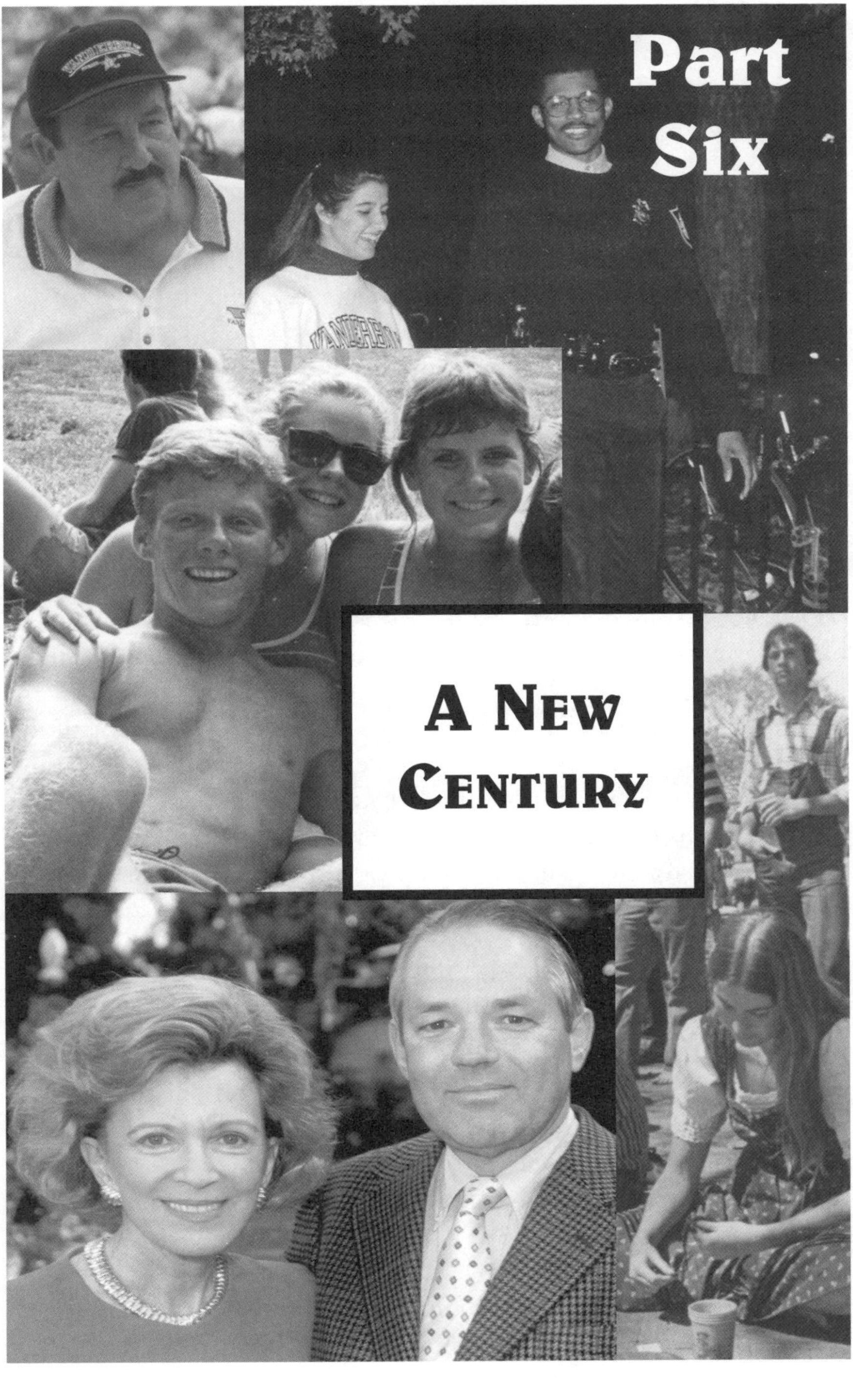

A New Century

PEABODY COMES INTO THE FOLD

For the first half of the twentieth century George Peabody College for Teachers was a strong force for improving public education in the South. It trained thousands of teachers. It helped rural school districts design school buildings and reorganize inefficient school systems. It had one of the South's finest library schools and one of the best administrative schools for principals and superintendents.

But by the 1960s Peabody College had financial problems. Along with the unprecedented growth of public colleges and universities after World War II came a rise in the number of public teaching colleges. Many of those institutions were modeled after Peabody, but charged far less in tuition. The rise of public colleges was the main reason Peabody's summer enrollment declined from 1,745 in 1965 to 639 in 1973. But it wasn't the only reason; by the mid-1970s, most baby boomers had completed school and there was a national glut of teachers.

The cost of a college education also began to rise dramatically in the 1960s. A private school like Vanderbilt largely offset such rising costs with endowment. But Peabody couldn't raise much endowment for the obvious reason that its alumni tended to have modest incomes. In 1944 investment income made up twenty-six percent of Peabody's income. Two decades later endowment only accounted for about eight percent of income.

Speculation that Vanderbilt and Peabody might eventually merge had been around since the schools became neighbors in 1914. But through the 1960s the only concrete example of the schools' working together was the Joint University Library, built for students of both institutions. Under the conditions of the General Education Board's funding of the library, Vanderbilt and Peabody were supposed to eliminate overlapping courses and positions. But in the 1940s and 1950s that didn't happen as the GEB had intended.

Then, in 1961, new Peabody president Felix Robb and Vanderbilt chancellor Harvie Branscomb commissioned an in-depth study of how the two schools could better work together. The study came out about a year later and recommended the formation of an organization called the Nashville University Center, to include not only Vanderbilt and Peabody but also Scarritt College and Fisk University. The study recommended that the four schools work together through the Nashville University Center to develop a common calendar, a foreign language center, study programs, a center for performing arts, a faculty club, a university press, and intramural and intercollegiate sports.

Vanderbilt's trustees vetoed the idea of the Nashville University Center in June 1962, and it is easy to imagine why. For starters, it's hard to envision a school with Vanderbilt's high academic requirements putting together academic programs with the other three colleges. In addition, the idea of working in tandem with Fisk was out of the question in the early 1960s, when neither Vanderbilt nor Peabody had black undergraduates. Nevertheless, it is interesting to ponder what might have happened if the four schools had implemented the plan. Nashville might have gotten a performing arts center long before it did. Vanderbilt football players might have had the option of attending Fisk. Scarritt might have survived, and Fisk may have avoided its financial problems of the 1980s and 1990s.

There were other attempts to build a working relationship between Vanderbilt and Peabody in the 1960s and early 1970s. One was a plan called "Peabody Plus" that was put forward by Peabody faculty and called for a close alliance, but not a merger, with Vanderbilt. That blueprint was rejected. However, in 1972 Vanderbilt and Peabody worked out a deal under which Peabody students could play for Vanderbilt sports teams, a measure that was worked out to help the Commodore football program.

John Dunworth became Peabody's new president in 1974. Within months of his arrival he announced several steps designed to improve the school's financial outlook. One was for the school to "spin-off" its demonstration school – renamed the University School of Nashville – to a board of directors controlled by parents. Other steps included the elimination of academic programs in business education, home economics, modern languages, accounting, and professional music training (which resulted in the creation of an independent Blair School of Music). Dunworth's moves were generally unpopular with Peabody faculty and alumni, and may have contributed to the disappointing results of a fundraising campaign then underway. In 1977 Dunworth took another step to generate cash flow when he began leasing empty dormitory space to Vanderbilt.

Despite the cost-cutting moves Peabody was a sinking ship by the late 1970s, with a flat endowment and declining enrollment. Sometime around 1977 Peabody chief financial officer Jim Whitlock conducted a lengthy study of projected enrollment, endowment, and inflationary costs that convinced Dunworth that the school could no longer survive alone. When Dunworth expressed this sentiment to the board, not everyone agreed. Peabody chairman Horace G. Hill Jr. was so upset at the idea that Peabody could not longer stand alone that he resigned as a trustee. "Horace's philosophy is that he didn't like to change much of anything, whether it was the way his stores were run or the way Peabody was run," Peabody board member Edward G. Nelson said many years later. "The idea that he would merge the school that he and his father had done so much to help years earlier was something he couldn't stand."

In the summer of 1978 Dunworth and Peabody Dean Tom Stovall approached Vanderbilt President Emmett Fields about the idea of a merger between the two institutions (Chancellor Alexander Heard was out of the country at the time). Fields told Dunworth that Vanderbilt would be interested in taking over Peabody's real estate and continuing the school's graduate programs. But Fields said Vanderbilt had no interest in continuing the mission of training undergraduates for teaching careers. He also said that the timing was bad, since he was in the middle of instituting a belt-tightening "reassessment" program at Vanderbilt. Dunworth and Stovall broke off the talks.

Convinced that drastic action was necessary, Dunworth and Stovall then began to consider the idea of merging their institution with a college or university outside of Tennessee. Under this vague blueprint, Peabody would sell its real estate to the highest bidder and move its faculty and staff to another state, much like a relocating company. To this end, Dunworth and Stovall visited officials at Duke University and George Washington University. "There were people at both schools that were very interested in the idea," Stovall said years later.

To this point Peabody's negotiations had not become public knowledge. But the next phase would. For several months Stovall had been talking to members of the Tennessee Higher Education Commission and the Tennessee Board of Regents about the idea of a cross-town enrollment deal to help Tennessee State University develop a doctoral program. In December 1978 Stovall explained Peabody's financial problem to a Tennessee Board of Regents official, who suggested a merger between Peabody and TSU. In January 1979 those merger talks began. By February 13, when *The Tennessean* first reported the story about negotiations between the two institutions on its front page, Dunworth, Stovall, TSU President Frederick Humphries, and the Board of Regents had come up with a draft of a merger agreement. Under it, the state would take over Peabody's campus and endowment, Peabody's students would begin paying (much lower) state tuition, and most of Peabody's academic programs would continue.

On March 9 the Tennessee Board of Regents approved the idea of a merger between TSU and Peabody. Still, the proposed merger faced an uphill battle in the legislature. Among the harshest critics was Rep. John Bragg, the chairman of the House Finance Committee, who pointed out that the cost of operating Peabody (at least $3.4 million per year) would have to come out of another school's budget. Other key players who were skeptical of the merger included Lt. Gov. John Wilder and House Speaker Ned McWherter. "They want to get it funded in time to start classes this fall?" McWherter asked a reporter. "Well, when I was five, I wanted a little red wagon for Christmas."

Meanwhile, Peabody faculty members were powerless to affect the fate of their institution. Some thought that they'd be better off merged with Vanderbilt; others favored TSU. A few, who were frequently quoted in the newspapers, still believed their school could survive independently if competently run. "The Dunworth line is that Peabody is a victim of national enrollment trends," said Shirley Newton, vice chair of the Peabody faculty. "I'm saying Peabody is a victim of Dunworth."

One thing that was little discussed during the merger talks with TSU was the fate of outside-funded Peabody programs that had working relationships with Vanderbilt. The most important of these was the Kennedy Center, a mental retardation research and training institution that worked closely with the Vanderbilt Medical Center and received about $3 million annually in federal money. The Kennedy Center had been started in the mid-1960s, in part with a $500,000 gift from the Kennedy Foundation. On March 14, 1979, Kennedy Foundation trustee Sargent Shriver said he was concerned about the idea of a Peabody-TSU merger. "My initial judgment is that it would be much better for the Kennedy Center to be connected to Vanderbilt than with any other institution in Nashville," Shriver said. Shriver's comments were criticized by TSU president Humphries, who said that they drew "a harsh reaction" from the black community.

By this time Vanderbilt Chancellor Heard and the Vanderbilt Board of Trust had reconsidered the idea of a merger with Peabody. If Peabody merged with TSU, Vanderbilt students would lose the option of cross-enrolling in Peabody classes and Vanderbilt would lose the use of Peabody dorms. Since about half of the Vanderbilt football team attended Peabody at this time, it was tempting for observers to focus on the effect of a TSU-Peabody merger on Vanderbilt's win-loss record. But as Vanderbilt officials pondered the implications of a TSU-Peabody merger, real estate concerns also came to the forefront. By the late 1970s Vanderbilt had almost completed its arduous battle to acquire most of the property south and west to Blakemore Avenue. The process had taken two decades and millions of dollars and cost the university the goodwill of many Nashville residents. And even though the acquisition gave Vanderbilt enough land for the foreseeable future, there was no way to predict the long-term needs of a university with a regional medical center and a commitment to big-time sports. The Peabody campus, meanwhile, already had several usable and beautiful structures, plus a lot of dormitory space that Vanderbilt desperately needed. A Peabody-TSU merger would create a neighbor that had power of eminent domain, something that could cause Vanderbilt complex legal problems in the future.

There was one other aspect of a Peabody-TSU merger that no Vanderbilt official would voice in 1979 (nor would they voice it two decades later). From the time Roger Williams University left the area

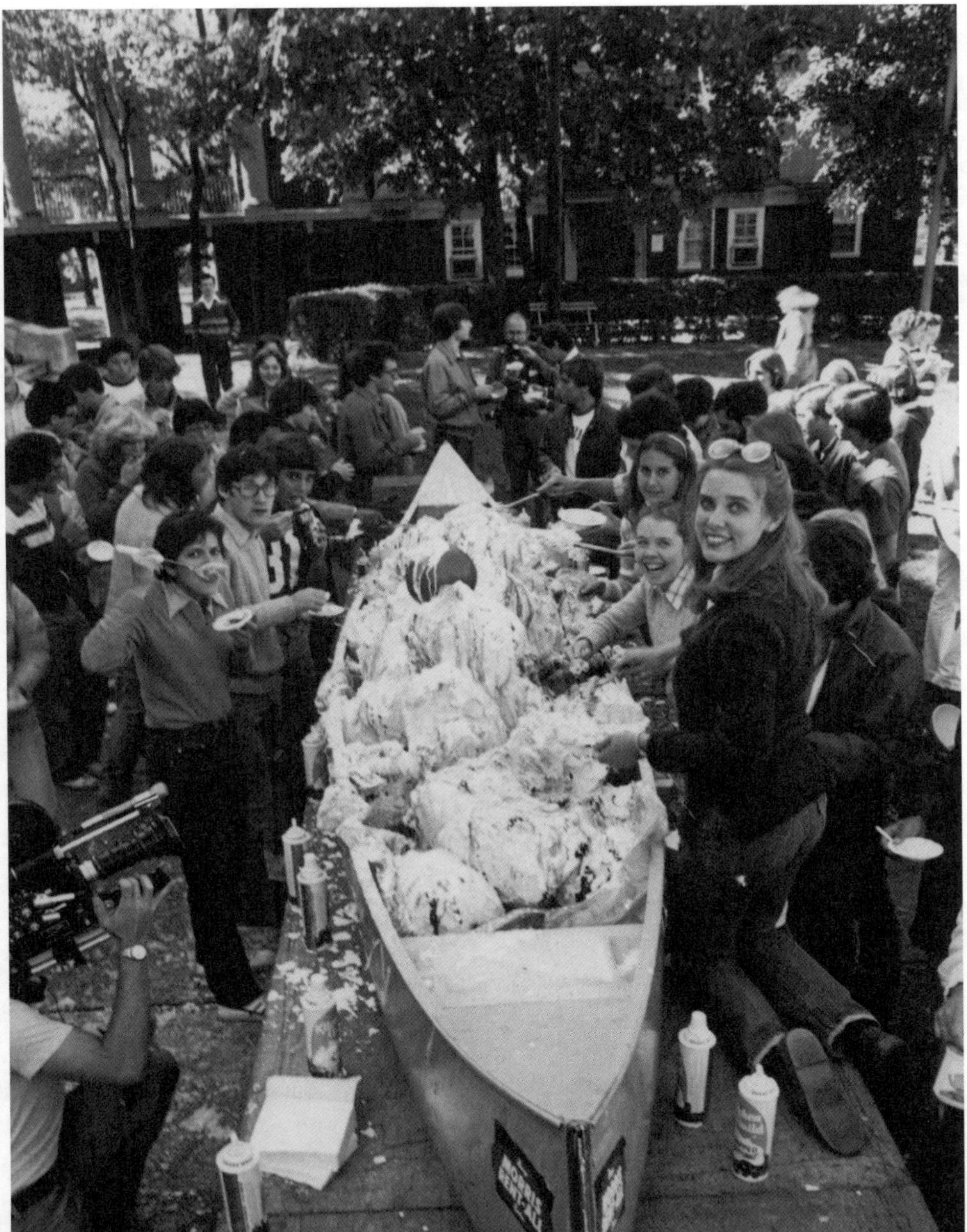

Shortly after the 1979 merger between Vanderbilt and Peabody, the administration organized this mixer between students of the two schools
Photographic Archives, Vanderbilt University

in 1909, Twenty-first Avenue had been a white corridor, lined all the way from downtown to the edge of Nashville with white schools, white neighborhoods, white churches, and white-owned businesses. Given Nashville's history, it was hard to imagine residents and trustees agreeing to the idea of TSU taking over the Peabody campus.

These issues moved Heard and the board of trust quickly to work out a deal with Peabody. On a weekend in early March 1979 the chancellor had a long meeting with Vanderbilt board chairman Sam Fleming. Fleming followed up by meeting with Peabody chairman Robert Gable. On March 19 Heard presented a merger plan to the Peabody board. After a six-hour debate the board approved the proposal unanimously. Seven decades after Peabody's move across town, its merger with Vanderbilt was complete.

Under the terms of the Vanderbilt-Peabody merger, Peabody retained its teacher education and research missions, but did away with its liberal arts, music, and arts departments. After one-time merger expenses were paid, Vanderbilt would take over Peabody's remaining $9 million in endowment and the Peabody campus. Vanderbilt agreed to contribute $700,000 a year toward Peabody's operation for ten years, after which the school would reassess the continuation of Peabody's teaching program. Four members of the Peabody Board of Trust were given seats on the Vanderbilt Board of Trust. Enrolled Peabody students continued to pay previous Peabody tuition rates; future Peabody students would be paying higher Vanderbilt tuition rates.

The Vanderbilt-Peabody merger was generally viewed favorably in most Vanderbilt circles, not the least important of which was the athletic department. "This marks a new era of Vanderbilt commitment (to the team)," newly hired Vanderbilt football coach George MacIntyre said. "It really excites me." Frank Mordica, a Peabody student who played tailback on the football team, had a rather humorous response to the news. "I know a lot of the players were wondering what might happen if Peabody merged with Tennessee State," Mordica said. "I was starting to wonder if I could start for TSU."

But not everyone was happy about the marriage between the two schools. During the next few months Peabody dismissed thirty-eight faculty members, twenty-three of whom had tenure. Despite

Vanderbilt's attempt to accommodate as many Peabody staffers as possible, some of them either lost their jobs permanently or "went through a humiliating reclassification procedure at Vanderbilt," according to a history of Peabody. The merger was also emotional for Peabody alumni and students, who were proud of the independent legacy of their school and who loved its small college atmosphere. Peabody had three sororities prior to the merger, all of which ceased to exist after 1980.

Two decades after the merger between Vanderbilt and Peabody, it is difficult to imagine Peabody as a part of TSU. Because of this it is tempting to say that Dunworth and Stovall were using the threat of a merger with TSU to get Vanderbilt's attention. However, when interviewed many years later, Dunworth said that the idea of a Peabody-TSU merger was no ploy. "The negotiations with TSU were serious," said Dunworth, who went to the University of West Florida after the merger was finalized. "I can say that unequivocally. I don't know whether people believe it or not, but they were."

Typical and Atypical Coeds

The history of women at Vanderbilt in many ways mirrors the history of women in America. Among the more significant milestones:

1879 – Kate Lupton, the daughter of a chemistry professor, takes and excels in classes on just about every subject offered on campus and graduates from Vanderbilt with a masters degree. Lupton was never actually admitted to the school because at the time the idea of accepting female students was out of the question. But apparently, no one had the heart, or nerve, to tell her she couldn't come to class.

1887 – After several young women (usually the daughters of professors) attend and pass classes without paying tuition, a faculty committee recommends to Chancellor Landon Garland that qualified female applicants be accepted for admission. The proposal starts a campus debate that leads to several letters for and against female students.

Vanderbilt coeds, circa 1892
The Stella Vaughn Family Collection, Photographic Archives, Vanderbilt University

"If we let women attend college and learn the science, they no longer make good wives," one piece states. "No man wants to come home at night and find his wife testing a new process for manufacturing oleomargarine, or sitting in the observatory, sweeping the heavens for a comet." In the end, the Vanderbilt Board of Trust does not act on the recommendation.

1892 – With little acclaim, Vanderbilt begins allowing women to register for classes and receive degrees. That year there are about a dozen female students on campus. By the end of the century female students win academic awards, form a sorority, and even organize a basketball team. However, male students are not allowed to watch the women play because it is considered inappropriate.

1904 – Vanderbilt women form their first sorority, Kappa Alpha Theta. The second sorority, Delta Delta Delta, follows seven years later.

1905 – Vanderbilt boys' practice of yelling "heads out" every time a girl walks past Kissam Hall becomes so frequent that Professor Wilbur Tillett condemns it at chapel. *The Hustler* defends the action. "When he (the student) cries 'heads out' he does it not to place his victim in an embarrassing position, but merely as a means of giving vent to his pent-up vitality. Indeed, if all ladies that pass Kissam Hall should show their disapproval of such conduct and should impress upon the students the fact that they felt that they were being treated in an ungentlemanly way, we have not the slightest doubt that 'heads out' would be condemned by the students as vehemently as by any others."

1915 – Female journalists are so numerous on campus that they publish a special women's version of the school publication *The Observer*. Meanwhile, female students begin dominating academic honors, which frustrates some male students.

1918 – While many young men are away fighting World War I, young women take advantage of the opportunity to register for classes at Vanderbilt. Women take over most of the leadership positions on campus, including senior class president.

1921 – Citing a shortage of adequate housing, the board of trust votes to limit the number of female students living on campus to fifty (while not restricting the number of women who can take classes).

1925 – Anna Russell Cole, the mother of board of trust chairman Whitefoord Cole, donates ten thousand dollars to Vanderbilt to fund the position of dean of women, a job first filled by Ada Stapleton. Largely through Stapleton and Cole's influence, Vanderbilt coeds form four new sororities and women enroll in the medical school and the school of engineering.

1933 – A rule on campus prohibits women students (but not their male counterparts) from smoking. And unlike male students, women must attend weekly gym classes – classes so unpleasant that they actually became the subject of a *Hustler* editorial. The article says that women's gym classes have "developed into a tyranny, with the gymnasium instructor as the tyranness. It seems that co-ed gym has become more of a reform school or prison than a recreation period."

1939 – One of the more established traditions on the Vanderbilt campus is the annual selection of a female student as a "Typical Vanderbilt Coed." The TVC award, which is considered an honor, is based on the results of a survey that genuinely tries to determine what the typical Vanderbilt female student is like in a particular year. For

Delta Delta Delta sorority members prepare for an event
Photo courtesy of Paula Lovell

example, the two hundred TVC surveys filled out in 1939 indicate that Vanderbilt women favor marriage over a career, do not favor making dates more than a week in advance, do not lose their temper, and consider three children to be the ideal number.

1940 – McTyeire Hall opens as Vanderbilt's first women's dormitory.

1943 – During the war women again take over many of the leadership positions on campus, including *Hustler* editor. In fact, *The Hustler* has three consecutive female editors during the war – Betty Freeman, Gloria Gilbert, and Betty Brunner. And during the 1944-45 school year, females make up two-thirds of the student body. "The 1945 woman steps out of college today with the job exactly suited to her talent, desire and capabilities awaiting her," one *Hustler* article says at the time. "Regardless of what her tastes and talents may be, the number and variety of positions available are boundless."

1946 – Young men return from the war and again become the majority on campus. A couple of years later Chancellor Harvie Branscomb states his intention to keep male students at least a two-to-one majority because, in his opinion, "once the number of women rises too high, the men cease coming. Then the women cease coming."

1949 – A topless female (shown from behind) is photographed in the student publication *The Masquerader*. Chancellor Branscomb bans the publication. The topless female is never publicly identified.

1952 – A student named Caroline Lowe becomes the one of the first female *Hustler* editors outside of a world war era. However, *The Hustler* continues to have an indisputable male slant. Throughout the decade, the publication runs sexy photographs of Vanderbilt coeds, often in shorts and tight sweaters, featured as the "Coed of the Week."

1955 – Beauty pageants abound on campus. Two of the biggest are the *Hustler*-sponsored Maid of Cotton and the Miss Commodore contest, sponsored by the school yearbook.

1993 Homecoming Queen Heidi Gillingham
Vanderbilt News and Public Affairs

1967 – In its debut issue, a campus publication called *Dirty We'jun* features an article by a female reporter complaining that she can't get birth control pills on campus. "Why is it that on this supposedly liberal campus – at a time when sexual relations are becoming as much a national part of dating as stopping at a restaurant after the show – that Vanderbilt is still in the 'hold your hand, may I kiss you good night' stage?" she asks.

1969 – Under pressure from students (female and male), the Heard administration does away with mandatory midnight curfews for sophomore, junior, and senior women. The next year, *Hustler* columnist Kathleen Gallagher points out that with the new freedom comes added responsibility. "Gone forever are the orgies of farewell in the (Branscomb) Quad lobby at closing hours . . . Formerly, whether you were having a great time, hated your date, were bored stiff, or had an exam at 8:00 the next morning, you felt that you owed it to your date to stay out until curfew. The responsibility for ending a date lay not with the individual involved, but with an arbitrary set of rules." At about the same time the administration does away with the rules that prohibit women from wearing pants and shorts on campus.

1972 – Under pressure from students and faculty, the board of trust discards a policy that limits female enrollment to one-third of the student body, allowing the number of women in the school to rise to about half by 1980. Alumna Mary Jane Werthan becomes the first female trustee. Also, female students gain access to indoor sports facilities in McGugin Center after employing some unusual protest methods. At one point, students Widget Judd and Mae Go shock the campus by climbing into the sauna bath at McGugin nude, to the pleasant surprise of a student named Tom Davis who was already sitting in it. "After some initial embarrassment and surprise, we all talked very normally about things in general," Davis says. A few days later, the athletic department announces a policy under which women can use the sauna for two hours a day, two nights a week.

1973 – In a form of mass protest against all things sexist and elitist, the largest vote-getter for the annual Lady of the Bracelet award is the entire group of senior class females.

1975 – Sallie TeSelle is named dean of the Vanderbilt Divinity School, becoming the first female dean of any division of Vanderbilt University (other than the School of Nursing).

1977 – Under pressure from a faculty commission Vanderbilt forms a women's center and begins hiring more female professors. Meanwhile, under Title IX of the Civil Rights Act, the university is ordered to take steps to provide equal opportunities for male and female athletes. By the end of the year Vanderbilt has formed intercollegiate women's teams in tennis, swimming, basketball, and track. The next year Karen Thompson becomes the first girl in the history of the school to be offered a sports scholarship.

1981 – Dozens of Vanderbilt women line up at the Holiday Inn to apply for the honor of posing for *Playboy* magazine's special "Women of the Southeastern Conference" section. Four are selected, and three of them – JoAnne Riggs, Marlene Hall, and Donna Crouch – pose partially nude in the national magazine. The Vanderbilt bookstore quickly sells out of the issue.

1991 – With the hiring of Jim Foster as head coach, the Vanderbilt women's basketball team becomes one of the strongest in the country. Two years later the team competes for the national championship and a six-foot-ten player named Heidi Gillingham is chosen by her fellow students to be homecoming queen. Gillingham's many honors result in a glowing story in *Sports Illustrated*, in which she is described as "regal, serene and fond of wearing elegant clothes sewn by her mother."

WOMEN'S DORM TO INTERNATIONAL HOUSE

McTyeire Hall is unique to Vanderbilt in many ways. It is the oldest dormitory standing at the school (not including dorms on the Peabody campus). It was the first dormitory built for women. It is the only Vanderbilt dormitory to have been saved from the wrecking ball by its own tenants. And it was one of the first student residences in the United States built around an international theme.

The story of McTyeire begins with a terrible fire. After Wesley Hall burned in 1932, the remains of the building sat for years while the university settled with the insurance company. For financial reasons the school chose not to rebuild Wesley, but to buy the old YMCA College building across Twenty-first Avenue and convert it into the new home of the divinity school. In 1940 the old bricks from Wesley Hall were used to build a new dormitory for female students. The building cost $150,000 and was named for Bishop Holland McTyeire. It was and remains the only thing on campus named for the most important person in the school's history.

For a generation of students the name "McTyeire Hall" was synonymous with Vanderbilt girls. In the 1940s and 1950s McTyeire's lounges were the site of countless semi-formal teas, socials, and open houses, all of which took place under the watchful eye of the dormitory's house mother. The girls who lived in McTyeire also had their own sets of rules. In the 1940s McTyeire residents were required to be in by 10:15 p.m. on weekdays and by forty-five minutes after the end of a dance on weekends. Smoking was allowed in rooms, but not in halls. Drinking was not permitted in the dorm. McTyeire girls were also required to attend church services at least twice a month. "This is for your own good and satisfaction and to prove to the folks at home that you are not trodding the downward path in this mad whirl of college life," the school newspaper explained.

McTyeire served its purpose as the home of most Vanderbilt women until the mid-1960s, when the massive Branscomb Quadrangle was opened. From that point the dormitory's longterm future came into question. In 1971 McTyeire became one of Vanderbilt's first coed dorms, used mostly by graduate students. Its cafeteria became a pub that occasionally featured live music, to the dismay of some residents who wished to study late at night.

In early 1974 the Heard administration considered tearing down McTyeire and the small house next to it to expand the medical center. (The administration wanted more land for the medical center in case public opposition prevented a proposal to close down Garland Avenue to through traffic.) The board of trust approved the plan and the U.S. Department of Health, Education and Welfare came through with a $7.7 million grant to help fund it.

A few weeks later students and faculty learned about the plan. In March 1974 a body called the Physical Facilities Committee asked that McTyeire and the old house next to it be saved "for reasons historic, humanistic, and aesthetic." About that time a few students including undergraduate Mary Sue Price began circulating a petition asking that McTyeire Hall and the old house be saved. Price pointed out that McTyeire had many unique qualities, including "the formal lounge with piano and a much used fireplace used informally for study breaks in the winter; and more importantly, the closeness that they [McTyeire's residents] report feeling tucked away from most other dorms." Eighty-eight residents of McTyeire and Landon House, another small dorm to be razed under the same project, signed the petition.

The opposition to the project made Chancellor Alexander Heard pause. In the summer of 1974 he instructed campus planners to rethink the demolition of McTyeire. By November of that year planners had gone back to the idea of expanding the medical center to the South (after the Metro Council approved closing Garland Avenue as a through street). Under the new blueprint, the school decided to put the new medical building on the south side of Garland where the old Vanderbilt Theater building was then located. Meanwhile, Vanderbilt would develop a new auditorium (later called Langford Auditorium) as a part of that medical center building, while refitting Neely Auditorium into a new Vanderbilt theater.

McTyeire was thus saved, although it was still unclear what would happen to it. Through the rest of the 1970s the building continued to be used as a dormitory and graduate student pub, but it needed renovation. In 1980 trustee Cliff Garvin arranged a $500,000 donation to Vanderbilt through the Exxon Education Fund. With that money, Provost Wendell Holladay, Dean of Housing K. C. Potter, and Vanderbilt professor Robert Baldwin came up with a plan to renovate McTyeire Hall and convert it into an international-themed dorm. The dormitory was set up with separate German, Spanish, French, and Russian halls. As a part of living in McTyeire, students were required to speak foreign languages on the hall and eat breakfast and dinner in the dormitory cafeteria. To the delight of the International House's organizers, more than two hundred students applied to live in McTyeire in the fall of 1981, the first year it opened as an international house.

THE TRADITION THAT IS ALWAYS UGLY

During the second half of the twentieth century the Vanderbilt football team was consistently one of the weakest in the country on the field. In fact, from 1953 until the end of the century, Vanderbilt had eleven football coaches. Nine of them left with losing records. Since so many coaches came and went that it's hard even for fans to remember them all. For some reason, everyone who went to Vanderbilt is under the impression that the nastiest departure of a football coach took place during their tenure. But they were all unpleasant.

In 1953 head coach Bill Edwards resigned after four seasons. Not only was Edwards accused of having a mediocre win-loss record (he won twenty-one and lost nineteen games), he was blamed for a drop in football attendance that resulted in a $90,000 loss for the athletic program. Edwards' replacement was Virginia head coach Art

Guepe. "Virginia's loss, Vandy's gain," a *Hustler* headline chirped. Guepe said that he thought he could succeed at Vanderbilt even though he would have two fewer coaches and ten fewer scholarships than Edwards – reductions imposed by the Branscomb administration to reduce the athletic department's financial deficit. "I will try awfully hard to give Vanderbilt a respected football team," Guepe said.

The Guepe era had one glorious year, as Vanderbilt fielded an 8-3 team that beat Auburn in the 1955 Gator Bowl. The team then won five games in each of the 1956, 1957, 1958, and 1959 seasons. But the fans were restless; toward the end of the 1959 season, a group of students hung an effigy of Coach Guepe from a tree near Kissam Quadrangle. "Somebody has a queer sense of humor," the coach said when he heard about the prank. "Or perhaps it's the thing to do nowadays. A few years ago, people were eating goldfish." Then the bottom fell out, and the Commodores won only six games in the next three years combined. In November 1962 the student senate passed a measure asking that Guepe be fired. A few weeks later, Guepe was gone, leaving behind the most insightful quote in Commodore football history. "Vanderbilt," he said, "tries to be Harvard and Yale five days a week and Alabama on Saturday."

Guepe was replaced by Jack Green. Four unsuccessful seasons later, *Hustler* reporter Paul Kurtz led the charge to get rid of Green. In a column headlined "Let's sack Jack," Kurtz wrote, "The football program at Vanderbilt is horrible. Any intelligent observer of the Vanderbilt scene can see this . . . Losing has become a habit under Jack Green, though the system has been responsible." A few weeks later, Bill Pace took Green's place, and Jess Neely was hired to fill the vacant athletic director position. "We are not interested in creating a jock cult," Neely said in one of his first interviews after being hired. "We believe that Vandy can win in the SEC without undermining the academic principles that bring most of our players here."

Pace remained at Vanderbilt for five years, during which the team only won five out of twenty-five SEC games (three of those against Kentucky). By the fall of 1972 some people at Vanderbilt were ready to give up on big-time football. "The truth is that Vanderbilt doesn't need, and can't afford, intercollegiate football – at least not on the scale it is attempting to play on now," *Hustler* sports editor John Bloom wrote. However, the administration decided that the problem wasn't with the system but the coach. Pace resigned under duress and was replaced by twenty-eight-year-old Steve Sloan.

Vanderbilt had a great season in 1974, fielding a 7-3-2 team that went to the Peach Bowl and tied Texas Tech 6-6. Texas Tech officials were so impressed by Coach Sloan that they immediately hired him and most of his staff. Sloan thus became the only head coach in two decades to leave Vanderbilt with a winning season.

Former Memphis State head coach Fred Pancoast was hired to replace Sloan. Pancoast's term began well, as the team went 7-4 and beat Tennessee his first year. However, the Commodores went 2-9 in 1976 and 2-9 in 1977, a year in which a Nashville newspaper reported that a group of alumni was willing to pay Pancoast $100,000 to step down. The coach resigned the next year after the team started the season 1-6.

About the time Pancoast resigned, Vanderbilt hired a new athletic director named Roy Kramer. Kramer said he thought Vanderbilt could field a better team if the school took some steps to upgrade the program, such as building better practice and training facilities and expanding the stadium. "I do not believe we (the administration) have ever made an honest attempt to be competitive in this great conference," Kramer said. The new athletic director hired a head coach named George MacIntyre, who had been a defensive back coach at Vanderbilt when Sloan was the head coach. "The complexion of Vanderbilt has changed during the past two years," MacIntyre said after being hired.

MacIntyre's first year was a 1-10 disaster that included a 66-3 loss to Alabama. The Commodores then got progressively better, winning two games in 1980, four in 1981, and eight in a glorious 1982 season that included wins over Tennessee and Florida and a trip to the Hall of Fame Bowl in Birmingham. But in 1983 things began to decline. Vanderbilt went 2-9 in 1983, 5-6 in 1984, and 3-7-1 in 1985. MacIntyre resigned before the last game that year. "If a person wants to enroll in challenging courses and play against some of the best football teams in the country, then Vanderbilt is the right choice," he said. "Vanderbilt must be able to make a concession to help recruiting. The money and the facilities are fine."

MacIntyre was replaced by Watson Brown, a former quarterback for the Commodores who had been MacIntyre's offensive coordinator during the 1982 bowl season. Brown's tenure was disappointing. After four straight losing years Vanderbilt opened the fifth season of Brown's term against Southern Methodist University, which was still recovering from a two-year break from the sport for violating NCAA rules in the mid-1980s. The Commodores lost 44-7. One of the Vanderbilt faithful in attendance at Texas Stadium that day was Chancellor Joe Wyatt. "It was not even close," Wyatt, a Texas native, said years later. "There was SMU with a bunch of guys that no one else would recruit trying to play football and they just absolutely killed us. We obviously hadn't prepared and hadn't paid any attention to what we were doing." It was the beginning of a 1-10 season in which the Commodores gave up an incredible 457 points. Brown was fired a few hours before the last game of the season that year. Many alumni and fans called the chancellor's office to criticize the handling of Brown's dismissal. "We are totally disgusted at the way Watson Brown was fired," one fan said. "In our opinion it was a tasteless act by the Vanderbilt administration."

Gerry Dinardo, former offensive coordinator at Colorado, was the next Vanderbilt coach. Dinardo stayed four seasons, during which his team won four games twice and five games twice, mainly by running an "I-bone" offense that rarely threw the ball. But Dinardo's teams were no match for traditional rival Tennessee. Among the losing scores to the Volunteers during Dinardo's tenure were 45-0, 62-14, and 65-0 (a home game in which Vanderbilt trailed 44-0 at halftime). But Dinardo wasn't fired, nor did he resign under duress. He was hired to be the head coach of Louisiana State University.

The next coach was Rod Dowhower, who brought to Vanderbilt the most extensive professional football coaching resume in Vanderbilt history. "There is a genuine sense of satisfaction with the present and excitement with the future as Dowhower and his new assistants come to Nashville," *The Hustler* rejoiced at the time. "Some of football's best offensive minds have worked with Dowhower." However, Dowhower only stayed two years, with the team winning two games each year. The high point of the Dowhower era was a

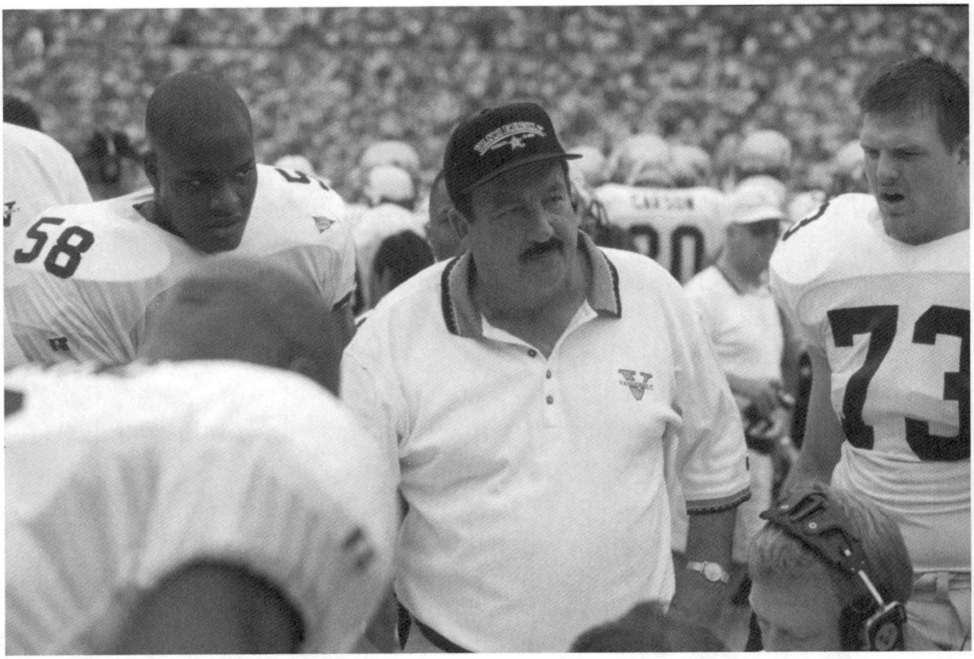

Woody Widenhofer, coach of the Vanderbilt football team from 1997 to 2001
Vanderbilt News and Public Affairs

nationally televised 14-7 loss to Notre Dame, a game in which Vanderbilt led for part of the fourth quarter. Vanderbilt's defense was so good that year that Dowhower was replaced with defensive coordinator Woody Widenhofer, whose coaching career had included a stint as linebacker coach for the Pittsburgh Steelers.

Expectations were high for Widenhofer, and the Commodores fielded a good defense during most of his tenure. But the offense wasn't good enough. Vanderbilt went 3-8 in 1997, 2-9 in 1998, 5-6 in 1999, and 2-9 in 2000 (a season that included an opening day home loss to Miami, Ohio). In the fall of 2001 Widenhofer announced his resignation after a 71-13 embarrassment at the hands of Florida, a game in which Vanderbilt trailed 65-0 in the third quarter.

Vanderbilt hired Furman football coach Bobby Johnson to replace Widenhofer. Johnson's first season had few bright spots; the Commodores won two and lost ten, one of those defeats being the team's second straight loss at home to Middle Tennessee State.

Attendance fell to alarmingly low numbers; people wearing orange easily outnumbered people wearing black at the Vanderbilt-Tennessee game in Nashville that year. But at the end of his first year Johnson was, naturally, optimistic.

The Business School in the Funeral Home

By the end of the twentieth century Vanderbilt's Owen School of Management would be housed in a marvelous structure and be considered one of the top graduate business schools in the country. But it didn't start off that way. Vanderbilt's graduate business school began as an unusual experiment in organization and philosophy. And it was housed in a funeral home.

Starting in the late 1950s several members of the Vanderbilt Board of Trust began talking about the idea of a graduate school of business at Vanderbilt. In 1965 Chancellor Alexander Heard appointed a committee of faculty and trustees to study the idea of a business school. That committee recommended that Vanderbilt move ahead with a graduate school that would provide "professional education rather than vocational training." But the committee estimated that $5 million in endowment would be needed to start such an institution.

Because of the cost Heard was not enthusiastic about a business school. But the trustees voted to start it anyway. In 1966 board member and Genesco executive Matt Wigginton began raising money for the new school. Wigginton's strategy was to convince at least 250 Nashville area businesses to pledge a thousand dollars per year for five consecutive years. That sum would be enough to get the school off the ground and give it enough time to raise the rest of the money for endowment.

Things were going very well through the summer of 1968, by which time there had been several positive developments. Wigginton succeeded in raising the $250,000 per year. Igor Ansoff, a professor at Carnegie-Mellon with extensive private sector experience, was hired to be the business school's first dean. Vanderbilt trustee David K. (Pat) Wilson donated the Cosmopolitan Funeral Home building on West End Avenue, adjacent to the Vanderbilt campus, for use as a business school. "My company [Cherokee Insurance] had acquired another company that owned a small chain of funeral homes, and we didn't really want to be in the funeral home business," Wilson explained years later.

The most important development was the decision by trustee Ralph (Peck) Owen to financially support the school. After graduating from Vanderbilt in 1928, Owen and several colleagues including Brownlee Currey Sr. started a brokerage house called Equitable Securities. In the 1930s and 1940s Equitable filled a void in the South that had been left behind by Caldwell & Co., a municipal bond house that went bankrupt during the Great Depression. By World War II Equitable had ten offices around the country and was considered the dominant bond house in the South. After the war it helped take several southern companies public, including Holiday Inn, Spur Oil, and Georgia Hardwood Lumber (later Georgia-Pacific). Along the way Equitable made many sizable investments – the most important of which was the 1949 purchase of thirteen percent of the stock in American Express Corp.

By the late 1960s Owen was extremely wealthy and Equitable Securities was winding down its era as a Nashville-based public company. Owen wanted to do something big for his community. But after a career of hiring Vanderbilt graduates and having to teach them the basics of the securities industry, he felt strongly about Nashville's need for a graduate business school. Around 1968 Owen agreed to contribute close to $2 million dollars to the business school's endowment (although he asked that his donation remain anonymous for as long as possible).

Vanderbilt spent a year renovating the funeral home while Ansoff put together a curriculum and a staff. In the fall of 1969, when about fifty students enrolled in Vanderbilt's new graduate school of management, they signed up with an unusual organization. Compared to most other graduate business schools, the curriculum Ansoff put together was strong on behavioral courses but weak on quantitative ones. Unlike the rest of the university, the school of management didn't operate on the semester system but on a system of "learning modules," where students worked on a subject until they had theoretically mastered it and then moved on. The first year was fairly structured, with each student required to take subjects such as accounting, economics, business strategies, and marketing. The second year was independent study, with each student expected to work out a thesis idea with a faculty member. All grading was pass-fail.

Eventually, Ansoff's program would be done away with. It didn't fit in with the other business schools in America and wasn't what the Nashville business community wanted. But the system had its defenders, such as 1972 graduate Frank Bumstead. Bumstead was twenty-eight and had already served a tour of duty in Vietnam when he started at the management school. He said he spent his entire second year at the school working on a thesis about the impact of America's break from the gold standard. "I worked hard and learned a lot," said Bumstead. "The model worked for me because I really wanted to learn. But I think the model worked better for people who were eager learn like me, not people who were just coming out of college and wanting to be professional students.

"Igor [Ansoff] was a very independent and bright man who had a vision of how to build a graduate business program in a different way than anyone else had. He placed a significant amount of the responsibility for learning on the student and not on the faculty member or the system. The advantages of that learning model probably existed for fewer students than he had hoped. And it didn't generally play well to corporate recruiters because it was so different."

Within three years of its organization the school of management was being criticized by many of its Nashville donors. Among their complaints were that the school's curriculum was too "touchy-feely," that the pass-fail system was unique in the world of business schools, and that its graduates were inclined to work for not-for-profit organizations or become entrepreneurs rather than go to work for existing companies. In 1973, the same year the school of management became subsidized by the university's general fund, Ansoff was replaced as dean by James Davis. Davis would remain interim dean for three years, during which his greatest accomplishment was keeping the school afloat. Davis began to move the school in a direction of a more traditional business school. He also tried to build better ties with Nashville's business community, bringing in many local business leaders to give guest lectures. It was also during Davis' tenure that the management school hired its most acclaimed faculty member, former governor of the Federal Reserve System Dewey Daane.

In 1974 Chancellor Heard appointed a committee to come up with a series of strategies for the business school. A year later the board heard the alternatives. Among them were the ideas of closing the school down entirely at one extreme and building the school into one of the best in the country at the other. After a long debate the board voted not to shut the school down but to try to build it into a "second-tier" business school. The vote was close; during the meeting a measure to shut down the school failed 18-16.

A few months later Vanderbilt hired Sam Richmond to be the management school's new dean. Richmond quickly set to work building a program along the lines of a traditional business school like Stanford and Wharton. He made major shifts in the curriculum. "There is a return to basics," an alumni publication said. "Its curriculum has made about a 95 percent revolution from the original conception of the school's course of study." Richmond brought in more and better faculty, more students, and better qualified students. He also went to great lengths to encourage ties with the Nashville business community.

Richmond succeeded in part because of the financial support of Nashville's business community. The most generous supporter remained Peck Owen, who continued to give money to the endowment. In 1977 Owen agreed to allow the management school to be named for him and his wife Lulu.

By 1979 the Owen School of Management was on firm ground. The school had made the transition to a more traditional business school curriculum. Its faculty had grown from twelve to twenty; its student body from about 150 to 250. Long-term support from the local community was also solidified with the successful launch of an executive MBA program in 1978.

The only thing the school didn't have was an adequate building; after all, it was still in a structure that had originally been built as a funeral home. In 1980 the Vanderbilt Board of Trust launched a fund drive for the building headed by trustees Bronson Ingram and Gerald Averbuch. Meanwhile, campus planners decided that the management school would be built on the site of the old Mechanical

Engineering Building, a structure that had been added on to many times in its ninety-year history. School officials hired St. Louis architect Gyo Obata, telling him that their intention was to tear down the old frame and build a new one in its place. After Obata examined the ME Building, he began working on a different plan, under which the original ME Building (but not its additions) would be saved and be made a part of the new Owen complex. Construction began in the summer of 1980, on the same day that alumnus and trustee Thomas Walker announced that he would give the school $1.5 million to build a library collection.

Grenada Liberation Day and the Return of Prohibition

The Reagan era was one of conservatism in American life, and no place in the country was more conservative in the mid-1980s than Vanderbilt University. A look through the key events in the life of students during the 1984-85 school year, as reported in *The Hustler*, makes this clear.

In 1984 the Tennessee legislature, under pressure from the federal government, raised the legal drinking age from nineteen to twenty-one. This policy change had extensive ramifications on the Vanderbilt campus. By the spring of 1985 the university had banned kegs from campus and outlawed the use of organizational money for alcohol, theoretically prevented fraternities from having beer at parties. Vanderbilt even eliminated happy hour at Sarratt Student Center's Overcup Oak pub. None of these steps was popular on a campus where a survey revealed that 92 percent of students consumed alcohol. But there were no organized protests against the new rules.

Among *The Hustler's* more popular regular features that year were the nationally syndicated Bloom County comic strip and the movie reviewer Joe Bob Briggs. Frequent advertisers included the Today contraceptive sponge, Dodge Cleaners, the Vanderbilt Tanning Spa, Domino's Pizza, Spinnakers restaurant, Stage Deli, AT&T, the National Security Agency, and Cantrell's night club. One of the favorite hangouts was a new restaurant called the San Antonio Taco Co., started by graduate student Robin Delmer and alum Richard Patton.

In September 1984 the Vanderbilt football team, under head coach George MacIntyre, had its best start since the McGugin era. By early October the team was 4-0, ranked in the nation's top twenty, and celebrating a 30-21 upset at Alabama. "A taste of sugar?" read *The Hustler* headline after the win over the Crimson Tide, referring to the fact that at that time, the Southeastern Conference champion automatically went to the Sugar Bowl. Unfortunately, the fifth game didn't go so well. The undefeated Commodores were upset by winless Tulane. Next came a loss at LSU. Then a disastrous 62-35 loss at

A group of Vanderbilt freshmen in the fall of 1983
Vanderbilt News and Public Affairs

Georgia. Vanderbilt finished 5-6, in what turned out to be the second out of at least twenty consecutive losing seasons.

No sooner had the season ended than the Vanderbilt football program became engulfed in the greatest controversy in it history, with the Tennessee Bureau of Investigation investigating the use of steroids among Vanderbilt athletes. Eventually, Vanderbilt football trainer E.J. "Doc" Kreis left the school after he was indicted for supplying steroids to thirty-three Vanderbilt athletes, most of whom were football players. As a result of the scandal, the university instituted a policy under which incoming athletes had to agree to undergo periodic steroid testing, making it one of the first schools to take such a step.

In the fall of 1984 most students didn't have computers yet, but they were beginning to learn how to use them. To this end Vanderbilt opened a new computer "microlab" in Garland Hall, equipping it with fifty-six Zenith Z-150 PC microcomputers. A few weeks later the Joint University Library installed "coin operated" microcomputers that cost two dollars per hour to use. By the end of the year the Vanderbilt bookstore was advertising the sale of a new Macintosh computer with an external disk drive and printer for $2,215.

At a student-run debate a few days before the 1984 presidential election between incumbent Ronald Reagan and Democrat Walter Mondale, Young Democrat Bill Carey (this author) said that "just because Daddy is voting for Reagan is no reason to vote for Reagan." Young Republican Stephen Vaughn, on the other hand, asked the three hundred or so debate attendees, "now that we have come this far [from the Carter years], why should we turn back?" A few days later, 88 percent of students polled said that they intended to vote for Reagan. Then, just before the election, *The Hustler* contained an insert called "The Prouder, Stronger Times," paid for by the Reagan-Bush campaign. The insert, which ran in many college newspapers across the country, contained articles with headlines such as "Stars shine for Reagan," "Reagan finds support on campus," and "Campuses no longer just for liberals."

Concerts during the school year included Elvis Costello, the Stray Cats, Stevie Ray Vaughn, REM, the Replacements, the White Animals, John Prine, Cyndi Lauper, Wynton Marsalis, General Public,

Steve Earle, Guadalcanal Diary, and Albert Collins.

In October 1984 the Vanderbilt College Republicans and United Students of America Foundation celebrated "Grenada Liberation Day" to honor the first anniversary of the U.S. military's invasion of that tiny Caribbean island. For the occasion, student organizers brought to campus one of the American medical students who was rescued as a result of the invasion. The next week graduate student Douglas Foxvog expressed his disgust with the event in *The Hustler.* "This is traditional gunboat diplomacy," Foxvog wrote. "It was condemned throughout Latin America and the third world as well as by our allies in Europe. We should be ashamed, not proud of this action."

In a newly published review of colleges called *Lisa Birnbach's College Book*, the author called Vanderbilt students "narrow minded, racist, and job-crazed" and said that at the Vanderbilt campus the Greek system is "oppressive and anti-intellectual." *The Hustler* took the insults seriously. Reporter Chris Crain did a four-part series in which he concluded that Birnbach did almost no research of any kind before she reached her conclusions about Vanderbilt.

Speakers during the school year included feminist Gloria Steinem, former Secretary of the Interior James Watt, *Roots* author Alex Haley, U.S. senatorial candidate Al Gore, journalists Sam Donelson and Roy Blount, Atlanta mayor Andrew Young, Tennessee Governor Lamar Alexander, and evangelist Josh McDowell. The most controversial was "Gonzo" journalist Hunter S. Thompson. Thompson, who drew $5,000 for his visit, called 1980s college students "a generation of swine," and said that President Reagan was a "old, senile man . . . The next four years are going to be a real adventure for all of you."

The Hustler began calling for more security, especially for men's dorms, which had little or no protection at that time. In January the administration responded to the concern by placing security phones throughout the campus. School officials also announced that they were looking into the idea of issuing what it called "super student ID cards" that would unlock dorms only to authorized people.

In the spring of 1985 Vanderbilt announced plans for a $9 million campus recreation center – complete with four basketball courts, a swimming pool, and luxurious weight rooms – to be built on the south end of campus. When the complex opened four years later, students no longer had to wait their turn to use Memorial Gymnasium to play basketball or work out.

Hustler columnist Jeff Sadow wrote one ultraconservative column after another, including one headlined "Homosexual promiscuity must be ended." An excerpt from the article, which inspired quite a bit of hate mail: "Two decades ago there were no homosexuals, only individuals who committed homosexual acts. As long as one indulged in these acts in private, society winked its eye and ignored the individual."

A conservative group called Vanderbilt Students for Life organized an event called the Abortion Holocaust Lecture Series to take place the same week as University Chaplain Beverly Asbury's Holocaust Lecture Series. Abortion Holocaust Lecture Series speaker William Brennan (a Catholic activist not to be confused with Supreme Court Justice William J. Brennan) delivered a speech comparing the U.S. Supreme Court's Roe v. Wade decision to Hitler's extermination of the Jews. "Doctors today are using the law as a crutch just as Hitler did," Brennan said.

Students were beginning to criticize new chancellor Joe B. Wyatt for his failure to socialize with them. "Is the man [Wyatt] alive?" student Jeff Harris wrote. "The students have no idea. All we ever get of him (or his clone) is an occasional glimpse at Parents Weekend or the freshman picnic. Is it against his religion to make an informal, unannounced appearance on campus?"

Electives, Dance Class, and Sex Ed

By the 1990s course work at Vanderbilt had very little in common with the curriculum being offered to previous generations of students. This happened gradually, but there are several key landmarks in the history of classroom teaching at the school.

For instance, it was once part of the chancellor's job to teach. Vanderbilt's first chancellor, Landon Garland, was a physicist and astronomer. The university built an observatory as one of its first buildings because of Garland's specialization. James Kirkland taught Latin, but stopped teaching around the turn of the century to focus on administrative responsibilities.

Early in the twentieth century so many courses were required that little time was left for electives. In 1912 freshman year consisted of year-long courses in English, Greek, Latin, mathematics, and a foreign language (French or German). Sophomore year consisted of year-long courses in English, Greek, Latin, history, and a foreign language. Juniors had to take year-long courses in chemistry, philosophy, and physics. Only then did the curriculums begin to vary, depending on majors.

One of the biggest turning points in Vanderbilt's curriculum came in 1919, when the school rescinded its requirement that undergraduates study Greek and Latin. This was a controversial move in the eyes of many alumni, who thought that the curriculum was being softened and believed young people should take Greek and Latin because they had. Ten years after the change Vanderbilt English Professor Edwin Mims wrote a long letter to alumni defending the school's switch to modern languages, literature, and sciences. "In truth," Mims wrote, "comparatively few students under the old regime ever got from these studies (Greek and Latin) any enjoyment or appreciation of literature."

Also in 1919 Vanderbilt began offering bachelor's degrees in business administration. During its first two years guest lecturers in the department included Nashville businessmen Whitefoord Cole, Lee Loventhal, William Nelson, Luke Lea, Edward Stahlman, and H. G. Hill Sr.

Vanderbilt created a Department of Physical Education and Hygiene in the early 1920s, in part to justify the hiring of athletic coaches as full-time employees. At the time there was an unprecedented emphasis on the role of P.E. within higher education. "Under the new system, every student should leave the university at least a better athlete than when he started, and a much larger number will leave it as superior athletes in particular sports," one publication explained. By the eve of World War II students had numerous physical education courses to chose from, including cross country, boxing, wrestling, tumbling, horsemanship, and even dancing. "Each Wednesday from three until six, Alumni Hall is inhabited with couples flinging a footsie to congas, rhumbas, and waltzes," *The Hustler* reported in the fall of 1941. However, mandatory physical education grew unpopular as the years passed, and became the target of student protests in the late 1960s.

In Vanderbilt's early years chemistry was the most emphasized science in the curriculum, which is why Chancellor Kirkland spent Mary Furman's legacy on a chemistry building. This situation changed in 1930 when, due to the lobbying of biology professor Edwin Reinke, the requirement that students take chemistry for a bachelor of arts degree was changed to allow them to take chemistry or biology. After World War II physics became the most popular science.

As recently as the late 1950s all engineering students were required to take a year of English, history, economics, and political science. This requirement, coupled with the fact that there were virtually no electives within the engineering school, meant that it was common for engineering students of that era and school to have some of their classmates in every single class for four years.

Through the 1960s every freshman in the school of Arts & Sciences had to take a year-long course called History of Western Civilization. Eventually, "Western Civ" became one of the least-liked classes on campus. The discontent boiled over in 1968, when fifty students walked out of a Western Civilization lecture to demonstrate their boredom. The next year, in a development the history department said was unrelated to the protests, the decision was made to alternate lecturers for each of the mandatory Western Civilization classes.

During the late 1960s there was an unprecedented rise in the number of students majoring in philosophy. In 1968 the school graduated thirty-five philosophy majors. Three years later it graduated ninety.

During the 1969-70 school year the nursing school began teaching a class called Preparation for Parenthood that contained sex education as part of the class. It became quite popular. "The only handicap in the course is the size of the audience, which prohibits personal discussion to a large degree," a *Hustler* article about the class said. In the mid-1980s the psychology department went a step further, teaching a class called Human Sexuality. It, too, drew quite a few students.

Vanderbilt began teaching Afro-American studies in 1972 and women's studies in 1975. For many years both programs were interdisciplinary, where classes would be taught by guest professors from other departments such as sociology, history, and psychology.

During the 1980s there was a notable rise in the number of students majoring in Russian. Then, after the fall of communism in the Soviet Union, the number dwindled to almost nothing, and Vanderbilt stopped offering a Russian major.

By the end of the twentieth century the rise in specialization had created a situation where students had more choice in what to study in college than previous generations could have imagined. In 2002 the economics and psychology departments each offered over a hundred classes. Vanderbilt also offered a major in women's studies and minors in Jewish studies and film studies.

The Chancellor Who Thought About Money

When Harvard administrator Joe Billy Wyatt was chosen to be Vanderbilt's chancellor, a lot of people weren't sure if he was up to the task. Wyatt's academic credentials included an undergraduate degree from the University of Texas and a masters degree in mathematics from Texas Christian University. He did not have a Ph.D.; a notable deficiency at a university that had made doctorates a virtual requirement.

But the three-member search committee of trustees Sam Fleming, Pat Wilson, and Bronson Ingram saw something in the tall Texan, and they offered him the job in 1982. "They told me that the goal was for Vanderbilt to become one of the top universities in the country in terms of undergraduate and graduate studies and in terms of research," said Wyatt. Wyatt, whose son was a sophomore at Vanderbilt at the time, remembered his first encounter with the Nashville media. "At my first press conference, when I was introduced as the next chancellor at Vanderbilt, about eighty percent of the questions had to do with athletics. They could have cared less about what the real issues were at Vanderbilt. They just wanted to know what this guy from the Ivy League was going to do to the sports teams."

Wyatt spent the first couple of years assessing the situation and came to four main conclusions. One was that Vanderbilt did not have a national fundraising machine. "Vanderbilt had a campaign organization, but if you look at the previous fund drives, you will see that the focus was heavily Nashville," he said. "The fact of the matter is that Vanderbilt had successful graduates all over the country, many of whom the school had lost track of." The second was that the university had historically not placed a high a priority on getting research grants. "It just hadn't been emphasized." The third was that the school's reputation academically was not as great as many alumni and faculty believed. This was confirmed in 1983, when the National Research Council published a ranking of graduate programs at U.S. universities that showed many Vanderbilt departments ranked lower than many had expected. "That was a real eye-opener," Wyatt said.

Wyatt's fourth conclusion was rather obvious. Because of the financial problems that Vanderbilt (and many other schools) had faced in the 1970s, the school's physical plant was in bad shape by the mid-1980s. In some cases, such as the many dormitories built prior to 1960, buildings were safe and solid but not modernized. But in other instances, such as Old Science and Kirkland Hall, buildings were decrepit. "Kirkland Hall was a slum," Wyatt said. "It was not particularly clean and not particularly attractive, and was chopped up into little warrens. There was a rusty dumpster sitting right out front. When you walked in the door, you saw no one; you saw opaque doors and halls and that was it. And this was the focal building of the university."

Wyatt attacked these deficiencies by increasing Vanderbilt's revenue on all fronts and investing the money in new people, new programs, new buildings, and renovations. By the time he retired eighteen years later, he had succeeded in doing what his search committee asked and presided over the most trouble-free era in school history in the process. "My predecessors are the ones who had to deal

Vanderbilt faculty members give two visiting Russian scientists a tour of the Free Electron Laser Center
Vanderbilt News and Public Affairs

with controversy, whether with the fraternities, integration, or social unrest," he said. "I didn't have very many moments of anguish."

When Wyatt took over in 1982, Vanderbilt was receiving about $42 million per year for sponsored research. By the end of his era that number was $214 million. The change took place largely because Wyatt made sponsored research a priority, adding staff to the school's sponsored research office and giving faculty as much assistance and as much prodding as possible to apply for research grants.

Detailing Vanderbilt's expanded research programs would require several chapters. But one program that merits mention in this brief space is the Free Electron Laser Center. In the mid-1980s the Office of Naval Research wanted a place to develop and test free electron lasers, which produce a narrow, intense beam of infrared light that could be put to a variety of medical and industrial uses (brain surgery, for example). A group of faculty members including physics professors Norman Tolk, Richard Haglund, and Glenn Edwards and several from the medical school got excited about the project and approached the administration about the idea. Wyatt told the group to submit a bid immediately and even asked Tolk to explain the proposal to the board of trust. To the euphoria of the physics department, Vanderbilt was chosen as the site for the $8 million Free Electron Laser Center in 1986. For the rest of the century scientists came from as far away as Europe and Japan to conduct tests at the Vanderbilt Free Electron Laser Center, located next to McTyeire Hall.

Another way Wyatt increased Vanderbilt's revenue was by raising tuition. When Wyatt took over, Vanderbilt tuition was $6,100 per year. By the end of his tenure Vanderbilt's tuition was $25,190, an increase that far exceeded national inflation rates.

The third increase was in endowment. In 1989 Vanderbilt started what it hoped would be a $350 million fund drive. Wyatt convinced trustee Bronson Ingram to lead the effort, which turned out to be one of the most important things the chancellor ever did. "Bronson really took it seriously," Wyatt said. "Those of us who were working on the campaign literally met every two weeks for a couple of hours or longer for six years. He is the real hero of the effort."

As a part of the fund drive, Wyatt and Ingram made appearances before alumni in about fifty cities, a process made easier by the fact that Ingram owned an airplane. "At these events, we would have dinner, then Bronson would say a few words, and then I would talk for maybe five minutes," Wyatt said. "And then four or six local alumni of different generations would make statements about what Vanderbilt meant to them. You would just hear wonderful stories through this process. It was very, very successful."

At some point during the campaign, Ingram told Wyatt he intended to make a sizable gift, but he wasn't sure whether to do it in cash or stock. "He was talking about a pledge of about $100 million, but he told me that if he made the gift in stock that it might be worth more," Wyatt said. "I chose the stock."

Bronson Ingram died of cancer in 1995, only months before Ingram Micro, a computer hardware and software distributorship controlled by his family, went public. Shortly after Ingram Micro's initial public offering the Ingrams announced they would give the school a gift of Ingram Micro stock that was (at the time) worth about $340 million. It was the largest gift ever made to an American private university and guaranteed that Vanderbilt's $350 million fund drive instead raised $557 million. The Ingram donation was so large that Wyatt compared it in significance to Cornelius Vanderbilt's 1873 decision to endow the school in the first place.

Unlike so many aspects of the school's history, the story behind the Ingram donation is not ironic or cloaked in intrigue. "Bronson simply fell in love with the university and thought that giving a lot of money to it could really make a difference and help make something splendid happen in our own backyard," said his widow Martha Ingram, who became chairman of the Vanderbilt Board of Trust in 1997. "He was crazy about Joe Wyatt; they had a close relationship and a symbiotic friendship. And even when he was sick with cancer, it brought a smile to his face every time he thought about the fact that he gave the first gift and would give the last gift in the fundraising campaign."

Martha and Bronson Ingram
Photograph courtesy of Robin Ingram Patton

The Ingram family channeled most of the money into several divisions of the university in which they had special interest. First on the list was a scholarship program called Ingram Scholars, set up for students who devoted a large amount of time to community service. "He wanted to start a scholarship program, but didn't want to start one just for people who grabbed their education without regard to their fellow man," Martha Ingram said. By 2002 Vanderbilt had sponsored nearly a hundred Ingram scholars.

The Ingram family also gave $56 million to the Vanderbilt Cancer Center. Orrin Ingram, the eldest of Bronson Ingram's three sons, directed a fund drive that raised another $100 million for the cancer center. "He knew that it was too late to save his father, but not too late to save others," Martha Ingram said. By 2002 the Vanderbilt Cancer Center had more than 250 full-time physicians, making it one of the largest such facilities in the United States and one of the few comprehensive cancer centers in the country.

Other major projects the Ingrams sponsored included the Owen School of Management, the Vanderbilt Children's Hospital, the Vanderbilt Athletic Department, and the Blair School of Music. In 2002 Blair opened a new performing arts center, appropriately named the Martha Rivers Ingram Performing Arts Center.

The fund drive made it possible for Vanderbilt to undergo a period of expansion and improvement. On the new construction front, Vanderbilt built a classroom and office building called Wilson Hall, the Eskind Biomedical Library, a student recreation center, two large parking garages, and a major expansion to Stevenson Science Center. Meanwhile, almost every structure on campus (other than the Carmichael Towers and Branscomb Quadrangle) got a major facelift during the Wyatt years. Two of the more notable projects were the renovations of Old Science (which then became known as Benson Hall) and Kirkland Hall.

Building upgrades were accompanied by faculty upgrades and expansions in curriculum. Twice during the Wyatt era the university approved more stringent requirements for faculty appointment and tenure. Most of the school's graduate programs expanded during the Wyatt years, especially in technical areas. Perhaps the most notable growth of any department was in biomedical engineering, a department that rose from obscurity to a faculty of fifteen, the largest division of the Vanderbilt School of Engineering.

For these and other reasons Vanderbilt moved up in national rankings during the Wyatt years. Before 1989 Vanderbilt's undergraduate programs had never been ranked among the top twenty-five national universities in the annual *U.S. News & World Report* survey. Starting that year Vanderbilt was ranked regularly, and placed twenty-first in 2001. In graduate rankings, Peabody College came in seventh among schools of education; the law school was ranked seventeenth; the medical school sixteenth.

Every leader has his detractors, and Wyatt had his. Four noteworthy complaints recurred during the Wyatt years. One was that faculty, staff, and students saw less of him than they did his predecessor. After his retirement Wyatt said he was aware that people criticized him for not being more visible. But he said it wasn't because he was aloof. "In some ways it was against my instincts to be seen so little," he said. "Back when I was at Harvard, I was an associate at a dormitory, taught two courses, and was an advisor for a number of graduate students. But when I got to Vanderbilt, I concluded that I had to focus my effort on certain things at the expense of others. I knew that there would be some expense in terms of image. So be it."

The second complaint was that by emphasizing fundraising, capital upgrades, and expensive research projects that the undergraduate life of the school was de-emphasized. This perceived shortcoming came to a head in the fall of 1995, when twenty-five senior professors sent Wyatt a letter asking that he step down as chancellor, saying the school needed "distinguished educational leadership." Among the faculty members who signed the letter was philosophy professor John Lachs, who told a reporter a few days later that "the board's avowed goal is for us to be in the top ten. But we're not going to do that with slicker brochures and nicer lawns." Many faculty members came to Wyatt's defense, including history professor Paul Conkin and education professor Terrence Deal. But among other things, the incident was a reminder that not everyone on the faculty appreciated a chancellor who behaved more like a chief executive officer than a scholar.

The third complaint had less to do with Wyatt personally than with educational trends in general. With the dramatic increase in tuition during his tenure, a Vanderbilt education became less accessible to middle-class students. With tuition over $25,000 per year by the year 2000, the notion of a student working his way through college, as many did in the twentieth century, became an outmoded one. Students without generous scholarships had to pay, and that often meant taking on a lot of debt.

Wyatt acknowledged the problems caused by rising tuition. "Keeping it affordable is a real problem, and that is why you have to do what we did and raise money for endowed scholarships. That and faculty chairs were the highest priority in the campaign that Bronson and I did together." In fact, 115 endowed scholarship funds came out of the fund drive. "But the bottom line is that the cost of college is huge because the things you spend money on keep adding up," Wyatt said. "When I went to college during my senior year the very first computer showed up, and it wasn't much of a computer. Today, I don't know how many tens of millions of dollars worth of computers exist here and at every other major university. It is an added cost; nothing has gone away. Then you have the increased cost of every kind of laboratory. Then you have the increased costs of running a residential campus, with all the infrastructure and security it entails."

Students in a biomedical laboratory in the late 1990s
Vanderbilt News and Public Affairs

The other thing for which Wyatt was criticized

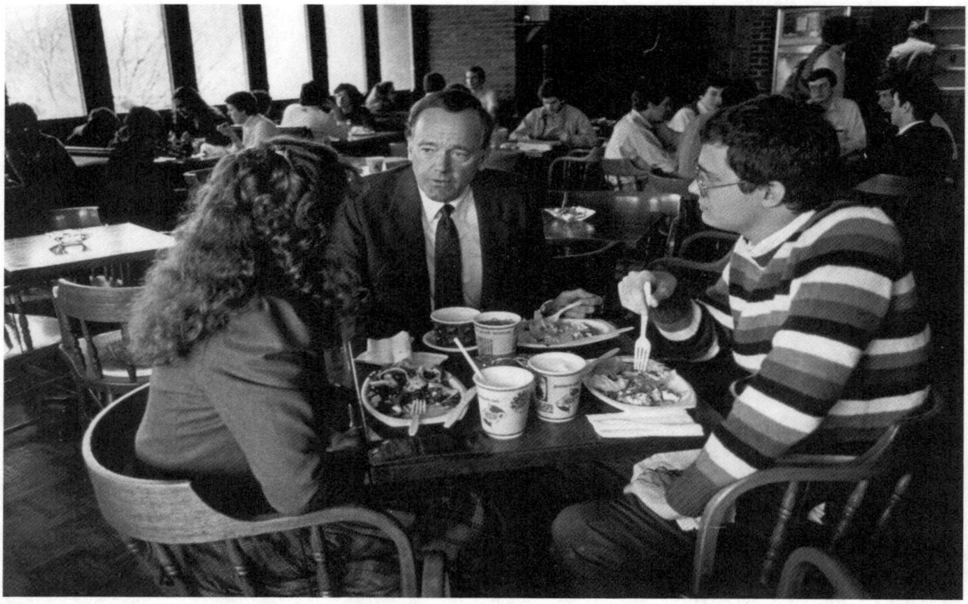

Chancellor Joe Wyatt does one of the things he was criticized for not doing enough of - hanging out with students in Sarratt Student Center.
Vanderbilt News and Public Affairs

was the lack of varsity sports success. Many people blamed defeats on the chancellor, saying in letters to the editor, in party conversation, or on talk radio shows that he did not do enough to help the Commodores win. This criticism reached its climax in April 1995, when a star basketball player from Nashville's Goodpasture High School named Ron Mercer was denied admission to Vanderbilt because his grades and standardized test scores weren't high enough.

Wyatt did not make a habit of talking to reporters about his opinion of big-time college sports, and it turns out that there was a reason. Like many Texas natives, Wyatt loved sports in general and football in particular. But he was concerned during his tenure that intercollegiate sports had become less of an educational experience and more of a training ground for professional leagues. Wyatt did not think Vanderbilt should lower its entrance requirements or create curriculums to make it easier to recruit athletes, in opposition to the trend in higher education circles in the 1990s. "My belief was and is that if you make true students out of athletes, then an institution like

Vanderbilt, Princeton, or Duke can certainly be competitive in some sports," he said. "But it is tough for an institution like Vanderbilt to try to do this while competing in the Southeastern Conference. In the SEC, you have this unusual situation where you have one private university and all the rest are very, very large public institutions. And these programs are so bloody expensive. There is such an effort to keep up with the other schools in every way.

"It sort of reminds me of the nuclear arms race during the height of the Cold War, where the Russians would design a new missile and then we'd design a new missile, and then they have fourteen and we'd have to have seventeen, that sort of thing."

About five years into his tenure Wyatt participated in a discussion with several other colleges who were members of the American Association of Universities about the idea of forming a new sports conference. The idea never made it very far because of logistics. "There were several meetings, and some of the other schools included Stanford, Tulane, and Duke," Wyatt said. "But the thing that shot the idea down in flames was the travel time that would be involved with such a conference. It was pretty obvious that if you make the athletes travel that much that you will undermine their academic program even more than you already are, so that was a real non-starter."

With the idea of another conference out the door and with the board of trust convinced that their school could and should remain in big-time sports, Wyatt made several futile attempts to reform the SEC and NCAA. One was the idea of tying the number of athletic scholarships to graduation rates, a suggestion that never made it past the joking stage at conference meetings.

Many supporters of Vanderbilt's athletic programs argued that success in sports would help fundraising. Wyatt never believed there was a connection. "The credible studies I have seen show that there's not much of a correlation between the track record of athletic programs and fundraising. And I would say that's not why people give significant money to universities. They give significant money to universities because they believe the university changed their life and changed their potential for a life above what they ever could have accomplished."

HARASSMENT AND OUTLAWED INSULTS

American colleges have had the reputation of being places where people can speak their minds and freely study what they want. But in the early 1990s Vanderbilt was beginning to look like a place where those freedoms were limited. It was the era of political correctness.

One of the first debates that might be classified as PC in nature was an argument about renaming a dormitory. In the 1930s the Daughters of the Confederacy contributed $50,000 toward the construction of a dormitory at Peabody College (which was independent from Vanderbilt at that time). In 1989, a time when many black groups in the South were criticizing the presence of things named after the Confederacy and Confederate heroes, a campus organization called the Racial Environmental Project held a forum about whether to rename Confederate Hall. The debate raged for weeks and got the attention of many people from off campus. "If that (the name of Confederate Hall) is changed because of the intolerance of some individuals, I am afraid that the name of your fine university will be next," a lady with a Daughters of the Confederacy group in Florida wrote *The Hustler*. "Commodore Cornelius Vanderbilt was one of the gentlemen who helped pay Jefferson Davis' bail for his release from a Union prison following the war. If these disgruntled people don't know that fact, we had better not tell them."

Perhaps the most cogent comment during the debate came from Vanderbilt Divinity School Professor Eugene TeSelle. TeSelle suggested that they leave the name of Confederate Hall alone but rename the Socio-Religious Building for Roger Williams University, the black school that left the site after its two buildings burned down in 1905. For the time being the name stayed, but a plaque explaining its origins was placed on Confederate Hall.

The PC phenomenon picked up speed during the next few years with a campuswide debate about homosexual rights. It peaked in the 1992-93 school year, when student Katie Gieringer filed a complaint about material that professor Don Evans had presented to his

West Side Hall is converted to the Vanderbilt Admissions Office, in one of many construction projects at Vanderbilt in the 1990s
Vanderbilt News and Public Affairs

Fine Arts 109 class. In the complaint, Gieringer claimed that Evans had shown the class material by the controversial photographer Robert Mapplethorpe, pictures of women's breasts, and even nude photographs of himself.

Dean Francille Bergquist conducted an investigation into the charges against Evans by talking to other students in the class. Evans did not find out about the accusations until a few weeks later. Soon Gieringer's complaint had been made known to the school's Opportunity Development Center. A few weeks later Opportunity Development Center director Pat Pierce said Gieringer's complaints provided "sufficient basis to support the allegations of sexual harassment" against Evans because his presentation "created a sexually hostile environment for several students." Meanwhile, Evans hired an attorney and wrote a long letter to Arts & Sciences dean John Venable in which he defended his actions in class. Evans wrote that he had only shown the students photographs that were a part of the curriculum of the class. As for the nude photographs of himself, Evans said that those were shown "as a means of demonstrating my development as an artist."

On February 12 more than three hundred students marched in Evans' defense. Among the organizers of the march were students Clay Hensley and Deanna Augsburger, an artist who a few months later had one of her paintings removed as a part of an exhibit at the Student Recreational Center because it depicted nudity. The next week a petition defending Evans drew thirteen hundred signatures. By this time *The Hustler* had published many letters defending Evans' right to teach his class the way he wanted, plus a couple defending Gieringer's right to complain. "What is wrong for Vanderbilt's administration to want faculty to zip their fly?" a student named John Mason wrote. "What does it have to do with the future of liberal education?" Meanwhile, in sharp contrast to past Vanderbilt chancellors such as Kirkland and Branscomb who did not hesitate to speak out about campus controversies, Joe Wyatt remained silent throughout the debate.

Then, in the middle of the Evans controversy, a second debate about free speech arose on campus. In the fall of 1992 Wyatt asked a student and faculty policymaking group called the Community

Affairs Board to review the school's official policy on free speech in light of a recent U.S. Supreme Court decision. In February 1993 that group voted thirteen to seven to recommend a campus policy under which personal insults would be outlawed on campus. Specifically, the proposal said that "speech intended to insult or stigmatize an individual or small group of individuals that is addressed directly to the individual or group of individuals and makes use of words or non-verbal symbols commonly understood to convey hatred or contempt" would no longer be allowed at Vanderbilt. Among the members of the Community Affairs Board who voted for the insult ban was a student named North Grounsell. "With no rule you have under-regulation," he said. "I would rather have over-regulation."

Many faculty members immediately attacked the proposal, seeing it as a bizarre attempt to ban free speech. "Anyone who would vote to prohibit insults is a scum-sucking geek," philosophy professor Crispin Sartwell wrote *The Hustler*. Many student groups also spoke out against it, including the Student Government Association and a student homosexual group called Lambda.

Also in the spring of 1993 the Vanderbilt Honor Council heard twenty-eight cases of alleged cheating, the highest number ever reported at the school. A group of students tried unsuccessfully to start a newspaper especially for female students called *Muliebrity*. And in February of that year, students footed the bill to bring rapper Sister Souljah to campus. Souljah gave one of the most radical talks in the history of the campus, a speech that made Stokely Carmichael's controversial address in 1967 seem conciliatory by comparison. "White people are just not intelligent," Souljah said. "Intelligence is the ability to analyze a situation, give a new outlook and to grow and to expand." No one apparently raised the point that had the ban on insults passed, speakers like Sister Souljah could no longer be invited to campus.

Eventually both the Evans case and the proposed insult ban went away. After the administration's lengthy investigation into his class Evans agreed that in the future he would warn students about material that was possibly offensive. And Vanderbilt general counsel Jeff Carr recommended to Chancellor Wyatt that the no-insult policy not be instituted.

NOBEL WINNERS AND JUNGLE ADVENTURERS

There are many influential faculty members during the period after World War II whose careers are not discussed elsewhere in this book.

Chief among them are Earl Sutherland and Stanley Cohen, the only two Vanderbilt professors to have won the Nobel Prize for Medicine. Sutherland came to the university as a researcher in 1963 and eight years later won the award for his discovery and research of "cyclic AMP," a substance found in every human cell that is vital to the way hormones work. Sutherland left the school two years after receiving his award, an embarrassing departure for the Vanderbilt Medical School.

Cohen is a biochemist who in 1959 moved to Nashville from Washington University in St. Louis, where he and colleague Rita Levi-Montalcini had extensively researched cell-growth factors in animals. By 1986, when Cohen and Levi-Montalcini received the Nobel Prize, their work had led to better treatment for burn victims and cancer patients.

Another academic superstar in the late twentieth century was Walter Sullivan, who earned his BA from Vanderbilt in 1947 and was hired by the English department a few years later. For the remainder of the century he was a stalwart in one of Vanderbilt's finest departments. In 1998 *The Hustler* praised Sullivan for fifty years of service and said that a class with him was more than just a course on creative writing. "It's really an advanced course on life, courtesy of a southern gentlemen, the likes of whom many of us came here to meet."

Just about every student who attended Vanderbilt in the 1970s, 1980s, or 1990s remembers philosophy professor John Lachs because he never kept a low profile during his career. Lachs was born in Hungary and came to Vanderbilt in 1967. He carved out a niche as a philosopher who publishes books and gives talks about how his field relates to real life. But hundreds of his students remember Lachs because of his devotion to teaching and his efforts to get to know them. "Lachs is a superb lecturer and he is very engaging as a person," said Michael Franks, a philosophy major from the class of 1971 who helped start *Versus.* "When I took his classes and turned in papers, not only would a graduate student comment on the papers in writing but he would comment on the papers and on the graduate student's comments." During his career, Lachs was also one of the key faculty members who supported and participated in activities in the McGill Hall philosophy dorm, Vanderbilt's first experiment at a "themed" dormitory.

By the time he got to Vanderbilt in the early 1980s, Paul Conkin seemed to many to be the quintessential intellectual, so versed that he was almost intimidating. But his background was a humble one. Conkin attended a one-room school in East Tennessee and read a book a night as a child. After he got his Ph.D. in history, Conkin began writing books almost as fast as he read them; it reportedly took him one month to write the 1965 volume *The New Deal.* "Things often make sense in the middle of the night," he once told a reporter. "I write furiously, seizing the moment, and then later check what I have written against my notes and endnotes. The point is to use creative enthusiasm." Conkin went on to write about twenty-five other scholarly books on subjects as diverse as Lyndon Johnson, American intellectuals, and the Tennessee Valley Authority. After he arrived at Vanderbilt, Conkin took it upon himself to complete a Vanderbilt history book started over a decade earlier by history professor Henry Swint. *Gone with the Ivy,* a tome researched with the help of more than twenty graduate students, was published in 1985 and is considered one of the finest scholarly university histories ever written.

While getting his Ph.D. at Harvard in the 1970s, Arthur Demarest chose Mayan culture as his specialty, a wise move, it turned out, because there was much about Mayan culture yet to be discovered. In 1988 Demarest became the director of the Dos Pilas Project, a multidisciplinary expedition with more than forty scholars and a hundred workmen located in the Guatemalan rain forest. That project was credited with making countless discoveries about the Mayan empire – including evidence that the Mayan culture may have ended because it became too warlike. Then, in 2000, Demarest was walking through the jungle when he fell into a hollow full of snakes. It turned out to be the remains of the largest Mayan palace discovered in more than a century. Demarest's adventurous career led to inevitable comparisons with big-screen archeologist Indiana Jones, something the Vanderbilt anthropologist didn't care for. "Indiana Jones would last maybe five seconds in real archeology," Demarest once told a reporter. "Indiana Jones swashbuckled through a mythical, generic, non-English-speaking Third World of swarthy people with threatening, incomprehensible ways, defending them with American heroics and seizing their treasures."

A law professor with a specialty in Constitutional law, James Blumstein made news as soon as he arrived at Vanderbilt in 1970. Blumstein found that Tennessee law required him to wait one year before he could legally vote. He sued the state, claiming that the law violated his Constitutional right of suffrage. Blumstein represented himself in the case, which went all the way to the U.S. Supreme Court. The Vanderbilt professor won in March 1972, and hundreds of thousands of American citizens who had been denied the right to vote because they had recently moved were granted that entitlement. "I heard that I had won the case on the radio," said Blumstein.

OPEN CAMPUS TO VANDERBUBBLE

In the 1970s and early 1980s Vanderbilt was a relaxed, tolerant, and relatively open campus. The school encouraged visitors more than at any other time in its history. There was little if any enforcement of drug laws and, at a time when the drinking age was nineteen, not much done to discourage students from consuming alcohol. Campus security consisted of students employed to sit at the door of women's dorms to theoretically prevent unauthorized people from entering. But in practice, students wandered in and out of dorms and lecture halls at all hours of the night without having to answer to anyone.

Meanwhile the Vanderbilt campus was showing wear and tear. Many structures, such as Old Science, Kirkland Hall, and Peabody's Socio-Religious Building, needed renovation. No dorm built prior to the 1960s had air conditioning, a convenience post-baby boomers viewed as a necessity rather than a luxury. There wasn't much emphasis on campus landscaping. Rather than stay on the sidewalks, students made a habit of taking shortcuts through the grass, a practice that left a network of paths across the Vanderbilt campus.

All of this changed in the late 1980s and early 1990s. By the beginning of the twenty-first century the Vanderbilt campus was a safer, more sober, more comfortable, and more attractive place than students from the 1960s and 1970s would have ever imagined. Of course, this did not happen in a vacuum. The changes at Vanderbilt were largely driven by the rise in the drinking age, the national clampdown on illicit drug use, and an increase in national awareness about preventing crime. But overlooked as the changes were taking place were the ways they changed the experiences of students and the ways they affected Vanderbilt's public image.

Like every other college in the world Vanderbilt University always had its share of crime. During just about every year in the school's history there was some sort of crime wave, such as burglaries in the massive dormitory Kissam Hall. As far as weapons were concerned, some faculty members and students brought guns to school for hunting purposes. In fact, the sound of gunshots didn't alarm anyone, because both Bishop Holland McTyeire and longtime security guard James "Cap" Alley habitually wandered the grounds shooting sparrows.

Crime as a chronic problem didn't apparently become an issue on campus until the 1970s (about the same time that the number of female students was rising from one in four to one in two). In the fall of 1975 a report from the Vanderbilt administration revealed that so far that year there had been 432 reported thefts, eighteen reported assaults, and five attempted rapes on campus. Despite the numbers, which seem high in hindsight, Vanderbilt Vice Chancellor George Kaludis said there was no need to be alarmed. "I don't think we are at a stage for panicking," Kaludis said. "We are an urban campus, and sixteen thousand people pass through here each day . . . A part of the open campus philosophy is that you don't stop anyone who passes by and say 'what are you doing here buddy' without some cause." Students were merely advised to lock their doors and use the student escort service, which Army and Navy ROTC members started as a free public service in 1974.

Keeping a free and open campus was a recurring theme in the

1970s. Part of the reason for this was that the 1960s protest spirit had wedded students to the concept of freedom, interpreted to mean freedom from being asked who they were and what they were doing. But there were other reasons for the devotion to the concept of open campus. In the late 1960s and early 1970s Vanderbilt students, faculty, and administrators had gone to great lengths to increase the amount of contact that the school had with the rest of Nashville. One example of this phenomenon was the student-formed "Free University" (FUN) which offered instruction free of charge to anyone in Nashville on everything from art to short wave radio. The "open campus" policy also resulted in many Nashville residents taking part in Vanderbilt campus events, such as the Rites of Spring festival started in 1971.

Vanderbilt students relax on campus in the late 1970s
Photographic Archives, Vanderbilt University

Along with Vanderbilt's preference for an open campus came a curious drug policy. Starting in the late 1960s Vanderbilt students increasingly experimented with illicit drugs such as marijuana. About 1971 Vanderbilt began telling its security officers and resident advisors (upperclassmen paid to be in charge of dormitories) that the school would continue to assist Nashville's police department in finding drug dealers on the Vanderbilt campus, but that the school would no longer expel or suspend students for drug use. Campus police officers were instructed, however, to aid students "in immediate trouble due to bad reactions."

There were several reasons for such a policy, which could perhaps best be described as "don't ask, don't tell." The cause most often stated publicly was a fear that a complete policy of intolerance would discourage students from coming forward and telling someone if they had an addiction problem. Whatever the reason, many students (not surprisingly) loved the policy; in 1971, *The Hustler* called it "a liberal, vital and praiseworthy arrangement."

This dual policy of encouraging an open campus and not enforcing drug use laws remained on campus through the 1970s, but began to change in the early 1980s. With the election of President Ronald Reagan, the nation began to turn away from its tolerance of drug and alcohol abuse. State and federal laws were passed in the early 1980s requiring private colleges and universities to enforce drug laws. The big change, however, was the increase in the drinking age from nineteen to twenty-one. This began to be "grandfathered in" in Tennessee in the fall of 1986, resulting in huge changes in student life. As late as 1985 fraternities threw keg parties in their front lawns at which just about anyone, regardless of age, could walk up and get free beer. But with the rise in the drinking age Vanderbilt Dean of Students K. C. Potter began implementing policies meant to severely cut down on underage drinking. In 1986 Vanderbilt banned kegs on campus and enforced a policy under which organizational money – such as fraternity dues – could not be spent on alcohol.

By September 1989 campus police officers were instructed to stop all students carrying open beverage containers to see whether they contained alcohol. Although some students complained about the new policies, there were no organized attempts to reverse them.

Rather than fight the rules, students chose to either live within them or break them and hope to get away with it. Perhaps the best example of the latter took place in April 1989, when twenty-five Vanderbilt students or former Vanderbilt students were arrested as a part of a citywide crackdown for manufacturing false identification cards.

Along with the new alcohol and drug policies came far more emphasis on campus security. In 1981, the same year Vanderbilt security received an annual $400,000 funding increase, *The Hustler* ran several front-page articles about crime, using a map on one occasion to illustrate the relative proximity of public housing projects to the campus. The next summer a Vanderbilt student named George Brown was killed at an off-campus bar called the Gold Rush. By the mid-1980s *The Hustler* devoted more space than ever to campus crime, even creating a regular feature called "Police Beat" that contained paragraph-long summaries of the latest burglary or assault. Although there was no evidence that crime was on the increase, the newspaper (as did many other media outlets in the 1980s and 1990s) made it sound as if there were. Students, especially women, were warned not to walk across campus alone at night and told to use free escorts. Campus security beefed up its numbers and began installing security phones throughout the campus.

If it was hard to argue against the increased security measures, it was more difficult after February 1989. That month a German exchange student named Tomas Weser was walking from the Alpha Chi Omega sorority house to the Mayfield House dormitories when he was shot to death at the corner of Twenty-fifth and Highland Avenues. The crime paralyzed student activities for months and may have done more to change student behavior regarding crime prevention than anything that has ever taken place at Vanderbilt. "No one has to walk alone at Vanderbilt," *The Hustler* said the next week. "It is simply too dangerous and should not be done." That summer the university built an eight-foot iron fence around the West End and Twenty-first Avenue sides of campus, a step that symbolized a change from open campus to closed campus. "We want to show that Vanderbilt is a place where one needs a reason to be and not just another end of town," university architect Dave Allard said as the fence went up. For the first time since cows and pigs occasionally wandered across West End Avenue, Vanderbilt University was flanked by a wall.

Meanwhile, dorm life at Vanderbilt was becoming safer and more comfortable than at any other time in its history. Starting in 1985 the school began to renovate every dorm on campus that had been built prior to 1960, installing air conditioning, new heating, and new plumbing in the process. The wave of renovations started with the old Peabody dorms (Confederate, Gillette, North, West, and East), then moved onto the dorms surrounding Alumni Lawn (Vanderbilt, Barnard, Tolman, Cole, and McGill) and finished with McTyeire Hall in 1993. The dormitory upgrades were the major reason the Wyatt administration was credited with reducing the amount of so-called "deferred maintenance" on campus from an estimated $170 million in 1984 to less than $50 million a decade later. Security and dormitory upgrades were also the main reason that the cost of campus housing far exceeded inflation during this period.

A typical campus scene from the 1990s
Vanderbilt News and Public Affairs

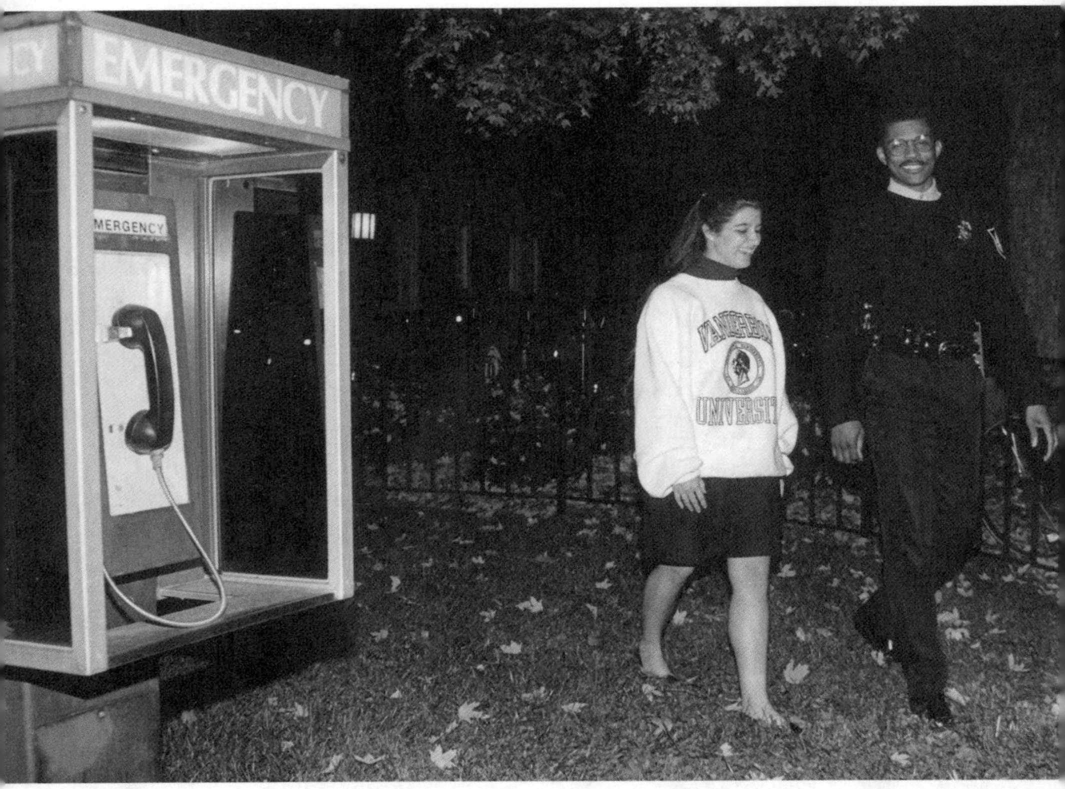

A student escorted by campus security
Vanderbilt News and Public Affairs

Architecturally, the renovations succeeded in preserving the original exterior appearance of every structure. But inside, life in a Vanderbilt dorm changed forever. Students would no longer get to experience the discomfort and inconvenience of loud, inefficient steam heaters. They would not have to learn how to fall asleep in the unmitigated heat of a Tennessee September night. But perhaps the most important change, at least from an institutional point of view, is that as the dorms were renovated the security inside them was greatly increased. By the early 1990s every dormitory on campus was protected by a full-time guard and an electronic turnstile that required valid student identification for passage. No one, not even visiting alumni, could wander into dormitories anymore. Vanderbilt had become a controlled atmosphere, referred to by its own students as the "Vanderbubble."

Conclusion

It was obvious from the beginning that Gordon Gee was going to be a different kind of chancellor. When search committee chairman Denny Bottorff called Gee's home to notify him that he had been selected to replace Joe Wyatt, a man with a British accent answered the phone. It was George Harrison of the Beatles, who had become friends with Gee because his son attended Brown University, where Gee was the president.

During the next two years Gee would change a lot of things about Vanderbilt University. One of the most important was the perception of the chancellor among students, faculty, staff, alumni, and Nashville residents. From the moment he arrived at Vanderbilt, Gee was engaging, available, and friendly to just about everyone. During his four-month transition period he established an office in Sarratt Student Center where students could drop by to see him. He met with alumni groups, faculty groups, and student groups. He even shocked many people (such as this author) by learning some people's names before he met them for the first time.

This pattern of being accessible continued after Gee succeeded Wyatt on July 1, 2000. The bow-tied chancellor made a habit of answering every single letter and e-mail that came his way. Gee became the first chancellor in Vanderbilt history to maintain regular open office hours. He organized and took part in road trips to Vanderbilt football games; he frequently ate at the school cafeteria; he even made the occasional appearance at a late night fraternity party. On one such night, Gee maintained, he walked into a costumed event wearing a tuxedo and bow tie, which he had worn to another party he had attended earlier that night. A female student (who was probably a bit tipsy) came up to the chancellor, put her arm around him, and exclaimed, "What a wonderful costume! You're dressed just like Gordon Gee!"

Being friendly and outgoing came naturally to Gee, but his ability to charm everyone from reporters to alumni was important because he did not intend to be a caretaker. After almost a year of talking and listening to people, Gee began to reveal the things that he wanted to emphasize as chancellor. Gee pointed out that he didn't need to "fix" Vanderbilt, because it wasn't broken. But he said that as chancellor, he intended to make major changes to the landscape, and to the institution.

One of the most important things that Gee said he hoped to achieve was a better cooperation between different departments of the school, particularly the academic departments. Under Wyatt, Vanderbilt strictly enforced its long-standing policy under which every academic department was required to balance its own budget every year, an approach that became known as "every tub on its bottom." Although this rigid system seemed logical, and fostered responsibility within Vanderbilt's departments, it had the unfortunate affect of discouraging creative academic initiatives that transcended bureaucratic boundaries, such as interdisciplinary majors. Gee said he was going to try to change that system, and early in his tenure restructured Vanderbilt's budget process to encourage more cooperative activity among the schools. One of the bigger things he did in this effort was help create a $100 million internal grant program called the Academic Venture Capital Fund meant to fund interdisciplinary research. "Assuming that the money is spent wisely, this is the most significant effort to accelerate the development and enhancement of its academic research programs in the modern history of Vanderbilt," Vanderbilt vice chancellor for health affairs Harry Jacobson said when the fund was created.

Gee also tried to put more emphasis on relations with the Nashville community. He made appearances on local television shows and local talk shows that had never featured Wyatt. On one such appearance in the spring of 2002, Gee (a Mormon) said he was opposed to Tennessee's passage of a lottery because of its effect on the poor – one of the first times in decades that a Vanderbilt chancellor spoke out publicly on a political issue that concerned something other than the school's narrow interest. Another time, during the search to replace Woody Widenhofer as head football coach, Gee went on talk radio and explained in detail the lengths to which he had gone to find the best replacement for the job. On the intercollegiate sports front, the new chancellor said in dozens of interviews that he was committed to the idea of Vanderbilt staying in the Southeastern Conference. But, echoing his predecessors, he said he had no intention of changing Vanderbilt's academic standards in order to help out the win-loss record. "We are not like the other schools in the SEC," he once told a group of alumni. "We are not a university in order to have a football team. We are a university that has a football team."

Another thing Gee said he intended to do was to bring about a better relationship between administration and faculty. To this end the chancellor met with every single academic department during his first year and made it a part of his regular routine to attend every meeting of the faculty senate.

However, the thing Gee spent most of his first two years talking about was the idea of a renewed emphasis on student life, especially for undergraduates. "We have students for 168 hours a week, and they only attend class for 18 of those hours," Gee said. "I think we need to put more emphasis on what they do for the other 150 hours." Gee took several steps toward emphasizing campus life, such as creating a full-time vice chancellor of student life and hiring David Williams to fill that position. But the most important thing Gee did in this regard is start Vanderbilt down the path of being a true residential college.

Chancellor Gordon Gee
Vanderbilt News and Public Affairs

By "residential college," Gee did not just mean a campus where students lived (with over 90 percent of its students in on-campus housing, Vanderbilt already was that). Gee meant a residential college in the Ivy League sense; where undergraduates were assigned to be members of a "college" of other students and faculty members their freshman year, and stayed with that "college" of students and faculty members, in the same dormitory, for their entire four years. A residential college in Gee's mind was a campus filled with small and medium-size dormitories, each with its own meeting rooms and eating facilities. If Vanderbilt could make the transition to residential college, Gee argued that the students and faculty members would be happier and have a more fulfilling experience at Vanderbilt. Student retention rates, not as high at Vanderbilt as they were at other academically inclined schools, would rise.

Through the latter part of 2001 and all of 2002, students, faculty members, alumni, and trustees reacted to the idea of a residential college in different ways. A lot of people loved the idea. But many students and alumni were concerned that the residential college Gee envisioned would destroy the school's fraternities and sororities. (Some argued that there wasn't much difference between a residential college and a fraternity or sorority, except that in a residential college the institution made assignments, while in a Greek system the students made assignments.) Other students, alumni, and faculty members didn't understand how the residential college would coexist with existing theme dorms such as McGill and McTyeire. As for the trustees, their main concern was money. Some of Vanderbilt's dormitories could be retrofitted into the residential college idea without too much trouble; but not the four Carmichael Towers dormitories, which were far too large and not really configured to encourage student interaction.

Gee heard all these concerns and admitted in some cases that he didn't have the answers to all the questions. But by the spring of 2002 the new chancellor had sold the idea to the Executive Committee of the Vanderbilt Board of Trust, and particularly to board of trust chairman Martha Ingram. By the 2002 Vanderbilt Reunion (which was, for the first time, combined with the school's fall homecoming festivities), Gee was openly talking about the idea of building more small and medium-size dormitories on the southwest end of campus, and about the long-term idea of tearing down the four Carmichael Towers. He has begun to put a price tag of at least $100 million on converting Vanderbilt into a residential college – money that he hoped to raise as a part of the school's next fundraising campaign. And he announced that by 2006, Vanderbilt would renovate some of the buildings in the Alumni Hall area – such as McGill Hall, Tolman Hall, and Cole Hall dormitories along with Alumni Hall, which was in dire need of upgrade by this time – and convert them into the first residential colleges on campus. Meanwhile, he had begun to consider the idea that the residential college concept might only apply to upperclassmen, so that freshmen could continue to live in Branscomb and Kissam Quadrangles.

Gee made another newsworthy change on the Vanderbilt landscape in 2002. In September of that year, the school made the surprising announcement that Confederate Hall had been renamed Memorial Hall. Gee said it was awkward for Vanderbilt to continue with a dormitory that honored the pro-slavery Confederacy – especially when black students were routinely assigned to live in that dormitory. "The university needs to be a place where all ideas are welcome, and when we have certain symbols that limit the ability of people to speak up and speak out then those symbols need to be taken away and we need to realign our values and our symbols," he said. A few students, alumni, and trustees were opposed to the move, one of them being trustee Ridley Wills II. Quoting the plaque on the side of the building, Wills pointed out that the women of the United Daughters of the Confederacy had contributed $50,000 toward the structure to "honor of their fathers and brothers who fought in the war between the north and the south" and to help educate teachers "in a region sorely in need of them." Wills, the son of Fugitive poet Jesse Wills, added that "it's hard for me to find anything offensive in that. Three of my four great-grandfathers either fought for the Confederacy or served in the Confederate government." A few weeks after the renaming, the Daughters of the Confederacy sued Vanderbilt, asking for a court order that would force Vanderbilt to return the dormitory to its original name.

It's impossible to know how the men who led Vanderbilt University through the trials and tribulations of the late nineteenth and early twentieth centuries would have taken all these changes. Of course, Bishop Holland McTyeire would have kicked and screamed at the idea of renaming Confederate Hall; the former newspaper editor would have argued that the university was started by the pro-Confederate wing of the Methodist Church, and that the institution could not ever hide that fact by renaming what is only the most obvious link to that heritage. But it's easy to imagine Chancellor James Kirkland loving Gee's general theme of putting more emphasis on the idea of a campus where the administration, faculty, and students knew each other better and spend more time together. Of course, Kirkland didn't exactly keep office hours, and he probably wasn't as approachable as Gee. But it is easy to tell from reading *The Hustler* that he kept up with just about everything that was happening on campus, that he knew many of the students, and was that he was ready at all times to jump headlong into the latest campus debate. Kirkland's 1915 vision of a school where every student lived on campus, spent a lot of time at a student center, and had plenty of opportunities to take part in school activities that were in some way related to their class life was too ambitious for its time, which is why it failed. As Vanderbilt moves into the twenty-first century, it's hard to know whether Gee's vision of a campus where students and faculty would be matched up for good in family-like dormitories will suffer the same fate.

Additional Information About Selected Photographs

Bishop Holland McTyeire - circa 1880 ------------------- **30**
Credit: Carl Giers/Photographic Archives, Vanderbilt University

Overview of Vanderbilt Campus ---------------------------- **36**
written of reverse of photographic mount:
View looking South from Kirkland Tower - Science and Wesley Halls
Credit: Marvin Wiles/Photographic Archives, Vanderbilt University

Aerial View of campus towards Downtown --------------- **84**
handwritten on original mount below image:
View of Nashville in June 1888 from the window in No. 3 Marked thus x
written on reverse of photo mount:
view from Wesley Hall
Engineering Hall construction in foreground
Credit: Photographic Archives, Vanderbilt University

Graduating Class of 1896 ------------------------------------- **89**
Peabody Collection
Credit: Charles Whitson/Photographic Archives, Vanderbilt University

Vanderbilt Students playing hooky ------------------------ **96**
scrapbook page, handwritten caption: Four Jacks. (the day we "cut".)
From Alumnus magazine caption from donor (Earl F. Scott):
(The photograph) "represents a day in the spring when we thought that we should have a vacation, on account of some holiday. The faculty did not agree with us, and we took it anyway. I expect there were more than 'four-jacks' in this picture!"
Credit: Photographic Archives, Vanderbilt University

Mechanical Engineering Laboratory --------------------- **98**
Stamped on reverse of photo:
Banner July 1940
Photo Frank Gunter Nashville Banner Nashville Tenn.

Source: News Office Vanderbilt University
Nasville 4, Tennessee
written on reverse of photo:
Vanderbilt University - a laboratory session in Mechanical Engineering
Credit: Frank Gunter for The Nashville Banner/
Photographic Archives, Vanderbilt University

FIREFIGHTERS TRY TO SAVE COLLEGE HALL -------------------------- 133
April 20, 1905
Kirkland Hall burning
from the Stella Vaughn Family Collection
Credit: Photographic Archives, Vanderbilt University

DELTA GAMMAS IN 1931 -- 183
Delta Gamma chapter of Delta Delta Delta,
Vanderbilt University, 1930-31
names of individuals in photo available on request
Credit: George Dickson/Photographic Archives, Vanderbilt University

VANDERBILT VS. AUSTIN PEAY - 1938 --------------------------------- 217
info on reverse of photo: January 13, 1938
Vanderbilt vs. Austin Peay, Clarksville, score 49-30
Ross Hanna, number 17, A'40, from Little Rock, Ark., makes a basket in the game with Austin Peay at Clarksville, Tenn., on January 13, increasing his total as high point man of the Commodores, while William Harlan, 18, Mt. Pleasant, Tenn., and John Milliken, 19, Bowling Green Ky., watch.
Commodore 1938, page 181
Credit: Photographic Archives, Vanderbilt University

VANDERBILT VS. KENTUCKY - 1955 ----------------------------------- 220
VU vs. Kentucky, 1955
reverse of photograph stamped Tennessean Library November 6, 1955
caption from newspaper pasted to reverse of photo:
-Staff photo by Joe Rudis
"Go...go...go for a touchdown!" roar the Commodores to their teammates on the field as Charlie Horton crunches through the Kentucky line and brings the ball within feet of another six points. Minutes later, the score made, the whole team

lined the edge of the field to scream its praise. From left are Don Karr-89, Jack Hudson-35, Carroll Toups-70, Pat Swan-74, and Monte Williamson-64.
Credit: Joe Rudis for The Tennessean/Photographic Archives, Vanderbilt University

stamped on back of photo: Tennesseean Library April 24 1955
caption pasted on back of photo:
-Staff photo by Bobby Moore
Boys aren't the only Vanderbilt students who can wear shorts these university coeds prove to three of the many boys who have adopted Bermuda shorts for campus wear. From left, Jimmy Patterson, Bob Walker, and Larnie Harper look at Frances Shanks, Carolyn Warren, and Lynn Smith, who also have discovered that shorts are nice for outings. A university rule prohibits women students from wearing shorts on campus. This spring short pants have not only become popular for wearing to classes and picnics but are being worn to formal dances.
Credit: Bobby Moore for The Tennessean/Photographic Archives, Vanderbilt University

written on reverse of photo: 1940 New Coaches, left to right:
Head coach Henry "Red" Sanders - backfield
Paul "Bear" Bryant - line coach
Herc Alley - end coach
Jim Scoggins - freshman coach
Credit: Van Irwin, Jr./Photographic Archives, Vanderbilt University

back of photo stamped March 8 1953
Tennessean Library
Newspaper caption for image pasted to back of photo:
Garry Fitts, being dragged from car in foreround, and Bary Hubbard, arm and back visible in background, are hauled out for a ducking in Watauga lake at Centennial park as punishment for dashing a bucket of cold water upon five other V.U. students as they played cards on the front porch of DKE fraternity house. The outraged ones are, from left, Bill Hardegree, Rodes Hart, John

Sources

Author's note: *Rather than pepper the text with endnotes, I decided to list sources cited and sources consulted in the same place. I also chose to separately list three books that I consulted for so many subjects that I would otherwise have to repeat the titles again and again. Of these three I must emphasize Paul Conkin's* Gone with the Ivy, *a volume that is so thorough that I don't believe I could have written this book without it.*

Many of the newspaper and magazine clippings listed here are on file at the Nashville Room of the Downtown Public Library. Ask for it by name; it's officially called the Ingram Vanderbilt History Collection.

I should also point out that many of the other cited sources are available at the Special Collections Office of the Jean and Alexander Heard Library.

Works consulted for several subjects

Conkin, Paul. *Gone with the Ivy: A History of Vanderbilt University.* Knoxville: University of Tennessee Press, 1985.
McGaw, Robert. *The Vanderbilt Campus: A Pictorial History.* Nashville: Vanderbilt University Press, 1978.
Mims, Edwin. *Chancellor Kirkland of Vanderbilt.* Nashville: Vanderbilt University Press, 1940.

Interviews

Leonard Alberstadt, Lamar Alexander, Nelson Andrews, Robert A. Baldwin, Steve Baker, Dan Barge Jr., George Barrett, John Beasley, James C. Bradford Jr., John Burch, Jeff Carr, Paul Conkin, Wilbur Creighton Jr., Larry Daughtrey, Maclin Davis, Don Doyle, Winfield Dunn, John Dunworth, Marshall Eakin, John Flexner, Tony Fort, Michael Franks, Gordon Gee, John Hardcastle, Charles Hawkins, Alexander Heard, Martha Ingram, John Mayo, Robert McGaw, Edward G. Nelson, Chuck Offenburger, Richard N. Porter, K.C. Potter, William (Dixie) Roberts, James Sandlin, Michael Schoenfeld, M. Lee Smith, Robert Street, Mary Teloh, Eugene TeSelle, Edward Thackston, Ridley Wills, Joe B. Wyatt.

Works Consulted by Subject

PART ONE: MCTYEIRE'S MIND TO METHODIST COLLEGE

Mr. Aartson's ferry rides

Hoyt, Edwin P. *Commodore Vanderbilt.* Chicago: Reilly & Lee Co., 1962.
Hoyt, Edwin P. *The Vanderbilts and Their Fortunes.* Garden City N,Y.: Doubleday & Co., 1962.
Lane, Wheaton J. *Commodore Vanderbilt: An Epic of the Steam Age.* New York: Alfred A. Knopf, 1942.
MacDowell, Dorothy Kelly. *Commodore Vanderbilt and his Family.* Dallas: Taylor Publishing Co., 1989.
Minnigerode, Meade. *Certain Rich Men.* Freeport, N.Y.: Books for Libraries Press, 1970.

Cornelius fights a war over Nicaragua

Greene, Laurence. *The Filibuster: The Career of William Walker.* New York: Bobbs-Merrill Co., 1937.
Hoyt, Edwin P. *Commodore Vanderbilt.* Chicago: Reilly & Lee Co., 1962.
Hoyt, Edwin P. *The Vanderbilts and Their Fortunes.* Garden City N,Y.: Doubleday & Co., 1962.
Scroggs, William O. *Filibusters and Financiers: The Story of William Walker and his Associates.* New York: MacMillan Company, 1916.

Nashville 60, Louisville 57

Carey, Bill. *Fortunes, Fiddles and Fried Chicken: A Nashville Business History.* Franklin, Tenn.: Hillsboro Press, 2000.
Nashville Christian Advocate, April 3, 1850.
Pilkington, James Penn. *The United Methodist Publishing House: A History Volume I.* Nashville: Abingdon Press, 1968.

McTyeire the warmonger

Nashville Union-American, May 4, 5, 6, 7, 9, and 11, 1873
Martin, Albert William Jr. *Holland Nimmons McTyeire and the Negro.* Master of Arts Thesis, Vanderbilt University Divinity School, 1961.
Nashville Christian Advocate, April 25; May 2, 9, 16, 23, and 30; July 18; Aug. 1 and 8, 1861.
Pilkington, James Penn. *The United Methodist Publishing House: A History Volume I.* Nashville: Abingdon Press, 1968.
Republican Banner, May 7, 9, 10, and 11, 1873.
Tigert, John J. IV. *Bishop Holland Nimmons McTyeire: Ecclesiastical and Educational Architect.* Nashville: Vanderbilt University Press, 1955.
Vernon, Walter Newton Jr. *The United Methodist Publishing House: A History Volume II.* Nashville: Abingdon Press, 1989.

The man who slugged Jefferson Davis

Alexander, Thomas B. *The anatomy of the Confederate Congress: a study of the influences of member characteristics on legislative voting behavior, 1861-1865.* Nashville: Vanderbilt University Press, 1972.
Ball, Clyde, "The Public Career of Colonel A.S. Colyar: 1870-1877," in the *Tennessee Historical Quarterly* (Volume 12, Numbers 1-3).
Foote, Henry S. *Casket of Reminiscences.* Washington, D.C.: Chronicle Publishing Co., 1874.
Foote, Henry S. *War of the rebellion; or, Scylla and Charybdis. Consisting of observations upon the causes, course, and consequences of the late Civil War in the United States.* New York: Harper & Brothers, 1866.
Nashville Union and American, Oct. 15, 1871; May 21, 1880
Nashville Daily Gazette, Oct. 27, 1861; Nov. 7, 1861.
Republican Banner, July 8, 1860; Oct. 18 and 26, 1861; Nov. 7 and 8, 1861.
Warner, Ezra J. *Biographical Registry of the Confederate Congress.* Baton Rouge, La.: Louisiana State University Press, 1975.
Yearns, W. Buck. *The Confederate Congress.* Athens, Ga.: University of Georgia Press, 1960.

THE BATTLE OF THE BISHOPS

Martin, Albert William Jr. *Holland Nimmons McTyeire and the Negro.* Master of Arts Thesis, Vanderbilt University Divinity School, 1961.
Nashville Christian Advocate, Jan. 20, 1872; March 2, 9, 16, and 23, 1872; April 6 and 27, 1872; May 4 and 18, 1872;
Pilkington, James Penn. *The United Methodist Publishing House: A History Volume I.* Nashville: Abingdon Press, 1968.
Tigert, John J. IV. *Bishop Holland Nimmons McTyeire: Ecclesiastical and Educational Architect.* Nashville: Vanderbilt University Press, 1955.
Vernon, Walter Newton Jr. *The United Methodist Publishing House: A History Volume II.* Nashville: Abingdon Press, 1989.

THE SCANDALOUS SISTERS AND THE BIG DONATION

Gabriel, Mary. *Notorious Victoria: The Life of Victoria Woodhull, Uncensored.* Chapel Hill, N.C.: Algonquin Books, 1998.
Goldsmith, Barbara. *Other Powers: The Age of Suffrage, Spiritualism, and the Scandalous Victoria Woodhull.* New York: Knopf, 1998.
Johnston, Johanna. *Mrs. Satan: The Incredible Saga of Victoria Woodhull.* New York: G.P. Putnam's Sons, 1967.
Underhill, Lois Beachy. *The Woman Who Ran for President: The Many Lives of Victoria Woodhull.* Bridgehampton, N.Y.: Bridge Works Publishing Co., 1995.

THE BISHOP WITH THE BAD BACK

Nashville Union and American, April 26 and 29, 1874.
Original bill of complainants and answer thereto of defendants in the Chancery Court of Davidson County; College of Bishops of the Methodist Episcopal Church, South, and the Board of Trust of Vanderbilt University.
Tigert, John James. *Bishop Holland Nimmons McTyeire: Ecclesiastical and Educational Architect.* Nashville: Vanderbilt University Press, 1955.

MCTYEIRE IGNORES THE LOCAL RAGS

Carey, Bill. *Fortunes, Fiddles and Fried Chicken: A Nashville Business History.* Franklin, Tenn.: Hillsboro Press, 2000.

Nashville Union and American, April 26, 1874; May 4-9, and 11, 1873.
Martin, Albert William Jr. *Holland Nimmons McTyeire and the Negro.* Master of Arts Thesis, Vanderbilt University Divinity School, 1961.
Nashville Christian Advocate, April 25; May 2, 9, 16, 23, and 30; July 18; Aug. 1 and 8, 1861.
Pilkington, James Penn. *The United Methodist Publishing House: A History Volume I.* Nashville: Abingdon Press, 1968.
Republican Banner, May 7, 9, 10, and 11, 1873.
Tigert, John J. IV. *Bishop Holland Nimmons McTyeire: Ecclesiastical and Educational Architect.* Nashville: Vanderbilt University Press, 1955.
Vernon, Walter Newton Jr. *The United Methodist Publishing House: A History Volume II.* Nashville: Abingdon Press, 1989.

CORNFIELD TO COLLEGE

Hustler, Jan. 15, 1954.
Jacobs, Dillard. *Ten Squared Years: A Story of the First Century of Vanderbilt University School of Engineering.* Nashville: Vanderbilt Engineering Alumni Association, 1975.
Nashville American, May 28, 1905.
Nashville Banner, Aug. 15, 1905.
Nashville Daily American, Sept. 3, 1875; Oct. 5, 1875.
Nashville Union and American, April 26 and 29, 1874; July 3 and 4, 1874; Sept. 13, 1874.
Republican Banner, Sept. 16, 1873.
Vanderbilt Alumnus, Nov.-Dec. 1927.

PART TWO: THE BISHOP'S SCHOOL

MCTYEIRE HIRES AND FIRES THE DREAM TEAM

Alberstadt, Leonard. *From Top to Bottom: A Small Science Department's 120-Year struggle to develop and survive at Vanderbilt University.* Self-published, 1995.
Nashville American, June 15, 16, 18, and 19, 1885; Sept. 20 and 21, 1885.
Nashville Christian Advocate, April 20, 1878; June 1, 8, and 29, 1878.
Tigert, John James. *Bishop Holland Nimmons McTyeire: Ecclesiastical and Educational Architect.* Nashville: Vanderbilt University Press, 1955.

THE SEASON OF THE *AUSTRAL*

Vanderbilt Alumnus, Feb. 1917; March 1917; Feb. 1923; Feb. 1924; Jan. 1926.
Vanderbilt Austral, March-June 1879.

BARNARD AND HIS $250 COMET

Carey, Bill. *Fortunes, Fiddles and Fried Chicken: A Nashville Business History*. Franklin, Tenn.: Hillsboro Press, 2000.
Lagemann, Robert T. *To Quarks and Quasars: A History of Physics and Astronomy at Vanderbilt University*. Nashville: Vanderbilt University Department of Physics and Astronomy, 2000.
Nashville American, June 22, 1885.
Richardson, Robert. *The Star Lovers*. New York: Macmillan, 1967.
Vanderbilt Alumnus, Jan. 1922; Nov. 1952; Dec. 1952.

THE BLACK SCHOOL ACROSS THE STREET

Hubbard, G.W. *A History of the Colored Schools of Nashville, Tennessee*. Nashville: Wheeler, Marshall and Bruce, 1874.
Lovett, Bobby. *The African-American History of Nashville, Tennessee: Elites and Dilemnas*. Fayetteville, Ark.: University of Arkansas Press, 1999.
Nashville American, Jan. 25 and 26; March 19; May 23 and 24, 1905.
Nashville Banner, Sept. 19, 1885; January 25, 1905; May 23, 1905.
Nashville Globe, Feb.1, 1907; May 17, 1907; Oct. 4, 1907; Nov. 1 and 15, 1907; Jan. 3, 1908.
"The Nashville Institute and Roger Williams University: Benevolence, Paternalism and Black Consciousness, 1867-1910," by Eugene TeSelle. *Tennessee Historical Quarterly*, Winter 1982.
Torrence, Ridgely. *The Story of John Hope*. New York: Mcmillan Co., 1948.

THE GHOST OF BEN KING

Nashville American, Sept. 13, 16, 19, and 22, 1885.

Kill the sparrows, save the starlings

Abbott, John Paul, editor. *Students' Handbook of Vanderbilt University.* Nashville: Young Men's Christian Association, 1925.
Hustler, April 26, 1913; Feb. 24 and 28, 1995.
Jacobs, Dillard. *Ten Squared Years: A Story of the First Century of Vanderbilt University School of Engineering.* Nashville: Vanderbilt Engineering Alumni Association, 1975.
Nashville American, May 25, 1905.
Nashville Banner, Jan. 7, 1958.
Tigert, John James. *Bishop Holland Nimmons McTyeire: Ecclesiastical and Educational Architect.* Nashville: Vanderbilt University Press, 1955.
Torrence, Ridgely. *The Story of John Hope.* New York: Macmillan Co., 1948.
Vanderbilt Alumnus, April 1917; Jan. 26; Feb. 1932.

Nashville gets a teaching school

Allen, Jack, "The Peabody Saga," in *The Peabody Reflector,* Summer 1980.
Crabb, Alfred Leland. *The Geneology of George Peabody College for Teachers,* 1935.
Dorn, Sherman. *A Brief History of Peabody College.* Nashville: Peabody College of Vanderbilt University, 1996.
Hoss, Elijah. "The Vanderbilt Matter," a pamplet written about 1910 related to the relationship between the Methodist Episcopal Church, South, and Vanderbilt University.
Nashville American, Aug. 4 and 8, 1909; Nov. 13, 14, 15, 17, and 18, 1909; Dec. 15 and 16, 1909.
Nashville Daily American, April 2.,3, 4, 9, 10, 14, and 16, 1880.
Peabody Reflector, Summer 1980.

Vanderbilt in 1901

Hustler, Sept. 1901-June 1902; Oct. 4, 1957.
Nashville Banner, Nov. 20 and 27, 1901.

A DEPARTMENT OF TINKERS AND BUILDERS

Carey, Bill. *Fortunes, Fiddles and Fried Chicken: A Nashville Business History.* Franklin, Tenn: Hillsboro Press, 2000.
Hustler, May 5, 1967; Nov. 5, 1965.
Jacobs, Dillard. *113 is a prime number: a supplement to Ten Squared Years: Outlining the history of the Vanderbilt University School of Engineering through 1988.* Nashville: Vanderbilt University Engineering Alumni Office, 1988.
Jacobs, Dillard. *Ten Squared Years: A Story of the First Century of the Vanderbilt University School of Engineering.* Nashville: Vanderbilt Engineering Alumni Association, 1975.
Nashville American, Jan. 4, 1889.
V Square: The Vanderbilt Engineering Magazine; May 1954.
Vanderbilt Alumnus, Feb. 1923.

A SUICIDE AND A CASTLE

Hustler, April 6, 1944.
Nashville American, Aug. 18, 1905.
Nashville Banner, Nov. 5 - Dec. 3, 1901.

DOG BREEDERS AND X-RAY EXPERIMENTS

In Memoriam: Herbert Cushing Tolman, Published by the Vanderbilt Chapter of Phi Beta Kappa, 1926.
Lagemann, Robert T. *To Quarks and Quasars: A History of Physics and Astronomy at Vanderbilt University.* Nashville: Vanderbilt University Department of Physics and Astronomy, 2000.
Nashville Banner, Feb. 25, 1918.
Nashville Tennessean, Oct. 30, 1954.
Science, April 10, 1896.

THE SCHOOL WITHOUT A BUILDING

Branscomb, Harvie. *Purely Academic: An Autobiography.* Nashville: Self-published, 1978.
Daily American, June 21, 1876.
Vanderbilt Alumnus, Jan. 1916; Nov. 1922; Jan. 1923; Jan. 1927; April

1932; Jan. 1944; March 1944; Sept. 1946.

THE GAME THE WAY IT USED TO BE

Nashville Christian Advocate, Feb. 4, 1897; Dec. 9, 1897.
Danzig, Allison. *The History of American Football.* Englewood Cliffs, N.J.: Prentice-Hall Inc, 1956.
Hustler, Sept. 22, 1904; Oct. 11, 1906; Nov. 5, 1908; Oct. 20, 1921.
Nashville American, Aug. 18, 1905.
Nashville Banner, Nov. 28, 1890; Oct. 14, 1922; Jan. 20, 1936.
Nashville Tennessean; Dec. 15, 1918; Jan. 20, 1936.
Russell, Fred. *50 Years of Vanderbilt Football.* Nashville: Fred Russell and Maxwell Benson, 1938.
Vanderbilt Alumnus; Nov. 1920; Feb. 1921.

THE FUNDRAISING CAMPAIGN THAT FAILED

Mims, Edwin. *Chancellor Kirkland of Vanderbilt.* Nashville: Vanderbilt University Press, 1940.
Nashville Union and American, May 6, 1873.

THE TRAMP OF THE UNBORN

Hoss, Elijah, "The Vanderbilt Matter," a pamplet written about 1910 related to the relationship between the Methodist Episcopal Church, South, and Vanderbilt University.
The Independent, May 11, 1905; May 31, 1906; Jan. 3, 1907; April 6, 1914; June 1, 1914.
Literary Digest, July 5 and 19, 1913.
Martin, Isaac Patton. *Elijah Embree Hoss: Ecumentical Methodist.* Nashville: Parthenon Press, 1942.
Mims, Edwin. *Chancellor Kirkland of Vanderbilt.* Nashville: Vanderbilt University Press, 1940.
Nashville Banner, Feb. 21, 1913; June 21 and 26, 1913; March 21, 30, and 31, 1914; April 1, 1914.
Nashville Christian Advocate, July 18, 1913.
The New York Times. June 21, 1910; March 22, 1914.
The Outlook, April 11, 1914.

Original bill of complainants and answer thereto of defendants in the Chancery Court of Davidson County; College of Bishops of the Methodist Episcopal Church, South, and the Board of Trust of Vanderbilt University.
Pilkington, James Penn. *The United Methodist Publishing House: A History Volume I.* Nashville: Abingdon Press, 1968.
Vernon, Walter Newton Jr. *The United Methodist Publishing House: A History Volume II.* Nashville: Abingdon Press, 1989.

PART THREE: MR. KIRKLAND'S SCHOOL

ONE CAMPUS, MANY PLANS

Agreement between the U.S. Navy and Vanderbilt University related to establishment of Vanderbilt Naval ROTC Unit, dated March 17, 1945 and revised in 1976.
Hustler, Feb. 19, 1954; May 13, 1955; Nov. 4, 1955; Nov. 1 and 8, 1957; Oct. 23, 1964; Sept. 22, 1967; Oct. 13, 1967; Dec. 10, 1968; Sept. 28, 1971.
McGill, Ralph. *The South and the Southerner.* Boston: Little, Brown and Co., 1959. (Quoted from p. 70.)
Nashville American, Aug. 18, 1905.
Nashville Banner, Aug. 15, 1905; March 6 and 14, 1958; Oct. 7, 1960.
Nashville Tennessean, May 6 and 7, 1957.
Tigert, John James. *Bishop Holland Nimmons McTyeire: Ecclesiastical and Educational Architect.* Nashville: Vanderbilt University Press, 1955.
Vanderbilt Alumnus; Jan.-Feb. 1928; June 1952; Summer 1986.
Vanderbilt magazine, Winter 1978.

PEABODY GOES ITS OWN WAY

Allen, Jack, "The Peabody Saga," in *The Peabody Reflector*, Summer 1980.
Brown, Dorothy Louise. *Maycie Katherine Southall: Her Life and Contributions to Education.* Self-published, 1981.
Crabb, Alfred Leland. *The Geneology of George Peabody College for Teachers*, 1935.
Dorn, Sherman. *A Brief History of Peabody College.* Nashville:

Peabody College of Vanderbilt University, 1996.
Hustler, Nov. 18, 1916.
Nashville American, Aug. 4 and 8, 1909; Nov. 13, 14, 15, 17 and 18, 1909; Dec. 15 and 16, 1909.
The George Peabody School for Teachers: Steps Leading up to its Establishment, Nov. 1909.

Mr. Flexner changes everything

Flexner, Abraham. *The American College: A Criticism.* New York: Arno Press, 1908.
Flexner, Abraham. *Medical Education in the United States and Canada: A Report to the Carnegie Foundation for the Advancement of Teaching.* New York: Carnegie Foundation, 1910.
Flexner, Abraham, *I Remember: The Autobiography of Abraham Flexner.* New York: Simon and Schuster, 1940.
Jacobson, Timothy. *Making Medical Doctors: Science and Medicine at Vanderbilt since Flexner.* Tuscaloosa, Ala: University of Alabama Press, 1987.
Strauss, Lewis L. "Lasting Ideals of Abraham Flexner," in the *Journal of the American Medical Association*, July 30, 1960.

The abandonment of Galloway Hospital

Flexner, Abraham. *The American College: A Criticism.* New York: Arno Press, 1908.
Flexner, Abraham. *Medical Education in the United States and Canada: A Report to the Carnegie Foundation for the Advancement of Teaching.* New York: Carnegie Foundation, 1910.
Flexner, Abraham, *I Remember: The Autobiography of Abraham Flexner.* New York: Simon and Schuster, 1940.
Hustler, Jan. 13, 1917.
Jacobson, Timothy. *Making Medical Doctors: Science and Medicine at Vanderbilt since Flexner.* Tuscaloosa, Ala: University of Alabama Press, 1987.
Journal of the American Medical Association, July 30, 1960.
Vanderbilt Alumnus, Jan. 1920; April 1921; May 1921; Oct. 1923.

HAZING AND THE BALDHEADED BROTHERHOOD

Hustler, Nov. 25, 1898; March 16, 1905; Sept. 27, 1906; Oct. 4 and 11 1906; Nov. 19, 1908; Jan. 17, 24, and 31, 1917; Feb. 21, 1917; Oct. 13, 1921; Nov. 3, 1933; April 14, 1939; Oct. 20, 1939; March 16, 1973; Jan. 16, 1981.
Nashville American, Nov. 19, 1909.
Vanderbilt Alumnus, Jan. 1917; Nov. 1920; March 1921; Feb. 1923; Feb. 1924.

VANDERBILT'S WEIRD WAR EXPERIENCE

Commodore, 1919.
Hustler, May 18, 1918; Nov. 11 and 25, 1918; Jan. 6, 1919; Feb. 8, 1919; Feb. 4, 1920; May 5, 1920.
Tennessean magazine, Sept. 8, 1957.
Thomison, John, "The 1918 Influenza Epidemic in Nashville," in the *Journal of the Tennessee Medical Association*, April 1978.
Vanderbilt Alumnus, Nov. 1918; March 1919; April 1920; May 1920; Feb. 1921.
Vanderbilt Tennessean, Oct. 1, 1918; Nov. 28 and 30, 1918; Dec. 8 and 29, 1918;

THE MAYOR AND CHAIRMAN DECLARE MARTIAL LAW

Hustler, May 3, 1919.
Nashville Banner, May 2-3, 1919.
Nashville Tennessean, May 3, 1919.

PHILOSOPHERS AND POETS

Blotner, Joseph. *Robert Penn Warren: A Biography*. New York: Random House, 1997.
Bradbury, John M. *The Fugitives: A Critical Account*. Chapel Hill, N.C.: University of North Carolina Press, 1958.
Hustler, April 13, 1922.
McGill, Ralph. *The South and the Southerner*. Boston: Little, Brown and Co., 1959. (Quoted from p. 75.)

Purdy, Rob Roy, editor. *Fugitives Reunion: Conversations at Vanderbilt.* Nashville: Vanderbilt University Press, 1959.
Stewart, John. *The Burden of Time: The Fugitives and Agrarians.* Princeton, N.J.: Princeton University Press, 1965.
Sullivan, Walter. *Allen Tate: A Recollection.* Baton Rouge, La.: Louisiana State University Press, 1988.
Tate, Allen. *Memoirs and Opinions: 1926-1974.* Chicago: Swallow Press, 1975.
Watkins, Floyd C.;, Hiers, John T.; and Weaks, Mary Louise. *Talking with Robert Penn Warren.* Athens, Ga.: University of Georgia Press, 1990.
Young, Thomas Daniel. *Gentleman in a Dustcoat: A Biography of John Crowe Ransom.* Baton Rouge, La.: Louisiana State University Press, 1976.
Young, Thomas Daniel; Watkins, Floyd; and Beatty, Richmond. *The Literature of the South.* Glenview, Ill.: Scott, Foresman and Co., 1952. (Quoted from p. 235.)

The first of its kind

Hustler, Sept. 28, 1905; Feb. 24, 1915; Nov. 30, 1916; Nov. 10 and 28, 1921; Dec. 8, 1921; Jan. 19, 1922.
Nashville Banner, Sept. 22, 1922; Oct. 14, 1922.
Nashville Tennessean, Oct. 14 and 15, 1922.
Vanderbilt Alumnus, April 1919; Oct. 1919; May 1920; Oct. 1920; Dec. 1920; Oct. 1921; Nov. 1921; Feb. 1922; Oct. 1922; March 1923; May 1924.

The name that won't die

Vanderbilt Alumnus, May 1919.
Nashville Banner, Feb. 20, 1932.
Nashville Tennessean, May 2, 1919; Feb. 20, 1932.
Tate, Allen. *Memoirs and Opinions: 1926-1974.* Chicago: Swallow Press, 1975.
Thompson, Bard. *Vanderbilt Divinity School: A History.* Nashville: Vanderbilt University Press, 1958.
Vanderbilt Alumnus, May 1919.

Waller, William, editor. *Nashville: 1900 to 1910.* Nashville: Vanderbilt University Press, 1972.

BUCK GREEN OF VANDERBILT

Buck Green of Vanderbilt, a videotape kindly loaned to the author by Michael Schoenfeld.
Vanderbilt Alumnus, All issues from 1925-27.

THEY TAKE THEIR STAND

The American Mercury, March 31, 1931.
Blotner, Joseph. *Robert Penn Warren: A Biography.* New York: Random House, 1997.
Bradbury, John M. *The Fugitives: A Critical Account.* Chapel Hill, N.C.: University of North Carolina Press, 1958.
Forum, Aug. 25, 1925.
Nation, May 27, 1925; July 1, 15, and 22, 1925; Aug. 5, 1925; Sept. 30, 1925.
New York Times, July 12-25, 1925; Oct. 19, 1925; Nov. 15 and 19, 1925; Dec. 9, 1926.
Outlook, May 27, 1925; July 22, 1925.
Saturday Review of Literature, Dec. 20, 1930.
Stewart, John. *The Burden of Time: The Fugitives and Agrarians.* Princeton, N.J.: Princeton University Press, 1965.
Sullivan, Walter. *Allen Tate: A Recollection.* Baton Rouge, La.: Louisiana State University Press, 1988.
Watkins, Floyd C.;, Hiers, John T.; and Weaks, Mary Louise. *Talking with Robert Penn Warren.* Athens, Ga.: University of Georgia Press, 1990.
Young, Thomas Daniel. *Gentleman in a Dustcoat: A Biography of John Crowe Ransom.* Baton Rouge, La.: Louisiana State University Press, 1976.
Young, Thomas Daniel; Watkins, Floyd; and Beatty, Richmond. *The Literature of the South.* Glenview, Ill.: Scott, Foresman and Co., 1952.

The best and worst of times

Hustler. Sept. 29, 1933 through April 20, 1934.

A library for four schools

Hustler, Sept. 28, 1905; Jan. 19 and 26, 1940; Sept. 29, 1961.
Kulhman, A. Frederick. *The story of the Joint University Libraries of Nashville, Tennessee; including their origin, purposes, legal establishment, operation, problems and achievements, 1930-1972.* Nashville, 1973.
Nashville Banner, Jan. 17, 1936.
Nashville Tennessean, Nov. 6, 1938.
Vanderbilt Alumnus, Nov. 1938; Dec. 1938; Dec. 1941.

The other, equally controversial *Hustler*

Hustler, Oct. 20, 1888; Nov. 26, 1908; April 11, 1914; Feb. 27, 1918; Jan. 12, 1934; Jan. 22, 1943; March 28, 1952; April 30, 1954; Jan. 6, 1961; Nov. 8, 1963; Dec. 6, 1963; Dec. 15, 1967; Jan. 9, 1968; Oct. 3, 1975.
McGill, Ralph. *The South and the Southerner.* Boston: Little, Brown and Co., 1959.
Versus, Dec. 1968 – Dec. 1970.

PART FOUR: MR. BRANSCOMB'S SCHOOL

Cigarettes with lipstick on them

Hustler, Sept. 1941-Sept. 1945.

The man who wrote about what he saw

Blotner, Joseph. *Robert Penn Warren: A Biography.* New York: Random House, 1997.
Bohner, Charles H. *Robert Penn Warren.* Boston: Twayne Publishers, 1991.
Bradbury, John M. *The Fugitives: A Critical Account.* Chapel Hill, N.C.: University of North Carolina Press, 1958.

Nation, Aug. 24, 1946.
Purdy, Rob Roy, editor. *Fugitives Reunion: Conversations at Vanderbilt.* Nashville: Vanderbilt University Press, 1959.
Stewart, John. *The Burden of Time: The Fugitives and Agrarians.* Princeton, N.J.: Princeton University Press, 1965.
Warren, Robert Penn. *All the King's Men.* New York: Harcourt, Brace and Co., 1946.
Watkins, Floyd C.;, Hiers, John T.; and Weaks, Mary Louise. *Talking with Robert Penn Warren.* Athens, Ga.: University of Georgia Press, 1990.
Young, Thomas Daniel. *Gentleman in a Dustcoat: A Biography of John Crowe Ransom.* Baton Rouge, La.: Louisiana State University Press, 1976.
Young, Thomas Daniel; Watkins, Floyd; and Beatty, Richmond. *The Literature of the South.* Glenview, Illinois: Scott, Foresman and Co., 1952.

Sneaking into the Tunnels

Hustler, Oct. 26, 1951; March 28, 1952; Jan. 23, 1953; Feb. 20 and 27, 1953; April 3, 1953; May 1, 1953; Jan. 15, 1954; Dec. 10, 1954; Feb. 11, 1955; Nov. 14, 1958; Dec. 4, 1959; Feb. 12, 19, and 26, 1960; Feb. 7, 1969; Sept. 17, 1971; March 16, 1972; Feb. 12, 1974; Dec. 6, 1974; Jan. 27, 1976; Sept. 12, 1978; Feb. 20, 1981; March 17, 1981; April 21, 1981; Jan. 17 and 27, 1989; March 31, 1989; Feb. 28, 1995.
Vanderbilt Alumnus; Jan. 1917; Nov. 1920; March 1921; Feb. 1923; Feb. 1924.

The helpful bridge builder

Carey, Bill. *Fortunes, Fiddles and Fried Chicken: A Nashville Business History.* Franklin, Tenn.: Hillsboro Press, 2000.
King, Adeline. *My Purpose Holds: The Life of A.J. Dyer* (Unpublished manuscript, on file at the Dyer Observatory.)

The gym with the benches in the wrong place

Hustler, Nov. 21, 1952; Oct. 23, 1953; Feb. 16, 1968.
Neal, Roy. *Dynamite! 75 Years of Vanderbilt Basketball.* Nashville: Burr-Oak Publishers, 1975.
Russell, Fred Russell. *Bury Me in an old Pressbox.* New York: A.S. Barnes & Co., 1957.
V Square: The Vanderbilt Engineering Magazine, May 1954.

Harvie versus the football team

Branscomb, Harvie. *Purely Academic: An Autobiography.* Nashville: Self-published, 1978.
Hustler, Dec. 8, 1939; March 29, 1940; Oct. 12, 1951; Feb. 29, 1952.
Nashville Banner, Oct. 3, 1951.

Lust, repression, and good clean fun

Chase, May 1954
Hustler, April 16, 1954; May, 1954; Sept. 24, 1954; Oct. 1, 1954; Dec. 3 and 10, 1954; Jan. 21, 1955; Dec. 6, 1957; Jan. 17, 1958.
Masquerader, Oct. 1949.

The medical school nearly goes away

Hustler, Oct. 15, 1954; Nov. 5, 1954.
Nashville Tennessean, Oct. 3, 6, 9, 14, and 29, 1954; Nov. 3 and 4, 1954; Jan. 14, 1999; March 19, 2000.

Visits, bizarre and fortuitous

Collins, Robert D. *Ernest William Goodpasture: Scientist, Scholar, Gentleman.* Franklin, Tenn.: Hillsboro Press, 2002.
Hustler, April 15, 1909; Nov. 10, 1921; Oct. 18, 1940; Feb. 4, 1955; March 1, 1957; March 3 and 15, 1972; Nov. 8, 1974.
Nashville Daily American, Sept. 3 and 4, 1875.

HARVIE VERSUS THE FRAT BOYS

Branscomb, Harvie. *Purely Academic: An Autobiography.* Nashville: Self-published, 1978.
Hustler, Feb. 16, 1940; April 12, 1940; Nov. 8 and 15, 1951; April 11, 1952; Nov. 14 and 21, 1952; April 17 and 24, 1953; Nov. 13, 1953; Feb. 5, 1954; April 2, 1954; Oct. 29, 1954; Feb. 25, 1955; Oct. 28, 1955; Feb. 3 and 10, 1956; May 10 and 17, 1957; Nov. 7, 1958; March 13, 1959; April 24, 1959; May 1, 8, and 15, 1959; Sept. 25, 1959; Oct. 23, 1959; Oct. 7, 1960.
Masquerader, Volume 2, Number 3.
Nashville Banner, May 11, 1919.
Vanderbilt Alumnus, May-June 1959.

VANDERBILT GETS IN BED WITH BIG BROTHER

The American City, June 1961.
Branscomb, Harvie. *Purely Academic: An Autobiography.* Nashville: Self-published, 1978.
Nashville Banner, April 6, 1959; Oct. 7 and 8, 1960.
Nashville Tennessean, June 27, 1935; Sept. 6, 1935; July 26, 1936; Aug. 2, 1936; Jan. 24, 1937; Nov. 1 and 2, 1938; May 20, 1940; May 29, 1949; June 21, 1949; April 15, 1959; Dec. 20-22, 1960; Feb. 3, 1961; Aug. 12, 1961; Jan. 10, 1963; June 10, 1963; Aug. 10, 1963.
Vanderbilt Law Review, Volume 27, 1974.

BRANSCOMB DECIDES TO STAY PUT

Branscomb, Harvie. *Purely Academic: An Autobiography.* Nashville: Self-published, 1978.
Nashville Banner, Oct. 7 and 8, 1960.
Nashville Tennessean, Aug. 12, 1961; April 30, 1962; Jan. 20, 1969
Vanderbilt Law Review, Volume 27, 1974.

THE INTERNATIONALIST AND REVISIONIST

Fleming, Denna F. *How do we make the victory stick? A series of radio broadcasts by Dr. Denna F. Fleming.* New York, Woodrow Wilson Foundation, 1945.
Fleming, Denna F. *The Cold War and its Origins: 1917-60.* Garden City, N.Y.: Doubleday, 1961.
Hustler, Oct. 6 and 20, 1933; Feb. 23, 1934; Feb. 27, 1953; Nov. 12, 1965; March 18, 1970.
Nation, Jan. 8, 1968; April 15, 1968.
New York Times, Dec. 24, 1961; Nov. 12, 1965; Sept. 24, 1967; Jan. 14, 1968; Dec. 8, 1968; March 8, 1970

JAMES LAWSON REFUSES TO QUIT

Branscomb, Harvie. *Purely Academic: An Autobiography.* Nashville: Self-published, 1978.
Halberstam, David, *The Children.* New York: Random House, 1998.
Hustler; May 8, 1953.
Johnson, Dale. *Vanderbilt Divinity School: Education, Contest, and Change.* Nashville: Vanderbilt University Press, 2001.
Nashville Banner, Feb. 29, 1960; March 1-7, 1960.
Nashville Tennessean, Feb. 13, 14, 16, 19, 21, 23-29, 1960; March 1-7, 1960.
U.S. News and World Report, Feb. 24, 1956.
Washington Post, June 1, 1960.

BRANSCOMB GETS IT FROM THE LEFT

Branscomb, Harvie. *Purely Academic: An Autobiography.* Nashville: Self-published, 1978.
Halberstam, David. *The Children.* New York: Random House, 1998.
Hustler, March 4, 1960; March 3, 1961.
Johnson, Dale. *Vanderbilt Divinity School: Education, Contest, and Change.* Nashville: Vanderbilt University Press, 2001.

PART FIVE: BREAKING WITH TRADITION

THE CHANCELLOR, THE FUTURE GOVERNOR, AND THE REFERENDUM

Hustler, Jan. 5, 12, 19, and 26, 1962; Feb. 9, 16, and 23, 1962;

A SPLIT-LEVEL HOUSE FOR A BASSET HOUND

Hustler, Sept. 18, 1964; Nov. 28, 1964; Feb. 25, 1966; Nov. 4 and 11, 1966; Dec. 16, 1966.

TOLERANCE AND RAP FROM THE 11TH FLOOR

Dirty We'jun, 1967.
Hustler, Nov. 8, 15, 22, and 25, 1963; Dec. 6, 1963; Oct. 15 and 22, 1965; Dec. 3 and 10, 1965; Feb. 11 and 18, 1966; March 25, 1966; April 1, 1966; Oct. 7 and 28, 1966; Feb. 28, 1967; Sept. 22, 1967; Oct. 6, 10, and 13, 1967; Nov. 10 and 17, 1967; Dec. 8, 1967; March 9 and 19, 1968.

GAMES, TRAGEDIES, AND EMBARASSMENTS

Hustler, Dec. 5, 1958; Dec. 6, 1963; April 17, 1970; Sept. 13, 1974; Oct. 31, 1978; Dec. 5, 1978; Jan. 16, 1979.
Nashville Tennessean, Dec. 31, 1955; Jan. 1-3, 1956.
Vanderbilt magazine, Winter 1979.

A VANDERBILT GUEST STARTS A RIOT

Heard, Alexander. *Speaking of the University*. Nashville: Vanderbilt University Press.
Hustler, Feb. 14, 1967; March 3, 10, and 17, 1967; April 7 and 21, 1967.
Nashville Banner, April 3-15, 1967.
Nashville Tennessean, April 5-15, 1967.

Heard gets it from the right

Heard, Alexander. *Speaking of the University.* Nashville: Vanderbilt University Press.
Time, April 21, 1967.

Dinah, Dickey, and the president of Panama

Carey, Bill. *Fortunes, Fiddles and Fried Chicken: A Nashville Business History.* Franklin, Tenn.: Hillsboro Press, 2000.
Hustler, March 7, 1941; Jan. 7, 1955; April 25, 1989.
Vanderbilt Alumnus, Oct. 1928.
Vanderbilt magazine, Winter 1996.
Versus, Nov. 1974.

Changing the game

Hustler, April 15, 1966; May 6, 1966; March 13 and 18, 1970.
Neal, Roy. *Dynamite! 75 Years of Vanderbilt Basketball.* Nashville: Burr-Oak Publishers, 1975.
Nashville Tennessean, March 8 and 9, 1970;

Sarratt and the quiet lounge

Hustler, Jan. 8, 1954; Jan. 10, 1969; Feb. 7, 1969; Sept. 26, 1969; March 31, 1970; Sept. 3, 1971; Sept. 6, 24, and 27, 1974; Nov. 8, 1974.
Vanderbilt Alumnus, March 1954; April 1954; Winter 1974.

Protesting everything

Hustler, Sept. 1968 through May 1970. Issues cited and of particular interest include Nov. 10 and 17, 1967; Feb. 6, 1968; March 9 and 19, 1968; April 5, 9, and 26, 1968; Sept. 24, 1968; Oct. 1, 11, 15, and 25, 1968; Nov. 26, 1968; Dec. 6, 1968; Jan. 7 and 10, 1969; Feb. 7, 1969; Feb. 3, 1970; Feb. 3, 1976.
Nashville Banner, Feb. 27, 1968; Feb. 20, 1969.
Versus, Feb. 20, 1969; March 6, 1969; Sept. 11, 1969.

VANDERBILT GETS ITS SLUM

Newsweek, Oct. 11, 1971; Nov. 1, 1971.
Vanderbilt Law Review, Volume 27, 1974.

THE TIRE SHOWROOM ON WEST SIDE ROW

Versus, Oct 2, 1969; April 16, 1971.

STREAKERS AND COED DORMS

Hustler, March 12, 15, 22, and 26, 1974; April 23 and 26, 1974.
Official record of the 1974 Tennessee State House of Representatives, Legislative Days 67 and 76.
Official record of the 1974 Tennessee State Senate, Legislative Days 78 and 80.
Tennessean, March 20 and 21, 1974; April 3, 1974.

PART SIX: A NEW CENTURY

PEABODY COMES INTO THE FOLD

Allen, Jack, "The Peabody Saga," in *The Peabody Reflector*, Summer 1980.
Dorn, Sherman. *A Brief History of Peabody College.* Nashville: Peabody College of Vanderbilt University, 1996.
Nashville Banner, March 3, 8-20, 1979.
Tennessean, Feb. 16, 1979.

TYPICAL AND ATYPICAL COEDS

Austral, June 1879.
Dirty We'jun, Sept. 1967
Hustler, March 16, 1905; Oct. 20, 1933; April 21, 1939; Oct. 17, 1941; March 5, 1945; March 7, 1952; May 16, 1952; Feb. 6, 1953; April 16, 1954; Feb. 8, 1972; April 18, 1972; May 2, 1972; Aug. 29, 1975; Oct. 3, 1975.
Playboy, Sept. 1981.

Sports Illustrated, Nov. 29, 1993.
Vanderbilt Alumnus, Oct.-Nov. 1951.
Vanderbilt magazine, Winter 1995, Winter 1996.

Women's dorm to international house

Hustler, Feb. 9, 16, and 23, 1940; Sept. 12, 1940; April 7, 1970; March 15 and 22, 1974; Nov. 19, 1974; Dec. 10, 1974.
Vanderbilt magazine, Winter 1982.

The tradition that is always ugly

Hustler, Jan. 28, 1949; Feb. 13, 1953; Nov. 6, 1959; Nov. 24, 1961; Dec. 1, 1961; Nov. 18, 1966; Sept. 26, 1967; Oct. 31, 1972; Oct. 31, 1978; Dec. 5, 1978; Dec. 4, 1990; Jan. 17, 1995.

The business school in the funeral home

Bell, Madison Smartt, *History of the Owen School: From its early origins to 1984.* Nashville: Owen Graduate School of Management, 1985.
Vanderbilt Alumnus, Winter 1978.

Grenada Liberation Day and the return of prohibition

Hustler, Aug. 1984-May 1985.

Electives, dance class and sex ed

Alberstadt, Leonard. *From Top to Bottom: A Small Science Department's 120-Year struggle to develop and survive at Vanderbilt University.* Nashville: Self-published, 1995.
Hustler, Oct. 24, 1941; Feb. 25, 1968; May 1, 1970; Sept. 26, 1975.
Vanderbilt Alumnus, March 1921; March-April 1929.

The chancellor who thought about money

Chronicle of Higher Education, Oct. 10, 1990; Jan. 5, 1996; April 26, 1996.
Hustler, April 7, 1995.

Lagemann, Robert T. *To Quarks and Quasars: A History of Physics and Astronomy at Vanderbilt University.* Nashville: Vanderbilt University Department of Physics and Astronomy, 2000.

HARASSMENT AND OUTLAWED INSULTS

Hustler, Jan. 27, 1989; Oct. 13, 1989; Nov. 1992-Dec. 1993.

NOBEL WINNERS AND JUNGLE ADVENTURERS

Atlanta Journal-Constitution, Jan. 24, 1993.
Current Science, Nov. 17, 2000.
Hustler, Nov. 20, 1998.
Vanderbilt magazine, Winter 1996.

OPEN CAMPUS TO VANDERBUBBLE

Chronicle of Higher Education, Oct. 10, 1990.
Hustler, Sept. 28, 1971; March 16, 1973; Sept. 23, 1975; Jan. 16, 1981; Oct. 2, 6, and 16, 1981; Aug. 10, 1982; Feb. 3 and 7, 1989; March 17, 24, and 28, 1989; April 14, 1989; Sept. 5 and 22, 1989.

A

B

C

D

E

F

G

H

I

J

K

L

M

N

O

P

Q

R

S

T

U

V

W

Y

Z